D0948218

INTERNATIONAL STUDIES

Hitler's Strategy 1940–1941
The Balkan Clue

INTERNATIONAL STUDIES

PUBLISHED FOR THE CENTRE FOR
INTERNATIONAL STUDIES, LONDON SCHOOL OF
ECONOMICS AND POLITICAL SCIENCE

The Centre for International Studies at the London School of
Economics was established in 1967 with the aid of a grant from
the Ford Foundation. Its aim is to promote research and
advanced training on a multi-disciplinary basis in the general
field of International Studies, particular emphasis being given
initially to contemporary China, the Soviet Union and
Eastern Europe and the relationship between these areas and
the outside world. To this end the Centre offers research
fellowships and studentships and, in collaboration with other
bodies (such as the Social Science Research Council),
sponsors research projects and seminars.

The Centre is undertaking a series of publications in
International Studies.

Other books in the series: Lucjan Blit, *Origins of Polish Social-
ism*; Eugen Steiner, *Slovak Dilemma*.

Whilst the Editorial Board accepts responsibility for recommending the
inclusion of a volume in the series, the author is alone responsible for the
views and opinions expressed.

Hitler's Strategy 1940–1941
The Balkan Clue

MARTIN L. VAN CREVELD

CAMBRIDGE
UNIVERSITY PRESS

Published by the Syndics of the Cambridge University Press
Bentley House, 200 Euston Road, London NW1 2DB
American Branch: 32 East 57th Street, New York, N.Y.10022

© Cambridge University Press 1973

Library of Congress Catalogue Card Number: 72-97885

ISBN: 0 521 20143 8

First published 1973

Printed in Great Britain
by Western Printing Services Ltd, Bristol

TO MY WIFE

CONTENTS

MAPS

ACKNOWLEDGEMENTS

The author and publisher are grateful to Her Majesty's Stationery Office for granting permission to reproduce material from *Documents on German Foreign Policy, Series D, Vols. X–XII.* And to Sidgwick and Jackson Limited for material from H. R. Trevor-Roper: *Hitler's War Directives, 1939–45* (1966).

PREFACE

Although a full scale study of the German campaign in the Balkans of spring 1941 is conspicuously missing from the historical literature on World War II, this work does not aim to fill this gap. Rather, its purpose is to examine the relationship between Hitler's overall strategy during the years 1940–1 on one hand and his policy towards two neighbouring, related countries in southeastern Europe on the other. Thus, it is intended both to examine the effect of Hitler's strategy as a whole on one particular part of his policy, and also to use that part as a measuring rod by means of which it is possible to see whether German strategy in this period conforms to the picture generally painted by modern scholarship. In the process of checking Hitler's strategy as a whole against his policy towards a particular area it was found necessary to throw overboard fairly important bits of the traditional view on both.

This is a study of Hitler's strategy and of a particular part of that strategy. It is thus not concerned with the details of military operations except in so far as they are relevant to that subject. The actual campaigns have therefore been allocated only a few pages and discussed simply in outline. The deployment for these campaigns and subsequent regrouping, on the other hand, have been described in some detail because of their importance in the preparations for Hitler's Russian campaign. This book is therefore the opposite of what one would normally expect from an operational study; much space and attention are devoted to background, preparations and consequences, little to actual military operations.

This study aims to examine the relationship between Hitler's strategy as a whole and his policy towards a particular area. It therefore consists of chapters examining the latter in some detail which alternate with others concerned with a less exacting survey of the former. Although the context and limited scope of this study make it impossible to examine Hitler's strategy in anywhere near sufficient detail to establish new interpretations I did not feel this should prevent me from expressing my views about this subject even when they do not coincide with what is usually believed. However, it was felt that in such cases some documentation at least was necessary, and thus such questions as when Hitler decided to abandon his invasion of the United Kingdom, or what was the nature of his relationship with Russia in

October–November 1940, are discussed in more detail and with the aid of more documents than would be possible or necessary in a study concerned solely with Hitler's policy towards Greece and Yugoslavia.

For the sake of simplicity, the book is divided into two parts: one dealing with the period from April to November 1940, the other with the one from December 1940 to June 1941. It is assumed that Hitler's greatest worry during the first of these periods was how to solve the English problem, while the Russian problem formed the centre of his interests in the second. This, of course, is to some extent an over-simplification. Hitler was concerned with the problem posed by the Soviet Union long before November 1940, and the English one continued to worry him long after that date. Moreover, the two problems were interrelated in his mind. Yet it would seem that this way of dividing up the sequence of events provides a framework that is more or less adequate in order to understand his policy towards Greece and Yugoslavia, if nothing else. I therefore decided to adhere to it despite all difficulties. By implication, Hitler's objectives in and attitudes to these two countries during the first period must be seen mainly – though not exclusively – as functions of his efforts to defeat England, while his determination to smash Russia largely dictated them during the second. Within this framework, however, almost infinite room for manoeuvre remains. Into this, other factors can, and will, be introduced.

My gratitude is extended to my supervisors at the London School of Economics, Professor J. Joll and Mr D. C. Watt, who read all or parts of my thesis and made many necessary corrections; to the staffs of the Foreign Office, Admiralty, Imperial War Museum and Wiener Libraries, all of whom were always more than willing to help in the tracing of source material; to Professor A. Hillgruber, who was kind enough to answer several queries and send over some unprinted material in his possession; to Miss Vera Roitman, who did a professional job on the maps, and to Mr Geoffrey Warner, formerly of Reading University, who showed unexampled generosity in offering me hospitality at his home, lending me considerable quantities of unpublished material, allowing me to use his own manuscripts, and discussing the present work with me during a great many unforgettable hours. I am also in debt to the Ford Foundation, which helped finance my studies and to the Central Research Fund of the University of London, which was so generous as to enable me to buy material without which this book could not have been written.

M. v. C.

ABBREVIATIONS

AOK	Armeeoberkommando
BFOD	British Foreign Office Documents
DBFP	*Documents on British Foreign Policy*
DGFP	*Documents on German Foreign Policy*
FCNA	Führer Conferences on Naval Affairs
FRUS	*Foreign Relations of the United States*
GFM	German Foreign Ministry
g.Kdos	Geheime Kommandosache
GMR	German Military Records
GNR	German Naval Records
IMR	Italian Military Records
IWM	Imperial War Museum
KTB/Halder	*Kriegstagebuch*/Halder
KTB/OKW	*Kriegstagebuch des Oberkommando der Wehrmacht*
KTB/SKL	Kriegstagebuch der Seekriegsleitung
ObdH	Oberbefehlhaber des Heeres
OKH/Genst.d.H/Op.Abt.	Oberkommando des Heeres/Generalstab des Heeres/Operationsabteilung
OKL/ObdL	Oberkommando der Luftwaffe/ Oberbefehlhaber der Luftwaffe
OKW/WFSt/Abt.L.	Oberkommando der Wehrmacht/ Wehrmachtführungstab/Abteilung Landesverteitigung
SDFP	*Soviet Documents on Foreign Policy*
St.S.	Staatssekretär
TMWC	*Trial of Major War Criminals*
TWC	*Trial of War Criminals*
Unst.S.	Untersstaatsekretär

PART 1

HITLER, SOUTH EASTERN EUROPE AND
THE WAR AGAINST ENGLAND
APRIL–NOVEMBER 1940

BETWEEN THE AXIS MILLSTONES

On 9 August 1940 an unusually long dispatch from the embassy in Rome lay before the officers of the military attaché branch at the Oberkommando der Wehrmacht (OKW) in Berlin. Deciphered, the telegram read:

General Roatta[1] invited me today and asked me to transmit the following wishes of the Italian general staff:
The general staff of the army received from the political leadership the order to prepare a plan for an attack on Yugoslavia, predicated on the commitment of Italian forces against the northern border of Yugoslavia through Carinthia and Styria... The initiation of these preparations did not mean that Italy meant to attack on shortest order, but only meant preparation by the general staff for a contingency that might arise in 2 months, in 1 year, or perhaps not at all.[2]

General von Rintelen[3] who sent the telegram added that Roatta had explained that an attack across the Julian Alps alone was not feasible and that the employment of an Italian army numbering 8 to 10 divisions from Austria was necessary. Consequently the Italian general staff had a few requests to make: would their allies please help with supplies, the use of railroads, hospitals (with German personnel) and, most important, 5000 motor vehicles? And could the necessary staff talks start as soon as possible?[4]

Could they? In order to fully understand both the Italian request and the German answer, it is necessary to go back and consider the importance of Yugoslavia to Hitler, Mussolini, the Axis and the war. The starting point in so doing is March 1939.

YUGOSLAVIA – THE FORBIDDEN FRUIT

While it would be possible to write books about Hitler's attitude to, say, Russia or England, it is singularly difficult to get a clear picture of his thoughts on southeastern Europe in general, and Yugoslavia in particular. As an Austrian, he told Mussolini, he was 'familiar with all these regions and the mentality of their inhabitants';[5] words, however, which mean little because Hitler considered himself a specialist on almost any subject. In his *Mein Kampf* there are some singularly unflattering references to Germany's World War I Balkan allies: he calls them 'old impotent *Gerümpel*' (trash) and 'rotten bodies'. To him the region was a barbaric and inhospitable one, infested by *Serbische Bombenschmeisser*, an uncivilized world.[6]

Although large parts of southeastern Europe had at one time or other been ruled from Vienna and still contained large German-speaking populations, Hitler never used these facts as he did in other parts of Europe. Like Bismarck before him, he seems to have been of the opinion that 'the territorial problems and internal relationships of the [Balkan] states' did not concern Germany.[7] He even went so far as to declare his 'absolute political disinterest' in this region in article 3 of the secret protocol of the Ribbentrop–Molotov pact of 23 August 1939.[8]

Economically, however, things were very different. In the event of a war against the west, such as Hitler had to reckon with, Germany would be blockaded and cut off from her overseas supplies; and six years of intensive effort had not, at the outbreak of World War II, guaranteed her anything like self sufficiency in the most essential war materials. The countries of southeastern Europe, poorly developed industrially but comparatively rich in natural resources, were the obvious source – situated at the Reich's very back door – from which to draw some of the deficient materials. Chief amongst those was oil. With wartime demand exceeding supply (home production plus operational reserves) by 4 to 6 million tons in 1939, Germany's situation in this respect was unenviable. The only source from which the gap could be bridged were the Ploesti oil fields in Rumania, producing six million tons in 1939. The capacity of these fields, moreover, could be considerably augmented.[9]

Great as the importance of oil undoubtedly was, it is an error – a very fashionable one – to allow it to overshadow the value of the other raw materials which the Balkans could, and did, supply. Among these, the most important were chrome, manganese, copper, lead, nickel, tin and aluminium, all of them indispensable for the production of arms and therefore to the war effort. Yugoslavia's share in the supply of these materials was by no means insignificant. In aluminium, for instance, she supplied about one third of Germany's demand. Her output in copper, lead and hemp, though by no means sufficient to cover German needs, was still about the only major source open to Germany in wartime Europe. Above all, her production of tin was large enough to satisfy almost all Germany's requirements.[10] As a source of raw materials, therefore, Yugoslavia ranked second only to Rumania.

Who should get hold of these resources was a problem that pre-occupied the leaders of the Rome–Berlin Axis for some time before the war. Though in principle the two dictators had divided their *Lebens-*

räume in such a way as to make the 'East' belong to Germany and the 'Mediterranean' to Italy, the boundaries between these areas had – deliberately so, on Hitler's side[11] – been left vague. Their definition, varying considerably from time to time and from capital to capital, was a cause of constant friction within the Axis, with Yugoslavia as a focal point.

Rome's position on this question is best summarized in the words of Attolico, its ambassador in Berlin, who asserted that 'the Mediterranean has certainly been assigned to Italy, and the adjacent countries and the Danube basin [*sic*] also belong to this area'.[12] By the time it was made, however, this claim had lost any semblance of reality. Much better equipped economically than either Italy or France, Germany began to acquire economic leadership in the region in 1936.[13] The annexation of Austria and Czechoslovakia turned such Italian preeminence as had existed in the Danube basin in the early thirties into a myth. The occupation of Czechoslovakia in particular gave the Duce a nasty jolt, because he regarded himself as the principal architect of the Munich settlement.[14] Hounded out of central Europe, he tried to make a stand over Yugoslavia. In a speech dated 26 March 1939, he said that 'geographically, politically, historically, militarily' the Mediterranean belonged to Italy, and that the Mediterranean included the Adriatic, so that Italian interests in relation to the Slavs there were 'preeminent but not exclusive'.[15] He then made representations in Berlin to see whether this attitude was shared there, only to receive an answer that was conciliatory in form but highly ambiguous in substance.[16]

How to get hold of Yugoslavia was another point on which the Axis partners differed. Hitler's approach to this problem was almost purely economic; the Balkans were one place where he does not seem to have had any territorial aspirations, and his main aim there was to secure, among that of other countries, Yugoslavia's output of raw materials. This was an aim that could best be achieved by friendly relations – and German–Yugoslav relations in the years immediately preceding the war were friendly – and by means of peaceful penetration, such as practised by Shacht. Mussolini, on the other hand, took a different view of the matter; not only did he have his territorial claims on Yugoslavia, dating from the *vittoria mutilata* of World War I – Dalmatia, etc. – but to him Yugoslavia was a French stooge specifically created with the intent of containing Italy, 'a typical Versailles creation'.[17] While Hitler wanted a viable – not to say strong – Yugoslavia with whom he could trade, Mussolini's aim was to dismember her – by political means if possible, by armed force if opportune.

The Duce's history as a Yugoslav-baiter was, indeed, a long one. His dispute with that country dated almost from his assumption of power, or even earlier if his role in D'Annunzio's 1919 Fiume expedition is counted. His lever for dismembering Yugoslavia was the Croat autonomist movement headed by Vladko Macek, and in particular the cut-throats of Ante Pavelic's more extremist Ustace organization. In 1937, however, Mussolini concluded that, following the decline of French influence as a result of Hitler's remilitarization of the Rhineland and the gradual disintegration of the Balkan Entente, his subversive policy was likely to drive an isolated Belgrade into the arms of a resurgent Germany. He therefore reversed his policy, effecting a *rapprochement* and signing a non-aggression pact with Yugoslavia in the hope of turning her into an Italian satellite and thus keeping her out of Hitler's reach. In this policy he found a convenient partner in the quasi-fascist government of Milan Stoyadinovic, a man ostensibly willing to play the role cast for him and who was also personally congenial to Mussolini.

The fall of Stoyadinovic in February 1939 put an end to this policy. Rome now decided to assign an independent Croatia, torn from Yugoslavia and linked to Italy by a personal union, the role previously earmarked for Yugoslavia.[18] Connections with Macek, allowed to lapse during the Stoyadinovic era, were re-established almost immediately.[19] Everything seemed to be going smoothly when the news of the Prague coup brought home to Mussolini the dangers inherent in such a policy. Disappointed because twenty years of conspiracy with Italy had failed to produce results, the Croat separatist movement might turn to Berlin. When Macek's first lieutenant, August Kosutic, went to Prague in mid March 'for personal reasons', Rome feared that the Croats had drawn the – for Italy – wrong conclusions from the Czech affair, and panicked.[20]

If further proof is needed of the way in which Yugoslavia formed the object of a dispute between Rome and Berlin, it is supplied by what followed. Afraid lest the Croats turn to Germany, Mussolini suddenly decided he had to do everything to strengthen Belgrade against them. Performing a complete *volte face*, he all at once discovered Italy was, after all, interested in a 'strong and united Yugoslavia', and even started to promote, after years of warmongering, Yugoslav–Hungarian friendship as a barrier against German expansion in the direction of the Adriatic.[21] To avoid jeopardizing Belgrade's position, moreover, he postponed his planned invasion of Albania until he could sound out Yugoslavia and perhaps offer her some kind of compensation.[22]

Mussolini, however, was too much of a Yugoslav-baiter to persist for long in this policy. Having received some kind of reassurances from Berlin to the effect that Germany did not lay exclusive claim to Yugoslavia, he soon resumed his connections with Macek. More dangerously still, he went ahead with his invasion of Albania. The character of that operation, however, underwent a change; it was turned into a demon-

stration of Italian independence *vis à vis* the Axis partner and interpreted as a measure designed to call a halt to German expansion in
southeastern Europe.[23]

To the Germans the occupation of Albania on 7 April 1939 was,
indeed, most unwelcome. Since their factories were working overtime
in preparation for war, they were sensitive to any upheaval that might
endanger the free flow of raw materials; moreover, they anticipated the
Anglo-French accusation that the Axis was out to dominate this
region.[24] The Italian action, while of little value strategically and
economically, lent substance to precisely that accusation. While
ostensibly congratulating the Duce on 15 April, therefore, Göring also
warned him not to repeat the Albanian adventure elsewhere; all the
Axis wanted from Yugoslavia was a benevolent neutrality that would
allow Italy and Germany to make all purchases necessary for the war
effort. Mussolini was not easily convinced; to him a reliable Yugoslavia
was an occupied, or at least a dismembered one.[25]

Ignoring Göring's warning, therefore, Mussolini went on intriguing
with Macek's envoys. Late in May his foreign minister Galeazzo Ciano
recorded in his diary an agreement that had allegedly been arrived
at with the Croats. The agreement provided for a Croat rebellion
financially supported by Italy to start within four to six months;
Italian troops would then be called in and an independent Croatia
proclaimed. This state would then enter in a kind of confederation
with Italy.[26] All this in defiance of Hitler, who continued to stress the
importance of a 'strong and united Yugoslavia'.[27]

Mussolini's hopes were soon dashed. Macek disowned the agreement
which, he claimed, had been negotiated behind his back.[28] Instead he
signed, on 23 August, a *Sporazum* (agreement) with the Yugoslav
minister president Dragisa Cvetkovic, which gave the Croats a considerable degree of autonomy and made Macek himself deputy premier.
With this Mussolini, who now had to fall back on the extremist Ustace
organization, effectively saw his hopes for dismembering Yugoslavia
buried.

Help came from an unexpected side. The shadow of war was hanging
over Europe, and Hitler began to realize that, in spite of the 'Pact of
Steel' signed between Germany and Italy on 22 May, Mussolini was
not going to enter the war. To get him in, the Führer unexpectedly
dangled the Yugoslav bait before Ciano's eyes on 12 August. Provided
the Axis countries covered each other's back, he said, they could
eliminate what he called 'the uncertain neutrals'; Italy, for instance,
should fall upon Yugoslavia who could be considered such an 'uncertain neutral'.[29]

War broke out on 1 September; Mussolini swallowed his pride and
stayed out. Nor did Hitler resent the fact for very long. After the

termination of the Polish campaign he realized that he could do without his ally whose 'nonbelligerence', moreover, served the useful purposes of protecting his southern flank and keeping open a door for overseas imports. Once Germany was at war and blockaded, Yugoslavia's importance as a supplier of raw material increased; on 5 October, therefore, an economic treaty was signed between the two countries, effectively tying almost the whole of the latter's output in raw materials to the former's use.[30] This in turn led to an immediate flare-up in German–Italian relations with Ciano instructing his representative in Belgrade to see what he could do to prevent agreement.[31]

Hitler's desire to keep the war away from Yugoslavia was not helped by that country's policy. Hemmed in as she was between Germany, Italy, Hungary and Bulgaria – all of them more or less hostile – Yugoslavia's only possible course was to stay out of the conflict, but her sympathies, particularly those of the army and air force, were clearly on the side of the allies. In September 1939, Prince Paul is reported to have said to the French minister, Brugere, that his country would enter the war on the side of the allies as soon as the latter seized Salonika – and thus secured an Italian-proof connection with Yugoslavia – and cleared the Adriatic and Mediterranean of the Axis.[32] Yugoslavia also participated wholeheartedly in the planning of the Anglo-French Salonika expedition in the winter of 1939–40.[33]

With spring and the fall of France Yugoslavia's pro-western policy crumbled. The outbreak of war had deprived Yugoslavia of her previous support in resisting the Axis, and the military defeat of the west left her at the mercy of Germany. Prince Paul, however, had foreseen this possibility as early as autumn 1939, and was looking for another ally capable of making Germany think twice. There was only one state in Europe strong enough to play this role: the Soviet Union.

Yugoslavia's relations with Moscow had not been good in the interwar years. Belgrade like Paris had served as an asylum for a great many White Russians, who were cordially received. Until 1939 Czarist Russia was represented in Belgrade by a Mr Strandtman, a former councillor at the Czarist embassy. In autumn 1939, however, Strandtman talked with Prince Paul, and then suddenly announced he was no longer representing a government that no longer existed. Prince Paul had evidently decided to improve his relations with Stalin; the opening of negotiations, however, was delayed until ugly rumours concerning a forthcoming Italian attack on Yugoslavia[34] forced Belgrade to act. In March, the Yugoslav foreign minister Cincar Markovic established contact with Moscow via Ankara. He pointed out Italy's expansionist tendencies and suggested that Russia ought not to tolerate this policy. In reply Moscow formally stated that it opposed Italy's Balkan aspirations, and came out energetically for the maintenance of the *status quo*.

Underscoring its point, the Soviet government expressed willingness to enter into negotiations towards an economic treaty; these began on 14 April and on 11 May ended with the signature of an accord. On 24 June, moreover, diplomatic relations between the two countries were established, and Belgrade sent Milan Gavrilovic, a leader of the Serb Agrarian Party and a confirmed liberal, to Moscow.[35]

As Italy came nearer intervention in the war, the likelihood that Yugoslavia would be drawn in increased. Having made his decision to join Hitler in March,[36] Mussolini was casting around for a victim small enough to suit Italy's limited resources.[37] The choice turned out to be a very limited one; as early as 1936 Stamage had recognized that, in the event of a European war, Italy's weakness would render her unable to attack anywhere except on the 'eastern front', that is either Greece or Yugoslavia.[38] Even Mussolini was forced to admit – heaven only knows what this must have cost him – that Italy would be unable to do 'anything spectacular',[39] and when he issued his so-called 'plan of war' on 31 March 1940 he envisaged offensive action only on the Balkan front.[40] Talking about Croatia, the Duce's hands 'fairly itched'.[41] At the end of April, he had his army chief-of-staff Marshal Rodolfo Graziani prepare a plan of war based upon an offensive against Yugoslavia, and the air force started to deploy accordingly.[42] His first reaction to the German invasion of the Low Countries of 10 May was to time the rising of Pavelic's Ustace, with whom an agreement similar to the one he had previously tried to obtain from Macek had been signed in January, for early June.[43] As late as 29 May he confirmed his directive to Graziani.[44] At this period, just as one year earlier, these measures had a pronounced anti-German edge; their purpose, among others, was to get hold of a disputed area while the Big Brother was engaged elsewhere – snatch as you can.

Mussolini's army and air force were just starting their preparations when a letter from the Führer arrived, and brought his plans to a halt. Hitler had learnt of his ally's intentions in April[45] and confirmation reached him in May.[46] After all that we have seen of his Yugoslav policy, it is not hard to see why he was unhappy about the Duce's plans. Hitler's overwhelming priority during this period was the west; here he had concentrated almost all his troops and hoped to gain a decisive victory. In this context Italy's plans presented a diversion, and one that was totally unrelated to the war against France and England. Moreover, they did not make strategic sense. Even if completely successful, nothing more than the transformation of the Adriatic into an Italian lake could be achieved. The Adriatic, however, is an inland sea with limited strategic significance; being in possession of both sides of the Straits of Otranto, Italy could seal it off in any case. A successful campaign, moreover, would have the disadvantage of finally settling the question as to whose sphere of influence Yugoslavia belonged to, and this in a way which was not, his declarations to the contrary notwithstanding, what Hitler wanted.

But would it be successful? Hitler and his army high command (OKH) were not sure. They doubted whether 'Yugoslav national structure' was as 'decayed' as the Italians tried to make out;[47] and World War I had taught them a healthy respect for the Yugoslav soldier.[48] Everything considered, therefore, they tended to share Graziani's scepticism.

Leaving these doubts aside, the Italian plan carried other dangers. Following the agreement of October, Yugoslavia's entire economy had been geared to the Axis, so that an attack on her could not but disrupt – temporarily at least – the flow of raw materials. Even worse, Yugoslavia's covetous neighbours – Hungary and Bulgaria – might seize the opportunity to intervene, possibly drawing in Rumania[49] as well. This in turn would spell disaster to German war production, dependent as it was on Balkan raw materials. Finally, there was the mystery of Yugoslav–Soviet relations. Little as Hitler knew about these, he suspected a military pact and was definitely worried.[50] A Balkan explosion, such as might be produced by an Italian attack on Yugoslavia, might provide the Soviets with an excuse to surge southward; whether they would stop before reaching the Ploesti oil fields was anybody's guess.

For all these reasons, Hitler did not dream of giving his ally the green light over Yugoslavia. On 18 April he sent him a letter in which, while denouncing 'the smaller neutral states' which 'think they can enjoy the privilege of gravely insulting or damaging . . . insolently a few great powers' invoking 'democratic freedom of the press and public opinion' to excuse themselves, he added that 'I . . . am naturally convinced that for us it is desirable to hold the Balkanic region . . . out of the war.'[51] On 26 April he was reported 'struggling with all possible means' to keep the Balkans quiet.[52] To make sure Mussolini did not move he refused Italy's request for arms,[53] and by 23 May he believed he had the 'reins well in hand'.[54] Four days later, however, his army commander-in-chief was still sufficiently nervous to tell the foreign minister, Joachim (von) Ribbentrop, that he personally should take care lest the Balkans be driven into disorder by Italy.[55] On 30 May a letter arrived from Mussolini, announcing that 'I hold it desirable to prevent the extension of the conflict to the *settore danubiano-balcanico* from which Italy too, derives supplies.'[56]

Strange as it may seem, this ostensibly conciliatory letter alarmed Hitler. He knew his co-dictator too well to take him at his word, and in any case had not yet forgotten the unpleasant way in which the Albanian affair was sprung on him. This time he did not want to take any chances. He therefore proceeded to write Mussolini a letter in which he assured his ally that he was 'in perfect accord' with his desire to keep the Danube basin and the Balkans out of the conflict. Moreover, he recommended that the Duce make a public statement to that effect. To allow his ally time to digest the message, Hitler also asked him to postpone his entry into the war from 5 to 10 June – ostensibly in order to allow Germany to finish off the French air force.[57]

This was a bitter pill for Mussolini, but not one that he could refuse to swallow. By 2 June he had made up his mind to comply;[58] with almost indecent haste Berlin dropped the ridiculous pretext it had dreamt up to delay his entry into the war and Italy was allowed to select any date she liked.[59] Ciano told the Yugoslav minister that his country would not be invaded if it behaved 'loyally', a grave statement of which the minister 'loyally' took notice.[60] The day after, the withdrawal of Italian forces and their transportation to Libya – where they would presumably be free from Hitler's meddlesome interference – began;[61] and on 10 June Mussolini, when declaring war, grudgingly announced his intention to spare not just Yugoslavia, but Greece, Turkey, Egypt and Switzerland as well.

Hitler had won a considerable victory in the tug of war between himself and Mussolini and had proved that he was perfectly able to hold his ally's Balkan plans in check when he wanted to. Behind Mussolini's back, he was already reassuring the Yugoslavs; tongue in cheek, the German minister in Belgrade explained that 'anybody could see that the interests of the Axis powers . . . were identical, and that Germany wanted to keep the peace in southeastern Europe'.[62] Thereupon the Yugoslavs claimed they were satisfied, at least for the time being.[63] In any case, they did demobilize in July.

The lull was to be of short duration. On 1 July Hitler met the new Italian ambassador, Dino Alfieri, and committed the error of talking somewhat strongly about Yugoslavia. Referring to a collection of top level allied documents for the conduct of the war that his troops had discovered in an abandoned railway carriage near Vitry la Charité, he said that it had been proved 'just how equivocal and hostile' Yugoslavia's attitude to the Axis had been. Italy, he said, would have (*dovrà*) to clear 'many problems' at her frontier 'at the right moment'.[64] No sooner had this news reached Mussolini than the Italian air force and army were ordered to redeploy in the Parma–Padua area, in view of possible 'complications in the direction of Yugoslavia'.[65]

Mussolini had obviously interpreted Hitler's words as a broad hint that Germany would not object to an Italian action. To make doubly sure he instructed Ciano, who was about to leave for Berlin, to inform Hitler of the need 'to split up Yugoslavia'.[66] When he raised the subject, however, the Italian foreign minister was treated to an angry lecture: The decisive question in this connection was whether it was a matter of indifference to Italy and the Duce which country had possession of the Dardanelles and Constantinople. If Italy should attack Yugoslavia, Hungary would immediately fall upon Rumania . . . the Russians would . . . bestir themselves, cross the Danube, and seek to establish a connection with Bulgaria.

Up to this point Hitler's exposition was reasonable enough; to give Ciano the creeps, however, he proceeded to paint a dark picture of the Bulgarians allowing the Soviets to cross their country and reach the Straits. So no Yugoslav adventures, please! Clearly alarmed by Hitler's show of anger, Ciano quickly interposed that 'personally he believed that the Yugoslav affair could be postponed until the war with England had been settled. The important thing now was to note that Yugoslavia was not a country friendly towards the Axis, and that in the new Europe . . . she could not assert to maintain her present form.'[67] Having made this attempt to save whatever could be saved, Ciano duly reported Hitler's words to Mussolini.[68]

Though the Duce was undeterred by the German *démarche*, he soon found that his own military advisors were none too happy about the whole affair. They would have preferred to wait until after the 'liquidation of our problems in North Africa', and in any case needed time to transport troops from the French frontier, evacuate civilians from the border areas and confiscate the necessary animals and vehicles.[69] Even in the most favourable circumstances, preparations could not be completed before the middle of September.[70] Since the Yugoslav armed forces were by no means negligible, success could be achieved only if part of them was tied down by the hostility of Germany and Hungary and the non-benevolent neutrality of Rumania and Greece. It was asking for a great deal to expect this combination of circumstances, and the Commando Supremo duly suggested German help could be dispensed with, provided an Italian army was allowed to operate from Austria.[71] Disregarding Hitler's warning, therefore, Mussolini on 22 July ordered Stamage to approach the Germans,[72] and on 11 August to have preparations completed by 20 September.[73]

The Italian request was not, of course, welcome in Berlin. Having twice before vetoed their ally's action, the Germans were furious. 'Unheard-of shamelessness!' bristled the army chief-of-staff, General Halder.[74] To put a brake on Italian enthusiasm, General Warlimont suggested that the plans of the Yugoslav fortifications on the German frontier, for which the Italians had also asked, be handed over to them 'omitting the appended OKH evaluation saying that the fortifications . . . would not present a serious obstacle to an army equipped with modern weapons.'[75] Even this, however, was too much for a cautious Hitler, who declared himself 'totally disinterested' in the Italian request and forbade the material from being handed over.[76]. On Hitler's order, OKW then instructed Rintelen to say to Roatta that 'no assurances of any kind have been made to the Italians by the Reich foreign minister ... OKW cannot discuss this suggestion until the political aspect has been clarified'.[77] This time, however, Berlin was clearly determined to make sure the message got through. Ribbentrop therefore had Alfieri pay him a visit, then handed him a stiffly worded, if polite, memorandum:

In principle it should be said that the Axis is at present engaged on a life to death struggle with England, and that it would therefore be inadvisable to tackle any new problems ... that did not absolutely have to be tackled in connection with the effort to crush England ...
    A new seat of conflict in the Balkans would in certain circumstances start a general conflagration. How would Greece react? How would it affect Hungary? Above all ... it should be remembered that Yugoslavia had close relations with Russia... Moscow would be brought into the picture ... in the end. Germany would be forced to ... shift its troops to the east.[78]

The Germans, then, professed several reasons for not allowing Mussolini to attack Yugoslavia; the need to concentrate on the war against England, a task to which the Italian plans bore no relevance, and the fear of a general conflagration in the Balkans with all the consequences this implied for certain highly inflammable materials in the area. Behind these two reasons we may safely assume another; Hitler's basic unwillingness to do anything that might help realize the Italian claim that Yugoslavia belonged to their exclusive sphere of interest. Finally, there was the mystery of Yugoslav–Soviet relations; little as Hitler knew about these, they caused him lots of worries. Berlin knew that Turkey was somehow connected with the *rapprochement* between the Soviet Union and Yugoslavia, and suspected the shadow of England behind Turkey. The foreign ministry considered there was a connection between the establishment of Soviet–Yugoslav diplomatic relations and the arrival in Moscow of Churchill's special envoy, Sir Stafford Cripps.[79] A very interesting dispatch from Gavrilovic to Belgrade, in which the newly appointed minister reported a conversation with Molotov and expressed his conviction that the Soviets were waiting for an opportunity to fall on Germany's rear, and expected Yugoslavia to join them, also reached Hitler during July.[80]
    Slowly, Alfieri read the German note. Then, as he was never noted for political (or any other) wisdom,[81] the Italian ambassador proceeded to commit a bad blunder; he introduced the subject of Greece into the conversation.

GREECE – THE VETO THAT NEVER WAS

Like Yugoslavia, Greece formed something of a problem for the Axis; the first thing to note, however, is that it was an infinitely less important

problem. Greece was considerably weaker than Yugoslavia in population and resources, while much less important economically to the Axis
war effort.[82] Unlike Yugoslavia, moreover, her geographical position
left scarcely any doubt as to the sphere of influence to which she belonged – that is, if the expression 'the Mediterranean and the countries
bordering on it' had any meaning at all.

Italian–Greek relations had never been particularly good. In 1922
Greece had the ill luck to be involved in the Corfu incident, which
ended in Mussolini's humiliation and which he regarded as a personal
affront. Although governed by a quasi-fascist regime since 1935,
Greece was too dependent – economically and militarily – on the
Mediterranean to be permitted much room for manoeuvre in her relations with the great power that, Mussolini's *Mare Nostrum* notwithstanding, ruled the Mediterranean. This dependence was accentuated
by the fact that Greek finances were to a large extent in British hands,
thus automatically determining the attitude of important Greek circles
towards Italy. To this must be added Greek participation in the sanc-
tions imposed on Italy by the League of Nations during the war of
Abyssinia.

As for Metaxas the dictator himself, he could not be accused of being
too pro-British. He had been deported by them for his Germanophil
tendencies during World War I, and as late as December 1939 there
were rumours that the existence of these tendencies caused the British
and the French to intrigue against his regime.[83]

Weak and relatively backward, Greece formed a natural magnet to
the resurgent Roman Empire – the parallel between the occupation of
Albania by Italy on 7 April 1939 and the establishment of a Roman
protectorate there in 229 B.C., the first step in Rome's subsequent
conquest of the Hellenistic world, was obvious. Though the Greeks
were unable to do anything to prevent Italy from occupying Albania
they were even more unhappy about it than the Yugoslavs, in particular
because they feared for Corfu and Crete.[84] The presence, against their
wishes, of the Duce's legions on their border naturally drove them
further into the arms of the west and resulted, on 13 April, in their
acceptance of a British guarantee. Now it was Italy's turn to be unhappy; as Greece had received assurances from Italy, wrote the semi-
official *Giornale d'Italia*, she 'had no need . . . of compromising
guarantees of distant countries'.[85] The Italians gave vent to their ill
humour when, a month later, they refused 'for obvious reasons' to
renew the Italo–Greek friendship pact of 1928.[86]

A few months of minor bickering between the two governments
followed: the Greeks repeatedly protested their determination to stay
neutral in any conflict between the great powers[87] and Italy tried to
find faults in this neutrality.[88] In this context, the most conspicuous

fact about this period is that, in marked contrast to their attitude towards Yugoslavia, the Germans to a large extent allowed Italy to have her way over Greece. The country did not form the object of a dispute between the Axis partners, and Hitler's intention seems to have been to encourage Mussolini in his belief that Greece, at least, belonged firmly to his own exclusive sphere of influence. Thus, the German *démarche* supposed to be addressed to Greece after the latter got her British guarantee was first sent to Rome for approval – a very rare procedure indeed – and then dropped altogether when Mussolini announced that the matter was not sufficiently important to warrant reaction.[89] In principle both Italy and Germany recognized that in the event of war Greece would be 'on the other side';[90] however, Ciano with some justice argued that she would be unable to do anything as Italy's occupation of Albania meant she held a pistol to Greece's head.[91] And in any case, the country was too remote, weak and unimportant for her hostile feelings to matter very much to the Reich. While the Italians were preparing their plans for an offensive against Greece, therefore, Berlin was indifferent.

The outbreak of war to some extent reversed this situation. While Berlin bickered with Metaxas over chartering part of the Greek merchant fleet to England,[92] Mussolini ostentatiously improved his relations with Greece. His reasons for so doing are a matter of conjecture; perhaps he thought Greece's geographical position was such as to make her relatively safe against German domination and wanted to secure her neutrality in case he decided to exploit German involvement elsewhere and forestall Hitler in Yugoslavia. This interpretation would also explain the simultaneous improvement in Italian–Turkish relations, and particularly why the Italians refused to censure the Anglo–Franco–Turkish pact in accordance with German wishes.[93] Be this as it may, on 6 September Mussolini seized upon a declaration by Metaxas in which the Greek dictator said he would welcome a *rapprochement* between Italy and Greece and began a series of consultations. These resulted, on 12 September, in an Italian declaration that she would not attack Greece even if she entered the war.[94] As further signs of goodwill both sides withdrew their forces to 20 km from the Albanian frontier, published a joint declaration of friendship on 3 November and had their respective presses adopt a more friendly tone towards one other.[95] Finally, Mussolini called home the notoriously anti-Greek commander of the Italian troops in Albania, General Guzzoni. Geloso, who replaced him, later received strict orders to confine his offensive plans to Yugoslavia alone.[96]

This show of friendship notwithstanding, Italo–Greek relations soon resumed their normal suspicious nature. The Italians would not believe that Greece was truly neutral; the Greeks protested their innocence time and again.[97] On 30 October the accusation that Greece allowed the British to maintain bases in the Aegean islands, which had such a magnificent future in store for it, appeared for the first time.[98] On the other hand, the Italians did take action when the Greeks complained that the British were threatening reprisals against their maritime commerce with Germany.[99] While all this took place, German–Greek relations were remarkably quiet; Berlin became jumpy only when it was rumoured that Greece planned to join the neutral Balkan block which the Rumanians were trying to construct.[100]

From the end of January to the end of April Greece vanishes completely from Italian diplomatic documents. It reappears dramatically on 30 April when Ciano instructed Emanuele Grazzi, his minister in Greece, to 'tell Metaxas that if he does not give me satisfaction about the mines of Lokris I shall take Corfu away from him'.[101] From this time onwards the situation developed rapidly; on 23 May Ciano predicted a 'decisive operation' against Greece which according to him was becoming 'a veritable aeronaval base' for the French and the British.[102] True, these growls did not come from Mussolini himself[103] but from the second man of the regime; Ciano's growls, however, could be dangerous because he had two creatures of his own in Albania who were perfectly capable of obeying him – even to the extent of provoking a conflict with Greece – in defiance of the general staff; Francesco Jacomini, lieutenant-general in Albania, and General Sebastiano Visconti Prasca, commander-in-chief of the troops stationed there.[104] Nor did the Italians make a secret of their intention to invade Greece – and possibly occupy Crete – if the British landed in Salonika.[105]

All this – when compared with his three-fold veto of Mussolini's Yugoslav plans, generated remarkably little excitement on Hitler's part. There are several possible explanations for this fact. To begin with, the Greek problem was much less important economically, militarily and politically than the Yugoslav one. Greece, unlike Yugoslavia, had never been the object of even a covert dispute between Germany and Italy, since her place in the latter's sphere of influence could scarcely be doubted. Unlike Yugoslavia, too, her bases and particularly her islands did have a potential significance in relation to the war against Great Britain;[106] strategically Salonika, the Peloponnese and Crete – unlike, say, Zagreb and Belgrade – were places worth possessing. If Greece, more remote from the centre of the conflict and less surrounded by hostile enemies, were attacked by Italy a general conflagration in the Balkans was less likely to occur. Last but not least, Greece did not possess anything like Yugoslavia's mysterious and confidential relationship with Russia; like their Turkish neighbours, the Greeks feared Soviet expansionist tendencies in the Balkans, while relations between Metaxas's staunchly right-wing regime and Moscow were of the worst.

It is further true, moreover, that Mussolini's Greek plans were not really out of step with Hitler's own. News about the allied plans for a landing in Greece and the establishment of a front at Salonika may have reached Berlin, where people had very unpleasant memories of a similar front dating from World War I. There would probably be no objection, therefore, to Italian action designed to forestall the danger. Such an assumption may explain why, on 25 April – that is, one day before he was 'struggling with all possible means' to keep the Balkans quiet – Hitler expressly authorized Mackensen to tell Mussolini that he 'would have no objection to the Duce's improving his strategic situation . . . very much as the Führer had done in the case of Denmark and Norway'.[107] In the event of a joint German–Italian Balkan campaign, which seems to have been at least considered in Berlin,[108] it would be Italy's job to hold Greece down.[109]

News reaching Hitler of Italian plans for Yugoslavia did, as we have seen, lead to German reassurances in Belgrade; when Athens asked for similar assurances, however, Berlin refused.[110] Instead, the foreign ministry pointed out to the Greeks that Italy's entry into the war had made them completely dependent on the Axis, and that they had better modify their policy accordingly.[111] Even more remarkable was Hitler's reaction to the Italian plans when they were first presented to him. Armed with (false) information supplied by the rabidly Graeco-phobe Italian governor of the Dodecanese Islands, Cesare de Vecchi, which purported to demonstrate that Greece had violated the rules of neutrality by allowing England to use her harbours and disclosing the whereabouts of Italian submarines,[112] Ciano on 7 July told Hitler that:

Italy was very dissatisfied with Greece, for Greece was supporting the English fleet so that it found Greek ports almost like the home country. Moreover, Greece was betraying to the English Italian submarines which surfaced in her waters . . . Italy also saw a danger in the statement in Churchill's latest speech to the effect that England would take the necessary steps to assure herself of absolute supremacy in the Mediterranean. It was not impossible that this implied the occupation of the Greek islands, such as Corfu and others, by the British . . . therefore Italy considered it advisable to proceed herself with the occupation of the Greek islands in the Ionian Sea, especially, however, of Corfu, and the adjacent islands, for Greece was impatiently waiting . . . to be violated by England.[113]

Though it may be doubted whether the prudish Führer enjoyed the metaphor, he did not, even according to the German records, protest against Italy's intentions; instead, he repeated his reference of 1 July to the 'extremely interesting documents' which Germany had found 'on all these questions', and which would be sent to the Duce – in spite of the fact that he did not really have any.[114] Ciano's record is even more explicit: according to him, Hitler said with reference to Greece that he was 'absolutely in favour' of Italian military action to prevent the occupation of the Ionian Islands by the British, adding that 'the Mediterranean . . . is a purely Italian matter, and that he therefore did not want to interfere in any way there, approving *a priori* any decision that may be taken by the Duce'.[115] This was certainly a far cry from the resolute veto imposed on Mussolini's Yugoslav plans during the very same conversation. Even if we assume that Ciano, who had a personal stake in the matter and regarded Greece as a possible extension of his Albanian '*granducato*', exaggerated Hitler's favourable reaction in order to persuade the Duce that an attack on Greece was preferable to one on Yugoslavia,[116] it is quite certain that Hitler did not protest. Of course he wanted peace in the 'Balkans'; the Mediterranean, however, had 'certainly been assigned to Italy', and Greece, if anything, belonged to the 'Mediterranean'. Hitler could not, after all, protest against defensive measures, against Great Britain! which Italy was contemplating in her own recognized sphere of influence.

This implicit division of southeastern Europe into a 'Mediterranean' Greece and non-Mediterranean 'Balkan', which seems to have had some reality if we are to judge by Hitler's actions of 25 and 26 April 1940,[117] was apparently grasped by the highly astute Ciano. When reporting to Mussolini on his next conversation with Hitler, therefore, he was careful to note that 'the Führer always thinks it extremely important for us to maintain the peace in the Danubian–Balkanic sector.[118] From now on the Italians worked on the assumption, which as we have seen had some basis in reality, that while the 'Balkans' had of course to be left in peace Greece did not belong to the 'Balkans' and could therefore be invaded with impunity.[119]

Preparations for such an invasion were now shifted into gear, but on a basis quite different from the one discussed between Hitler and Ciano. Far from stressing the defensive, anti-British character of their intervention, the Italians seized upon the discovery of the headless corpse of one Daut Hoxha, cattle thief, in Albania as a pretext to open a propaganda campaign against Greece. Jacomini, who well knew his master's mind, sent Ciano a magnificent memorandum in which he commemorated the Albanian bandit as being 'animated by a great patriotic spirit' and claimed that he had been killed on the orders of the Greek government for supporting the Albanian claim to Ciamuria.[120] He also referred vaguely to more Greek murders of Albanians 'who hoped for Italian help to rejoin the motherland' and to 'insults' and 'repression' to which the Albanians in Ciamuria-Epirus were subjected by their cruel Greek overlords.

Delighted with this opportunity to foment trouble that might lead to the extension of the Albanian frontier, Ciano immediately told Mussolini of the 'difficulties which had arisen on the Graeco–Albanian border'. The Duce responded by 'contemplating an act of force', and a 'surprise attack' upon Greece towards the end of September. He ordered the press to start to 'stir up the problem', and had Ciano summon Jacomini and Visconti Prasca to Rome.[121] They arrived that very evening (10 August) and Ciano told them that 'for political reasons' Mussolini intended to occupy Ciamuria. They were taken to see the Duce in the following morning, and Visconti Prasca advocated an attack in about fifteen days, since otherwise the Greeks would learn of it and take counter-measures.[122] 'Jacomini and Visconti Prasca consider the operation possible and even easy, provided it is carried out at once. The Duce, on the other hand, remains of the opinion that . . . the operation should be postponed until the end of September.'[123]

Alarmed by the press campaign directed against his country, the Greek Prime Minister appealed to Berlin.[124] Hitler, as we have seen, was quite prepared to allow the Italians to have their way over Greece and even help them a bit, provided the venture served some useful purpose against England. He could not, however, tolerate the occupation of the remote, strategically worthless Ciamuria under a ridiculous irredentist pretext and thus risk the transformation of the rest of Greece into a British base. The adventure planned by Italy had another drawback; Yugoslavia's Albanian minority was even larger than Greece's, and an Italian operation based upon the irredentist claim to Ciamuria might therefore turn into a highly undesirable precedent.

On 14 August, therefore, Ribbentrop asked Alfieri whether Italy intended to go to war over her claims in Ciamuria. He was put off by the ambassador's declaration that he did not know and would send for instructions.[125] Ciano answered his question by telling him to inform Ribbentrop that:

Our attitude towards Greece is determined by motives of a precautionary nature . . . we cannot ignore the possibility lest the English proceed to occupy some naval bases on the Greek coast. In that case, we shall have at hand all the military means suitable to prevent such a British action. An epilogue to this situation, which does not exclude the possibility of reconciliation, may be expected in the first ten days of September.[126]

This was an extremely well calculated answer, wholly in the spirit of the Hitler–Ciano conversation of 7 July, and one to which Berlin could not possibly object. However, the fine point was wasted on Alfieri, who did not put it to use. Having digested, on 16 August, the sour contents of Ribbentrop's *démarche* concerning Italy's Yugoslav plans, he asked him point blank: 'Was he right in assuming that the same applied to Greece?' 'Yes, yes, of course,' replied an astonished Ribbentrop, who had obviously not expected this question[127] and was caught with his pants down.

Alfieri had now heard enough. 'Both the Greek and Yugoslav questions', he wired to Rome, 'are seen by Ribbentrop as a function of the decisive struggle against England.' This was perfectly true in itself, but not in the sense Alfieri understood it; Berlin was in fact considering both questions from the point of view of the war against England, but while this point of view would in any case make an attack on Yugoslavia appear as a superfluous blunder it could also, under certain circumstances, justify the occupation of Greece. This point was in fact made by Ribbentrop who, while categorically rejecting 'even purely technical studies' concerning Yugoslavia because they were not 'immediately relevant to the defeat of England' and would only present a 'distraction to the general staffs',[128] also explicitly added he had 'nothing to say about preparations bearing a precautionary character' against Greece.[129] However, the importance of this distinction was lost on Alfieri, who proceeded to tell Ciano that 'as far as Russia is concerned, it is . . . necessary to do whatever is possible to . . . avoid making possible the realization of her expansionist tendencies . . . by means of acts which help to create situations favourable to her.' This, too, could refer only to Yugoslavia, an invasion which the Germans had originally intended to veto; it applied with far less force to Greece, whose geographical position compared favourably with that of Yugoslavia and which had not even recognized the Soviet Union.

With these factors in mind, Rome could only blink with astonishment at the news from Berlin. In view of past events there was very little room for surprise at Hitler's reaction to Mussolini's Yugoslav plans, but a German veto on an eventual preventive operation in Greece had clearly not been expected. Having as yet no inkling of the blunder committed by Alfieri, Ciano moodily confided to his diary that 'an eventual action against Greece is not at all welcome in Berlin; it is a complete order to halt all along the line'.[130] Soon, however, it turned out that things were not so bad after all.

PREPARING A 'COLPO DI MANO'

On 17 August 1940 the Italian government found itself in the embarrassing position of being forced to surrender, not for the first time, to an ultimatum from Berlin. That this was so, was partly the fault of Mussolini himself, for he had insisted on ramming the Yugoslav issue down the Nazi throat long after it had been made clear to him that Berlin was sick and tired of the subject; on the other hand, the unnecessary German 'veto' on action against Greece, was mainly due to

Alfieri's bad diplomacy – but this, of course, was a factor which Rome could not yet know.

As far as Yugoslavia was concerned unconditional surrender was the only way out. The campaign against her had been planned on the assumption that German help, at least to the extent of allowing Italian troops to operate from Austria, would be forthcoming; now that this hope had been disappointed the entire plan collapsed. The war of words against Yugoslavia was halted at once; contacts with the Hungarian general staff, which had already been initiated, were suspended immediately.[131] The general staff dropped its attempts to update the plan because the question was considered 'outdated'.[132] As the prerequisites of the campaign vanished into thin air, the operations department of Stamage appealed for fresh directives, to be fobbed off by Badoglio with the words '*i direttive sono: lasciar dormire*'.[133] Some kind of *schieramento* was still planned for the eastern frontier, but nobody in the army knew what it was to be like, nor cared very much.[134] Even Mussolini, an occasional fit of anger notwithstanding,[135] had to recognize the game was lost. On 12 September the operation was officially scaled down; the Duce now simply had in mind an invasion in support of a Croat rising which he still hoped was imminent;[136] by the end of the month even this *schieramento* had been practically abandoned and the order to demobilize the army was issued.[137] The final order, cancelling the entire plan, followed on 4 October.[138]

The story of Greece was more complicated. After the German *démarche* Ciano had called on Mackensen and promised him that 'for the moment' everything would be deferred 'as having only secondary importance to the supreme goal of the Axis powers, namely the defeat of England'. He was just going to send Alfieri a telegram that was 'largely inspired, or one could say, dictated by the Duce' in which Mussolini assured his nervous partner that, while no action against Yugoslavia was contemplated, 'the controversy with Greece would be dealt with by diplomatic means'. Significantly, he added that the fact that Italy was reinforcing her six divisions in Albania by another three was not to be construed as a prelude to military action.[139] Ciano next improved on his role as messenger boy and sent a watered-down version of this telegram to Berlin: 'the Italian government is in accord with the German government in the conviction that the war against England is one of fundamental significance also in respect of all objectives of political systematization'. This was clean language going back to his original instructions. 'No action of any sort is intended against Yugoslavia' – a promise which Ciano, with his marked preference for Greece, must have found easy to make – while 'THE ATTEMPT IS NOW BEING MADE [emphasis supplied] to transfer the controversy with Greece to the diplomatic plane.'[140]

Ciano was clearly recovering his nerve, and so was Mussolini. The latter's first reaction to the German *démarche* had been to draft a military directive indefinitely postponing the action against Greece and Yugoslavia;[141] he at first wanted to inform Hitler of this by telephone, but then countermanded his own instructions and decided to send it in writing.[142] Finally he did neither of these, but went back to his old policy of dispatching a letter in which he repeated that he was not going to alter his policy in the *bacino danubiano-balcanico*.[143] This was an elegant way out, using geographic rigmarole – nothing but a piece of Axis trickery.

Mussolini did not mean a word of what he said. Having examined the German 'veto' at leisure, he apparently concluded that it was not to be taken too tragically[144] and quickly came up with a new order: 'as to the Yugoslav affair ... ITS IMPORTANCE HAS LAPSED. [The general staff] is to hold ready for Greece ... possible lines of action are to be studied.'[145] Preparations then went on undisturbed. Ciano ordered Jacomini 'to slow down the pace' but 'to retain the potential effectiveness of measures already taken'; Roatta informed Visconti Prasca that the operation had been postponed from 1 September to 1 October and that the assembly of the troops required would be delayed accordingly.[146] Planning went on as usual, with Corfu and the islands commanding the Gulf of Patras being added – with the explicit aim of endowing the whole business with a more pronounced anti-British character – to the list of places to be occupied.[147] Even the troop transports, originally suspended, were resumed after a few days[148] – as clear a sign as any that the Italians had recovered their composure after the first impression of the German 'veto' had worn off. If the operation was further postponed, and scheduled for 20 October, this was the result not of German pressure but of transport difficulties.[149]

Why did the Italians give up Yugoslavia, while going ahead with their preparations for Greece? The answer is probably to be found in the fact that while no full scale invasion of the former was possible without German help, the latter was weaker and presumably liable to occupation without such aid. After all, Greece had a population of only 8 millions compared with Yugoslavia's 16.[150] Moreover, it seems likely that Mussolini and Ciano had made some kind of guess about Alfieri's blunder – in any case, the latter was never again utilized as an intermediary on this question – and correctly concluded that the Germans were more concerned with Yugoslavia than with Greece. Ribbentrop was reported to have said that 'every effort must be concentrated against England ... because there alone is the question of life and death';[151] therefore better drop the entire foolish claim to Ciamuria – which could not and did not interest Hitler – and stress the anti-British character of the Greek venture. This line was consistently adopted, and with considerable success. Mussolini's letter to Hitler of 24 August already contains no reference to the Daut Hoxha affair; instead, the 'efficient, continuous and verified complicity of Greece with Great Britain' was stressed and the 'fact' that 'all Greek ports are bases against us' emphasized.[152] The same line was adopted – with considerable success, that reminds one of the Hitler–Ciano conversation of 7 July – by Mussolini at his next meeting with Ribbentrop,[153] and so on to within four days of the actual attack by Ciano, Roatta and Badoglio.[154] At the same time, the irredentist claim to Ciamuria disappears never to be taken up again. The Italians had evidently reopened their old records and drawn the right conclusions. To attack Greece, it was Ciano's tactics of July, not Jacomini's of August, that were the right ones.

Meanwhile, they made some attempt to carry their 'controversy with Greece' into the 'diplomatic plane' as promised. For Ciano himself this was nothing new since he had always hoped that Greece would give way without war.[155] At the first shock of the German veto the Italians had justified their decision to bring up further forces by the need to exercise political pressure on Greece,[156] and there are some indications that this was not just an attempt to throw dust in their allies' eyes.[157] On 13 August, the German minister in Athens had seen Metaxas and demanded a change in Greece's policy; Metaxas, however, merely replied that he could not do so as long as England ruled the Mediterranean.[158] This was an old story that the Greek minister president had already used on a number of occasions; perhaps in order to show Athens exactly who ruled the *Mare Nostrum*, that typical *stile fascista* attack – the torpedoing of the old cruiser *Helle* right in the middle of a religious festival at Tinos – took place a mere two days later. Ciano next prepared a note for the Greek government, in which he claimed that 'the questions which divide Greece and Albania [*sic*] are not essentially dissimilar – in fact, they are very much similar – to those which exist in other zones of the Danubian–Balkanic sector, where frontiers were drawn with an eye more to opportunity than to justice. The solution could also be similar.' Ciano then asked the Greeks to agree to a solution 'on the same basis as the one adopted – or being adopted – in similar circumstances in the Danubian–Balkanic region', i.e. similar to the Second Vienna Award, under the terms of which two thirds of Transylvania were just being granted to Hungary.[159] However, the note was never delivered, perhaps because the Italians, as we have seen, had sufficiently recovered from the stupor following the German veto to fix a new date for the attack, and because Ciano, who wanted to have 'his' war against Greece, felt he could now dispense with such diplomatic niceties.

Berlin on the other hand seems to have regarded the proposal to transfer the controversy to the diplomatic plane more seriously. There, too, people had for some time hoped that Greece would cede without offering resistance,[160] and in any case there could be no harm in an attempt to bully her into submission. Even before 16 August Weizsäcker had coolly told Rizo Rangabe, whom Metaxas had instructed to inquire about Italian intentions towards Greece, that his country had better change its pro-British orientation.[161] Following the attack on *Helle* Rizo Rangabe reappeared in the Wilhelmstrasse and asked for an interview with Ribbentrop. He was told – quite truthfully – that the foreign minister was out of town and had to content himself with discussions with Woermann the undersecretary of state. The latter answered his questions evasively, stating merely that 'as his personal opinion' no attack on Greece seemed 'imminent'.[162] After the departure of the ambassador, Woermann proceeded to draw up a memorandum in which he asked Ribbentrop's permission to tell Rizo Rangabe that 'According to our information no Italian attack on Greece is imminent: it will only take place if Greece provokes Italy.'[163] Considering the supposed German veto on Italian action against Greece, and the German desire to keep the Balkans peaceful, this was the logical answer calculated to calm things down; but this does not seem to have been Ribbentrop's aim when he vetoed Woermann's memo and instructed him to treat the matter dilatorily,[164] thus keeping the pressure on Greece. Consequently, the unhappy ambassador was unable to get any new information; instead, his government had to suffer further agony when Erbach joined the war of nerves 'in close understanding with his Italian colleague, in an attempt to make it clear to the Greeks that their safety could be found only in understanding obeisance to the small and great desires of the Axis powers'.[165]

A week after his original application, Rizo Rangabe was finally received by Ribbentrop at the latter's estate in Fuschl. Far from being comforted, however, the unhappy ambassador was subjected to a series of savage threats: Germany

classified countries as those which aligned themselves with the Axis, and those which had aligned themselves with England. We considered Greece as a country which had gone over to England ... such an attitude seemed unwise to the foreign minister. For the coming centuries, Europe would be controlled by the Axis powers, and the attitude of the Axis towards the European countries would be guided by the attitude which these states maintained towards England in the fight which Germany and Italy were waging for their existence.

Rizo Rangabe was next confronted with a large number of accusations, which the Germans explicitly knew[166] were unfounded, regarding the aid Greece had allegedly given to the English, and advised 'to reach an agreement with the Italians'. Ribbentrop then stressed that 'the

Mediterranean was the sphere of interest of our allies', and that he was consequently determined not to interfere. Finally, the hapless Greek was treated to a typical piece of Nazi diplomacy; Ribbentrop warned him against any mobilization, since 'a mobilization had started the Czech crisis and had led to the total annihilation of Czechoslovakia'.[167] It remained for the Greeks to find out exactly what the Axis desired; here, however, they failed because the Italians could not or would not make up their minds.[168] As a result, the diplomatic campaign slowly petered out, despite some later outbursts in Berlin.[169]

Why did the Italians not pursue their war of nerves more vigorously, and why did the Greeks, who according to Grazzi were not averse to negotiations,[170] not yield? The reason is probably that though the Germans did not have to lie when informing the Italians of the harsh treatment meted out to the Greeks,[171] Rome does not seem to have believed these assurances. Thus Lanza, usually so well-informed, noted – quite wrongly, as we have seen – that Ribbentrop 'has given the Greek minister . . . full assurances and was at pains to demonstrate all the dangers and complications that would result from an Italian action in the Balkans.'[172] Ciano's note, too, seems to contain more than a hint of sarcasm. On the other hand, the Greek government received a message from Politis, its minister in Italy, according to whom Berlin, though recognizing the Mediterranean as an Italian sphere of influence, intervened in Rome and 'signified her wish that peace should on no account be disturbed in the Balkans'. This meant that 'Germany's objections are confined to the event of military action, whereas she continues under an obligation to . . . support Italy's efforts to solve by diplomatic means the questions regarded by the latter as affecting her vital interests'. According to Politis, Italy had asked that Corfu and Ciamuria be recognized as such.[173] All this fits perfectly well into the German attempt to intimidate Greece as described above, but was hardly calculated to affect the Greek Prime Minister who, as later events were to prove, remained steadfast.

This interpretation may also explain why for a further week after the German veto the Italians went on inventing charges against Greece;[174] Mussolini and Ciano must have hoped to achieve their aims within the framework of the 'small' diplomatic solution with German help, but then, as the reports concerning the activities of Rizo Rangabe in Berlin came in, concluded that their allies were double crossing them and plunged for a military solution. A fresh date for this was then decided upon. Quite naturally, the Germans were content to follow their allies' example and let the war of nerves against Greece die out.

Meanwhile, Italian military preparations for Greece remained very much alive. The Daut Hoxha affair had been dropped like a hot potato, but this did not imply a renunciation of the planned attack, nor even a change in the operational plan which still aimed at the occupation of Ciamuria rather than at the conquest of the entire Greek mainland. Conceived by General Geloso in July 1940 and later slightly modified by the general staff,[175] the plan was based on the remarkable assumption that one could fight a 'large' or a 'small' war according to one's own choice; the occupation of the whole of Greece would require twenty divisions, and since this number could not be brought up fast enough to suit Mussolini it was decided to conduct a 'small' campaign for the occupation of Ciamuria only; nine divisions only would suffice.[176] The whole thing was not even conceived as a 'war' against Greece, but, in the words of Visconti Prasca, as a *colpo di mano in grande*,[177] a kind of military parade carried out against slight opposition, which the bulk of the Greek forces concentrated on the Bulgarian frontier.[178] At the end of August it was decided to allocate a further division for the occupation of Corfu, while the transportation of the forces designed to raise the number of troops in Albania to the required level – 'Parma, Sienna' and 'Piemonte' divisions – was started early in September.[179] By the end of the month, these forces had arrived and were ready for action.[180] Ciano was determined to have 'his' war, and at no time after the beginning of September was there any doubt but that he would.[181]

It is almost unnecessary to add that these activities did not escape German attention. The military attaché von Rintelen had in fact reported the resumption of preparations almost as soon as the decision was made,[182] while the Greeks complained about troop concentrations on their border.[183] However, Berlin did not react to the news; late in August, people there had more important matters to think about.

GREECE AND THE MEDITERRANEAN

WAR IN THE PERIPHERY

Balkan problems were forcing Hitler to work overtime late in August 1940. Just when it seemed that he had successfully restrained the Duce's Yugoslav ambitions, another danger to peace in the Danube Basin arose: that of Magyar revisionism. The Hungarians, indeed, had chosen to revive their claim to Transylvania in April; and it had taken a stern Axis warning to prevent an explosion that would have been disastrous to German economic interests in the area. In August, however, there was no holding the Hungarians; Prime Minister Teleki and Foreign Minister Czaky announced their determination to solve the Transylvanian problem at all costs, even at the risk of war, and the two countries had in fact already begun to shoot it out. To Hitler such a war – particularly in view of the attractive prospects it would offer to the Soviets, who were apparently encouraging Hungary[1] – could not but end in disaster. He therefore summoned the parties to the Vienna Belvedere in order to impose the so-called Second Vienna Award.[2] Under the terms of this Hungary was granted about two thirds of her claims. For good measure, Bulgaria was also promised a slice of the Dobrudja in return for coexisting peacefully with Rumania. What was left of Rumania – the Russians had already taken their share in the Bukovina and northern Bessarabia – was then guaranteed by Germany. Hitler hoped that this settlement would take the fuse out of the Danube powder keg.

On his return from Vienna, Hitler found new problems awaiting him. The Führer discovered that, despite the far reaching improvement in his strategic position effected by the defeat of France the fundamental problem facing him had not really been modified. Now as before, there was an actively fighting opponent in the west, one which could, if driven to its limits, count upon the help of the United States. As the half hearted attempt to achieve a compromise peace had failed,[3] the 'life and death' struggle against Great Britain must go on. On 16 July therefore, after some preliminaries which are irrelevant to our subject,[4] the invasion of the British Isles was ordered.[5] Preparations for the landing were to be completed by the middle of August, but in fact by the 14th of that month doubts as to whether it was to be carried out had already appeared.[6] After the end of August Hitler's interest in the operation rapidly diminished,[7] while a variety of circumstances made its realization before the end of September impossible.[8] Long before that time the operation had for all practical purposes been cancelled and a different course adopted.[9]

The new plan to bring England down was less direct and more time consuming. It aimed to dispense with a straightforward invasion of the British Isles by hitting Great Britain at other vulnerable spots – particularly the Mediterranean, since that was about the only part of the British Empire that was within the reach of the Axis powers. The idea appeared for the first time in a memorandum prepared by General Jodl of OKW in January 1940.[10] For practical purposes, the starting date of the so-called 'peripheral' strategy must be fixed at 20 June, when Hitler called his naval commander-in-chief, Admiral Raeder, to discuss the German occupation of the Azores and other Atlantic Islands.[11] A somewhat more detailed discussion of these problems is contained in a Seekriegsleitung memorandum written eight days later: 'the delimitation of Russian and Italian interests, which is in progress,[12] gives room to hope that in the not too distant future these states will move in accordance with a plan inspired by Germany and with the support of German arms, with the goal of bringing down the British position in the Near East ... It is certain that in the near future five armoured divisions will be ... re-equipped for employment overseas, as will a series of infantry divisions.'[13] By 30 June a coherent plan of action had been worked out by General Jodl, who was always one of the main exponents of this approach.[14]

Since political means do not lead to the desired results, England's will to resist must be broken by other means.

a. Warfare against the British Isles. b. Extension of the war to the periphery ...

Germany's final victory is a question of time only...

As to (b): the war against England can be conducted only through or by means of states interested in the downfall of the British Empire ... these are, in the first place, Italy, Spain, Russia and Japan...

England cannot fight for victory any more, but only to maintain her colonies and world position. It can therefore be expected that she would be ready for peace, if convinced that this aim can still be cheaply achieved. On the other hand, she will resist to the bitter end any attempt to eliminate her.

The 'peripheral' strategy would consist of a series of attacks on the British world position, providing a progressive tightening of the screw until England was ready to yield in order to cut her losses. The first step in this direction, according to Jodl, was to be the occupation of the Suez Canal by the Italians, a measure which was in fact discussed between Hitler and the Italian ambassador only one day later.[15] The

Führer also wanted to take Gibraltar, thus anticipating both essential elements of the future strategy. Various other suggestions, such as an attack on the oil pipe terminus in Haifa, were considered during July.[16] By the end of August it had been decided that Suez and Gibraltar were the most promising targets.[17] By 5 September both proposals had received Hitler's blessing and preparations were under way.[18] Since at that time the war industry had already received instructions to prepare a programme based on the assumption that England would not collapse in 1940,[19] it must be concluded that Hitler had more or less made up his mind that an invasion of the British Isles would not be attempted. Accordingly, he was easily won over to the more detailed schemes submitted by Raeder on 6 and 26 September.[20] As early as 10 September a directive summing up the measures forming part of the 'peripheral' strategy – the future No. 18 – was being discussed.[21]

At the same time, Hitler scanned the horizon for possible allies in the struggle against England. Since Jodl had already listed them, it remained for him to endow this conception with typically grandiloquent names; he spoke about a 'continental block' and about 'an anti-British front stretching from Morocco to Norway'.[22] Italy, Spain, Russia and Japan were listed as potential allies. As the cooperation of Italy and Spain was needed for the realization of the most immediate plans – the occupation of Suez and Gibraltar – Hitler set out to win them over. Contacts with Spain, broken off in June, were resumed in September,[23] but negotiations with Serrano Suner the foreign minister proved tricky and unsatisfactory because Spain demanded a lot – particularly at France's expense, in North West Africa – and offered but little.[24] Italy, too, was sounded; on 10 September Rintelen, who had just returned from a visit to Berlin, met Badoglio for a long conversation about the new approach.[25] On 13 September a visit by Ribbentrop to Rome – supposed to open the way towards the signature of a Tripartite Pact between Germany, Italy and Japan – was announced;[26] by the time he arrived on the 19th, the Italians must have been aware, at least in outline, of the new German approach.

THE CHANGING ROLE OF GREECE

The German decision to abandon the landing in the British Isles and to concentrate on battering the English position in the Mediterranean had important implications for the Balkan countries, above all for Greece. Hitler's basic aim in the Danube region was not affected by his decision to turn to the Mediterranean; now as before, he needed the raw materials from that region, and was therefore interested in keeping the peace in Hungary, Rumania, Yugoslavia and Bulgaria.

Above all, he was anxious to keep his supply of raw materials out of Russian hands – he had irresponsibly committed the entire region to them the previous year. His anxiety had led to the Second Vienna Award, to the subsequent guarantee and to the dispatch of troops to Rumania.[27] From a strategic point of view, the decision to turn south did not open any new perspectives in that part of Europe, for England's interests there were nominal. Thus, southeastern Europe remained what she had always been – a source of raw materials, above all oil, and a prize for Germany and Russia to fight over; not, however, a region that was strategically important for the war against England.

As far as Greece was concerned, however, matters were radically different. From being an irrelevant appendix to the *settore danubiano-balcanico*, one that had better be left in peace in order to avoid unnecessary complications but was otherwise quite unimportant, Greece, and in particular Crete, turned into a potential base for operations against the entire British position in the Near and Middle East. The occupation of the Greek mainland, together with the Aegean Archipelago, would do more than merely open the way towards the effective use of the Italian-held Dodecanese Islands as an aeronaval base against Egypt; it would immensely reinforce the Axis position in the Mediterranean. Two imposing aeronaval systems, the Ionian–Libyan–Sicilian and the Greek–Aegean–Cretan, would interlock to form a large and well guarded basis for aeronaval manoeuvring on internal lines between its various parts, restricting the English to two mutually isolated strongholds in Alexandria and Gibraltar, and eventually forcing them to abandon the Mediterranean altogether.[28] The possession of the Peloponnese and Crete would secure the flank of the Italian advance into Egypt, and at the same time help construct a bridge for the sort of operations against Syria, which were being urged by Raeder as part of the 'peripheral' strategy. The possibility – not yet realized but always in mind – that Greece might be used by the British as an aeronaval base against Italy would be eliminated, and the Italo–German bases correspondingly advanced in the direction of Alexandria.[29] The base for an eventual two-pronged attack on Syria and Northern Iraq from both Egypt and Turkey, would have been secured. British sea communications in the eastern Mediterranean would be put in jeopardy, while those of the Axis from Constanta through the Dardanelles to Italy would be safeguarded. The occupation of Greece and her islands would, in sum be a huge step towards the expulsion of the British from their Near and Middle Eastern positions, the effect of which would be disastrous.[30] All this, it must be emphasized, came to be clearly recognized by both Hitler and the German armed forces high command.[31]

It will be understood, therefore, that during Ribbentrop's visit to Rome on 19–20 September the Greek problem, if not the Yugoslav one, presented itself in a completely new light. Although within the framework of the Mediterranean warfare against Great Britain it may not yet have been examined in sufficient thoroughness its fundamental importance must have been pretty clear. Even though Ribbentrop refused to admit to his hosts that the landing in England had been a flop – he may not have been informed himself – the Italians were not misled; to them, probably as a result of the Rintelen–Badoglio conversation, it was quite clear that 'Germany will not carry out the landing in England, and the war will be completely transferred to the Mediterranean. Instead of fighting England on her own soil, an attempt will be made to defeat her in Egypt.'[32] In this context, certain aspects of the Italian plans for Greece might well be discussed; and Mussolini, aided by Ciano, set out to explore them. The adroitness displayed in the process shows that the lessons of July and August had not been forgotten.[33]

While Mussolini and Ciano regarded the talks as an opportunity to forward their own plans, Ribbentrop found himself in an unpleasant position. He had come to Rome in order, among other things, to announce the imminent signature of the Tripartite Pact between Germany, Japan and Italy. The relevant negotiations had been carried out almost exclusively between Germany and Japan[34] so that the Italians were effectively faced with a *fait accompli* to which they were asked to add their signature. To win them over, Ribbentrop had to explain to them their share in the division of the world, and particularly to reassure them that German incursions into their recognized sphere of influence (as had occurred in August) would not be repeated. At the same time he was to sound Italy about the formation of a German–Russian bloc, an awkward mission, as Germany herself had intervened to prevent an Italo–Soviet *rapprochement* in July. Ribbentrop, in short, was at a disadvantage, and in no position to raise objections to any demands the Italians might make.

This being so, the Nazi foreign minister tried to forestall such demands. Contrary to what might have been expected, it was he, not the Italians, who raised the question of Greece and Yugoslavia; bundling the two questions together, he 'emphasized' that they formed an 'exclusive . . . Italian interest', and tried to deal with them by saying that although 'at the present time' it was better to concentrate our 'entire effort' against England, Italy could count on Germany's 'sympathetic support' in dealing with these states at some future date.[35] This provided the Duce with the opening he had been waiting for. Ribbentrop was looking for fresh ways to combat England; he, Mussolini, would provide him with one. Both the German and the Italian records of the conversation agree that the Duce, evidently intent on avoiding the pitfalls of August, did not waste a single word on the

Albanian irredentist claim to Ciamuria; instead, he proceeded with vehement denunciations of Greece as an English stooge. Deftly using the comparison between Greece and Norway – it was one that Hitler himself had put into his mouth,[36] and to which Ribbentrop could not possibly object – he emphasized the importance of Greece within the framework of the Mediterranean war against England, and pointed out that the Greek harbours could, if necessary, serve as a refuge for the British fleet after the expected fall of Egypt. Belatedly, Ribbentrop realized that by raising the issue he had set a trap for himself. Rather lamely, he countered that the escape of the British fleet to Greece would be a good thing, because it would be easier to bombard there.

Mussolini had won an impressive victory. He had succeeded in establishing the need for Italy 'to proceed towards the liquidation of Greece', while 'at the same time' admitting that 'the principal objective was to defeat England' – all this without evoking German protest. He had not, indeed, extracted an unequivocal go ahead, but the consequences of Alfieri's blunder of August had been more than compensated for: the Germans were returning to their former willingness – expressed in July – to tolerate an Italian attack on Greece in certain circumstances. However, and this is the crucial point, the circumstances themselves had altered. The character of the Italian attack on Greece had completely changed: from a defensive measure against the unlikely eventuality of a British occupation of the Greek islands – not considered that unlikely any more[37] – it was now implicitly recognized as part of the Mediterranean offensive against England. Mussolini had recognized that 'the principal objective was to defeat England' (according to the Italian record) and promised 'first of all to carry out the attack on Egypt' (according to the German one); for the rest, he had his way. As he expected the second stage of his Egyptian offensive, the advance from Sidi al Barrani to Mersa Matruh, to start in mid-October,[38] this arrangement did not even involve a delay in his original timetable. Above all, he had received what amounted to tacit German approval for his plans for Greece; and Mussolini, it must be remembered, had a knack for 'tacit approvals'. The fact that he did get it should not perplex us too much. After all, the Greek operation, if carried out in the sequence mentioned at Rome, that is after the occupation or at least closing of the Suez Canal, would make perfect strategic sense even in the sober eyes of OKH.[39]

Mussolini did not receive a similar German authorization on Yugoslavia. Indeed, it is doubtful whether he asked for one. The Italian invasion of that country, it will be remembered, could not be carried out without German help, and consequently very little was done to prepare for it. The available evidence does not make clear what exactly was said about the subject. According to the German record, Mussolini followed Ribbentrop in lumping the country together with Greece and in stressing his desire 'to remain at peace' with both; according to the Italian one, which seems more credible, he scarcely mentioned it at all. Strategic considerations made it very difficult to present Yugoslavia as a target in the war against England, and it is unlikely that Mussolini tried. The savagery of the German reply to his former attempt must have been in his mind; and in any case, an attack on Yugoslavia would place him in the uncomfortable position of having to ask for German help. All these considerations must have made Mussolini play down his plans for that country; and the order for demobilization, issued a few days later, confirms this interpretation.

GREEN LIGHT AT THE BRENNER

On his return from Rome, Ribbentrop found the atmosphere in Berlin was undergoing a change. The talks with Serrano Suner about Spain's entry into the war had been difficult, and the Führer, prodded on by von Stohrer (German ambassador to Madrid), OKW, Halder and the Seekriegsleitung,[40] all of who combined to emphasize the manifold drawbacks of the Spanish alliance, began to have second thoughts. Spain offered but little in the way of military assistance, but asked an exorbitant price for her help. Not only would she require generous German aid in military equipment, raw materials and food-stuffs,[41] but her demands in North West Africa, where she hoped to take over a sizeable chunk of the French Empire, were such that any attempt to put them into practice would lead to the immediate defection of the whole of French Africa to de Gaulle and the British. This was something which Hitler, who did not have a strong navy, would be in no position to prevent. As the Spaniards were not even ready to cede the Canary Islands to Germany as Hitler had asked in order to protect this strategically important area,[42] Hitler was, probably much against his will,[43] forced to try and persuade the French to defend their colonies themselves.

During the second half of September, therefore, France loomed ever larger as a possible partner. The various stages in Hitler's decision-making need not concern us here, but the most important single factor seems to have been the determined and successful resistance put up by the French to the British attempt to seize Dakar on 23–5 September.[44] On 23 September a French request for an anti-British alliance was being examined 'with great interest'.[45] By the 25th, although the Führer was regarded by his collaborators as getting nearer a line of thought that would lead him into an alliance with France, the situation was still 'entirely fluid'.[46] It must have been sometime after this date that he told Raeder that he would 'probably' rather collaborate with

France than with Spain, because the latter was offering too little and demanding too much.[47] On 26 September he was already contemplating a meeting with Pétain,[48] and by 28 September he made up his mind. On that day he agreed with Ciano on a meeting with Mussolini to be held on 4 October, in order to discuss the new approach.[49] During the next few days his decision to try and win over Italy to a policy of cooperation with France seems to have hardened.[50]

Italian resistance, indeed, was the most immediate obstacle to any kind of German–French cooperation, however limited. From July onwards, the Italians had left no stone unturned in their efforts to drive away even the shadow of such a possibility.[51] They also objected to the release of any French forces for the defence of the French Empire,[52] so that Hitler was forced to use a trick when allowing French forces stationed in Africa to take part in the defence of Dakar.[53] The French would not defend their colonies if convinced they were to be handed over to Italy; Mussolini therefore had to drop his claims, as well as agree to a partial French rearmament in order to make the defence possible.[54] Hitler aimed to obtain this consent during his meeting with Mussolini.[55] Far from being ready to sacrifice French interests to Spain and Italy, as he had wanted during the time of Ribbentrop's visit to the Italian capital,[56] he now wanted to limit his ally's claims on her. This applied to Spain too; the question of her entry into the war was no longer considered 'acute'.[57]

Quite clearly coming to the Brenner in order to ask Mussolini to co-operate in something that would involve at least the temporary renunciation of the latter's most cherished war aims, placed Hitler in a relatively weak position: he could not make further demands, nor deny any requests the Duce might make. In particular, he would have to avoid rousing his ally's resentment by imposing a veto on his plans for Greece, rumours about which were circulating in Berlin.[58] From the records of the conversation, it would seem that Hitler succeeded in persuading the Duce to follow his example in his French policy,[59] without apparently offering any real compensation. The Italians, summing up the results of the conference for their own purposes, concluded that it meant that more attention would in the future be given to the Mediterranean, and particularly 'the eastern Mediterranean', which was considered 'good for us'.[60] Nowhere in the records of this conversation are the Balkans mentioned – a fact that is suspect in itself, because they had figured in practically every other important German–Italian communication since April.

The lack of any reference to the Balkans, however, does not prove that the matter was not touched upon by Hitler and Mussolini. The Brenner meeting of 4 October 1940 is one of the most 'fishy' in the history of World War II, in that it was hard to get a good account of it,[61] and because it gave rise to 'a heap of ambiguities in the [foreign] ministries of both sides'.[62] Even for the German ambassador in Rome it was impossible to find out 'whether the subject of Greece was not considered from a new point of view',[63] while one of Hitler's closest associates, puzzled by the latter's reluctance to put a brake on his ally's plans, concluded that 'it is not impossible that the Führer has reached an understanding with Mussolini concerning the attack on Greece during their meeting at the Brenner'.[64] The SKL even claimed to possess reports to the same effect.[65] So mysterious were these conversations that when Ciano later claimed that Hitler had allowed Mussolini to go ahead Ribbentrop felt unable to dismiss this as a tactical manoeuvre designed to throw sand in his eyes. He had to refer the statement to Hitler himself,[66] who did not repudiate it. The cumulative evidence that something about Greece did in fact pass between Hitler and Mussolini at the Brenner is therefore considerable. Mussolini knew some German, and used that language during at least part of the conference;[67] is it impossible that, in the break between the two sessions, the two leaders exchanged a few words between themselves? We shall never know. However, there is no real need to go as far as that. Assuming that the subject was left unmentioned, Mussolini would probably have interpreted Hitler's silence as tacit confirmation of what he regarded as the outcome of his talks with Ribbentrop.

In fact there is some evidence that he did more than that. Returning from the Brenner, he had Graziani issue the army circular that put a final end to what was left of his plans to attack Yugoslavia.[68] At the same time he had some new ideas about Greece:[69]

Today [5.10.1940] a message from the Duce arrived . . . it contains a short note for Badoglio . . . in which are enumerated the new aspects examined with the Führer . . . to this one, another for Graziani is appended . . .

This note [Badoglio's] contains new points that demonstrate the Duce's thoughts. Side al Barrani is a tactical success; Mersa Matruh will present a strategical one. . . Having reached Mersa Matruh, it will remain to be seen which of the two pillars of the British Mediterranean position is to fall first; the Egyptian or the Greek . . .

The action against Greece reappears and does not seem to be limited to the realization of immediate aims, but to aim at the elimination of an English stronghold. Not Ciamuria but Salonica and the Greek naval bases, that is the whole of Greece.

The meeting with Hitler had then given Mussolini a number of fresh ideas, the most important of which were 1. that Greece was to be attacked only after the occupation of Mersa Matruh (and the subsequent blocking of the Suez Canal by German bombers, which was proposed by Hitler) and in connection therewith; 2. that to be effective within such a framework, the invasion of Greece would have to aim not only at Ciamuria, but also at the occupation of the entire Greek mainland, and probably the islands too.[70] Since at that time Mussolini hoped to begin the advance on Mersa Matruh in the middle of the month, an attack on Greece at its end would be by no means unreasonable strategically.

Whether it is Mussolini's thoughts alone that are expressed in this directive, or whether they reflect something that had been discussed – at least in outline – at the Brenner, is hard to say. The language used on the significance of the capture of Mersa Matruh certainly suggests some military influence, and since Mussolini was not accompanied by any of his own generals at the meeting[71] it is as likely as not that he picked up the phrase about 'tactics' and 'strategy' directly from the chief of OKW, Field-marshal Keitel. However, speculation of this kind cannot yield definite results; it is to German plans of the same period that we must turn.

Both defensively and offensively, the Germans did in fact have some plans for the eastern Mediterranean. It will be remembered that in July and August Hitler and Ribbentrop respectively had authorized Italy to take precautionary measures against Greece in case a British landing in Crete were planned: and as during the autumn the British seemed to be concentrating their main strength in the Mediterranean it was felt in Berlin that this possibility was an increasingly real one.[72] In response to a Greek inquiry the British had said on 5 September that if there were a Greek–Italian war they would try to 'forestall' the Italians in Crete, and a force was in fact being held ready for the purpose.[73] This fact did not stay entirely hidden from Berlin's eyes, in that SKL received a report from Egypt that the English and Australian troops on the Suez Canal were busy carrying out embarkation and disembarkation manoeuvres on the Timsah Lake, at Ismailia and at Port Fuad. 'Together with other reports' this was regarded as a sign that the British were planning to occupy Crete, most probably in connection with the Italian offensive from Libya. On their side, the Greeks were reported to be preparing Crete and Lemnos 'for the landing of troops on a grand scale',[74] not Italian troops, to be sure. In view of these facts, SKL had its own interpretation for the meeting of 4 October:[75]

According to reports from several sources (in the first line the air force liaison officer) Italy plans to attack Greece on 26.10, possibly with Bulgarian help . . .

No official confirmation so far. The foreign ministry is not yet convinced of the correctness of the reports. Basically, it has been agreed with the Italians that a military offensive in the Balkans is to be written off in favour of the main war against England. However, reports lying before SKL say that during the talks between the Führer and the Duce the former had given Italy a free hand in case a military offensive against Greece becomes necessary to forestall an English initiative.

Defensively, therefore, Hitler was still committed to the line he had adopted in July and August, i.e. authorizing preventive measures. In a wider context, however, he was now committed to the 'peripheral' strategy, that is to offensive action in the Mediterranean. The decision which had just been made, to cooperate with France rather than with Spain, meant – as General Marras correctly surmised – that Gibraltar became the second priority, while the eastern Mediterranean would now become the centre of attention.[76] During October, this approach accordingly became the subject of serious study in the various German staffs. Operations on a large scale, against Egypt as well as against Syria (via Bulgaria and Turkey, ultimately aimed at Iraq) were being examined.[77] Into such a framework, operations against Greece, and particularly against Crete, could be made to fit without any difficulty.[78] An OKW study prepared on the question showed that, within this context, the advantages of a successful occupation of the whole of Greece would be very great – while the consequences of a failure would be equally grave.[79] The upshot of the investigation, conducted at both OKH and OKW and lasting for about two weeks, was a proposal which Jodl prepared to submit to Marras.[80] In this note, a combined German–Italian offensive in the eastern Mediterranean, including Crete and Greece in the last stage, was proposed:[81]

The following order of operations seems expedient:
1. The continuation of the Italian offensive in Libya, in order to take Mersa Matruh as soon as possible.
2. After the occupation of Mersa Matruh, continuation of the attack on the English naval squadron at Alexandria by all possible means.
3. After sufficient weakening of this squadron, the start of operations against Greece with simultaneous occupation of Crete.

Jodl also warned against any Italian action aimed at occupying only part of Greece, because this would inevitably lead to a British landing in what was left. His memorandum therefore contains both essential points of Mussolini's directive; the need to defer the Greek operation until after the seizure of Mersa Matruh,[82] and the importance of conquering the whole of Greece. The memorandum, prepared while Hitler was away in France, became redundant with the outbreak of the Italo–Greek war. Outdated, it was probably filed and never looked at again. Still, it is very much in line with Hitler's statement of 20 November, when he wrote to Mussolini that it would have been better to postpone the invasion of Greece until after a 'lightning like' occupation of Crete.[83]

The resemblance between the three above-mentioned documents – Mussolini's directive, Jodl's memo and Hitler's letter – is too great to be attributed to sheer chance. All three contain the same basic elements which, considered strategically, did after all make perfect sense. To argue that Mussolini, OKW, Halder and Hitler all arrived at the same solution independently is most unlikely. It is much more probable that Hitler, who had an excellent eye for strategy, told Mussolini at the Brenner that he could go ahead, provided that: 1. he waited until after the fall of Mersa Matruh; 2. made sure no part of Greece eluded his grasp.

To fulfil both these conditions, in fact, was just what Mussolini set out to do. Possibly losing patience with Graziani, who disobeyed the order he had received on 5 October to resume his advance by the middle of the month and kept postponing it,[84] he summoned Badoglio and Roatta to meet him on the 14th at the Palazzo Venezia. There, he informed the two flabbergasted generals of a radical change in his plans for Greece. There was no longer any question of occupying Ciamuria; he wanted the whole peninsula. This order was clearly designed to forestall a British landing, and the Italian general staff interpreted it as such.[85] Though one need not, in the light of the directive of 5 October, take Roatta's assertion that 'this was the first time on which I and the general staff received notice of this plan' too literally, there can be no doubt that he was stunned. Asked by the Duce how many troops would be needed, he answered that twenty divisions – engaged simultaneously at the beginning of the attack – were required. The transportation of those forces would require three months, so that the offensive could not be opened before February 1941. The Duce seemed to agree, ordered Roatta to cancel all demobilization measures – just initiated – and to prepare a timetable for the transfer of the twelve divisions needed to raise the total number of troops in Albania to the desired level. Roatta was also to prepare an operational plan for the commitment of these large forces, a plan which 'would not be put into effect before three months had passed'.[86]

By the next day, he had changed his mind again. Three months now seemed too long to wait for the elusive glory he desired. He therefore summoned another conference to the Palazzo Venezia. This time Ciano, Jacomini, Visconti Prasca and Soddu – but not, interestingly enough, the commanders of the air force and the navy – were also present. Seizing upon an old SMG memorandum, which requested 12 days notice before the start of the limited operation,[87] he now called for the attack to begin on the earliest possible date, that is 26 October. At the same time, he divided the operation into two stages; an initial advance into Ciamuria, followed later by a 'march on Athens'. By means of this piece of cleverness he obviously hoped to avoid the need to bring up further forces, and thus save three months.

With the problem of occupying the whole of Greece without wasting time now solved to his own satisfaction, Mussolini's attention was now drawn by Badoglio to the other part of his supposed agreement with

Hitler, i.e. the coordination of the invasion of Greece with the Italian offensive in Egypt. There were two sides to the question, the chief of staff explained:[88]

That of Greece and that of British aid. Like you I am of the opinion that there will almost certainly be no British landings. The British are far more preoccupied with Egypt than with Greece and will not willingly put their troops on board ships in the Mediterranean. Therefore, the only possible assistance will be with aircraft.

In anticipation of this it would be possible to make the operation against Greece coincide with the attack on Mersa Matruh. In this case it would be difficult for them to disengage aircraft from Egypt to send to Greece. We would do this because Graziani could also be ready by the 26th of the month.

To this Mussolini replied:

I should like Graziani's operation to take place some days beforehand. Then the fact of the conquest of Mersa Matruh will make the possibility of such assistance still more difficult, especially in view of the fact that we shall not halt there. Having lost their pivotal point, Egypt, the British Empire will be in a state of defeat, even if London can still hold out ... in addition there is the morale factor. This African success would give impetus to the soldiers in Albania.

That is why I should like to synchronize the two operations, with the African one slightly in advance.

In principle, at least, the Italian plan of attack was perfectly in accord with what the Germans would like it to be. The operation aimed at the conquest of the whole of Greece, and was coordinated with the Egyptian campaign. If everything went well, both parts of Mussolini's directive of 5 October would be fulfilled. The only sour point – admittedly an important one – was Crete. But the Italians were loath to employ their navy in an all out attempt to seize that island – unlike the British, they were in no position to replace their lost ships[89]– and in any case it is hard to see how Crete could be reached by the Italians with Greece between them and it. The occupation of the island, as the Germans discovered to their cost in May 1941, was difficult enough even when the Greek mainland was available as a base. In October 1940 the Italian staffs did in fact consider the operation, only to reject it.

ON THE WAY TO FLORENCE

Mussolini made his decision to attack Greece on 15 October; even though the German foreign ministry was professing a strange and unusual 'inability' to go to the heart of the matter,[90] Berlin soon knew everything about the plan. Thus, OKW on 18 October received notice from Rintelen that the attack would start on 26 October.[91] This was correct, except that Rintelen could not know that Badoglio had just succeeded in having the opening of hostilities postponed by two days.[92] There followed a long series of reports from the German representatives in Belgrade and Ankara, as well as the consul general in Tirana and the German general at the headquarters of the Italian air force, von Pohl, who also named the 26th.[93] Some of these reports – notably those sent by Mackensen – arrived in Berlin before Hitler's departure on his voyage to France and Spain, and are known to have been submitted to him. The first of these was a rather ambiguous telegram No. 473/40 g. of 18 October, which stated that Ciano was all for the attack, Badoglio against and Mussolini hesitating.[94] There followed No. 1883 of 19 October, in which the attack was announced in no uncertain terms and the date given as the 23rd.[95] Upon this Ritter, the director of Ribbentrop's office, prepared a strong *démarche* aimed at making Mussolini stop in his track. Ribbentrop, however, vetoed this draft as too explicit, and ordered Ritter to ask Mackensen to address a 'friendly inquiry' to Ciano. Before Ritter could carry out these instructions, however, a third telegram from Mackensen, No. 1884 dated 19 October, arrived. This time Mackensen reported that Ciano had told him that Hitler had approved Mussolini's plans to attack Greece.[96] Was this just a trick on Ciano's part? Ribbentrop, who had been present at the Brenner and may be assumed to have been as well informed as anybody of what had taken place there, did not think so. On receiving Ciano's statement he ordered Ritter to hold back his instructions to Mackensen until the matter could be cleared with the Führer. He then sent another collaborator, von Steengracht, to ask Hitler whether Ciano's words were based upon truth and what to do about them. Steengracht saw to it that No. 1884 was submitted to the Führer, then telephoned the latter's reply back to Ritter; Hitler had decided that 'no questions should be addressed to Rome'.[97] Mackensen next received a pointed reply to his question as to what to do about the news concerning the attack: 'you will notice that on this point we are at present sending you no instructions of any kind, and are not even directing you to make official inquiry as to whether there is some truth in the story or not'.[98] One would be hard pressed to imagine clearer terms in which Hitler, whose order directly inspired this telegram, could have expressed his reluctance to interfere with Mussolini's Greek plans.

Meanwhile, there were other things to occupy his mind. The decision to opt for France rather than for Spain had opened a number of extremely complicated political questions, which, he must have felt, he alone was able to solve. While hoping to win over the French, he still needed the Spaniards cooperation for the seizure of Gibraltar. The claims of the latter thus imposed a limit on what he could offer to the former. At the same time, he would have to keep a wary eye on his Italian partner, whose suspicions of the French were by no means lulled. Consequently, he decided to make what was for him an unprecedented gesture; he would travel to France in order to meet Pétain, and to Spain in order to meet Franco.[99] The fact that this was the first and the last time in Hitler's entire career as a dictator that he left his headquarters for anybody less than the Duce is a singular indication of the importance he attributed to the whole affair.

At 2330 hours on 20 October,[100] therefore, he set out on a journey that would finally take him over almost 4000 miles. His aim was to try, by means of personal encounters, to persuade the French, Spaniards and Italians to forget their differences and cooperate in the construction of a 'continental bloc' directed against England. This was a truly Herculean task, one that, as he himself chose to put it, could be carried out only through a 'grandiose fraud'.[101]

Hitler's special train, nicknamed 'Amerika', travelled through Aachen, Namur, Yvoir and Vendôme to arrive at Montoire, where he was to meet the French premier, Laval, at 1800 hours on the 22nd.[102] Ribbentrop's special train, 'Heinrich', carrying the Nazi foreign minister and his numerous staff, had arrived half an hour earlier, complete with two documents which merit some attention. Drafted on the way to Montoire,[103] they consisted of a letter summing up – in advance – the results of the meeting, as well as a draft of a German–Italian–French protocol. The contents of both documents are roughly similar; in return for recognizing France's 'rightful place in Europe' after the end of the war, the Axis powers wanted her to cooperate militarily against England, particularly in Africa.[104] Whether Hitler did or did not actually see the documents in question[105] is not really relevant; they do, in any case, represent what he would have liked to be the outcome of his talks with Laval and Pétain.

At 1830 hours the German ambassador to Paris, Abetz, arrived bringing Laval with him. The Hitler–Ribbentrop–Laval meeting started an hour later. Laval was not authorized to sign any agreement, but the record does show a clear willingness on his side.[106] After spending the night at the railway station, Hitler travelled on to Hendaye on the French–Spanish border. There, on 23 October, he met Franco and his newly appointed foreign minister, Serrano Suner. In a conversation lasting for three and a half hours, nothing was achieved. Franco would not promise to enter the war, and repeated his enormous demands.[107]

The failure of the talks at Hendaye naturally made the forthcoming meeting with Pétain appear even more important. If the journey was not to end in a fiasco, and if part at least of the 'continental block' idea was to become a reality, France had to be won over, and Hitler was clearly determined to do this.[108] Pétain, in fact, turned out more reserved – and the meeting with him less of a success – than Laval,[109] but Hitler does not seem to have noticed the fact.[110] The old Marshal's personality left a tremendous impression on the ex-*Gefreiter*,[111] while OKH, OKW, SKL and the foreign ministry were all convinced that the meeting had been a great success.[112] Cooperation was agreed upon in principle, while the details were to be settled in the near future.[113]

It was time, after this great achievement, to cast a wary eye towards the other end of the Axis and make sure it would not mar the results just obtained by raising excessive claims on France. The news of Hitler's journey to France, which reached Rome on 20 October,[114] had been met with ill-disguised anger. His meetings with Laval and Pétain had caused many sour faces to appear at the Italian embassy in Berlin,[115] while putting Mussolini in a 'black mood' because 'the Germans prefer the French to us'.[116] Italy's resentment was expressed in more than mere words. As soon as Hitler set out on his journey, the Italians started to foment trouble by demanding control of the French Mediterranean coast and Marseilles.[117] Interpreting French policy as designed to delay the cession of colonies in the hope of future British and American aid, they hinted darkly at some kind of conspiracy between Pétain and de Gaulle.[118] To make sure Hitler's French policy would not poach on their preserves, they prepared a long list of territorial and economic concessions which were to be demanded of France.[119] All this scarcely foreshadowed any good in connection with the attempt to win over the French; if Italy was to be prevented from spoiling the tender roots of the Franco–German understanding, something had to be done fast.

In the evening of 24 October, therefore, Ribbentrop rang Ciano in Rome. He gave him an account of the talks at Hendaye and Montoire, but the telephone connection was bad and the Italian foreign minister did not conceal his 'fears and suspicions'.[120] Ribbentrop subsequently sat down and wrote him a letter, in which he explained that, while the outcome of the negotiations with Spain had not been satisfactory, France had agreed in principle to cooperate. The Führer, he added, would soon send the Duce a letter to explain these matters in more detail, and also wanted to meet him – somewhere in northern Italy – in the near future.[121] Ribbentrop next had this draft – which bears the date 24 October – typed out on the large-lettered 'Führer' typewriter, and sent it to Hitler for approval. It came back bearing a pencilled note: '*Führer . . . einverstanden*', signed by Walter Hewel the representative of the foreign ministry at Hitler's headquarters.[122] At 0400 hours on the 25th Ribbentrop's message was sent to the foreign ministry in Berlin, where it arrived at 0650. It was given a new number – 1500 – and forwarded to Rome, where it arrived at 0800 hours.[123] Mackensen asked for an audience with Ciano, and delivered the message at 1230 hours on the same day.[124] Hardly able to contain his joy over the great prospects opened by the German–French *rapprochement*, Ciano thanked the ambassador and told him he was looking forward to the Hitler–Mussolini meeting, which according to him was to take place on 3 or 4 November.

Shortly after Mackensen's departure, the telephone in Ciano's office rang again. Ribbentrop was on the line. He minced no words in explaining his purpose; he wanted the meeting between Hitler and Mussolini to be advanced to an earlier date. Ciano did not like this sudden change of plan – he suspected that Hitler's intention, in rushing to Italy so soon after his meeting with Petain, was to make her renounce her claims on France – but he could not disagree. A meeting was summarily fixed for Monday, 28 October, in Florence.[125] Having laid down the phone, Ribbentrop informed Berlin, where his telegram arrived at 1508 hours.[126] Weizsäcker then informed Mackensen, and told him the boss wanted him to come to Florence for the occasion.[127]

What made Ribbentrop – and behind him, Hitler – change his mind? Historical scholarship, mostly based on statements made by various participants after the war,[128] has it that it was the announcement of Mussolini's imminent attack on Greece, in whatever form it was transmitted to Hitler, that caused the latter to redirect his train to Florence. On the other hand, it is remarkable that neither the OKW nor the Halder diaries, both first class contemporary sources, mention this reason. The SKL diary says the visit had been planned for some time as part of Hitler's policy towards France and Spain, but its timing is supposed to have been determined by the news of the Italian attack.[129] However, this account is too muddled – it makes Hitler learn of the attack on the 27th, while in fact the decision to travel to Florence had been made 48 hours earlier – to receive much credence, particularly because SKL had to rely on OKW reports for similar matters.

A close examination of the facts will show how dubious is the theory that the announcement of Italian action caused Hitler's decision. Throughout his journey in France, the rain of reports warning against this eventuality had gone on. The German general at the Italian headquarters of the air force sent two urgent telegrams on 21 and 24 October;[130] from Belgrade came disturbing news;[131] while both Mackensen and Rintelen kept sounding the alarm.[132] None of this affected Hitler in the slightest. Such was the stream of reports, and such Hitler's reaction – or lack of reaction – that both OKW and the navy high command concluded he must have had given his ally the green light at the Brenner, as Jodl noted, 'without informing his close collaborators'.[133]

In order to find out why Hitler changed his plans, therefore, we must reconstruct the events that led to that decision. Among the documents that can be shown to have been received by Hitler on 25 October there are two that concern the Greek affair and may therefore be relevant to the Führer's decision to travel to Florence. One is a telegram from Mackensen, the other a letter from the Duce. Mackensen's telegram arrived at the foreign ministry in Berlin at 1300 hours, and was forwarded to 'Heinrich' – and presumably to 'Amerika' as well – at 1340. In this dispatch, Ciano's *chef de cabinet*, Filippo Anfuso, was reported as informing a circle of friends confidentially that the attack on Greece was certain to start *'noch dieses Wochenende'*.[134] Despite some assertions to the contrary, it is impossible to show that it was this telegram that made Hitler change his mind and formed the reason behind Ribbentrop's second telephone call to Ciano. Not only does most of the evidence we possess point in another direction, but it is impossible to assume that Hitler divided this telegram into a 'serious' and 'non serious' part. Either he believed in its contents, or he did not. If he did, he should have advanced the date of his meeting with Mussolini still further or, failing that, ring up the Duce.[135] If he did not, there was no reason to act at all. But to assume that the message made Hitler change his plans, yet was not considered sufficiently urgent to justify an even earlier meeting is clearly beyond the bounds of credibility. Rather than serving as proof of Hitler's intention to stop Mussolini, therefore, this document tends to demonstrate the extent to which Hitler was prepared to ignore even the most urgent warnings about the Italian plans.

Mussolini's letter is a curious document, and a very clever one. Bearing the postscript 'Rocca delle Caminate [Mussolini's villa in the Romagna] 19 October 1940/XVIII', it was in fact sent to Berlin on 22 October at the earliest.[136] It arrived there by means of a special envoy late at night on the 24th.[137] It was then translated into German and sent to Hitler's special train. It is not clear by what means this was done,[138] nor at what hour Hitler received the letter. However, it seems likely that he got it somewhere near 1400 hours on the 25th, while his train was on the way back from Montoire to Yvoir.[139]

In his letter, Mussolini dealt exhaustively with the subjects discussed between himself and Hitler at the Brenner. Most of his venom, as could be expected, was directed against France:

our informants . . . are unanimous . . . that the French hate the Axis more than before. . . Vichy is in contact with London . . . the overwhelming majority of them place their hopes in the US, which will assure Great Britain's victory. In this atmosphere, one cannot think of their collaboration. Nor should we seek it. If that were to happen, the French . . . would believe that the victory over Great Britain was due to them only . . . and they would be capable of presenting us with the bill. While dismissing, therefore, the idea of French adherence to a continental block I nevertheless believe that the moment has come for a redefinition of the shape of colonial and metropolitan France.[140]

There followed a sizeable list of the Duce's ideas on how to clip France's wings, crowned with the ominous statement that he regarded the time as ripe to put them into practice.

Passing over to other problems, the Duce referred to 'the English positions on the continent'.[141] This was a clever opening gambit, comparable to the waving of a red rag in front of a bull. 'In case the war should be prolonged', the Duce went on, 'I believe you would be in accord with me on the absolute necessity of getting rid of the remaining English positions on the European continent. This is another condition of the victory.' The logic was impeccable, and could not but sound a responsive echo with Hitler. Mussolini now proceeded to calm Hitler down by assuring him that, though there were no doubts about the fundamental hostility of Yugoslavia, he was not going to alter his policy towards that country, which was one of 'watchful vigilance'.

Having thus prepared the way, Mussolini came to the crux of the matter, selecting his words with extreme care worthy of a student of Machiavelli:

As regards Greece, I am resolved to put an end to the delays, and very soon. Greece is one of the main points of English maritime strategy in the Mediterranean. The king is English, the political classes are pro-English, and the people immature but trained to hate Italy. Greece . . . had made her air and naval bases available to Great Britain, as is revealed by the documents which von Ribbentrop has had the kindness to send me after the discovery at Vitry la Charité. English officials have recently taken possession of all airfields in Greece. In short, Greece is to the Mediterranean what Norway was to the North Sea, and must not escape the same fate.

Using Hitler's own expression, Mussolini thus went back to the tone that had done so well during July and September. The operation was presented as a defensive measure directed against Great Britain; no mention whatever was made of the irredentist claim to Ciamuria that had led to the German 'veto' of August. This, however, was not enough. Following the Brenner meeting, Mussolini had realized the need to incorporate his Greek adventure into a wider context:

As regards Egypt, the resumption of operations is dependent on a formidable effort of logistical preparation, comparable to the one you had to carry out in preparations for the landing in Great Britain. In any event, I hope I shall be able to launch operations simultaneously on the Greek and on the Egyptian front. Following the conclusion of this second stage of the offensive, which will seize the strong point of Mersa Matruh (230 Km. from Alexandria) it remains to face the decisive battle of the Delta.

Having put his attack into a context he knew was acceptable to Hitler, while at the same time donning the latter's very own kind of reserve parachute, Mussolini passed on to the problem of Spain, which he wanted to keep in reserve as a kind of trump card for the Axis to play at the right moment. Always jealous of his position with Hitler, he preferred that country to keep quiet in her present non-belligerent attitude rather than face the danger of being supplanted as Germany's first ally. Finally, he took care – most probably, in good faith – to link his letter to what had passed between himself and Hitler:

I have written a long letter . . . I could not refrain from passing in review for you my thoughts on the numerous questions which were the subject of our meeting at the Brenner.

In view of the motives attributed to Hitler in making his journey to Florence, it is best to allow our sources to tell of his reaction to the news contained in this letter in their own language.

When . . . on or around 25 October . . . we learnt . . . that the Greek action was to begin in a few days, I [Weizsäcker] set about making a very clear *démarche*. I drew up an unambiguous instruction to Rome that we should not allow our ally, who was weak enough in any case, to bring new countries into the war without our advice and consent as allies. Ribbentrop approved this, but Hitler said he did not want to cross Mussolini. Hitler's silence meant indirectly giving Italy the sign to go ahead with her . . . step in the Balkans.[142]

Nor was Weizsäcker the only person to try and make Hitler see the light. Keitel later told Rintelen that

[his] and General Pohl's information had made it clear to [him] that something was wrong, particularly when Mussolini told Hitler in a letter of 23 October that it would not be possible to stand the continuous provocations from the Greek side, but without saying anything more about his plans. [Keitel] . . . told [Rintelen] he had suggested to Hitler, who was then on his journey to France, to warn the Italian government . . . to hold their hands off Greece. But Hitler decided in favour of a personal conference with Mussolini and changed the date of the meeting between them from 5 November to 28 October.[143]

Hitler's attitude on the 25th, therefore, was exactly similar to his reaction on the 19th. On both occasions reports concerning the imminence of an Italian action were brought to his attention; on both occasions he rejected those suggestions out of hand. Even Mackensen's telegram, announcing the attack for the end of the week, failed to move him.

What did? Once more, we must allow our sources to tell their own story. 'The meeting at Florence was the result of a letter from the Duce, in which he gave expression to his anxiety lest Italy's claims are endangered by the cooperation with France. He fears an increase in French strength.'[144] And again: 'after the discussion with France, the Duce wrote an emergency letter to the Führer in which he gave vent to his anxiety lest France will be aided too quickly (fears military measures in the colonies). Result: meeting at Florence. In this meeting, the Duce was fully convinced of the correctness of the Führer's policy towards France.'[145] As if to make sure the message got through, Hitler himself told his top brass on 4 November that 'the meeting at Florence was in the first line for the purpose of removing Italian objections raised by the Duce against partial French rearmament in the colonies because he believed that Germany is allowing the French too much freedom, and that Italian demands are thus receiving no consideration'.[146] The argument is clinched by a note made by von Etzdorf, who wrote:

Conversation with Duce:
  In a letter to the Führer the Duce has expressed Italy's fear of too close a relationship between Germany and France and the possibility of a revival in French power.
  The main theme of the conversation is to soothe these fears and to discuss the details of future relations with France.
Italy and Greece:
  Apparently not envisaged as a subject for the discussion between the Duce and the Führer. The Führer does not want to obstruct [Bremsen] any more, in view of Germany's action in Rumania.[147]

The above statements originate on three different dates and from two separate persons, one of them Hitler himself. They were recorded by two of Germany's top officers and by his liaison man with the army, all of them in daily contact with the Führer. It is almost impossible to imagine anything clearer. Mussolini's letter, not Mackensen's telegram, made Hitler rush to Florence; the two pages about France, not the passage about Greece, were the immediate cause. His aim was to talk Mussolini into cooperation with France, not to talk him out of his attack on Greece.

  Given the situation, there was little else he could do. His journey to France and Spain was, all things considered, only a qualified success. The talks with Franco had failed completely – Hitler was under no illusions on that point – and thus the beginning of some kind of understanding with France was the only result he could show for his efforts. Now, this tender understanding was being put in jeopardy by his ally, who went back on what had been agreed between the two of them at the Brenner and 'dismissed the understanding with France out of hand'. If given a chance, his exorbitant claims on France could, and would, put an end to whatever agreement had been reached with the French. French resistance would become harder, their colonies, under the threat of being taken over by Italy, would desert to de Gaulle and the British. No more 'anti-English' front; no more 'continental block'. By every and any means, Mussolini had to be prevented from officially raising the demands he had just listed in his letter.

Instead of returning to Berlin, where he had been expected on Sunday, 27 October,[148] Hitler therefore redirected 'Amerika' to Munich, where he arrived on the 26th, closely trailed by his foreign minister in 'Heinrich'. After spending a night and a day there, he left for Florence at 1800 hours of the 27th. Meanwhile, further news from Italy arrived. At 1200 p.m. on the 27th, Rintelen had called up Bürckner from OKW/Ausland and told him it was now 'practically certain' that the attack would start early next morning. The message was passed on to Jodl,[149] who compared it with other reports lying before him and concluded that Rintelen was right. OKW next informed the foreign ministry, where Ritter transmitted both the report and Jodl's *Stellungnahme* to 'Heinrich', then on its way to Florence.[150] Now Jodl was the one general in whose judgement Hitler trusted. Ritter's message must have made it clear to him that he would arrive too late. A telephone call to the Duce, however, might still halt the attack. But Hitler did not make use of this last-moment opportunity presented to him. Indeed, there is no indication that he considered it in the first place. Instead, 'Amerika' continued its voyage southward among the snow-covered Alps.

At 1000 hours on the 28th, while the train was passing through Bologna, news arrived. The Italian attack on Greece had started.[151] Hitler's immediate reaction is known to us from the diary of his army *aide de camp*, Major D. G. Engel. The Führer was 'swearing and cursing', but the main target of his anger, curiously enough, was not the Duce himself. Rather, he fumed at the German 'liaison staffs and attachés', whom he accused of being 'idlers, but no spies', a fact that had 'spoilt many a plan of his'.[152] In view of the foregoing, this was simply not true. For the last ten days Hitler had been bombarded by a hail of reports concerning the imminent action, some of them giving precise dates. There was scarcely a German official anywhere near Italy who did not sound the alarm. Ritter and Ribbentrop, Weizsäcker and Keitel, had called his attention to the news. He had even (supposedly) redirected his train to meet Mussolini and stop him. And now he was shouting he knew nothing of the entire business and blaming his subordinates. What was he up to? There is no certain answer, but an interesting guess can be made. On later occasions, after the Italian offensive had turned into a fiasco, Hitler repeatedly assured his military advisers – that is, the people who had not accompanied him on his journey and therefore had no first-hand knowledge of what had happened – that he had 'known nothing' about the attack and was 'completely surprised' by it.[153] He seems to have taken other measures to make this version seem credible. An investigation aimed at discovering the culprit for his supposed 'ignorance' was launched,[154] and – a highly suspicious fact – the original of another telegram from Mackensen, sent from Rome at 2250 hours of the 27th and transmitting Ciano's official announcement of the ultimatum to Greece was destroyed by a *Zerreismaschine*, i.e. deliberately.[155] Is it possible that Hitler, anticipating that Italy might eventually fail, was creating an 'alibi' for himself? One would not put it past him. He was actor enough to put on a show.

Scarcely an hour later he needed all his acting talents when he arrived at Florence, only to find a beaming Duce meeting him at the station with the unforgettable words 'Führer, we are marching! This morning a victorious Italian army has crossed the Greek border!'[156] Hitler contained himself admirably – assuming, of course, that he was really angry in the first place. If he was, then the Italians got no inkling of his resentment. Neither Ciano nor Mussolini ever seem to have connected the forthcoming visit with the Greek affair;[157] at Florence, it was scarcely mentioned at all. Instead of making a fuss, Hitler opened the conference by congratulating and encouraging his ally, actually offering him German parachutists with which to occupy Crete.[158] The subject was then put on one side, not to reappear during the seven hours of Hitler's visit. If Hitler was really angry, this was a remarkable *tour de force* on his side; or was it?

Like most Hitler–Mussolini conferences, this one, too, developed into a Führer monologue. A wide range of subjects was covered, or rather rambled over, which we can safely leave aside. The core of the meeting was formed by Hitler's report on the conversations he had just had. Hitler told of his talk with Franco, whom he did not like a bit, and with Laval, who had made a scarcely better impression on him. For Pétain he had nothing but praise. Here was a man with whom something could be done. Hitler informed Mussolini that Spain was not, regrettably enough, going to enter the war at an early stage, and once more explained the importance of arriving at an agreement with France. He then reassured his ally that he did not, however, intend that country to take Italy's place as Germany's senior partner, and also succeeded in trimming the Duce's demands, or rather in having them deferred into the remote future. At 1800 hours[159] the Führer once more boarded his train and travelled back to Munich, leaving behind a Ciano who happily noted that 'the conference has shown ... that German solidarity has not failed us'.[160] For his part, Hitler was under the impression that he had successfully carried out his main purpose, i.e. making the Duce fall into line with his French policy.[161] Both sides therefore came away satisfied from this meeting, although for quite different reasons.

IN THE WAKE OF THE ATTACK

Returning from Florence and considering the Italian action, Hitler does not appear to have had much cause for resentment. Several of the reports reaching him stressed the connection between the invasion of Greece and the forthcoming attack on Egypt,[162] and were therefore perfectly in line, if not actually with what he had discussed with Mussolini at the Brenner, then at least with the new 'eastern Mediterranean' approach that was just emerging from the studies conducted at OKH, OKW and SKL. Like the Italians,[163] he probably did not expect the attack to develop into a real 'war', and, should this nevertheless happen, then Greece would be defeated within a very short time.[164]

It is usually alleged that Hitler was angry with Mussolini because he feared lest the Italian action might cause the entire Balkans to go up in flames. There is not a scrap of evidence for this. Indeed, if the Führer ever bothered to read the reports reaching him he should have known that the Italians were right in assuming no diplomatic complications. The countries whose intervention was at all possible were Yugoslavia, Bulgaria and Turkey. Now Yugoslavia was known for weeks to favour a neutral attitude, provided the Italians did not demand rights of transit; her attitude was again confirmed a few days before the Italian attack took place.[165] Italian attempts to get her in notwithstanding,[166] Bulgaria held in check as she was by the Turks, was not making any aggressive noises.[167] Within a few days of the start of hostilities this attitude of hers was confirmed.[168]

Since it was fear of Turkey that prevented the Bulgarians from joining Mussolini, Ankara therefore held the key to peace in the Balkans. Ten days prior to the outbreak of hostilities the Turkish cabinet had held a meeting and decided not to interfere. Notice was given to the Greek government.[169] After the Italian attack the Turks did, to be sure, move their army into Turkish Thrace, but only in order to hold Bulgaria in check. She did not intend to attack Italy, while the Bulgarian government was warned – both before and after the start of the war – that it had better stay quiet.[170] The warnings worked; Bulgaria did remain neutral. So did Turkey.

Assuming Italy was going to invade Greece and occupy her entire territory in one hard, swift blow, it is hard to see why Hitler should have objected. Greece was, after all, a small country; Italy a 'great power', and an 'Axis' one at that. Nobody, least of all the Greeks themselves, expected her to hold out for as much as two weeks, not to mention five months. Though a general war in the Balkans was not in Germany's interest, a lightning occupation of Greece might well make the other states, particularly Yugoslavia, more amenable to German wishes. To this should be added Hitler's realization that his unilateral action in Rumania had hurt Italian pride and that consequently he wished to handle 'the other end of the Axis' with care; also, that Greece was at best a doubtful candidate for his new Europe. Though the attack may have been a tactical error from the point of view of sequence and timing, it still fitted into Hitler's overall 'peripheral' strategy. Provided it was quickly successful, it could, in Jodl's words, do but little harm and much good in this context. It is to the state of the latter that we must now turn our attention.

THE DECISION TO OCCUPY GREECE

WAR IN THE EASTERN MEDITERRANEAN

On his return from the meeting in Florence on 29 October Hitler had reason for qualified optimism when considering the record of the six weeks that had passed since his decision to turn to the 'peripheral' strategy. France had ostensibly been won over, and talks between Ribbentrop and Laval for the signature of an agreement were expected to take place in the near future.[1] Italy had also been persuaded to cooperate, and at the same time had consented to postpone her demands on France to a more convenient time. The only blot on the fine picture was Spain, which had not yet been made to commit herself. However, Hitler still hoped to achieve the *Einklang* of Spanish policy with that of the Axis, and 'coerce' Franco to enter the war.[2] The 'guidelines' for future German–Spanish cooperation had been laid down between Ribbentrop and Suner at Hendaye, and Hitler clearly hoped to have this secret agreement signed and ratified within a short time.[3]

While tackling political problems himself, Hitler generally left military preparations to his staff. These preparations – and this is typical of the way he worked[4] – were not made dependent on the results of the political measures; that is, they were to be pushed ahead even before the completion of the latter, so as to have them ready for immediate execution in case of success. Thus, the diary of the army chief-of-staff bristles with references to preparations for action against both Gibraltar and Egypt from about the middle of September onward.[5] Reconnaissance parties were sent out, forces and specialized equipment prepared, plans studied and directives issued. For our purposes, it is the preparations for the eastern Mediterranean that are most interesting. The dispatch of one air corps and two armoured divisions to Libya was considered. Their employment was, of course, subject to Mussolini's approval and dependent on the course of Italian operations.[6] Understanding of the latter is therefore essential to any analysis of German strategy in the eastern Mediterranean.

In Libya the Italians had two armies, one of them, the 10th, facing Egypt with 10 divisions. Opposing them were British forces consisting of about 3 divisions. Marshal Rodolfo Graziani who was in charge of the Italian offensive against Egypt planned that it should fall into three stages. The first of these would consist of an advance over some 100 km to Sidi al Barrani. The second would bring his forces to Mersa Matruh. The third and most important would involve the advance to Alexandria and occupation of that city and of the Suez Canal. Given the lack of roads and supplies in the desert, each of these stages would have to be separated from the next one by a considerable pause during which waterlines would be laid, roads constructed and materials brought up. The whole operation could therefore reasonably be expected to last for at least several months.

The Germans, it will be remembered, had been considering the transfer of forces to Libya since August. Their first offer to this effect had been transmitted to Rome even before Graziani went over to the realization of his 'first stage' on 13 September; it remained unanswered.[7] Jodl then approached the Italian military attaché, General Marras, who passed the German proposal on to Badoglio and promised an early answer.[8] In the meantime, OKW instructed OKH to make all the necessary preparations, so as to prevent time being wasted when the Italian answer came.[9] Within a few days, the German military attaché in Rome reported that, contrary to expectations Badoglio and Roatta were not at all eager to have German armoured units in Libya and would prefer Stukas.[10] Asked for his opinion on 10 September, Graziani himself evaded the question.[11] In a SMG conference on the 25th Badoglio was more straightforward:

The Germans have offered two armoured divisions. Roatta, who has studied the question, concluded that the transport of a single division will require six months. We must take cognizance of the fact that in Africa we need *uomini*, and that the *uomini* we have there are superior to the German soldiers.

Consequently, if the matter is considered at all, it must be limited to the cession of material, not of men.[12]

Badoglio, however, did not transmit his refusal to Berlin, again leaving the German offer unanswered: Hitler therefore raised the subject at the Brenner on 4 October. Like other aspects of the same conversation, this one, too, gave rise to conflicting interpretations. According to the Italian record, Mussolini refused Hitler's offer of 'special units for the attack on Egypt', saying that while he did not need them for the 'second stage' of the offensive he reserved the right to inform the Führer of his needs for the third.[13] While the German record agrees that the Duce refused German aid for the second stage, it is less clear on the third; Mussolini is quoted as saying that 'he might be forced to utilize the aid of Germany for the third phase, i.e. the battle of Alexandria... For the operation against Alexandria he would request of Germany 50 to 100 heavy tanks of 30 tons'.[14] While not daring to reject all help, therefore, it would appear that the Duce was 'forced' to agree to German material being sent to Libya somewhere in the future.[15] To the Germans, however, this was not enough. Determined to gain a foothold in North Africa, they tried to ram through their original proposal, and sent General Ritter von Thoma at the head of a small staff to Rome, whence he was to continue to Libya to reconnoitre after conducting technical conversations with the SMG.[16] The Italians, disagreeably surprised, decided to get rid of him and sent him on to the desert after only two days in Rome, with Badoglio sarcastically observing that 'as long as [he] was in Libya there was no danger of the Germans sending their troops there'.[17] Meanwhile, in a masterpiece of ambiguity, he told OKW that:

> [there was] a need for an early meeting between [him] and Marshal Keitel in order to agree on operational plans for the winter . . . the focal point of the war must be transferred to the Mediterranean, in order to drive the English out of Egypt and Gibraltar. . . Marshal Badoglio believes that Mersa Matruh will be captured in 2–3 weeks after the waterline Sollum–Sidi al Barrani is ready as ordered. Despite the reinforcement of the English troops in Egypt . . . he believes that the Nile Delta and the Suez Canal can be reached. Palestine and East Africa will then fall of themselves. The Italian air force in East Africa is too weak to prevent the passage of English supplies through the Red Sea.[18]

Badoglio thus informed the Germans that the objectives discussed at the Brenner would be reached – implicitly dispensing with German aid – while at the same time making sure he could not be blamed for failure to keep his promise. The studious avoidance of any reference to German aid was conspicuous, and Keitel, obviously angry, brusquely decided to postpone the meeting until the political situation had been clarified.[19] Having successfully evaded the German offer, Badoglio went on to convince Mussolini. Using Graziani's repeated postponement of the start of the 'second stage',[20] he finally extracted from the Duce recognition that no advance past Mersa Matruh was possible at all, and that German aid was therefore superfluous. Thus the German attempt to insist on the commitment of German troops for the 'third stage' led, on 29 October, to its complete abolition by Mussolini and Badoglio.[21]

While Hitler's efforts, conducted through OKW, to promote the 'peripheral' strategy by having the Italians accept a German expeditionary force in Libya came up against a wall, OKH also encountered difficulties. On 23 October the German armoured and air force units for Libya were ready,[22] but their transportation was delayed by the return of von Thoma from Africa. His report, which was everything but flattering to the Italian army, could be summed up as follows: 1. Should German help be offered, Graziani intended to postpone his advance on Mersa Matruh until after the arrival of the expeditionary force. 2. In that case the German units would be forced to use Tripoli, a thousand miles behind the front, as a supply base. 3. Graziani did not want German help to begin with.[23] Still worse was a report the next day from another officer, Meyer-Rick from Fremde Heere West. According to him, the English would fall back on the Nile forcing the German and Italian army – assuming they ever reached Mersa Matruh – to fight with their backs to the desert against a British force that had already grown to 200,000 men. Consequently, much stronger German forces than originally envisaged would be required, and Greece would probably be drawn into the war through the occupation of Crete, which was essential for the solution of the transport problem.[24] All these, needless to say, were decisions which OKH could not make on its own; it would be necessary to wait until Hitler returned from France.

On his return to Berlin on the evening of the 30th,[25] Hitler immediately had to face the fact that, while his political measures creating the basis for realizing the 'peripheral' strategy in the western Mediterranean had more or less succeeded, the corresponding military measures in the eastern Mediterranean faced ruin because of Italian inefficiency and reluctance. He promptly ordered Thoma to report to him in person.[26] After hearing the general's report, Hitler decided to dispense with the idea of a German expeditionary force in Libya 'for the time being' for the following reasons: 1. The Italians just did not want any German troops.[27] 2. The unfavourable impression received by Thoma at Graziani's headquarters. 3. Logistical and technical difficulties.[28] The decision, and this point is crucial to our analysis, did not mean a renunciation of the expeditionary force, but only its postponement until after the capture of Mersa Matruh. Preparations for the employment of German air force units from there against Alexandria and Suez were to go on.[29] Rather than implying a fundamental alteration in the eastern Mediterranean part of the 'peripheral' strategy, therefore, this decision merely reflected Hitler's belated recognition that the reluctance and military incapacity of his ally were likely to defer its realization.

'A SECOND RATE SUBSTITUTE'

We have followed the vicissitudes of the German offer for help in Libya at some length, because they demonstrate how strong Hitler's commitment to the 'peripheral' strategy was – he kept up his pressure for about six weeks and did not give up entirely despite the manifold obstacles and repeated postponements caused by the attitude of his ally – and because they are intimately connected with what was to happen in Greece after the start of the Italian invasion. From the point of view of the 'eastern Mediterranean' strategy there was a close resemblance between the Italian advance on Mersa Matruh and the attack on

Greece. Both were directed against the British, though in both cases it was the territory of third parties that was chosen as the theatre of operations. Each of them would, if successful, result in reducing by half the distance between the Italian bases and the British main base in Alexandria.[30] Each of them separately, and certainly both taken together, could, if properly exploited, help to bring about a radical change in the balance of power in the eastern Mediterranean. An Italian conquest of Egypt would, of course, finally put an end to the British position in the Balkans, while the occupation of Greece would in turn forward and supplement the seizure of Egypt. Even greater was the interdependence of Crete and Egypt. The domination of each of these was crucial to the holding and capture of the other. From the British point of view, the possession of Crete would mean a very serious obstacle on the flank of the Italian advance in Egypt; conversely, it would be practically impossible to solve the supply problem involved with the attack on Alexandria (not to mention Palestine or Syria) without secure possession of the island. The German staffs might disagree as to whether it should properly be seized after the occupation of Mersa Matruh or as a precondition for it; nobody in OKW, OKH or SKL doubted its importance, and Hitler fully shared this opinion.

With or without Crete, the occupation of Greece and the Aegean Islands by the Italians would – if successful – be of considerable strategic significance for the balance of power in the eastern Mediterranean. The trouble was, the Italian invasion was anything but successful. By the end of the second day, Visconti Prasca's armies had penetrated to a depth of only 10–12 kms into Greek territory, and only the *Alpini* of the 'Julia' divison were still advancing at all.[31] Torrential rain delayed the advance, while the Italians, having failed to foresee this possibility, did not have enough engineers and bridging equipment at hand.[32] By the late afternoon of the 30th matters had already reached such a state that Badoglio, blaming the weather which prevented the effective employment of the air force for the small successes booked by his troops, asked for a rapid reinforcement of the German military mission in Rumania, so as to 'put pressure on Turkey'.[33] At the same time, clarification of the Italian operational plans was finally obtained; this, too, was disappointing. Not only were the preparations revealed as hopelessly inadequate, but it now appeared that the attack simply had no strategic aim at all. Instead of racing for Salonika, the Italians wanted to try and fight their way south from Albania into the strategically worthless region of Epirus down to the Gulf of Arta; assuming they ever reached there, they would regroup and march on Athens.[34]

The slow advance of the Italian offensive – in what was strategically the wrong direction – was not at all in accordance with Hitler's 'peripheral' plans; what was more, it made it possible for the British to occupy Crete and send air force units to Greece itself, an opportunity which they grasped on 6 November. Having kept his mouth shut at Florence, and, as far as we know, immediately afterwards,[35] Hitler finally exploded on 1 November, when Rintelen's reports had made it crystal clear that the offensive was firmly bogged down. Belatedly, he came to judge the operation – which he had probably authorized and in any case refused to veto – 'negatively in every respect'. He was 'very angry at the Italian machinations' and his disappointment with the martial inefficiency of his ally such that he had lost 'any inclination for military cooperation with him'.[36] He then proceeded to demonstrate that this was no more than a momentary burst of irritation by postponing his decision as to whether to send troops to Libya and made it dependent on Thoma's report. When the African project was allowed to fall through two days later Greece was not even mentioned, and the decision justified on perfectly rational grounds that were shared by the sober OKH.

Even before making that decision Hitler, in accordance with his usual method, had taken steps to provide for an alternative course of action. Informing Jodl of his growing doubts concerning the effectiveness of the Italian offensive in Egypt, he told him that 'should the employment of German troops in Libya be written off, a second rate substitute – an advance from Bulgaria to the Aegean – may become necessary'. Disappointed with the Italian performance, Hitler was casting around for means to carry out the 'peripheral' strategy without them and, if necessary, in spite of them. It was within this framework that the idea of an invasion of Greece from the north – coupled with a German attack on Gibraltar, from which he now intended to exclude the Italians[37] – presented itself to him. 'If Greece were lost and Egypt menaced', he reasoned, 'England would practically be driven out of the Mediterranean.'[38] He therefore had the subject incorporated into the agenda of a scheduled conference with his senior military advisers, the aim of which was to discuss and coordinate all military measures designed 'to make England admit the war is lost', as Halder put it.[39]

At 1430 hours on the 4th, therefore, a select group of senior officers – consisting of Keitel, Jodl, Brauchitsch, Halder, Deyhle and Schmundt – gathered at the Reichskanzlei to meet the Führer. One by one, Halder reported on the results of the studies conducted by OKH about the various aspects of the 'peripheral' strategy, and asked for a decision from Hitler.[40] The results of the conference were as follows:

1. Gibraltar. Halder regarded the problem as 'difficult, but certainly soluble', and warned Hitler that 'the Rock alone will not do'. The Führer expressed his hope that Franco would enter the war, and ordered preparations to go on. He also said that the question of the Atlantic Islands (Canaries, Azores) was being examined.

2. Libya. Halder reported what he had learnt from Thoma about Italian reluctance and inefficiency, adding that in order to be really effective the German expeditionary force would have to be large enough to effect preparedness for 'continental operation'. Hitler, who had already been put into the picture by Thoma himself, agreed. Basing his decision upon Italian reluctance, logistic and operational difficulties, he confirmed his determination to allow the project to fall through for the time being.

3. Turkey. Halder reported on the study made by his *Oberquartiermeister* I (and effective second in command) General Paulus, for an advance from Bulgaria through Turkey to Syria.[41] Hitler rejected these plans as too sanguine, for they would bring Russia into the picture.[42]

4. Greece. Here the idea seems to have been Hitler's own, for there is no reference to it in Halder's *Vortragsnotiz*. He ordered OKH 'to prepare to assist [?] a rapid invasion of Turkish Thrace'. In all probability, we can assume with Jacobsen that this operation was meant to subdue Turkey quickly if a Turkish–Bulgarian war were to break out, an ominous possibility which might well set the Russians racing southward.

However, Hitler seems to have said more than this. Though for some reason Halder did not record any further utterances of his on this subject, we find him and Brauchitsch discussing the measures to be taken by OKH for 'Bulgaria/Greece' two hours later.[43] Since this discussion is entitled '*Ergebnis der Führerbesprechung*', it is quite clear that Hitler must have said something more about Greece than would appear from the record in Halder's diary. His words were recorded by the OKW diarist, Helmut Greiner: 'OKH will prepare, if necessary to occupy . . . Greek Macedonia and Thrace in order to create the prerequisites for the employment of German air force units against the British bases threatening the Rumanian oil fields'.[44] These two sources, both first-hand records of the conference, therefore give us two different reasons for whatever German action was to be taken in the Balkans. Nor does the confusion end there. The SKL diary, recording the information supplied by Jodl about the conference, has a third version: 'the Führer considers the Rumanian oil fields menaced from Lemnos! Therefore IMMEDIATE [emphasis in the original] dispatch of anti-aircraft units, fighters and interceptors to Rumania. . . The support of the Italian offensive against Greece by German troops . . . is being ordered. . . The aim is to advance over Rumania and Bulgaria against Greece in the direction of Salonika–Larissa . . . the commitment of troops for supporting Bulgaria against Turkey . . . will be ordered'.[45] The three records, coming from two distinct persons, conflict; the result is utter confusion.[46] As sources explaining Hitler's objectives in Greece they are singularly inadequate.

In our attempt, therefore to learn something more about Hitler's aims in giving orders to prepare for an attack on Greece, we are forced to fall back upon other, less direct, evidence. For one thing, the very fact that the subject was brought up in a conference that was designed to coordinate the measures of the war against England, and in the first place those forming part of the 'peripheral' strategy, is of course important. So is the fact that it was first mentioned in connection with the Egyptian offensive and as a 'second rate substitute' for that. The significance of these facts is pointed out by Halder's ADC, Major Mueller-Hillebrand:

It was necessary to incorporate any form of war in the Balkans in the plans for the war in the Mediterranean, since here one would everywhere meet the English head on. Therefore, the plans for a German attack from Bulgaria against northern Greece were already included in 'directive No. 18', issued on 12 November, which enlarged about the planning and direction of the war in the Mediterranean. For Hitler had occupied himself with the question of securing the Mediterranean for the warfare of the Axis.[47]

The decision to invade Greece with German troops coming from the north via Rumania and Bulgaria must therefore be viewed in a context of 'securing the Mediterranean for the warfare of the Axis', that is not an Italian or even Balkan one.[48] From the start, it was directed against the British. It was regarded as part – perhaps not one that had been included in that form in the preliminary studies, but still a part – of the 'peripheral' strategy.

As a Mediterranean and 'peripheral' operation, the invasion of Greece was incorporated into the order which summed up all the measures Hitler expected to take against the British in the Mediterranean during the winter. On 4 November Hitler had ordered OKW to prepare such an order, to be signed by him and issued as a 'war directive'.[49] A first draft was ready on 5 November, but was rejected by Jodl because it gave too much prominence to operation 'Sea Lion', the landing in the United Kingdom, which Hitler still thought might take place in the spring.[50] On 7 November Warlimont submitted to Jodl a second draft, in which the necessary corrections had been introduced.[51] On 12 November this one was issued, signed by Hitler as 'war directive No. 18'.[52] In providing 'for the conduct of the war in the near future', it laid down the following directives on each of the main problems:

1. Relations with France.
The aim of my policy towards France is to cooperate with that country in the most effective manner possible for the future conduct of the war against England. For the present France will assume the role of a 'nonbelligerent' power and will thus be required to allow German war measures on French

territory and particularly in the African colonies. She will also be required to support these measures with her own forces as far as may be necessary. The most urgent duty of the French is to secure their African possessions (West and Equatorial Africa), defensively and offensively, against England and the de Gaulle movement.

Thus France received first priority. The French were reported to be 'very satisfied' with the results of their talks with Hitler,[53] and on 30 October Pétain had broadcast to the French nation his readiness to cooperate with Germany.[54] Consequently, OKW was busily negotiating the details of the future military *Zusammenarbeit* between the two countries by means of the armistice commission.[55] Next came Spain:

Political measures to bring about the entry into the war of Spain in the near future have already been initiated. The aim of GERMAN [original emphasis, designed to exclude the Italians] intervention in the Iberian peninsula . . . will be to drive the English from the Western Mediterranean. To this end:
  a. Gibraltar is to be captured and the Straits closed.
  b. The English are to be prevented from gaining a footing at any other point on the Iberian peninsula or in the Atlantic Islands.

There followed a series of more detailed orders for a fairly large operation, designed to occupy Gibraltar, the Canaries, Azores, Madeira and parts of Morocco. This was the 'peripheral' strategy at its largest and most sanguine, involving cooperation with both France and Spain. It aimed to drive the British out of the western Mediterranean as well as to secure the coast of North West Africa for the Axis. But Hitler had not forgotten the eastern Mediterranean:

The employment of German forces will be considered . . . only after the Italians have reached Mersa Matruh.
  One armoured division . . . will stand ready for service in North Africa.

Until the Italians reached Mersa Matruh Alexandria and Suez were beyond the reach of the German air force, and this made the transfer of forces to Libya pointless. Hitler therefore fell back on his original idea, of sending his troops there only for the 'third' stage, even though he now realized that it was as likely as not that this stage would never materialize. Still, in the faint hope that the Italians would finally get moving in December, he gave orders for preparations to continue.[56] Meanwhile, a paragraph concerning the 'second rate substitute' for the Egyptian operation was incorporated into the directive:

Commander-in-chief army will be prepared, if necessary, to occupy from Bulgaria the Greek mainland north of the Aegean Sea. This will enable the German air force to attack targets in the eastern Mediterranean, and in particular those English air bases threatening the Rumanian oil fields.

The object of German intervention in Greece was exactly the same as that of the expeditionary corps in Libya; to provide air bases for use against the British in the eastern Mediterranean. Hitler was so eager to achieve this aim that, two weeks later, he decided he would rather not wait until the realization of the other parts of his programme. Instead he would try to induce the Italians to accept the employment of the German air force from bases in the Italian Dodecanese.[57]

As a substitute for the Italian offensive in Egypt, the German plan for an invasion of northern Greece naturally gained in importance the more remote the prospect of an Italian success became. Suppose the Italians did not capture Mersa Matruh, the question whether it would be enough to occupy northern Greece alone would arise. It is therefore probably no accident that the SKL, which among the branches of the Wehrmacht seems to have had the least confidence in the Italian prospects – even before the start of the Greek war – was the first to raise this issue on 8 November, demanding that not only Salonika, but the whole of Greece be occupied.[58] After the talks between Keitel and Badoglio, held at Innsbruck on 14–15 November, had made it abundantly clear that no Italian advance in Egypt would ever materialize,[59] the Wehrmachtführungsstab, too, joined in this demand:

Large scale offensive action by Italy can no longer be expected. It seems that the Italians have by no means envisaged the occupation of southern Greece. Under these circumstances eventual German intervention gains in significance. OKW has recognised the need for eliminating any British forces on the Greek mainland (Peloponnese, Salonika).

The air force has been ordered to examine how and from what bases an effective operation against the British positions and navy in the eastern Mediterranean is possible.[60]

At Innsbruck Badoglio had promised that the Italian offensive in Albania would be resumed with twenty divisions in mid-February, but given the interdependence of the Greek and the Egyptian offensives, and the Italian plan not to occupy southern Greece, this was no longer sufficient. Consequently, on 19 November, Hitler seems to have ordered the extension of the German invasion of Greece to include not only the Aegean Coast but the entire Greek mainland.[61] This decision naturally required the commitment of more forces than had originally been planned and wrought havoc with the build-up plans which, as we shall see, were fairly advanced. We therefore find Halder complaining about the 'deficient connections between ourselves and OKW', and the 'heap of unnecessary work loaded on the general staff' because of insufficient clarity in the OKW directives, which 'did not say what was wanted in Bulgaria, but only prattled about the strength of the troops required and even about specific units'. Unable to see a way out of confusion, Halder consoled himself by noting that the Führer was once more showing some interest in operation 'Sea Lion', which was 'the most

certain way to get at England'.[62] In any case, the OKW directives –
however confused – had to be obeyed; and by 20 November Halder
already had a fairly clear idea of what the operation would be like.

PRELIMINARY MILITARY CONSIDERATIONS

On 4 November 1940 OKW was faced with a new task; that of preparing, within the framework of 'directive No. 18' and the 'peripheral'
strategy, an invasion of Greece from the north, i.e. via Bulgaria. Two
hours after the conference at the Reichskanzlei, Halder and Brauchitsch
sat down to have a first look at the requirements of the campaign Hitler
had just ordered.

Since the conclusion of the armistice with France in June, the German Wehrmacht had, in Hitler's words, been the world's largest unemployed army. Its four army groups and ten armies lay scattered all
over Europe, garrisoning the occupied countries and preparing for all
kinds of eventualities, such as the protection of the Rumanian oil fields
against the Russians or the capture of Gibraltar. None of these forces
was engaged on active military operations, though many of the divisions
were temporarily not combat-worthy because of the cession of nuclei
earmarked for the establishment of new units.[63]

Compared with these huge forces, the requirements of the Greek
campaign at first appeared modest enough. The obvious units to select
were XXXXth army corps and 2nd and 9th armoured divisions subordinated to it, because they were closest to the scene of action. Having
been transported to Vienna in August in order to occupy, if necessary,
the Ploesti oil fields,[64] they had to a large extent been relieved of their
tasks by the concentration of the mighty *Heeresgruppe* B with its 35
divisions in Poland, and by the dispatch of a German army mission
to Rumania proper after the Second Vienna Award.[65]

The XXXXth corps would be joined by another, still unspecified,
corps consisting of 2 mountain or infantry divisions. In addition, it
would be necessary to bring up *Heerestruppe* – artillery, communications and engineering troops of all kinds, whose proportion in relation
to the number of organic divisions would have to be rather high because
of the difficult terrain in the Balkans. Even so, the force envisaged was
small enough to be put under the command, not of an army but of
Panzergruppe Kleist – so called after its commander, Ewald von Kleist
then a colonel general – which status was somewhere between that of
an army and a corps.[66] Urged on by various rumours of preparations
made by the Russian Black Sea fleet, the appearance of Soviet officers
in Istanbul and a British landing in Salonika,[67] OKH must have felt
that haste could do no harm; as early as 4 November, therefore,
General Greiffenberg of OKH introduced Colonel Zeitzler, chief-of-

staff to *Panzergruppe* Kleist, to his unit's new tasks, so that the staff could start its preparations immediately.[68]

Four divisions seemed a modest number to start with, but when Colonel Heusinger, chief of the operations department at OKH, submitted his first plans to Halder on 6 November it appeared that the chief of the general staff had underestimated the strength of the forces required. The 60th and SS 'Adolf Hitler' – both motorized elite units – divisions were added to XXXXth corps, raising the number of large units under its command to four. XXXth corps, which at that time was still under the command of army group B in Poland and had to be released on the next day, was selected to join it. The 164th and 78th infantry divisions, as well as 6th and 5th mountain divisions, were placed under its command.[69] Within the space of two days, therefore, the forces earmarked for the Greek operation had grown from 4 to 8 divisions – with the number of army troops increasing in proportion.

On the next day, 7 November, Halder summoned his ADC – Major Gehlen – and Colonel Heusinger to have a first look at the concentration and deployment of the forces. Hitler's directive had specified that the attack was to come from the north via Bulgaria, and in order to reach that country it would be necessary to march from the Reich through either Poland or Hungary into Rumania. Politically, the question of the attitude of the last named countries was not regarded as a problem; both had been driven into the arms of Hitler by their fear of Stalin and could be regarded as safe German satellites. Hungary had already consented to the passage of German troops on their way to the Rumanian oilfields on 30 September, and when Hitler on 20 November asked Premier Teleki for rights of transit for additional troops these were granted without further ado on the next day.[70] General Ion Antonescu of Rumania, informed of the German plans by Keitel on 23 November, also raised no difficulties; his only request was that the burden of supplying the troops should not fall on his country, as the German army mission sent to Rumania in October was already devouring a very considerable part of the Rumanian budget.[71] This request was readily granted by Hitler, and OKH now had to bring up all supplies for over 100,000 men from Germany – a task which, in view of the state of the central European road network, was likely to cause great difficulties and perhaps delay.

From the operational point of view, the order to concentrate on the Bulgaro–Greek frontier and carry out the operation from there was, indeed, a difficult one. The Greek border was heavily fortified by the so-called 'Metaxas line', a modern series of fortifications constructed between 1936 and 1939. An attack in this direction would not point towards the heart of Greece, but only to Greek Thrace. Moreover, the deployment area was remote and hard to reach. Rumania, through which the troops would perforce have to pass on their way to Bulgaria, could in theory be reached through either Hungary or Poland, but in effect she was cut off from the latter country in 1939 when the Russians invaded eastern Poland and, despite some last moment German attempts to save it from their clutches,[72] took possession of part of the vital Breslau–Lwow–Cernauti railway. The remaining rail communications crossing the Carpathians from German-occupied Poland to Rumania were considered practically unsuitable for troop transports.[73] The attitude of Hans Frank, the Nazi governor of Poland who had built his own kingdom there, was not helpful either.[74]

Only by way of Hungary, then, could one reach Rumania. Once there, however, the troops would be faced with the plain fact that there were no bridges over the Danube between Rumania and Bulgaria. They would therefore have to travel by rail from Austria through Hungary into Rumania; get off north of the Danube; march to the river; construct temporary bridges; and finally, cross into northern Bulgaria. Even then their ordeal would be just beginning, for they would still face a march of several hundred miles right across Bulgaria to the Greek frontier; a lengthy, complicated and, for the troops, tiring operation. Given conditions in Bulgaria, which could safely be assumed to be bad enough, the build-up was bound to last for ten weeks if this route were selected.[75]

The first priority was to discover excatly what conditions would face the army in Bulgaria. On 8 November air reconnaissance over the country was therefore cleared.[76] The following day, Colonel Bruckmann, military attaché in Sofia, delivered a report about the Bulgarian army, road network and climate.[77] The picture painted was so dark that Halder decided to organize a regular reconnaissance staff under the command of Colonel Kinzel, head of Fremde Heere Ost department, to study conditions on the spot.[78]

Hitler's order to deploy in southern Bulgaria for an operation against Greece was, in sum, anything but easy to put into practice. Nor were the difficulties only of a geographical nature. Bulgaria had only one railway leading directly into Greece (Salonika) – the one branching off the Sofia–Istanbul line near Pythion and running south through the valley of Maritsa – and that one was too close to the Turkish border to be utilized. On their way south, the German troops would have the Turkish army looking over their left shoulder; and the attitude of Turkey to the entry of German troops into Bulgaria was by no means clear. On their right flank, the Germans would have another uncertain factor: Yugoslavia.

If the Bulgarian operation was a difficult one, it was the government of Belgrade that was in a position to make it very much easier. Hungary–Rumania was one route into Bulgaria; Austria–Yugoslavia was another, and an infinitely shorter and easier one at that. If Yugoslavia consented, it would be possible to transport the German troops by rail from Vienna and Klagenfurt over Belgrade directly into Sofia, thus solving the problem of crossing the Danube and cutting the distance which the troops would have to cover by road inside Bulgaria by half. Greece's border with Yugoslavia was not only longer than her frontier with Bulgaria, but also hopelessly unprotected and exposed. The two best roads into Greece, the one running via the Vardar Valley and the one running through the Monastir Gap, were also under Yugoslav jurisdiction. Should the Yugoslavs grant rights of transit, OKH reckoned that the build-up could be cut by four weeks; should it be possible to operate from her territory, circumventing the Metaxas line and making use of the best roads leading into Greece, the campaign itself would also be very much easier.

The attitude of Yugoslavia was of the greatest importance from yet another point of view. Even if Belgrade could not be persuaded to collaborate in the liquidation of Greece – and Hitler, as 'directive No. 19' shows, doubted this very much[79] – her neutrality was still crucial to the success of the operation. With its right flank stretching without protection over hundreds of miles, any German undertaking in Bulgaria not previously cleared with Yugoslavia was an extremely risky affair. This was dramatically illustrated by the example of the only other Bulgarian railway which was of any potential relevance to the German deployment; utilizing the valley of the Struma, it followed the Yugoslav frontier within a distance of 13 miles, at one point coming as close as 6 miles.[80] Belgrade, therefore, not only held the key to a much easier and quicker operation in hand; in the last resort, her attitude would determine whether Hitler could branch out into the eastern Mediterranean as planned, or whether he would be stuck in southeastern Europe.

During the first days of November, therefore, Germany diplomacy initiated moves the ultimate aim of which was not only to open the way through Bulgaria and, if possible, Yugoslavia, but to establish political control over those parts of southeastern Europe that were not yet under its sway. The capitals which Germany diplomacy would soon find itself approaching were Sofia, Belgrade and Ankara. However, there was another great power which had its vital interests in the area and wanted to have a say about its fate; in his efforts to incorporate the whole of southeastern Europe into the German sphere of influence, Hitler clashed head on with the Soviet Union.

PART 2

HITLER, SOUTH EASTERN EUROPE AND THE WAR AGAINST RUSSIA, NOVEMBER 1940 – JUNE 1941

FROM THE MEDITERRANEAN
TO THE EAST

In this context, the Russian problem is almost a new one. It is very probable that the mystery enveloping Soviet–Yugoslav relations played a part in Hitler's categorical and persistent refusal to allow Mussolini to attack the latter country, while fear lest the Soviets might exploit the Italian failure in Greece to forward their own aims – to advance in the direction of the Straits and ultimately, perhaps, to join hands with the British in Greece – may have played a role in his decision to build up his forces in Rumania and Bulgaria as a preliminary to the Greek operation. Apart from this, the Russian factor does not seem to have had much influence in this context.

From about July 1940 onward, German–Soviet relationships proceeded on several different levels. On one hand there was the idea – conceived by OKW and strongly sponsored by Ribbentrop in the foreign ministry[1] – of constructing an anti-British continental block, an idea which to some extent was taken up by Hitler himself.[2] On the other hand, there was the German–Soviet struggle for influence in eastern Europe, a struggle that stretched right across the continent from Finland in the north to Turkey in the south. Exploiting Hitler's involvement in the war against the west, the soviets had exceeded the provisions of their 1939 non-aggression pact with Germany and swallowed, in addition to the Baltic States and parts of Finland, the northern parts of Rumania. In the summer of 1940 the two countries were engaged in a race to incorporate the whole of eastern Europe in their respective spheres of influence. In this race Hitler, to whom the area was absolutely indispensable as a source of raw materials – particularly Rumanian oil and Finnish nickel – had scored an important victory in the form of the Second Vienna Award, from which the Soviets had been excluded. By the late autumn of the year he was on the verge of scoring further successes when both Hungary and Rumania agreed to join the Tripartite Pact. On the other hand, his success in bringing Bulgaria and Yugoslavia over to his camp was still very much in doubt.

Partly as a result of Soviet pressure in north and southeastern Europe, which threatened to deprive him of his economic hinterland, but also as the result of much wider considerations, Hitler had started to contemplate an attack on the Soviet Union towards the end of July. Speculating about the factors that held England in the war, he concluded that they were to be found in the hope for American and Soviet aid. There was nothing he could do about the former, but Russia was within reach and could if necessary, be crushed. This approach presented the additional advantage of relieving Japan of Soviet pressure and thus enabling her to hold the US in check, whether by threats or by actual warfare. These considerations led to an order to OKW and OKH to prepare the theoretical and organizational basis for an attack on Russia in the spring of 1941.[3] The importance of these preparations, started early in August and proceeding rather slowly and without any intervention from Hitler until early in December, should not be overestimated. They were based on oral commands only and at the time of 'directive No. 18' had not yet been presented to the Führer.[4] For our purpose, the important point is that Hitler thought he could proceed either with Russia or against her; either a far-reaching agreement, preferably involving her in a war against England must be achieved, or it would be necessary to smash her, because she was too dangerous a neighbour and could be expected to attack Germany once the US and England had completed their preparations in the west.[5]

From about the middle of September 1940, it was the 'with Russia' approach seems to have been foremost in Hitler's mind. The invasion of England had been abandoned, the war was likely to reach into 1941, Hitler therefore needed a secure back. He was increasingly inclined to listen to his foreign minister's plans, which now began to assume a more concrete form. Their main postulates were as follows. Germany would assume the leadership in an European coalition directed against England. Into this coalition he wanted to incorporate Russia and Japan, as well as Italy, Spain and possibly France, so as to create an anti-British bloc stretching from Tokyo to the Straits of Gibraltar. All these countries were to come to a mutual agreement and participate in the onslaught on the British Empire, each in its own designated 'sphere of influence'. By offering the Russians the prospect of expansion at the expense of Britain in the direction of the Persian Gulf and India, Hitler and Ribbentrop hoped not only to hurt the British but to 'divert' the Russians from their traditional European aims and relieve Germany of their pressure. This, in a very much abridged and simplified form, was the plan which Hitler had Ribbentrop – and who was better suited? – communicated to Mussolini on 19 to 20 September.

Though it would be wrong to regard the 'continental bloc' conception as synonymous with Raeder's 'peripheral' strategy – which also involved the use of other European states against England – the two programmes had much in common. Both aimed at bringing Britain to her knees 'by other means' than invasion. Both involved waging war against England with the help of other states. Both were ultimately based on the assumption that the war would not end in 1941, for otherwise both would, presumably, be dispensable and even dangerous in so far as they would result in the strengthening of other states, some of them not at all congenial. The idea of a 'continental bloc' was naturally much the larger of the two programmes, and supplemented the 'peripheral' strategy in a double sense; England would be faced with more enemies, and Hitler's back would be relieved of Soviet pressure.

It is therefore no accident that the two systems grew up together, as it were. The nadir of German–Soviet relations was probably reached early in September, after Hitler had excluded the Soviets from participating in the Vienna Award and guaranteed Rumania's frontiers against them; from that time onward there are clear signs that, although by no means ready to renounce the advantages he had won in eastern Europe (which he proved by sending his troops to occupy the Rumanian oil fields on 12 October)[6] Hitler hoped to improve his relations with the big eastern neighbour. Thus, the preparations for a Russian campaign in 1941 were increasingly pushed into the background until in October such a campaign was regarded as no longer probable.[7]

Even before then efforts to bring about a *rapprochement* with Russia had begun in earnest. The first step towards the establishment of a grand anti-British – and, incidentally, anti-American–coalition was the signature, on 27 September, of the Tripartite Pact between Germany, Italy and Japan. Both Ribbentrop and his Japanese colleague, Matsuoka, regarded the pact as a prelude to the definitive clarification of relations between the signatory powers and the Soviet Union, the one by incorporating her in the pact and the other by the signature of a Soviet–Japanese non-aggression pact, a goal in the attainment of which he hoped to enlist the good offices of Berlin.[8] The text, therefore, contained an article explicitly saying it was not directed against Russia.[9] To create the right atmosphere Ribbentrop had given Stalin twenty-four hours advance notice of the signature of the pact,[10] while Hitler ordered Soviet industrial orders to be given top priority – that is, even over German ones.[11] After spending four days – from the 5th to the 8th – in solitary contemplation at the Berghof, Hitler emerged with his mind made up. As a result, on 13 October, Ribbentrop sent a letter to Stalin, in which he explained Hitler's plans and invited Molotov to come to Berlin to discuss them.[12]

Stalin's reply turned out to be satisfactory; the Soviet dictator professed his general agreement to the plans suggested by the German government and agreed to have Molotov visit Berlin.[13] From Moscow, Ambassador Schulenburg reported that the Soviets were ready in principle to sign a pact with Japan.[14] It was therefore in optimistic mood that Hitler made Mussolini a party to his plans,[15] and on 4 November Ribbentrop was brimming over with confidence at the prospect of 'negotiating an agreement between the Tripartite Powers and Russia', based on mutual recognition of spheres of interest, abstinence from helping each other's enemies, friendship and collaboration, a definition of the 'direction of dynamism' – a euphemism for territorial expansion – of each signatory, and a revision of the Montreux Convention. Russia would then join the Tripartite Pact and share the spoils of the British Empire.[16] So confident was Ribbentrop that he prepared a draft for the German–Italian–Japanese–Soviet pact.[17] Should Hitler succeed in 'pulling off this trick' as he put it to his foreign minister,[18] England would be faced with the largest coalition of all time, stretching from East Asia to Western Europe. Whether or not this grand coalition would come into being depended on the outcome of the truly epoch-making visit to Berlin by Soviet foreign minister Vladislav Molotov.

From the German point of view, the talks with Molotov from 11 to 13 November turned out to be a disappointment. The Soviet foreign minister seemed to be an extremely tough negotiator and was not impressed even by Hitler's oratory. While expressing agreement 'in principle' to the ideas raised by Hitler and Ribbentrop, he refused to be 'diverted' into Asia and insisted on raising, one by one, precisely those European questions which had caused so much friction between the two countries in past months; Finland, Poland, Rumania and, particularly Bulgaria, Hitler's most recent focus of interest, which Molotov insisted belonged to the Soviet sphere of influence.[18a] In doing this, he allowed the long-term goals of Soviet foreign policy to come through with a frankness that must have shocked Hitler.[19] Even though Molotov had not explicitly rejected the German proposals and promised to submit them to Stalin; his insistence had made one thing clear to Hitler: the Soviet Union would not stand idly by and watch German troops enter Bulgaria.

DIPLOMATIC FAILURE IN THE SOUTHEAST

Considering the reputation she had acquired in the years immediately preceding World War I, Bulgaria's reaction to the outbreak of the Italian–Greek war had been remarkably restrained. The country was as much dependent economically on Germany as any other Balkan state; she also nursed revisionist claims to the Aegean Coast, taken from her by Greece in 1913. This could perhaps be satisfied by participating in an Italo–German campaign against Greece. All these factors notwithstanding, King Boris had refused to join Mussolini in his attack on Greece when the Italian dictator asked him to, refused to follow Slovakia, Hungary and Rumania in promising to sign the Tripartite Pact[20] and shown little enthusiasm, for taking part in the on-slaught on Greece, or even for German troops doing the dirty job for him and crossing his country on the way to Greece.

There were two reasons for this. First, there were the 37 divisions Turkey had concentrated in Thrace, and which it was loudly pro-claimed, were ready to march against Bulgaria if she joined Mussolini. Behind Turkey, moreover, the shadow of England lurked menacingly. London had already warned Bulgaria against changing her neutral policy when, on 15 October, it had erroneously been reported that German troops were about to march into the country.[21] Immediately on the outbreak of the Italo–Greek war, moreover, England had come out with open threats to Bulgaria.[22]

Even more powerful was the second argument against opening the doors to the German army: the Soviet Union. From the Soviet point of view, an alignment of Bulgaria with Germany was highly undesir-able because it would contribute to the consolidation of southeastern Europe under German domination and close the road to the Straits. Molotov had made this clear to Hitler, and the Soviets also protested against Bulgaria's reported intention to join the Tripartite Pact. What the Soviets might do in such a case was, of course, anybody's guess, but the way in which they had seized some islands in the northern arm of the Danube late in October, completely ignoring Hitler's guarantee to Rumania, as well as the enormous number of troops they were concentrating in Bessarabia,[23] was scarcely a good omen.

Bulgarian fear of Turkey and the Soviet Union came to light as soon as the Germans began their approaches. One of Hitler's first decisions after the Italian defeat in Albania was to set up an advanced air-raid system along the Bulgaro–Greek border as a precaution against possible British attacks on the Rumanian oil fields. A German note asking that 200 air force specialists be allowed to set up the system was therefore handed over to the Bulgarians on 6 November.[24] On the next day, the Bulgarians granted the request.[25] A few days later, however, they changed their mind; fearing that the presence of German army units might be disclosed to the British intelligence service, they now proposed to set up the air raid warning system themselves, with the help of only a few German instructors.[26] It took strong German representations before, on 20 November, the Bulgarians finally surrendered and agreed to have the system constructed and manned by German personnel; on 25 November the first stations were established.[27]

To persuade Sofia to take part in the attack on Greece, or even to abstain from doing so and allow only German troops to pass through her territory, was far more difficult. Geography had turned Bulgaria into the pivot of the German–Soviet struggle for influence in south-eastern Europe; situated between Hitler and Stalin, Sofia – for reasons that are only too easy to understand – never left any doubt that she would, in the last resort, choose the former. In the meantime, she wanted to defer her decision for as long as possible, so as to escape Soviet pressure and revenge. King Boris himself, whom Hitler received at the Berghof on 18 November, can scarcely have left the Führer in any doubt about the sympathies of his country; yet it seems that he refused to sign the Tripartite Pact, and would not, for the time being, allow German troops to enter Bulgaria.[28]

This reply did not and could not satisfy Hitler, to whom Bulgaria had become vital as a deployment area for the Greek operation. On 22 November, therefore, he sent the suave Franz von Papen, his ambassador in Ankara, to talk to Boris but to no avail.[29] Sofia feared the Soviets, and with good reason. On 18 November the Bulgarian minister in Moscow, Stamenov, had unexpectedly found himself facing Molotov, who proceeded to tell him the following: the Soviet Union was in doubt of Bulgaria's present position. Whenever the talk in Berlin turned to Bulgaria, the answer was that the Italians would also have to be consulted. Did Bulgaria have a treaty with Italy or an Italian guarantee? If so, Russia would also insist on giving a guarantee. In any case, she would not tolerate Bulgaria becoming a 'legionaire state' – presumably, that is, following Rumania into the German orbit. Molotov's *démarche* had caused anxiety in Sofia; the foreign minister had become 'dubious' and asked whether Bulgaria's accession to the Tripartite Pact could not be postponed 'so as to coincide with that of Spain'.[30]

It was an anxious Bulgarian minister, therefore, whom Hitler faced on 23 November. Draganov began by stating his government's readiness 'in principle' to sign the pact; but he still wanted to postpone action for reasons which he, Draganov, had been instructed to explain. The minister then tried to refer to Stamenov's talk with Molotov, but Hitler interrupted him. He had been told of that conversation, he said, and could assure Draganov that the facts were not as the Soviet foreign minister had presented them. It was the Russians who had insisted on giving a guarantee to Bulgaria just like the one Germany had given to Rumania; the Soviet guarantee, incidentally, was of a rather strange kind, because it included the statement that no harm would come to the dynasty, and that no attempts would be made to change the internal regime of Bulgaria. He, the Führer, had saved Bulgaria by evading the question and telling Molotov he would have to ask Rome.

Faced with this account of what had taken place in Berlin, Draganov could only reply that the Russians were 'a treacherous people'. His other arguments were similarly cut to ribbons by Hitler. The minister asked what Yugoslavia's attitude might be; Hitler countered by asking what Bulgaria would say if Yugoslavia was to join the Tripartite Pact herself. Draganov talked about the Turkish danger; Hitler retorted that the Turks knew very well that any move on their side would cause Constantinople to share the fate of Birmingham and Coventry. As to Russia, it was essential, and possible, to divert her from the Balkans to the east; Stalin was a good businessman, and upon recognizing there was nothing to be gained in Bulgaria he would turn elsewhere – as had been proved by the example of Rumania, whose sufferings at Russia's hand had been cut short once and for all by the German guarantee. To help Stalin turn eastward, Hitler declared himself ready to consider a revision of the Montreux Convention in Russia's favour. When Draganov took his leave the Führer fired his parting shot; should the Soviets march into Bulgaria, her fate would be similar to that of the Baltic States, and 'a few months of terror would then shape Bulgaria according to Russia's wishes'. Still, Hitler conceded, 'the arguments advanced by the minister, also as regards England, were not without merit'.[31]

On 3 December, Draganov was again summoned to the Reichskanzlei; again to no avail. The Bulgarians had in the meantime been subjected to the strongest Soviet pressure. After their offer of a guarantee was rejected, the Soviets had proposed a mutual assistance pact aimed at helping Bulgaria to fulfil her territorial aspirations at the expense of Greece, Turkey and Yugoslavia.[32] When this, too, was rejected they resorted to underhand means. On 28 November a great mass of pamphlets repeating the latest Soviet offer word for word, together with a precise description of the 'national aspirations' Russia was prepared to help Bulgaria in obtaining, appeared in Sofia.[33] As a result, on 3 December, Draganov again refused to surrender to the Führer's arguments; Bulgaria was ready to sign, only not quite yet.[34]

The minister's arguments must have convinced Hitler, if he had not yet realized it, that Bulgaria's problem was essentially one of security. King Boris had shown surprisingly little enthusiasm to take part in the Greek operation with his own forces, but his own conversations with Draganov persuaded him that Bulgaria was really prepared to sign the Tripartite Pact and allow German troops to pass if convinced that she was in no danger from Russia and Turkey. Though there was nothing he could do to make the Soviets stop their pressure on Sofia, Ankara could perhaps be persuaded that her interests would not be endangered by the presence of German troops in Bulgaria; and it was to Ankara that Hitler now turned.

During World War I, Germany and Turkey had been allies; in World War II Turkey found itself in England's camp. That this was so was to a large extent due to the most important postulates in Hitler's foreign policy during the period 1939–41, i.e. his alliance with Italy and his non-aggression pact with the Soviet Union. Italy, of course, was an old enemy of Turkey; Turkish fears of the Duce's Imperial ambitions in the eastern Mediterranean and especially his occupation of Albania caused them to enter into negotiations with the British and the French for a mutual assistance pact. After a short time, however, the Turks discovered that the western powers' fear of Mussolini joining Hitler in an eventual war was even greater than their own fear of him, and they exploited this in order to extract economic concessions. It was only after the signature of the Molotov–Ribbentrop pact, and particularly after the Soviets had joined Hitler in partitioning Poland, that they were jolted into signing.[35]

Berlin, of course, was anything but happy about the conclusion of the pact. Claiming that Italy was its principal target they tried to make their allies protest, but the latter appear to have appreciated the anti-Soviet edge of the pact and refused. Although the Turks defected on their alliance when Italy entered the war and again when Greece was attacked, German–Turkish relations steadily deteriorated. To a considerable extent this was the result of the discovery of the Vitry de la Charité documents. From these the Germans concluded that the Turks had conspired with the British and the French to bomb the Soviet oil fields in the Caucasus – a source of supply for Germany, too.[36]

In September 1940 the Turks started to sense once again an old and mortal danger; that of the establishment of a German–Soviet block. It was feared in Ankara that in order to obtain Soviet cooperation against England Hitler might well make concessions in the Straits – the more so, as his own interests were not directly involved. A greater danger to Turkey was inconceivable.[37] Convinced that Hitler was about to sell them to the Russians – if, indeed, he had not already done so[38] – the Turks tried to forestall him by themselves coming to terms with Stalin: they now hoped to conclude a friendship pact with him which would guarantee their frontiers in return for free passage through the Straits.[39]

Just when it was thought in Ankara that some headway was being made in this direction,[40] the announcement of Molotov's visit to Berlin struck like a bombshell and drove the Turks into a panic. With good reason, too; although out of consideration for Italy, Hitler was not prepared to grant Stalin the bases on the Straits the latter asked for, he was certainly not above putting the Turks under pressure by means of a German–Soviet *rapprochement*;[41] nor would he hesitate to pay for Stalin's cooperation at Turkey's expense.[42] In the last fews day before the visit, Ankara made frantic attempts to embroil Stalin with Hitler by leaking reports about the latter's intention to attack Turkey and thus 'destroy completely Russia's influence in the Balkans';[43] to no avail. Molotov went to Berlin as scheduled, and to Ankara it seemed that the end had come [44]

Fortunately for the Turks, the German–Soviet talks did not proceed as Berlin had planned. Soviet demands in the Straits and elsewhere were such that even Hitler, for all his desire to establish a 'continental bloc', could not accept them. The talks had made it clear to Hitler that his move through southeastern Europe into the eastern Mediterranean would be opposed by the Soviets; consequently, German–Turkish relations underwent a sudden and dramatic change. No more could there be a question of 'selling' Turkey to Stalin; nor would it be possible to count on Soviet help to keep the Turks quiet during Hitler's march through Bulgaria. Just as Russia's attitude over the Bulgarian question had forced Hitler into long and difficult negotiations with Sofia, so her attitude on Turkey forced him to approach Ankara directly.

On 15 November, therefore, Hitler surprised Papen – who had come to Berlin on the eve of the Molotov visit on the assumption that German and Soviet troops would soon cooperate in altering the *status quo* in the Straits[45] – by ordering him to postpone his departure for Ankara by one week. What followed is not entirely clear. Apparently on 21 November,[46] Hitler seems to have conferred with Papen and provided him with a completely new set of instructions, of the nature of which we have only indirect information.[47] Papen then flew back to Ankara – inviting himself to talks with King Boris on the way – to find the Turks in a panic. On the night of 22 to 23 November, greatly frightened by rumours about the results of Molotov's visit to Berlin, the Turkish government put Turkish Thrace under martial law and alarmed the troops there.

Upon arriving at his post on the 23rd, therefore, Papen had nothing more urgent to do than to assure the foreign minister, Saracoglu, that it had all been a 'misunderstanding' and that the Axis 'was prepared to respect the possessions and sovereignty of Turkey and, in some circumstances, to give guarantees to that effect, if Turkey could make up her mind to cooperate in the new order in Europe'.[48] Six days later he repeated the same to President Inonü who, however, was not easily convinced. He asked Papen what Germany's attitude to the preservation of the peace in the Balkans was, and under what circumstances she would come to the aid of her ally; Papen answered that this would only happen if the British tried to build up a Balkan front. He was cut short by the president's statement that in his opinion German action against Greece in the spring was inevitable.[49] This, Papen thought, the Turks were determined to resist.[50] Still, the German ambassador did not give up; on 2 December he was able to send Ribbentrop a *resumé* of the points on which he thought agreement was possible.[51]

While negotiating with Hitler's envoy in Ankara, the Turks had also been active in Sofia. On 25 November their minister there had appeared in the foreign ministry and put forward his government's offer, under the terms of which Turkey would give guarantees that she would not attack Bulgaria, 'provided Bulgaria refrained from any hostile act'.[52] As the Germans themselves had no intention of attacking Turkey, nor of allowing Bulgaria to do so, Ribbentrop replied that 'I believe it would be advisable for the Bulgarian government to reply to the Turkish proposal with an offer to conclude a Bulgarian–Turkish non-aggression pact.'[53] While this answer was on its way, the Turks let the cat out of the bag: their minister in Sofia explained that 'hostile acts' also included the presence of 'foreign' – either red or grey – troops on Bulgarian territory.[54] Ribbentrop must have felt that he had been tricked, for he sent an angry telegram to Papen in Ankara: 'until you receive further instructions, please exercise great reserve in your conversations with the Turks. I assume you have not delivered anything in writing and request confirmation of the fact . . . for the time being, please do not carry on any further conversations regarding the question of the Straits.'[55] With this telegram Ribbentrop admitted that he had lost the first round in his efforts to make Turkey declare her acquiescence in the presence of German troops in Bulgaria; but perhaps it would still be possible to make such a declaration unnecessary by negotiating with Yugoslavia.

The Yugoslavia we left in August 1940 was in a very weak position; entirely dependent as she was on Hitler's grace to protect her from the greed of her Italian and Hungarian neighbours, her situation grew even worse during the autumn. With the expansion of German power into the southeast Yugoslavia gradually saw herself surrounded by a ring of steel and cut off from the Soviet Union, the only power that could still make Hitler think twice. As her neighbours prepared, during the late autumn, to join the Tripartite Pact Yugoslavia saw her independence slowly eroded as she was inexorably drawn into the German orbit.[56]

Just when Berlin began to think it had Yugoslavia where it wanted her – that is, ready to sign the Tripartite Pact[57] – Mussolini was defeated in Greece and thus the tables were turned. For Yugoslavia, this defeat was certainly a blessing. Had Mussolini won his war, she would have found herself surrounded on all sides by the Axis and forced to surrender her independence, presumably with parts of her territory; conversely, Mussolini's defeat immensely strengthened her position.

By botching up his Greek adventure the Duce had, in effect, thrown himself onto Belgrade's mercy. The Yugoslav army had only to move to the rear of his troops in Albania to make their whole position there untenable. By the middle of the month, moreover, Mussolini found himself in the humiliating position of having to beg Belgrade for transit-rights for his trucks to Albania – only to be resoundingly rebuffed. But Hitler, too, had been made dependent on the good will of Belgrade;

without her consent no German operation against Greece was possible
at all. Her cooperation on the other hand could save the Wehrmacht
lots of time and trouble. As negotiations with Turkey dragged on,
moveover, it became clear that Ankara would be much more coopera-
tive if the German troops were to march through Yugoslavia and not
through Bulgaria.[58] Made safe against attack by general winter,[59]
courted by the two strongest powers in Europe and holding the key to
the success or failure of the Axis war against Greece – indeed, of
Hitler's attempt to reach out into the eastern Mediterranean – Yugoslavia's position was an extraordinarily strong one.

Hitler's decision to attack Greece had made it essential to win over
Yugoslavia; early in November, the Germans believed they had discovered a suitable lever to do this in the form of Salonika. Both before
and after World War I the city had been the subject of a bitter dispute
between Yugoslavia and Greece. When it was finally awarded to the
latter, Yugoslavia was granted free harbour. As her sole port not facing
Italy, Salonika was naturally of the greatest importance to that country.
Wouldn't it be possible to win her over by offering her the city? During
the first half of November, the Yugoslavs gave every indication that it
would. As soon as the Italian invasion of Greece had started the Prince
Regent had summoned a conference attended by Cvetkovic, the Prime
Minister, Cincar Markovic, the foreign minister, Nedic, the minister
for war, and Antic the commander-in-chief.[60] The conference seems
to have resulted in Nedic instructing Colonel Vauhnik the military
attaché in Berlin, 'to put out feelers with the highest German authorities to find what steps would be appropriate to secure Yugoslavia's
interest in Salonika'. Direct negotiations with Italy, the military attaché
said, were 'out of the question', but in return for 'mediating in favour
of Yugoslavia, Germany might perhaps be able to make certain demands on Yugoslavia'.[61] Though Nedic was dismissed a few days later,
the stream of hints to the same effect did not cease.[62]

On 12 November there was another semi-official Yugoslav approach.
A well known pro-German journalist, Danilo Gregoric, visited Berlin –
presumably on the instructions of Cincar Markovic himself[63] – and had
a long talk with Dr Paul Schmidt the head of the press department at
the German foreign ministry. Yugoslavia, he said, wanted a *rapprochement* with Germany; behind their wish loomed the question of Salonika.
Perhaps it would be possible to negotiate a Yugoslav–German agreement, according to which the Axis would guarantee Yugoslavia,
Yugoslavia would receive Salonika, and payment would be made in
the form of demilitarization of the Adriatic. Though Schmidt stated
that Ribbentrop was too busy to receive the journalist – for once, this
was true – the Reich foreign minister thought the matter sufficiently
important to receive Gregoric later on.[64] The meeting between the two,

of which no record has been found in the archives of the German foreign ministry, took place on the 23rd. According to Gregoric's own account, Ribbentrop undertook to send a telegram to Heeren and to invite Cincar Markovic to Berlin.[65] This account is confirmed by a telegram from Heeren to Ribbentrop of 24 November, in which he reports having carried out the instructions of the foreign minister and arranged the visit.[66]

While expecting the Yugoslav foreign minister, Hitler – who correctly recognized the Salonika question for what it was, i.e. an effective lever to apply to Yugoslavia – deemed the matter sufficiently important to raise it with Ciano on 18 November. Would Mussolini, he asked the Italian foreign minister, consent to an accord with Yugoslavia on the following basis: 1. An Axis guarantee for Yugoslavia's frontiers. 2. Demilitarization of the Dalmatian Coast. 3. In return, the transfer of Salonika to Yugoslavia. Ciano expressed his personal agreement and undertook to raise the matter with the Duce, who, he said, was sure to agree.[67] Mussolini, indeed, had already received a somewhat similar Yugoslav offer for an Italian–Yugoslav agreement, and had been receptive to the idea; to him, it was a heaven-sent opportunity to secure his rear in Albania, while Ciano thought a new Yugoslav–Italian accord might be useful if Rome should at any time decide on an anti-German line – that is, a return to the Stoyadinovic era.[68] On 22 November the Duce therefore agreed to the idea with some enthusiasm.[69] By then, however, it was too late. On 28 November the Führer exercised all his powers of persuasion on Cincar Markovic, trying to convince him that Yugoslavia should sign a non-aggression treaty with Germany and Italy. He promised in return to give her Salonika and, explicitly declared that he did not require rights of transit.[70] However, the series of Italian defeats in Albania, which had now begun in earnest, spoke even more loudly. Having no reason to fear Salonika would ever fall into Italian hands, the Yugoslavs saw no reason to commit themselves irrevocably to the Axis, and lost interest in the matter.

Hitler did the same, and at approximately the same time. The Yugoslav refusal meant to him a third rebuff at the hands of a Balkan country. However, an accord with Yugoslavia that would have given her Salonika made sense only as long as a German attack on Greece was planned, that is, as long as the 'peripheral' strategy was alive; in this context, his offer of Salonika to the Yugoslavs is an excellent 'external barometer' to gauge his intentions towards Greece. By the beginning of December, however, the eastern Mediterranean had ceased to be the focus of Hitler's attention.

THE END OF THE 'PERIPHERAL' STRATEGY

From the German point of view, November 1940 can fairly be said to have been the most crucial month of the entire war; not because of what was going on in southeastern Europe, but because of Russian–German relations. It was during this period that Hitler made the most important decision of his life – in a sense, his last important decision – and then set out irrevocably on a *va banque*, an all or nothing gamble, that was ultimately to lead him to his destruction.

Molotov's departure had left Berlin in a state of suspension. The talks had not led to any concrete agreement; and even though the military – Halder, SKL and OKW – were optimistic about the future of German–Soviet relations,[71] Hitler himself scarcely shared their confidence. His own realistic estimate of the chances of success was reflected in 'directive No. 18', which he signed during the visit, ordering 'all preparations for which verbal orders have already been given' to be pursued 'regardless of the outcome' of the talks with Molotov. On 15 November he told his closest associates that 'the talks have shown the direction in which the Russian plans are moving. Molotov has let the cat out of the sack. They did not even try to hide their plans. To allow the Russians into Europe, would mean the end of central Europe. The Balkans and Finland are endangered flanks.' Consequently, he ordered Engel and Schmundt, his adjutants, to co-ordinate with master-builder Todt in the selection of suitable locations for new *Gefechtstände* on the northern, central and southern sectors of the Soviet frontier, and to have them constructed as fast as possible.[72]

There followed a period of uncertainty lasting from 16 to 25 November. During this time the Soviets made uncompromising noises – they stepped up their interference in Bulgaria and denounced the accession of Hungary to the Tripartite Pact[73] – but Hitler does not seem to have given up all hope. On 18 November he told Ciano that 'it is necessary to apply strong measures in order to divert Russia from the Balkans and direct her southward', a sentence which he repeated almost verbatim in his letter to Mussolini two days later.[74] He also told Teleki the Hungarian prime minister, that:

Russia's conduct was either Bolshevist or Russian nationalist, depending on the situation... Nevertheless we could try ... to bring her into the great world wide coalition that stretched from Yokohama to Spain.

The Russians, indeed, hung 'like a threatening cloud on the horizon', but since they could also 'think realistically' it would perhaps be possible to 'divert them to the south Asiatic continent'.[75] Hitler was sceptical, but not entirely despondent; and when General Speidel, commander of the German air force mission in Rumania, asked for

instructions in case of a German–Soviet war the Führer had Jodl postpone the reply until the arrival of the Soviet answer.[76]

On 26 November, the Soviets did answer. Stalin had decided to
accept Ribbentrop's draft for a four-power pact subject to the following
conditions:

1. Provided that the German troops are immediately withdrawn from
Finland . . .:
2. Provided that within the next few months the security of the Soviet
Union in the Straits is assured by the conclusion of a mutual assistance pact
between the Soviet Union and Bulgaria . . . and by the establishment of a
base for land and naval forces of the USSR within range of the Bosphoros
and Dardanelles by means of a long-term lease.
3. Provided that the area south of Batum and Baku in the general direction
of the Persian Gulf is recognized as the centre of aspirations of the Soviet
Union.
4. Provided that Japan renounces her rights to concessions for coal and oil
in northern Sakhalin.[77]

These demands constituted an infinitely higher price than Hitler ever
dreamt of paying and, coinciding as they did with the Soviets' efforts
to establish themselves in Bulgaria, finally proved to him what he had
suspected all along; that no long term understanding with Russia was
possible. It was clear that the attempt to 'divert' Stalin into Asia had
failed, and that eastern Europe remained the centre of Soviet aspirations. The Soviet note was therefore left without a reply; General
Speidel, on the other hand, got his instructions the very next day.[78]
Hitler's attempt to reach an understanding with the Soviets had failed;
he now decided to go to war against them – the sooner the better.

This momentous decision – which had been crystallizing from the
time of the Molotov visit onward,[79] but probably not finalized until the
arrival of the Soviet note on 26 November – had immediate and far-
reaching consequences. Firstly, the war against Great Britain now turned
into a secondary matter, and the 'peripheral' strategy was therefore
eliminated at a single stroke. Secondly, the mess created by Italy's
failure in Greece turned from a rather secondary nuisance within the
framework of the 'peripheral' strategy (and not wholly unqualified, as it
had presented the Germans with the opportunity to install themselves
in the eastern Mediterranean while circumventing Italian objections)
into a first-class blunder from the point of view of the future war
against Russia. Let us take up each of these issues in turn.

The decision to attack Russia in the spring of 1941 meant the end of
the 'peripheral' strategy. Studies conducted at OKH and OKW had
demonstrated that Germany's forces did not suffice to carry out both;
as long as there was tension between Russia and Germany such strong
forces would be tied to the Russian border[80] that the peripheral

strategy could not be put into effect. Conversely, no attack on the Soviet Union could take place with large German forces bound to various operations within the framework of the 'peripheral' strategy, in theatres as remote from each other as Gibraltar and Egypt, Morocco and Greece. The realization of any of these programmes ruled out the other.[81] In November 1940, Hitler decided to opt for the Russian solution. His Mediterranean offensive against England had to be scrapped in consequence, and this was a factor about which Hitler was never in doubt.[82]

Easier said than done. On the night of 11–12 November a Royal Air Force attack on the harbour of Taranto cost Italy half its fleet, and resulted in a radical turn in the balance of forces between her and the British. By the end of the month, moreover, her armies in Greece were in full retreat before fierce Greek counter-attacks. If left on her own she was likely to collapse, thus incurring disastrous loss of prestige for the Axis and opening up a wide gap in Germany's own defences. Though Hitler probably resented the fact, he had no choice but to pursue some of his Mediterranean plans. However, the aim of these plans now underwent a basic transformation. Instead of forming part of an overall strategy designed to bring down England, they turned into makeshift measures designed to win time – essentially defensive actions aiming to prevent the complete collapse of Italy and an excessive strengthening of Britain's Mediterranean position.[83] In view of the coming offensive against Russia, it would be desirable to commit only a few forces to the Mediterranean, and to have them there for the shortest possible period. Moreover, the large-scale, prolonged operations would have to be abandoned in favour of the smaller, more immediate ones.

To reduce the size of his commitment in the Mediterranean was, in fact, just what Hitler set out to do. At the beginning of November, it will be remembered, he preferred cooperation with France – in the interests of preserving the relatively remote North African colonies – to collaboration with Spain; but by the middle of the month Italian defeats had made the closing of the Mediterranean a much more urgent task. On 11 November Suner was therefore summoned to Berlin.[84] The talks with the Spanish foreign minister on 18 November were inconclusive,[85] but the Germans were encouraged by the fact that he agreed to the establishment of a joint German–Spanish military commission to examine the tactical aspects of capturing Gibraltar.[86] Consequently SKL now hoped for an early materialization of operation 'Felix', as the Gibraltar venture was called.[87] The attempt to lure Spain into the war also meant that France, which had for some time been regarded by Hitler as the more likely partner, could henceforward be granted less consideration, and Hitler, who in the meantime may have suspected a secret Anglo–French agreement arrived at behind his back,[88] started to modify his attitude towards the latter country. On 18 November Halder noted that it had been decided to hold on to the original [i.e. 'hard'] line in Germany's attitude to France;[89] on 21 November a French request to transfer forces to Indo-China was brusquely rejected, as was a French protest against the dumping of 100,000 Lorrainers in unoccupied France.[90] Compared with Hitler's former plans for far-reaching collaboration with Vichy, this old-new 'with Spain' approach had the advantage – and this was undoubtedly the most important consideration behind it – that it was small enough to fit into the timetable for the future Russian campaign, which now started to assume concrete form.[91]

Hitler's decision to turn against Russia had similar results in the eastern Mediterranean. Here, the question of German intervention in Libya was eliminated once and for all – or so Hitler thought.[92] Having cut down three of the four elements forming the 'peripheral' strategy, Hitler turned to the Balkans. Here the problems involved were more complex because, unlike the other operations, the Italian attack on Greece had already begun – and failed – and could not, regrettably enough, be liquidated at the stroke of the pen. Here, other measures were called for.

Hitler's change of strategy had, indeed, given a nasty turn to the Italian defeat in Greece. As long as the 'peripheral' strategy was alive the failure of the Italian offensive was unpleasant enough; with the decision to turn against Russia it became an unqualified obstacle. Hitler desperately needed the Balkans to be stable and thus to form an effective cover for the right flank of his future Russian offensive; in no case could he base it on a British-infested Greece, particularly with the menacing example of the allied Salonika front of World War I before his eyes.[93] The first thing to do, obviously, was to show his displeasure to the Italians. Mussolini's knuckles – hitherto conspicuously spared[94] – were now severely rapped in Hitler's letter to the Duce of 20 November. Rather belatedly, Hitler discovered that 'when I asked you to receive me in Florence, I began my trip in the hope that I might be able to present my views to you before the beginning of the threatening conflict with Greece, concerning which I had been informed only in a general way'. There followed a long list of psychological and military consequences of the Italian failure, and of the measures Hitler intended to take to improve the situation. German troops were promised for the Mediterranean, but Hitler said he would 'probably' need them back by March or April, as they would be required for other tasks. Mussolini remained unmoved; on 22 November he answered that he 'keenly regretted' that 'the letter he had sent on 19 October, that is 9 days in advance', to announce his action had 'missed' the Führer [*sic !*] and his hope that the worst was over already.[95] Privately, however, he observed to Badoglio that 'on 19 October I wrote a letter to the Führer that I was taking over Greece. The Führer being on his way, the letter reached him on the 24th. The Germans therefore were not at all displeased and had all the time in the world to take the measures of which they thought I had not taken cognizance. The only reason for their displeasure is that matters have not proceeded as they should.'[96] Mussolini was perfectly right; and it was precisely for this reason that he did not, like Ciano before the beginning of the offensive, insist that Hitler had given him the go ahead.

From the German point of view, Mussolini's conciliatory reply was insufficient to retrieve the situation. Once he had decided to attack Russia in the spring, Hitler could not do without a stable, British-proof flank; preparations for the Greek operation therefore had to continue, even though they had lost their original purpose. On the other hand, there was the possibility that the same aims might be achieved by peaceful means; if the Greeks could be induced to bring their war with Italy to an end and throw out such British units as had already landed on their territory no military operation would be necessary. Once he had decided on the Russian operation, Hitler, at the beginning of December, thought this approach worth a try.

ATTEMPTS AT RECONCILIATION

'This is ridiculous and grotesque' Ciano reported his father-in-law as saying on 4 December, 'but it is a fact: we have to ask for an armistice'.[97] The outlook in Albania was in fact grim. Having been misled by a false movement Soddu – who had taken over from Visconti Prasca on 9 November – mistook the main goal of the Greek counter-attack. This mistake cost him Koritza on 22 November. This initiated an Italian retreat all along the line; Moschopolis and Progradets fell on 30 November, Premeti and Hagia Santa on 4 and 5 December respectively. With the capture of Argyrocastro on 8 December things also became lively on the left wing of the Greek offensive.

As the defeats of his troops in Albania multiplied, it seemed to Mussolini that there was only one way out short of a humiliating armistice; an agreement with Yugoslavia that would allow him to transport reinforcements and material, particularly lorries, by way of the latter's territory.[98] The Duce, it will be remembered, had agreed with the Führer's plans for an accord with Yugoslavia, and even consented to scrapping one of his original prerequisites for such an accord. During the first days of December, however, it began to look as if this gesture was not appreciated in Berlin, where people seemed to have lost interest in the matter. To remind them, Mussolini – who had no idea that Hitler had in the meantime lost interest in the Mediterranean – on 5 December dispatched Alfieri, who had been convalescing in Rome, to Berlin 'with the real, specific mission to request the Führer to bring about a speedy accession of Yugoslavia to the Tripartite Pact'.

Mussolini was out for disappointment. When Yugoslavia had first been discussed by Hitler and Ciano on 18 November the German dictator was reported to have grown 'warm, almost friendly'; this time, his reaction was decidedly less enthusiastic. Instead of warming to the subject, he merely replied that 'Yugoslavia . . . was very cool in her attitude'. Not discouraged by this lack of interest, Alfieri tried to make himself helpful by suggesting other ways in which Germany might contribute towards the liquidation of Greece by military means:

Perhaps [Alfieri said] it was possible for the Führer, so the Duce thought, to hit upon a diversionary manoeuvre, possibly by bringing Bulgaria to a partial mobilization merely for the purpose of effect. In this way also the pressure on the front would be reduced. Another possibility of lessening the pressure he [Alfieri] had already suggested to the Reich foreign minister on the day before.[99] It might be possible, namely by means of a 'journalistic indiscretion', to start a rumour abroad that Germany was concentrating rather large numbers of troops in Rumania. All this would, in the opinion of the Duce, contribute to relieving the pressure and splitting the enemy forces.

At this point the Italian ambassador was cut short by Ribbentrop who, obviously relishing the marvellous prospects for a general conflict in the Balkans, which an immediate Bulgarian mobilization would open, poured cold water on his suggestions by telling him that 'Bulgaria was even demobilizing, since she was now on the point of coming towards an agreement with the Turks.' Hitler then made use of the interruption to bypass the Duce's plans and open a discussion of 'the most important thing', which according to him was 'to bring order immediately to the front itself by using barbaric means', such as shooting of officers who deserted their posts, decimating the troops, etc. 'To be sure, he had already started to build up his forces in Rumania, and he hoped to be able to hold this Balkan position. [?] But the important thing was to raise the morale of the Italian troops. For that purpose, there was need for a man with iron nerves and barbaric determination who . . . would not shrink from serious measures'. By now the poor Alfieri was thoroughly alarmed in face of this show of Nordic *Furchtbarkeit*. He hastily interposed that the situation on the Greek front was not that bad after all, and that the Duce's ideas had been mere 'possibilities'.[100] Then he took his leave.

He left behind a troubled Hitler. Twenty days earlier the Führer had taken a lively interest in the Yugoslav question, but now, with the 'peripheral' strategy scrapped and the attack on Russia determined on, the Greek operation had lost its original *raison d'etre*; unprepared to offer anything but symbolic German military aid,[101] Hitler preferred to settle the conflict by diplomatic means, if at all possible. The first steps in this direction had, in fact, been taken even before Alfieri's visit. On 1 December Canaris told Rintelen for the first time that it was necessary to establish a cease-fire in Albania by German mediation.[102] On 5 December Hitler himself told his senior officers that:

> If the Greeks do not expel the English themselves, we shall have to carry out the Bulgarian operation. It is not impossible that the Greeks, too, are aware of this. . .

Since, in Hitler's words on the same occasion, 'the decision over the European hegemony falls in Russia', the Greek affair had developed from an essential part of the 'peripheral' strategy into an unpleasant, but alas necessary, diversion. Fortunately it was not as unpleasant as other operations taken from the framework of the 'peripheral' strategy would have been, because Greece's geographical situation made it possible to withdraw the troops committed there for the east, and because the forces concentrated in Rumania for the purpose would be available for the east even if the Italo–Greek conflict was terminated. This was precisely what Hitler wanted most:

> Should the Greeks drive out the English, no attack by us will be necessary any more. In any case, however, operation 'Marita' [as the Greek under-taking had been code-named] is to be prepared for.
>
> Operation 'Felix' will be carried out early in February. Under its impression, Greece may alter her attitude to England. For this reason, we maintain correct relations with Greece. Towards Greece we are a 'non belligerent' state.[103]

Unfortunately for Hitler it was only three days later, on 8 December, that the chief of his intelligence service reported from Madrid that Franco did not intend to enter the war.[104] As a result on 10 December the whole Gibraltar operation was scrapped.[105] Franco's refusal sounded the death knell of whatever was left of the 'peripheral' strategy; it meant that the Mediterranean would remain open to the British, and hence increased the problems of solving the Greek question by force of arms should that prove necessary. The change in Hitler's attitude is reflected in the fact that the original 'directive No. 19', which outlined a highly pugnacious plan for the capture of Gibraltar, was left unsigned.[106] Instead another directive bearing the same number was issued, ordering the occupation of unoccupied France if the de Gaulle revolt spread to North West Africa.[107] Hitler's attempt to branch out into the eastern and the western Mediterranean had ended in failure; and in both cases his reaction was the same, i.e. recoil back into Europe.

Pushing Franco into the war was not the only mission Canaris had to fulfil in Madrid. The German head of the Abwehr also paid a visit to an old crony of his, the Hungarian minister Andorka. Andorka subsequently approached the Greek minister, Admiral Argyropoulos, with the following German offer: 1. Subject to Greek consent, the German government would mediate a cease-fire in Albania. 2. German troops would guarantee the cease-fire by positioning themselves between the belligerent armies. 3. Greece was to keep all the territories it had occupied in Albania. 4. In return, she would drive out the British and become 'truly neutral' once more. Argyropoulos had the German offer transmitted to Athens, but never received any answer.[108] Not putting all their eggs in one basket, 'Hitler and Ribbentrop', that is the very highest German authorities, at about the same time seem to have approached a former Greek minister, Maniadakis, using the services of Professor Boehringer, the German cultural attaché in Athens, with an identical offer.[109] Furthermore, the German ambassador in Ankara during these days expressly aired his opinion that once Greece had defeated the Italians, she should conclude peace with them.[110] However, nothing came of any of these proposals.

The reason for this is a matter for conjecture – or rather, was until the recent opening of the British documents for 1940.[111] It seems that long before the outbreak of the Italo–Greek war the chief concern of Britain was to make sure that, should this eventuality arise, the Greeks would not give way without resistance. For this the foreign office gave the following reasons: 1. A war waged by Italy in Greece would divert the former from Egypt. 2. It would enable Britain to establish air and particularly naval bases in Greece which would 'make all the difference in the prosecution of the war in the eastern Mediterranean'.[112] With this object in mind, the British were busy 'maintain[ing] Greek determination to fight' and 'fortify[ing] the courage already shown by general Metaxas'.[113] Once the war had broken out, they were naturally suspicious of any hints of possible German mediation in the Italo–Greek conflict and did their best to forestall such a possibility.

Early in December a positive stream of such hints was reaching the foreign office in London. From Belgrade Campbell reported the 'lively interest' caused by reports in foreign papers of an impending meeting in Salonika between Metaxas and Saracoglu the Turkish foreign minister which was believed to be connected with 'certain proposals which von Papen had brought back to Ankara for solution of Italo–Greek conflict'. Though it was impossible to get confirmation of this news from official German sources, it was 'becoming clearer every day that Germany desired a rapid conclusion of the Italo–Greek conflict'. According to the Berlin correspondent of the Yugoslav newspaper *Vremde*, moreover, German officials had quite suddenly changed their former position and insisted that the conflict should be liquidated as soon as possible, and that 'all possibility of new conflict in Balkans should be prevented'.[114]

While London hurriedly instructed its Belgrade representative to 'do what [he] could in order to prevent the Yugoslav press lending itself to German propaganda in relation to Italo–Greek struggle',[115] the alarm was sounded from Madrid. The Greek minister, Sir Samuel Hoare reported:

gave me an account this afternoon of a conversation with the Hungarian minister who had come straight from the ... German ambassador. The German ambassador, who evidently wished his views communicated to the Greek, said that the Greeks should now approach Germany with a view to German intervention to stop the war on favourable terms to Greece. Germany did not want war to extend in the Balkans and Greece had everything to gain by a peace that could be made immediately after Greek successes. The Greek minister told the Hungarian for transmission to the German that a separate peace was no good for Greece and that the only chance of a general peace was the complete defeat of Italy.[116]

Although this was perfectly clear, and incidentally leaves but precious little doubt as to which side was to blame for the continuation of the conflict, the British were not yet satisfied. To begin with Palairet was sent to Metaxas and extracted from him a denial of the story that he was going to meet Saracoglu. Greece, the Prime Minister said, had also rejected a German proposal for the resumption of Greek–German economic relations, because she 'knew quite well that [Germany] wished to advertise Greece's consent to this as proof that Greek and English policy were divergent'. He also said 'most emphatically' that Greece would never agree to any attempt to drive a wedge between Great Britain and Greece.[117] In Ankara Knatchbull-Hugessen the British ambassador was next dispatched on a similar mission, but Saracoglu was recalcitrant and the British had to content themselves with a statement issued by the Turkish press bureau.[118] Even so they were not quite satisfied; they continued to put pressure on Metaxas to publicly reject the German overtures, until Palairet had to warn his superiors that, since the Greek Prime Minister was obviously determined to expel the Italians from Albania and had informed the Germans of this, it 'would be a mistake even to hint that we thought him capable of making a separate peace with Italy'.[119]

While it is easy to understand British motives in thus pressing Metaxas, the Greek dictator's reasons for bending to this pressure are harder to explain. One obvious explanation is that the Greeks were desperately in need of British aid, especially in the air, and that they rightly sensed that the two issues were linked. The flaw in this argument, however, is that if Metaxas had accepted the German proposals he would not, in theory at any rate, require further planes with which to fight Italy. Another explanation is that Metaxas really believed the German offer was intended only to drive a wedge between himself and the British. This would not be incompatible with the deep distrust of the Germans which he showed in his diary.[120]

The real reason, however, seems to have lain elsewhere. Psychologically the German proposals came at an unfavourable moment, just when the Greeks were beating back the Italians in Albania and Graziani's army was being pulverized by the Nile Army; they may have been, and probably were, regarded as signs of weakness. In the middle of December the Greeks were confident of their ability to throw the Italians into the Adriatic, and it is not impossible that they hoped to be able to do so without evoking German reaction. It was this assumption which lay behind a letter from George of Greece to George VI of England. In this the Greek king explained that, since Germany could not come to Italy's assistance for at least a few months and would scarcely risk antagonizing Turkey and Yugoslavia in so doing, it was now – after the British victory at Taranto – time for them to help Greece and deal Italy 'a crippling blow'.[121] From Britain, the Greeks 'wanted enough [aid] to enable them to overcome the Italians but not enough to provoke German intervention; the two aims were incompatible, but the Greek government affected not to recognize this'.[122] Although warned by the German ambassador in Ankara that Germany would not sit idly by and watch her ally destroyed,[123] it seems that the Greeks wanted the war isolated, but not terminated.[124] It was with this purpose in mind that Metaxas told the German minister that 'in the future, too, no disturbance of the correct relations between Germany and Greece as a result of English initiative was to be feared... He was assuming that even if the Greeks would not advance any further, the Italians would no longer be able to hold out in Albania.'[125] At the same time, his press was trying to drive a wedge between Germany and Italy by quoting 'various German authorities' to the effect that it was high time for Germany to leave Italy alone.[126] If Italy were to ask for an armistice, Metaxas said:

he thought [Germany] would form a defensive block in central Europe. Even if she occupied Trieste and other Italian ports our supremacy in the Mediterranean would, he said, not be in danger.

In such circumstances Greece and ourselves would continue to be separated from Germany by a belt formed by Yugoslavia, Bulgaria and Hungary, the neutrality of which it may be in nobody's interest to violate.[127]

Unbelievable as it may seem in retrospect, it was this kind of reasoning which led Metaxas and the Greek government to reject the German peace offer. The Greeks were wholly immersed in their own little war against Italy; they were quite unable to grasp its wider implications.

To Hitler, this was a highly unpleasant result. Having liquidated the 'peripheral' strategy, he lost his taste for the Greek operation as conceived in 'directive No. 18'. In order to obtain an Italo–Greek peace he suspended the talks with Turkey, virtually retracted his offer of Salonika to Yugoslavia, and talked around Mussolini's plans for German military assistance; all in vain. The prudent Führer, however, was not the man to be caught without another card up his sleeve, and while putting out feelers towards a cease-fire in Albania he also followed his usual method in ordering military preparations for an eventual invasion of Greece from the north to be continued regardless of the results of his diplomacy. If and when the effort to find a diplomatic solution for the Greek problem should fail, the German army was to be prepared to liquidate it by other means.

IN THE SHADOW OF 'BARBAROSSA'

'Directive No. 18' for the conduct of the war in the 'periphery' was drawn up by OKW in September 1940; ordered into being during the conference of 4 November; issued under Hitler's signature on the 12th of the same month; and lay stone-dead at its end. The section dealing with the Greek operation in particular looked like a pricked balloon. Hitler's decision to attack the Soviet Union, made just when preparations at OKH were getting under way, had cost the operation its original offensive aim of enabling the Luftwaffe to 'attack [British] targets in the eastern Mediterranean'; for early in December Hitler had lost any interest in either the British or the Mediterranean.

With its offensive aim, the operation also lost its defensive one. The possible development of a British airborne menace to the Rumanian oil fields had worried Hitler early in November, but by December it already seemed that these fears were largely unfounded. We have already seen that the Greeks were blind to the fact that Hitler could not sit by and watch his partner destroyed; however, their blindness did not extend to allowing the British to operate against Germany directly. Throughout November Berlin was receiving reports to the effect that the British plans for operations against the oil fields were causing friction between them and their Greek hosts,[1] and the reports were right. The British had in fact sent a few groups of fighters and fighter-bombers to Greece, but found themselves very restricted in their use. In dealing with Air Vice-Marshal d'Albiac the Greeks persistently refused the Royal Air Force the use of air fields in the Salonika area, the only ones from which the oil region could be reached. The RAF was limited to two air strips near Athens, Eleusis and Tatoi, both well out of range from Ploesti. As to the construction of new air fields, work was started on two only; one at Agrinion (on the west coast, north of the Gulf of Corinthos) and one at Araxos in the northwestern corner of the Peloponnese. Both were unmistakably directed against Italy.[2]

Berlin also seems to have warned the Greeks in no uncertain terms against allowing the British to bomb the oil fields, and expected the effects of that warning to last 'for the next few months'.[3] Reports coming from Greece emphasized the weakness and small size of the British force in the country, and by the middle of December SKL – as we have seen, a fervent supporter of the Greek operation – concluded that 'England had not so far shown any inclination to bomb any targets except for those under Italian dominion. . . this is not to be feared either, because the English must make do with the forces they have and do not want to risk German counter-measures.'[4]

With the scrapping of the 'peripheral' strategy the Greek operation lost its original, offensive purpose; during December attempts were accordingly made to liquidate the affair by diplomatic means. Should these efforts fail, however, the operation would have to be carried out – not so much because of the actual presence of a few thousand Englishmen in Greece, but because of the threat of a Salonika-front developing in the future. In view of Hitler's plans for a campaign against Russia, the appearance of such a front would be disastrous. Since by this time Hitler had already reached the conclusion that 'the decision over the hegemony in Europe will fall in Russia', the Greek operation had become a – regrettable – diversion. Still, the prospects of making it unnecessary by diplomatic action looked slim and when Hitler ratified the army's plans for an attack on Russia during a conference of 5 December, he reluctantly ordered preparations for Greece to go ahead.[5]

Undertaking 'Marita', as the Greek operation had now been dubbed, bore but little resemblance to the 'second rate substitute' as originally conceived. Its aim was defensive, not offensive. Its framework was continental-European, not eastern Mediterranean. In the words of Halder's ADC, 'Marita' had been 'taken out of its context and brought into close relationship with the plans for Russia. Its task now was to secure Germany's southern flank and eliminate the threatening danger before the start of the offensive against Russia.'[6] Greece, in short, was taken out of the 'Mediterranean' and annexed to Europe again. On 13 December the new character of the operation was officially laid down in a Führer directive:

Directive No. 20
Operation 'Marita'
The outcome of the battles in Albania is still uncertain. In the light of the threatening situation in Albania it is doubly important for us to frustrate English efforts to establish, behind the protection of a Balkan front, an air base which would threaten Italy in the first place and, incidentally, the Rumanian oil fields.

Compared with 'directive No. 18' the most conspicuous feature of this prelude is undoubtedly the lack of any reference to the eastern Mediterranean. The operation is said to be dictated by purely defensive reasons, pending the uncertain outcome of the battles in Albania; this makes it the exact counterpart of operation 'Attila' which Hitler was at the same time preparing in the west. The menace to the Rumanian oil fields is mentioned only 'incidentally', and the directive correctly recognizes that the British air bases in Greece were directed against Italy. These considerations led Hitler to order the following:

a. Establish in the coming months a constantly increasing force in southern Rumania.

b. On the arrival of favourable weather ... to move this force across Bulgaria to occupy the north coast of the Aegean and should this be necessary, the entire mainland of Greece.

There followed orders about the build-up in Rumania, of which more below. The directive goes on:

Undertaking 'Marita' itself will be prepared on the following basis:

a. The first objective of the operation is the occupation of the Aegean Coast and the Salonika Basin. It may become necessary to pursue the attack via Larissa and the Isthmus of Corinth.

...

d. It will be the task of the air force to give effective support in all phases of the advance of the army; to eliminate the enemy air force; as far as possible to seize the English bases in the Greek Islands with airborne troops.

The reference to the occupation of the entire Greek mainland was clearly a remnant of the 'large', original operation, and made sense only if it was intended to carry on into the eastern Mediterranean. As for covering the flank of the Russian campaign, this objective could clearly be achieved by occupying northeastern Greece alone. When it became clear that the British were only sending a few air force units and no ground troops to Greece the operation was therefore limited to this area, and it was only after larger British forces arrived in Greece in March that Hitler reluctantly extended it again.[7] The Russian campaign, which Hitler had still regarded as 'probable' on 20 November, had now become a certainty. The last paragraph of 'directive No. 20' accordingly linked operation 'Marita' with Hitler's eastern plans:

At the conclusion of undertaking 'Marita', the forces envisaged will be withdrawn for NEW EMPLOYMENT.[8] [emphasis in the original]

'Marita' would have to be over before the start of the eastern campaign, not only because its aim was to secure the latter's right flank but because the forces engaged on it would be needed in the east. Since it was this aspect of the operation – itself, of no very great significance – that was later supposed to have been of crucial importance for the outcome of the war, the relationship between it and the plans for an attack on Russia deserves more detailed examination.

'MARITA' AND 'BARBAROSSA'

In December 1940, preparations for an attack on Russia had already been in progress for six months. A host of operational plans had been examined; some practical preparations, such as the construction of roads and railways in Poland, and the enlargement of the army to 180 divisions, were also under way. During the last days of November wargames were organized in order to determine the basic lines of the deployment, under the direction of General Paulus, Halder's deputy at OKH.[9] On 5 December the plans were duly submitted to Hitler. On 18 December they were incorporated into 'directive No. 21'.[10]

The general form of the plan was determined by geography. The border between the Soviet Union and what could effectively be regarded as the German sphere of influence stretched over some 1500 miles across the European continent from the Baltic to the Black Sea. For operational purposes this gigantic front was divided into a northern and a southern sector by the Pripjet marshes, 250 miles long and 120 miles wide, which were – wrongly, as it turned out – considered unsuitable for large scale military operations. From the beginning, the German plans envisaged the division of the attacking forces into two main groups, one operating north of the marshes, the other south of them. The question as to where the main thrust was to be delivered, and therefore where the bulk of the forces was to be concentrated, was answered in different ways by the various officers responsible for the early plans. The one finally adopted by OKH foresaw the commitment of two army groups – Heeresgruppe – north of the marches and one south of them.[11] These three army groups, comprising some 140 divisions and 3600 tanks between them, represented the largest military force ever concentrated on a single front.

The operation itself was divided into three stages. The first consisted of frontier-zone battles. During the second and most important one the general line Smolensk–Dnjepr would be reached by a series of deep enveloping thrusts. The third consisted of a further advance up to the general line Archanglesk–Ural Volga, where Hitler is reported to have indicated the frontier of his future empire with a pencil-line on a globe. OKH hoped – rather than knew – that the Soviets would stand and fight in the western parts of their country, so that they could be surrounded and annihilated before distances and lines of communication became unmanageably long. For this purpose, the employment of armour on a grand scale was essential. In any case, the distances to be covered were such that it was of the utmost importance to start the operation as early as possible in the spring, so as to exploit the season.[12] Since the Russian operation could not be started before the Greek one securing its flank was more or less over, it was essential to speed up the beginning of the latter and to get it over with quickly. Moreover, war games were to show that the forces employed on 'Marita' could not be spared for 'Barbarossa', as the Russian campaign was known; without them, the third stage of the Russian operation could not be carried out.[13] Once the decision to attack Russia was made, therefore, the Greek operation fell completely under the gigantic shadow cast ahead by 'Barbarossa'; and the two operations would have to be coordinated with the greatest precision.

The existence of a close relationship between on the one hand the number of troops engaged and the time allowed for operation 'Marita', and on the other the starting date and therefore the prospects of 'Barbarossa' was recognized by OKH even before Hitler made up his mind to smash the Soviet Union. On 12 November in anticipation of 'directive No. 18' Halder noted: 'the Führer reportedly wants to employ up to 10 divisions [in Greece]. This raises difficult questions concerning the non-motorized units'.[14] Halder's troubles were only just beginning, for on 18 November Hitler – probably as a result of his conversation with King Boris, a statesman he held in some esteem – raised the number of divisions to 12, presumably in order to help guard against possible Turkish and Soviet surprises. This time the difficulties put in the way of 'Barbarossa' were such that Halder concluded that 'the Russian operation is apparently going to be cancelled'.[15] The arrival of the Soviet answer to the proposal to join the Tripartite Pact soon put an end to these speculations.

The growing number of troops to be employed in Greece, as well as the necessity to transport 16th armoured division to Rumania in order to protect the oil fields against the Russians,[16] provided good reasons for speeding up the transport movements. On 25 November a draft timetable was therefore submitted to Halder. Allowing the period from 7 to 25 December for troop preparation, this timetable planned transport movements to Rumania in three stages, the first of which was to leave Austria on 26 December and complete its concentration on the Danube on 15 January. Without allowing for any pause, troops would then enter Bulgaria on 16 January. The motorized forces would reach the Bulgaro–Greek frontier by 23 January, the mountain and infantry divisions on 4 February, so that the attack could go ahead on 11 February.

This timetable, made on the assumption that the first stage would complete its disentrainment in Rumania before crossing the Danube into Bulgaria, did not really satisfy Halder because he thought that 'the political leadership would demand greater security *vis-à-vis* Greece'. This meant that the concentration of German troops north of the Danube would create a power vacuum in Bulgaria, which Greece and even Turkey might – with English encouragement – feel tempted to fill.[17] Still, since it would not require the first stage to wait for the arrival of the two others before crossing the Danube, the proposed timetable was the quickest possible solution, and Halder 'in consideration of the eastern operation' dropped his reservations and allowed it to stand.[18]

Not for long: on 26 November Kinzel returned from his reconnaissance mission in Bulgaria, and reported his findings; it now became evident that OKH had greatly underestimated the difficulties of marching through Bulgaria. The country's only railway of any importance, running south from Sofia through the valley of the Struma past Dupnice and Melnik up to Marinipa was unsuitable for troop transports. In all there were only five roads leading into Greece from the north, all of them characterized by high passes, sharp curves and bridges that were too weak to take heavy equipment and could not bear more than one vehicle at a time.[19] All the roads were likely to be blocked by snow at any time until mid-April, while snowploughs were an unheard of invention. Bulgaria had no fuel, limited supplies and even less shelter to offer the troops; everything, even the barracks for those units that were to be stationed in Bulgaria, would have to be brought up from the Reich.[20]

So dark was the picture painted by Kinzel that OKH decided to send a second reconnaissance staff to Bulgaria, this time consisting of officers from the units that would later have to cope with the problems posed by the Bulgarian roads and climate. The Bulgarians themselves did not like the idea; they had just rejected the Soviet proposal for a mutual assistance pact, and were afraid lest the Russians should take military counter measures. Their demand for the greatest secrecy led to some delay, and it was only on 13 December that the mission, camouflaged as a car agency, equipped with special cross country vehicles and commanded by Colonel Zeitzler of *Panzergruppe* Kleist got under way. It lasted for two weeks, and at its end Zeitzler reported his findings to Brauchitsch and Halder. In essence, his reports confirmed Kinzel's; the weather and the state of the roads did not allow an operation against Greece to take place before March.[21]

In view of the Russian operation, which by this time had been definitely decided upon, Kinzel's report was bad news. The relationship between 'Marita' and 'Barbarossa' formed one of the key issues discussed between Hitler and his top brass during a conference on 5 December. As usual, it was Halder who did most of the reporting. In carrying out the attack on Greece, he explained, it would be necessary to overcome the difficulties created by the narrowness of the Struma Valley and concentrate the strongest forces opposite the Rupel pass at the extreme western end of the Bulgaro–Greek frontier, for it was there that the Metaxas line was at its weakest.[22] Another corps would advance into Greek Thrace from the extreme eastern end of the frontier, while the rest of the border would be covered by relatively weak forces. The armoured and motorized divisions could only be brought into action after the Rhodope mountains had been breached, that is in the second stage. In all, 13 divisions would have to be transferred to Bulgaria. Of these, 7 – including 5 infantry, 1 armoured and 1 motorized – were to carry out the actual attack. The remaining 6 divisions would serve as cover on the Turkish border, and the need to bring them up would result in some delay when compared with the original timetable.[23] The build-up plan was based on the assumption that Turkish intervention was possible, if improbable. For this reason the first two armoured divisions to enter Bulgaria were to race for the Turkish frontier. The forces earmarked for the attack proper would be the next to cross the Danube. These would in turn be followed by more infantry divisions which were to deploy on the Turkish border and thus relieve the armoured divisions to join the attacking forces. The build-up would require a total of 78 days, so that an immediate order was necessary if the operation was to start early in March. The operational plan was based on the breaching of the Metaxas line at its weakest point, then racing down the Vardar Valley to the coast. By means of this manoeuvre, it would be possible to cut off Greek Thrace – together with the Metaxas line protecting it – from the rest of Greece. After the completion of this stage of the operation and the occupation of the territory north of the Aegean it would be possible to push on to Larissa and Athens. Depending on whether or not the operation was thus extended, it would be over by the end of March or mid-April.[24]

In reply, Hitler did not criticize Halder's operational plans but went on to discuss the political and strategic significance of the campaign. The decision over the hegemony in Europe, he declared, would fall in Russia, and the Greek affair was therefore a secondary matter dictated by defensive reasons. Hopefully it might be possible to end the Italo–Greek war by diplomatic means and have the British thrown out of Greece, but he doubted this and wanted preparations to go on in such a manner that the operation could start as soon as the weather permitted, that is at the beginning of March. The transportation of strong forces to Rumania would in any case not be wasted, since they would be available for 'Barbarossa' even if 'Marita' were cancelled.[25] The important problem now was the Soviet Union, which had recently given additional proof that it would exploit any and every opportunity to weaken the Axis. Preparations against her therefore had to be shifted into high gear. The attack would presumably start late in May.[26]

Having received this green light from Hitler, OKH pushed ahead with its preparations. The number of divisions earmarked for Bulgaria was now so large that they had to be put under the command, not of a *Panzergruppe* but of an *Armeeoberkommando*; originally OKH had designated Fieldmarshal von Kluge's Fourth army for the purpose, but von Kluge had given an extraordinary account of himself during the French campaign and after the decision to attack Russia was made OKH did not think it could dispense with his services during the period of preparations for the east.[27] Operation 'Marita' was therefore entrusted to Fieldmarshal Wilhelm List's Twelfth army, which at that time was under the command of *Heeresgruppe* B in Poland and was replaced there by Seventeenth army on 14 December.[28] On 9 December Halder signed and issued the deployment order for Twelfth army: 'the political situation may make it necessary to occupy Greek Thrace from Bulgaria. The extension of the operation to Thessaly is possible'.[29] The order did not – as a result of Hitler's conversations with King Boris and Minister Draganov – count on active Bulgarian participation, but the Bulgarians could be expected to help secure their borders with Greece and Turkey by means of their own troops. Greece was expected to fight, Turkey to sit by idly. Precautions against possible Turkish intervention were nevertheless to be taken. The build-up was to proceed in such a way as to make it possible for Twelfth army to march into Bulgaria within 12 hours at any time from 25 January 1941 onward, and to start operations for the occupation of Greek Thrace within 35 days of crossing the Danube.[30] On 11 December OKH issued a more detailed timetable for the transportation of the three stages to Rumania:

stage I buildup, 3–24 January: army high command 12th, high command *Panzergruppe* Kleist, high commands XIVth and XXXXth army corps, 5th, 9th, 11th armoured divisions, 60th motorized division, SS 'Adolf Hitler' (AH) division, 50th, 72nd, 164th infantry divisions, 1/3 army troops and 50 trains each for air force and supplies.
stage II buildup, 24 January–8 February: high command XIth corps, 2nd armoured division, 5th, 6th mountain divisions, 73rd infantry division, infantry regiment 125th, 2/3 army troops and 60 supply trains.
stage III buildup, 5–28 February: high commands XVIIIth, XXXth army corps, 46th, 76th, 198th, 294th infantry divisions, remaining supply trains.[31]

In all, the forces earmarked for Rumania consisted of seventeen and a third divisions, plus one air corps – General von Richthofen's No. VIII. The timetable for the transportation of these forces, however, was made obsolete even before it was issued, because OKH had once more underestimated the difficulties of the operation. On 10 December Halder received a report on the construction of bridges; it then appeared that the job would take no less than three weeks, and would require 70 to 100 trains of bridging equipment.[32] If the bridges were to be ready for the Danube crossing on 25 January as specified in the deployment order, haste was essential; the trains had therefore to be incorporated into stage I build-up, while nine companies of engineers and bridge builders were added to the transports of 16th armoured division.[33] This naturally resulted in delays, which by 20 December had already grown to five days. This, Halder calculated meant that the attack could not start on 1 March as planned, but only on 6 March.[34]

The delay in the starting date of 'Marita' in turn endangered the timely start of 'Barbarossa', so something had to be done about it fast. On 21 December, therefore, the commander of the German army mission in Rumania, General Hansen, joined forces with Minister Fabricius and went to see Antonescu. The unhappy Rumanian head of state was informed that circumstances had made it necessary to transport a larger force to Rumania than had originally been planned, and that Germany therefore demanded the introduction of a *Höchstleistungfahrplan*, that is the abolition of all civilian transports on the Rumanian railways and their use by German military trains only.[35] From the Rumanian point of view, this meant that while the German troops would have 52 trains a day rolling on each of their railways they themselves would be left with only one. They would be faced with economic ruin, and Antonescu therefore flatly rejected the demand.[36] Consultations followed which led, on 27 December, to the adoption of a compromise solution that gave only partial satisfaction to German demands.

Even more problematic for the timely start of the operation was the weather. On 24 December Halder noted 'abnormal snow storms' in Rumania, and while giving vent to his anxiety lest this should have an adverse effect on the morale of the Rumanian people and therefore on the position of Antonescu he expressed the opinion that 'the consequences for the expiration of "Marita" and the effects on "Barbarossa" could be far-reaching'.[37] Fortunately for the chief of the general staff his leave was just due, thus throwing the worries resulting from the really frightful weather now beginning on other shoulders. On 28 December a new timetable issued by the Oberkommando der Luftwaffe showed that the end of stage I build-up had been postponed from 24 January to 5 February.[38] Early in January, heavy snow forced the suspension of all transport movements to Rumania and inside the country.[39] As a result a fresh timetable was immediately issued by OKW, in which stage I build-up was stretched further from 31 December to 10 February, while stage II was not to start moving before 11 February at the earliest.[40] On 7 January, just when the transports were supposed to be resumed, the high command of the troops of the German army in Rumania, as Twelfth army was officially known, reported that 'the melting of the snow has turned all Rumanian roads . . . into impassable morasses. The majority of locations earmarked as quarters for the troops are therefore inaccessible.'[41] This promptly resulted in yet another timetable, in which the second stage was postponed to 17 February.[42] Nor was even this the last word, for on 13 January Twelfth army sent another message:

Heavy snow has blocked the roads in Wallachia to such an extent that the realization – especially the timely realization – of the deployment of the troops of the German army in Rumania is in serious doubt. The momentary state of the roads in most cases makes it impossible even for troops already detrained to reach their scheduled shelters. The supply services, too, are working under the greatest difficulties.[43]

Twelfth army asked the German army mission in Rumania for help in clearing the roads, but little could be done to ease the situation. By the end of January, when stage II ought to have been moving, only half of the first high command Twelfth army, high commands XIVth and XXXth army corps, as well as 5th and 11th armoured, 72nd and 164th infantry divisions – had arrived in Rumania. The armoured divisions were stationed in the Dobrudja, from whence they could easily race into Bulgaria to forestall possible Graeco–Turkish preventive measures; the rest of the troops were deployed in the Craiova–Giurgiu area.[44]

Preparations for the bridging of the Danube had also been delayed by the weather. It had originally been planned that the anti-aircraft units earmarked for the protection of the crossing would reach their positions on the river by 24 January, but the catastrophic transport situation had made it impossible for the trains carrying 99th anti-aircraft regiment to reach their destination. The regiment was therefore forced to get out south of the Carpathians, from where troops and equipment were to march to the Danube by – Rumanian – road.[45] This meant that the crossing, even by such troops as were available, had to be postponed. In order to save time, therefore, on 9 January Hitler ratified Brauchitsch's proposal to march the first stage over the ice 'as soon as the river is frozen'.[46] Fortune, however, was clearly hiding her face from the Führer; the days passed and the Danube refused to freeze. Even if it did, the crossing would have been obstructed as the Danube, with its strong current, does not form a continuous layer of ice but piles blocks on top of each other. For the formation of a reliable – that is, passable for light vehicles – layer of ice 14 days of severe frost were needed, which meant that no crossing could be expected before the end of January.[47] On 10 January Warlimont resignedly signed a directive to this effect.[48] Moreover, Twelfth army itself was unhappy about the entire plan; it was known that the local inhabitants used to drive 1 and 2 ton vehicles over the ice, but what would happen if an attempt were made to get the 16 ton vehicles of the army across was anybody's guess. Without actually saying so, the staff of Twelfth army therefore gave vent to its anxiety.[49] List's objections must have impressed Hitler, for nothing more is heard of the proposal.

The decision to desist from the plan to march stage I over the ice meant, in fact, that it was no longer possible to project even an approximate date for the start of 'Marita'. Large numbers of ships earmarked for the construction of the bridges had been concentrated

in the upper Danube, but during January chunks of drifting ice pro-
pelled by the strong current made it impossible to bring them up.[50]
Even when this obstacle had finally disappeared the actual work could
be expected to last for two to three weeks.[51] Not even in the most
favourable case could the order to proceed with the bridging be
expected before 26 January, for it was only then that the first armoured
division would have arrived in Rumania.[52] Finally, the numerous
delays apparently convinced OKH that its timetable for the march
inside Bulgaria was as irrealistic as the one for the march up to her
border. If the original directive had ordered Twelfth army to be
prepared to cross the Bulgaro–Greek border within 35 days of the
Danube crossing, this figure was increased by eight days to 43 on
6 January.[53]

By mid-January, only two weeks after the beginning of the transports, the weather had already caused such delay in the build-up for
'Marita' as to make the starting date of the attack unforeseeable and
coordination with 'Barbarossa' exceedingly difficult, if not impossible.
Everything had to be done in order to facilitate the task of Twelfth
army and thus cut the period its divisions would have to spend in
Greece; and in mid-January, just when OKH was again expressing its
fear lest 'Marita' might have an adverse effect on 'Barbarossa',[54]
Hitler believed that he had discovered a means to do just this. Italian
opposition, it will be remembered, had prevented him from sending
forces into the Mediterranean within the framework of his 'peripheral'
strategy. In January, however, it seemed that this opposition might be
dropped. In both Libya and Albania, Mussolini's armies had reached
the end of their tether.

THE ALBANIAN INTERMEZZO

December 1940 was a bad month for Italy's quest for glory in the
Mediterranean. Starting in the second half of November, the Greek
counter offensive was booking considerable successes; by 8 December
the fall of the main port at Durazzo seemed possible. This would mean
the complete collapse of Soddu's armies. The prospect had driven
Mussolini into such a panic that, on 5 December, he sent Alfieri – who
had been convalescing in Rome – to beg for help from the Führer.
Bad weather, however, delayed the ambassador, and it was not until
8 December that he met Hitler.[55] The latter had, as we have seen,
shown but very little enthusiasm for the proposals raised by the Italian,
since at this time his change of strategy had already led him to contemplate a solution by diplomatic means. Although Alfieri came away with
empty hands, the Commando Supremo had in the meantime been
remobilizing the divisions that had been demobilized after Mussolini's

order of 5 October and transferring them to Albania. As the initial numerical superiority of the Greeks was slowly cancelled out their offensive ground to a halt, and by the middle of the month the Italians had succeeded in establishing a new defensive line.

Soddu had just succeeded in pulling off this trick when disaster struck again. On 9 December the Nile Army under General O'Connor launched an attack which hit Rome 'like a bolt from the blue'.[56] Within a few days large parts of Graziani's army had ceased to exist, while the rest was falling back in disorder across the frontier into Libya. There followed one of the mightiest marches in the history of warfare, with the British advancing rapidly over hundreds of miles and taking one fortified Italian position after the other. Sollum fell on 17 December, Bardia on 5 January. Soon the capital of Cyrenaica, Tobruk, was also endangered.

OKW was kept informed about the situation by the military attaché in Rome. On 19 December Rintelen cabled that 'three weeks ago the situation in Albania was so critical that a heavy defeat had to be taken into account. The front has now been stabilized and is expected to hold. After the transfer of further divisions it will be possible to consider the preparation of an offensive for the spring.' The situation in Libya, he reported, was 'extremely unfavourable. Graziani is fighting a delaying battle near Bardia and Tobruk, which loss must be reckoned with. . . It has not yet been possible to see whether the British advance can be halted.' The Duce had therefore ordered Cavallero to ask Germany to hold one armoured division 'in readiness', and supply the material to equip no less than ten divisions.[57] Two days later, after a review of the situation with Ciano and Marras, Mussolini concluded that German troops would be of no use in Albania; in Africa, on the other hand, their presence was regarded as 'desirable'.[58]

The relatively euphoric mood in Rome did not last for very long. On 28 December Marras returned to his post as military attaché in Berlin and went straight to Keitel; although the Greeks were seldom attacking with more than one or two battalions, he explained, there could be no question of the Italian front in Albania being stabilized. Even now it was rather a matter of retreating *combattendo*. He was convinced that the engagement of only a few German mountain regiments would stabilize the front, not least because of the extraordinary effect on the morale of the Italian troops, as well as that of the Greeks. As for Libya, it was becoming clearer every day that Cyrenaica could not be held. Without German help the whole of Italian North Africa would be lost to the Axis. Here, too, the appearance of even a small German force would have such an effect on the morale of both friend and foe as to turn the tables.[59] On 3 January General Guzzoni, deputy chief of Stamage, seconded Marras's request; a few German units – Guzzoni specified 'armoured troops' for Libya and a 'mountain division' for Albania – would be enough to restore the situation.[60]

Hitler's goal, however, was different. To him a simple 'restoration of the situation' on the Albanian front was necessary but not sufficient; something had to be done to cancel out the delays in the transport movements for 'Marita', and for this purpose the commitment of German troops on the left wing of the Italian front in Albania, with a view of opening up the way to Salonika from the rear, presented a perfect opportunity. On 9 January the Führer summoned the chiefs of OKW and OKH to the Berghof to discuss these questions. The main topic was Russia which, Hitler said, had to be eliminated during 1941 so that Germany might be able to confront the combined forces of the Anglo-Saxon world – including the United States, whose entry into the war he now regarded as a certainty – in 1942. For this reason, it was absolutely essential for Germany to dominate the European continent. In this context it was necessary to support the Italians in Libya, not so much because of any immediate danger – the loss, Hitler argued, even of the whole of North Africa would not affect Germany's own strong position on the continent – but because its loss might bring about the collapse of Italy. The Xth air corps had, indeed, already been transferred to Sicily and was attacking the British navy with some success,[61] but this was clearly not sufficient to stave off the disaster now threatening the Italians in Libya. It was therefore necessary to dispatch a *Panzersperrverband* there, equipped with everything to stop the British. Ultimately, of course, these forces would have to be deducted from those earmarked for 'Barbarossa', and it was therefore imperative to keep them as small as possible. This consideration seems to have been the reason behind Brauchitsch's proposal for the dispatch of a surprisingly small force comprising in all only 8000 men and 1350 motor vehicles – considerably less than one division.

Hitler then came to discuss the situation in Albania. Recent reports from that area had indicated that the Italians were now at long last able to hold their own, and consequently there was no point in sending German troops there unless they could take the offensive. Such an offensive would be very useful in connection with the attack of the Twelfth army from Bulgaria, but could only be undertaken with considerably stronger forces, including armour, than those requested by the Italians. As it might be expected that German intervention in Albania would relieve the pressure on the Italians in Libya,[62] but more particularly as a result of the extremely tight timetable governing the return of the forces from 'Marita' for 'Barbarossa', it would not be a mistake if the offensive in Albania took place before that of the Twelfth army. Brauchitsch thereupon asked clearance for reconnaissance in Albania, which Hitler granted.[63] The request of the army commander-in-chief was of a rather peevish nature, because at that time General Rintelen was already at the Italian front.

On 11 January the results of the conference were laid down in a Führer directive:[64]

Directive No. 22
German Support for Battles in the Mediterranean Area

The situation in the Mediterranean area, where England is employing superior forces against our allies, requires that Germany should assist for reasons of strategy, politics and psychology.

Tripolitania must be held and the danger of collapse on the Albanian front must be eliminated. Furthermore, the Cavallero army group [i.e. the Italian army in Albania] must be enabled, in cooperation with the later operations of 12th army, to go over to the offensive in Albania.

I therefore order as follows:

1. Commander in chief army will provide covering forces sufficient to render valuable service to our allies in the defence of Tripolitania . . .

2. Xth air corps will continue to operate from Sicily . . .

3. German formations in the approximate strength of one corps, including 1. mountain division and armoured units, will be detailed and made ready to move to Albania . . .

It will be the task of the German forces:

a. To act as immediate stiffening in Albania in case further critical situations should arise.

b. To enable the Italian army group to go over to the offensive at a later date with the purpose:

1. Of breaking through Greek defences at a decisive point for extensive operations.

2. Of opening the passages west of Salonika from the rear, thereby supporting a frontal attack by the List army.

As the opening statements indicate, the overall aim of both operations was purely defensive, and it is here that the crucial difference between the present directive and 'directive No. 18' of November lies.[65] The transfer of German forces to both Libya and Greece had originally been conceived as part of a grand Mediterranean offensive against the position of Great Britain in the area; but the present directive only dealt with makeshift measures intended to relieve immediate dangers in a rather uncoordinated way. Even the eventual offensive operations planned for Albania were only meant to support the much larger – but still essentially defensive – operations of the Twelfth army. Convinced that 'the decision over the hegemony in Europe would fall in Russia', Hitler was bent on limiting his forces elsewhere to the indispensable minimum, and when Rommel arrived in Tripoli on 17 February he had at his disposal only one division.

While Hitler was so enthusiastically ordering into Albania much stronger forces than the Italians had asked for, Mussolini began to have second thoughts. On 4 January a long telegram from the military attaché in Berlin reached Rome. The Germans, Marras claimed, had arrived at the conclusion that the Mediterranean was just as vital for them as it was for Italy or England. They were determined to turn the Greek affair to their own advantage, and in this respect their present move into the Balkans was nothing but another step in their traditional pursuit of hegemony in southeastern Europe. Germany's principal aim was the occupation of Salonika, a city in which powerful German political and economic circles had for long shown great interest. The military attaché postulated a number of 'proofs' for his theory: 1. During his conversations with Badoglio at Innsbruck, Keitel insisted that Salonika should be occupied by German troops and even suggested German participation on the left flank of future Italian offensives in Albania. 2. Germany had virtually ceased operations against England, enabling her to concentrate on southeastern Europe and the Mediterranean. Finally, the assumption that Salonika was Germany's principal target explained why they were preventing Yugoslavia from participating in the liquidation of Greece, since the city would obviously be the Serbs' first objective.

Marras had more bad news. The Greeks, he declared, were unable to offer real resistance to the German advance and knew it. As for the British, they could not defend the Greek peninsula, nor wanted to transfer strong forces from Cyrenaica for the purpose. Instead they preferred to consolidate their hold on Crete. Under these circumstances it was possible that the Greeks would only offer token resistance to a German invasion from the north while holding out in Albania and thus depriving Italy of her just revenge. What was more, the strong and well equipped German forces could be expected to occupy rapidly not only Salonika, but Athens as well; in this context it was significant that OKW, when discussing the possibility of sending a mountain division to Albania, expressed the desire to have it link up with the forces advancing against Salonika. The only way out of this situation, Marras argued, was to conclude – as early as possible – political and military agreements with Germany on the coordination of future offensives against Greece. Since she was the weaker partner, all the advantages of such coordination would go to Italy.[66]

It goes without saying that Marras's report was hopelessly wrong; nothing was further from Hitler's mind than German expansion in the eastern Mediterranean, for at this time he was thinking of the Ukraine as Germany's future *Lebensraum*. Mussolini, however, did not know this and was greatly alarmed. He forwarded Marras's letter to Cavallero in Albania with the comment that something ought to be done in order to 'forestall' the Germans in Greece.[67] Cavallero replied with a long telegram in which he pointed out that the state of his forces made it impossible to go over to the offensive for the time being; instead, he suggested a political solution for a military problem, and seconded Marras's proposal that the German offensive be 'coordinated' with the Italian one.[68]

Cavallero's refusal to attack convinced Mussolini that a meeting with Hitler – which he had long avoided for fear of being scolded for his miserable failure in Greece – was necessary, and it was duly arranged to take place on 19 – 20 January. In the meantime, he and his senior officers began to take a new view of what they now regarded as the German efforts to rob Italy of her sphere of influence. On 11 January OKW informed Stamage that a small reconnaissance staff would leave Berlin for Albania on the 15th.[69] On 17 January Cavallero reported that five officers under the command of 'Colonel Jode' (= Alfred Jodl, an expert on mountain warfare) had arrived at his headquarters. OKW, Jodl told Cavallero, was planning an offensive from Albania late in March; he did not answer the Italian general's question as to whether this date coincided with the German advance from Bulgaria. Not one, but two German mountain divisions were going to operate on the Italian left flank in Albania, and to attack 'in conjunction with the Italian Alpine divisions'. Cavallero, of course, knew that OKW's intention to commit strong German forces in Albania was not at all in line with Mussolini's desires to 'forestall' them and, using 'pre-prepared data', demonstrated to Jodl that the extremely difficult supply situation made it impossible for him to have another corps in Albania. If, however, the Germans insisted on Italian participation in the final onslaught on Greece [sic] this could also be brought about in another way: he, Cavallero, would very much like to see an Italian motorized division operate in conjunction with the German troops from Rumania and Bulgaria.[70]

In their fear lest the issue would develop into a full size showdown over the question of spheres of influence, the Italians desperately groped for excuses that would enable them to sidestep Hitler's over-generous proposal to send not one, but two mountain divisions to Albania. On 18 January, that is on the day before Mussolini's departure for his meeting with Hitler, Roatta prepared a memorandum for this purpose. The Albanian ports, he argued, did not allow the maintenance of more than twenty divisions in Albania (although the Italians them-selves were to bring up no less than 27 by the end of February); and in any case, an offensive from the difficult Albanian terrain was unnecessary, because it was the task of the Italian troops, within the overall strategy of the Axis, to pin down the Greek army and thus open up the way for the Germans to advance from a deployment area where they did not suffer from logistical problems. Thus, German participation in Albania was both impossible and unnecessary. If Berlin nevertheless wanted to see the Italians taking a more active part in the war this purpose could best be served by the despatch of a few Italian divisions to Rumania, from where they could join the German forces in their march across Bulgaria.[71]

Whatever the purpose of this memorandum – either to exclude German troops from Albania, or to introduce Italian ones into Rumania – Hitler did not swallow the bait. Not only was the participation of Italian units in the offensive of the Twelfth army clearly out of the question, but he himself had already concluded that the Albanian project was impractical. On 15 January Rintelen reported to the Führer in person on what he had observed in Albania. The situation on the Italian front, he concluded, was bleak. No successful offensive was possible without more troops and equipment. The Italian soldiers were doing their best, but months of fighting without food, without boots and in extreme cold had sapped their strength. The terrain was very rough, creating great difficulties for the supply system. Mules were the only means of transport in many areas. Lateral communications along the front simply did not exist. The ports on which the entire army depended for its supplies were congested and ill-organized. Though an occasional Greek attack might still book some local successes – as witnessed by the capture of Klisura, where Rintelen himself narrowly escaped capture, on 10 January – the military attaché did not think the front was in danger of collapse. Offensive operations, however, could not be attempted.[72]

The pessimistic picture painted by Rintelen evoked no comment from Hitler, who ordered him to attend the conference that had, after infinite delays, been fixed for 19–20 January. Rintelen next travelled to Zossen, the seat of OKH, and reported to Brauchitsch.[73] His report must have made it clear that the main obstacle facing operation 'Alpenveilchen', as the project was now dubbed,[74] was the problem of supply and transportation; this resulted in OKW instructing the naval high command to investigate the practicality of sending simultaneous transports to Tripoli and Albania.

On 16 January Hitler again summoned his senior officers to the Berghof. The star of the occasion was General Paulus, who in the meantime had made some study of the possibilities of sending troops to Albania. It now appeared that Hitler had been over-optimistic when he expressed the hope that his forces would be ready for action in Albania even before the Twelfth army; true, 1st and 4th mountain divisions could be made ready for transportation by 20 January and 10 February respectively, but the fact that only one port was available – the one at Durazzo, Valona being 'totally insecure' – and even that one could take only three vessels at a time, meant that the transfer of the divisions from Brindisi could not be completed before mid-March.[75]

This, of course, meant that they could not start their attack until April – that is, until after the Twelfth army's advance would hopefully have made the entire project superfluous. These considerations, together with a considerable improvement in the situation on the Albanian front, convinced Berlin that the entire project could be dispensed with.

Operation 'Alpenveilchen' is another example of Rome interpreting a German project for military action in the Mediterranean as a foul Teutonic attempt to penetrate into Italy's 'living space'. From Hitler's point of view there was no point in sending a small force on a defensive mission, because Rintelen had informed him that the front in Albania could be held. The commitment of larger forces on an offensive mission that could have been of use within the framework of 'Marita' and even that of 'Barbarossa', on the other hand, was prevented by a combination of objective circumstances and Italian obstructionism. The Germans wanted to see the front in Albania held; they had but little confidence in the prospects of the new offensive the Italians had promised,[76] and, resigned as they were to having to carry out the liquidation of Greece with their own forces, advised their allies not to engage in offensives that were causing more harm than good.[77] Mussolini had started the Greek affair; as long as he did not botch it up even further, he could stew in his juice.

BULGARIA BETWEEN THE MILLSTONES

With the failure of the attempt to speed up the liquidation of the Greek affair by means of a German attack from Albania, Hitler again turned his gaze to the build-up for 'Marita'. Here things were on the whole going slightly better, and on 21 January the transport of stage I detachment was 'running on schedule',[78] although, to be sure, the schedule had already been revised four times. On the other hand, the diplomatic situation had scarcely improved. The attitude of Yugoslavia was still not clear. Russia was still showing every sign of unhappiness with the German presence in Rumania. Above all, Bulgaria's persistent refusal to name a date for joining the Tripartite Pact made it impossible to foresee the beginning, and therefore the end, of operation 'Marita'.

Although the German foreign ministry had started exercising pressure on Bulgaria immediately after Hitler's decision to attack Greece, the Bulgarians refused to commit themselves and the negotiations reached deadlock early in December.[79] As the month went by the Germans – most probably in connection with the attempts to find a diplomatic solution for the Italo–Greek war, which were incompatible with the promise of chunks of Greek territory to her neighbours and were in any case intended to make the operation unnecessary – relaxed their pressure not only on Bulgaria, but on Yugoslavia and Turkey as well. Ribbentrop even went so far as to veto the continuation of the negotiations with Turkey which Papen was conducting so enthusiastically. From these facts, it seems clear that sometime around 5 December Berlin lost interest in the attempts to open up the way to Greece; and we have already traced the course of Hitler's decision to revise his strategy and its implications.

Towards the end of the month the German attitude changed again. It now became clear that the efforts to end the Italo–Greek war were leading nowhere;[80] regrettable as it was, operation 'Marita' would have to be carried out. When, on 23 December, Bulgarian minister President Filov told the German minister of his willingness to go to Germany for talks his offer was regarded as a sign that Bulgaria was ready to modify its previous attitude. It was in a hopeful atmosphere, therefore, that the offer was accepted and the visit arranged for the first days of January.[81]

On the morning of 7 January Filov was received by Ribbentrop at the latter's estate in Fuschl. In preparation for the meeting the Nazi foreign minister had received two memoranda from his principal political and military advisers, which are of some interest because they show what the issues were. Weizsäcker stressed the need to arrive at an agreement with Bulgaria concerning the conduct of negotiations with Turkey; the importance of dissuading the Bulgarians from raising the Macedonian question, so as not to endanger a possible German–Yugoslav accord; Bulgarian accession to the Tripartite Pact, the state secretary suggested, was desirable but the Greek operation should not be made dependent on it. As to the territory that was to be promised to Bulgaria, the awarding of Salonika to Yugoslavia and 'the glacis on Greek soil ending in front of Edirne to the southwest' to Turkey.[82] In his memorandum Ritter explained that the main military problem involved was that of transit; OKW, in accordance with 'directive No. 20', wanted the Bulgarians themselves to provide cover on the Turkish frontier, and for this purpose it was necessary that they should enter into staff conversations with Fieldmarshal List 'as soon as possible'.[83]

After an inconclusive talk with Ribbentrop, Filov ascended to the Berghof in the afternoon of 7 January. If Hitler had hoped the talks would be easy he was in for a surprise. True, Filov started by stating his government's readiness 'in principle' to join the Tripartite Pact; however, his fears of Russian, Turkish and Yugoslav reactions were as lively as ever. Hitler tried to dismiss Turkey and Yugoslavia out of hand; Russia, he admitted, was 'more difficult', but 'as long as Stalin lived it was absolutely impossible that Russia should start anything against Germany, provided the spheres of influence were clearly delimited'. There followed a lecture about Germany's military strength, calculated both to impress and to intimidate the visitor.

Hitler 'deplored the Greek conflict for a variety of reasons' – the real nature of which he could not, of course, disclose to his visitor – but its liquidation presented no military problem to Germany. This was Bulgaria's opportunity to obtain 'further revisions in the form of an outlet to the Aegean Sea'. Russia, Hitler concluded, had recently shown considerable interest in Bulgaria; if she wanted to escape the fate of the Baltic States she had better sign immediately.

The Fuhrer's lecture left Filov unimpressed. True, he countered, the Soviets had of late shown unusual interest in Bulgaria; that was precisely why she was afraid to sign. The Turks were more dangerous than the Führer thought, and the award of Salonika to Yugoslavia would not be well received in Bulgaria. A disagreeably surprised Hitler now delivered another lecture, rambling from Russia to the United States and their 'unimportant' aid to Turkey; to no avail. Filov insisted that Turkey, Yugoslavia and Russia presented real dangers and could not be waved away. Bulgaria, he repeated, would sign – but only in her own good time.[84]

This was a diplomatic defeat, and Hitler resented it. Still, a partial result had been obtained; Ribbentrop had succeeded in extracting Filov's consent – 'in principle', to be sure – for the initiating of staff conversations.[85] This meant that the all important military preparations could go ahead. On 9 January Hitler accordingly cleared the beginning of talks with Bulgaria for the construction of quarters for the first troops to cross the Danube.[86] While the most urgent military measures were thus saved from further delay, the political situation was still far from rosy. Bulgaria, Hitler realized, was 'willing, but afraid';[87] though he could not admit this to Filov, the dangers of intervention by third parties were real and something had to be done about them.

This was the duty of the foreign ministry, which displayed unusual dexterity in accomplishing its task. Early in January the Germans still had but few forces in Rumania; nothing with which to oppose the 34 Soviet divisions in Bessarabia, 37 Turkish divisions in Thrace, and the million-strong Yugoslav army. To counter these forces, the Wilhelmstrasse – and behind it Hitler, who took a personal interest in the matter – had to rely on sheer bluff. While deliberately refraining from any official announcements, on 7 January Ribbentrop sent a circular to his envoys in Moscow, Ankara, Belgrade and Athens. Marked 'for the personal information of the ambassador [minister] and the military attaché', the circular in fact regulated the attitude to be assumed towards possible questions regarding the German military activities in Rumania. Ribbentrop directed that the transportation of German troops through Hungary and Rumania and their concentration on the Danube should be admitted; they could not be concealed anyhow, and the knowledge might have a beneficial effect on the Greeks. As to the

purpose of these measures, the foreign minister instructed his representatives to say that Germany had 'received reports of increasingly
large reinforcements of every kind in Greece', and authorized them to
mention the World War I Salonika front.[88] Any further inquiries
should be referred to Berlin. The note, together with the official silence
maintained by the foreign ministry, had the desired effect. From
Moscow and Ankara Schulenburg and Papen reported that although
the respective governments had not reacted officially to the news,
exaggerated rumours, fear and anxiety were in the air.[89]

If Berlin had ever hoped that fear would deter the Soviets from
opposing its plan to march through Bulgaria, these hopes were soon
dispelled. On 13 January the Soviet news agency Tass published an
official *démarche* clearly aimed at Sofia:[90]

If German troops really are present in Bulgaria, and if the further despatch of
German troops to Bulgaria is really taking place, then all this occurred . . .
without the knowledge and consent of the USSR.

. . . the Bulgarian government never approached the USSR with an enquiry
regarding the passage of German troops to Bulgaria, and consequently could
not have received any reply from the USSR.

As if this were not clear enough, the Soviet ambassador, Dekanosov
called on Weizsäcker on 17 January to deliver a tough statement.
According to all reports German troops were being concentrated in
Rumania in preparation for the march into Bulgaria. Their aim was to
occupy Bulgaria, Greece and the Straits. The British and the Turks
would undoubtedly try to forestall the operation, occupy the Straits
themselves and turn Bulgaria into a battlefield. This the Soviet Union
could not tolerate, since Bulgaria belonged to her security zone and the
entry of German troops into the country would therefore be regarded
as a 'violation of the security interests of the USSR'.[91]

Ribbentrop's circular thus had the effect of clarifying the Soviet
attitude, but not in the desired direction. From now on, there could be
no doubt whatsoever but that the Soviets would oppose the German
plans with all available means. Despite his brave words to Filov – and
despite the fact that the leading experts in the foreign ministry,
Weizsäcker and Schulenburg, were unanimous that the *démarche* should
not be regarded too tragically[92] – Hitler was not the man to take the
threats of his Georgian colleague lightly. On 18 January he reserved
clearance of the noticeable preparations for the Danube crossing to
himself.[93]

Ribbentrop's diplomacy had a more beneficial effect on Turkey.
Negotiations with Ankara had been abruptly halted on 5 December;
suspended, in complete disregard of Papen's urgent appeals,[94] for the
coming fortnight; and resumed only on 21 December, that is approxi-

mately at the same time as those with Bulgaria.[95] Despite declarations of enthusiasm,[96] the Turks had been dragging their feet and on 10 January Papen reported that in his opinion the only way to keep her out was to promise that the German troops in Bulgaria would respect a zone of 50 km (= 30 miles) from her frontier.[97] This, however, was a proposal which the foreign ministry could not accept, since if leaked to the Bulgarians it would supply them with proof that Germany was double-crossing them on the 'glacis' on Greek territory which Weizsäcker was planning to set aside for Turkey.

On 13 January there was a breakthrough. Saracoglu told the Bulgarian minister in Ankara that his government was now prepared to agree to the Bulgarian demand that third parties be left out of the talks between the two countries.[98] Whether this rather surprising Turkish surrender was a result of Ribbentrop's bluff we do not know,[99] but in any case it was a tremendous relief to the Bulgarians. Though Rendel, the English minister, could still threaten them with a Turkish invasion if they signed the Tripartite Pact, they were by now much more worried by a possible British bombardment and therefore requested immediate staff talks to clarify 'what German protection Bulgaria could be provided with'.[100] A conversation between Weizsäcker and Draganov on the same day also showed that something had changed in the Bulgarian attitude; though still making a point of listing all the manifold dangers facing Bulgaria and repeating Filov's assertion that the award of Salonika to Yugoslavia would not make a good impression on Bulgarian public opinion, Draganov now expressed his hope that an agreement on the territorial question could be arrived at before his departure for Sofia, that is within two days. He also brought his government's consent to the initiation of staff conversations, though for reasons of secrecy Sofia preferred them to take place in the Reich rather than on its own territory.[101]

This, then, was the beginning of the end as far as Bulgaria was concerned. After some wrangling between Weizsäcker and Ribbentrop – the former still insisted that the 'glacis on Greek soil' be reserved for eventual cession to Turkey[102] – the state secretary was, on 15 January, authorized to inform Draganov that Germany consented to Bulgaria's territorial demands. 'Bulgaria', he told the minister, 'must now state her full readiness to sign the Tripartite Pact in Berlin at a time to be set by us. Germany would thus determine the time itself, but taking into account that we would then be in a position to cope with all eventualities.'[103] With this reply in his pocket Draganov flew to Sofia, from whence the answer came on 23 January: Richthofen reported that Filov had said his country was ready to join the Pact, provided the German–Bulgarians staff talks emerged with some effective means by which Bulgaria could, and would, be protected. For the rest, Filov

wanted a written confirmation of what Weizsäcker had told Draganov.[104]

By placing herself under German protection Bulgaria must have
hoped to extricate herself from between the Turkish and Soviet millstones. Whether it was fear or greed that pushed her towards Hitler it is
impossible to say; however, the Bulgarians were so successful in pro-
tracting the negotiations (others might say, in getting a good price for
their neutrality) that Hitler and OKW had to go through many an
anxious moment. Her decision to opt for the Axis made it possible for
them to go ahead with the military preparations, but it soon turned out
that not all the difficulties had been overcome; more than a month was
still to pass before German troops could at long last cross the Danube.

ON THE WAY TO THE DANUBE

The military preparations for 'Marita' were, when we left them, in a
considerable mess. While the original timetable was based on the
assumption that stage I would be ready to cross from Rumania into
Bulgaria on 26 January, the weather had already caused such delay that
only four of the eight divisions comprising that stage had reached
Rumania by that date. According to the most recent timetable, issued
on 8 January, the last transports of stage I would not arrive in Rumania
until 16 February, while the tail of stage III now reached to 20 March –
rather than 28 February as originally planned.[105] Furthermore, the
state of the ice on the Danube made it impossible to foresee when the
bridging, and hence the crossing, could be effected.

That OKH regarded Bulgaria's surrender as a timely relief is, in the
circumstances, hardly surprising. The thing to do now was to rush
through the staff conversations, arrive at an agreement, and cross into
Bulgaria at the earliest possible moment. On 15 January, OKW was
hoping that all this could be done within two to three weeks.[106] This
timetable, however, like so many of its predecessors, was antiquated
almost before it was conceived. On 17 January the Soviet Union
issued the *démarche*, which has already been discussed, confirming
Halder's worst fears; the plan to have I detachment cross the river
before the arrival of the rest of the forces was politically unsafe. On 18
January Hitler admitted this by reserving the order to start noticeable
preparations for bridge construction to himself. On 21 January he
issued a new directive about the prerequisites that would have to be
fulfilled before the crossing could take place; a special force would have
to be made ready to protect Constata against a possible Russian attack,
and strong forces would have to be stationed in Rumania in such a way
as to be able to repulse an attack on the rear of the Twelfth army.
Moreover, Hitler now feared lest the British should bomb the Ploesti

oil fields when his troops marched into Bulgaria, and he therefore
ordered strong anti-aircraft units to be brought up for the protection
of both the oil fields and the bridges themselves.[107] All this meant an
additional burden on the Hungarian railways; further delay, Hitler
explained to Mussolini, was inevitable.[108]

The measures to be taken in order to protect Bulgaria against Soviet
and Turkish surprises had to be coordinated by the German–Bulgarian
staff talks. The Reich foreign minister had already given his consent to
such talks, and detailed Minister Benzler to the headquarters of the
Twelfth army in order to 'assist' List at the negotiations.[109] After a
meeting between List and his senior subordinate officer, General von
Kleist, talks were initiated on 22 January between a German delegation
under General Greiffenberg, the recently appointed chief-of-staff of
Twelfth army, and a Bulgarian delegation under General Boydeff.[110]
Since List did not want to leave his headquarters the talks did not take
place in Austria as the Bulgarians had requested, but at Predeal,
Rumania.

If the German side had expected the conversations to be easy they
were in for a nasty surprise. The Bulgarians began by demanding that
Germany 'should not schedule the accession to the Tripartite Pact
earlier than the start of military operations'.[111] Next, they wanted
military operations to be conducted in such a way as to leave their
army available for 'subsequent new arrangements in the Balkans';
obviously they hoped to press their claims for territorial revision after
the end of 'Marita', which did not suit Berlin at all. Furthermore,
Greiffenberg was authorized to offer the Bulgarians only very little in
the way of military protection – all he could point to were the two
armoured divisions which were being made ready to move into Bulgaria from the Dobrudja, but which of course could not defend the
country against British bombardment. The Bulgarians resented this.
On 23 January Filov again told Richthofen that his government
regarded the adequate protection of the country by German troops as a
conditio sine qua non for her participation.[112] By the time the foreign
ministry had, by way of OKW, asked List to comply it was too late;
Boydeff had already left for Sofia.[113]

From the German point of view the main problem was one of timing.
Here, too, the Bulgarians were anything but easy partners, for they
had in mind mid-March as the terminal date, and made even this
dependent on the delivery of war material Germany had promised but
not supplied.[114] On 24 January Halder discussed the question with
Brauchitsch. The chief of the general staff apparently did not take the
Bulgarian objections too seriously, for he made the following calculation: List needed two days for the final stage of his bridge construction.
The anti-aircraft units earmarked to protect the operation had already

arrived in Rumania,[115] and would be to hand to protect the bridges on 7 February. The two armoured divisions earmarked to protect Bulgaria against Turkey would be concentrated in the Dobrudja – where they were not dependent on the construction of bridges – by 1 February.[116] Halder now wanted to speed up the movement of some of the anti-aircraft units and to use them as protection inside Bulgaria; for this purpose, they were to be taken over the river by boat on 5 February. On the same day, the armoured divisions would also move. The bridges for the main forces would have to be constructed without anti-aircraft protection, but by the time they were ready such protection would be available and the crossing could thus take place on 7 February. In view of the fact that an early start to 'Marita' was desirable in order to relieve pressure in North Africa, not to mention operation 'Barbarossa', Halder considered it worth his while to submit this plan to Hitler.[117]

Soon, however, it became clear that the chief-of-staff's impatience had run away with him once more. On 25 January Brauchitsch had to inform OKW that preparations for bridging the Danube would be ready on 10, not on 7 February.[118] On 27 January Colonel Bruckmann raised the question of who should supply the German army units in Bulgaria and pointed out that the Bulgarians themselves would take 21 days to mobilize instead of the 17 Halder had reckoned with, and that there was still a host of uncompleted technical preparations.[119] When, therefore, Ritter on the same day asked Jodl about the date of the crossing the chief of the Wehrmachtführungstab could tell him nothing 'conclusive'. 'Personally', however, Jodl told the minister that the bridges could be ready within two or three days from 10 February onward; the bulk of stage I would by then have arrived in Rumania, but the commander of VIIIth air corps wanted to start the crossing only after establishing an air base inside Bulgaria. If this request were granted it would take 16 days to construct the base, since the Bulgarians could process only 6 trains a day out of the 100 needed for the purpose. Jodl also hoped that some of the units of stage II would be allowed to reach Rumania – as a precaution against the Soviets – before the crossing, all of which meant that the move into Bulgaria could not begin until 'considerably later' than 10 February. Jodl therefore did not believe the crossing could start before 20 February.[120]

On 28 January List reported on the conversations with the Bulgarian general staff. Bulgaria was 'absolutely willing', but anxious lest her defences should prove inadequate. This anxiety was justified in that the bulk of the Bulgarian army had not yet been mobilized and would require at least 17 days to deploy on the Turkish frontier. Halder's suggestion that anti-aircraft units should cross the Danube by boat was impracticable. Since protection for the bridges would not be available until 7 February, and all the units of the Twelfth army except the armoured divisions stationed in the Dobrudja were dependent on the bridges, even modest military protection for Bulgaria was impossible before mid-February. This being so it was necessary to hold off the crossing at least until some protection could be made available by other means, that is until after VIIIth air corps completed its deployment in Rumania on 10 February.[121]

Discouraging as this report was, it had one merit; it made it clear once and for all that the single factor contributing most towards the endless delays was the fact that no anti-aircraft units were immediately available to protect the bridges and Bulgaria. There was only one way to solve this problem, and solve it thoroughly; the anti-aircraft batteries earmarked for Bulgaria had to roll through Yugoslavia. This, List told the foreign ministry, would make possible a crossing of the Danube on 10 February or immediately after, and would also bring tremendous relief to the overburdened railways of Hungary and Rumania.[122] On 29 January a request from OKH to try and open the way arrived at OKW.[123] Political considerations, however, made it impossible to fulfil this request.[124]

On 28 January Hitler drew together the conclusions resulting from the German–Bulgarian staff conversations. They were:

The entry into Bulgaria will take place as late as possible – that is, in no case before 10 February – and not before:

1. The camouflaged preparations of VIIIth air corps . . . are completed.
2. The anti-aircraft and coastal defences for Constanta, Varna, Burgas and the crossing of the Danube are ready.
3. The concentration of German forces in Rumania makes the entry into Bulgaria necessary.[125]

The envisaged date for the start of operations (1 April) is to be maintained . . . the date after which the crossing of the Danube can be expected to be free from obstacles caused by the weather (ice etc.) is to be reported.[126]

The threat of foreign intervention had led Hitler to the conclusion that it was necessary to give the game away at the latest possible moment, that is to cross the Danube at the latest date compatible with the start of operations early in April. On 31 January OKW translated his instructions into an order, and since the date of the crossing was now contingent on the concentration of VIIIth air corps clearance was given for this operation.[127] At this point, however, the weather interfered once more; not only was the construction of bridges still being made impossible by the ice, but the melting of the snow made it impossible to bring up the air force units at the desired pace.[128]

Following his decision of 28 January to postpone the Danube crossing, Hitler summoned another of his habitual military conferences to the *Reichskanzlei* on 3 February. The main subject of the discussion was, as usual in this period, Russia. Halder delivered a long lecture about various aspects of the future Russian campaign, and the deployment order which OKH had just completed was submitted to Hitler.[129] On the face of it this order, envisaging an attack with three army groups, corresponded to Hitler's 'directive No. 21' for operation 'Barbarossa', but a closer scrutiny reveals that OKH was trying to trick the Führer by allocating considerably stronger forces than originally planned to the northern and central army groups, while weakening the southern one.[130] Since, for obvious geographical reasons, the forces to be employed on 'Marita' were now for the greatest part earmarked for this last army group, [131] this meant that their relative importance within this group greatly increased. As a result, it was now more than ever essential to 'counter the danger that the forces of "Marita" will be stuck'; in Halder's opinion, the Bulgarians would resist being left alone. More dangerous still was the attitude of Turkey, which had not yet committed itself and might intervene when the German troops entered Bulgaria. OKH had prepared a plan for a counter-attack, but such an operation would take so much time and so many forces that 'Barbarossa' would have to be postponed.[132] Since the outcome of the diplomatic negotiations with Turkey was still by no means certain, all that Hitler could do on this account was to express his hope that Turkey might stay quiet.

Turkey, however, was a consideration for the future. The immediate problem was Bulgaria. True, on 31 January Boydeff had returned to Predeal and with List now authorized by OKW to offer adequate protection the talks made rapid progress. It was agreed that the Bulgarians should start mobilizing on 6 February, so as to be ready on the frontier by 27 February. On 2 February, moreover, List could send his superiors a draft agreement.[133] Sofia had no objections to the article under which her forces would not be committed offensively against Turkey or Greece; those which dealt with making German protection available – including armoured, motorized and anti-aircraft units – were also ostensibly regarded with satisfaction. On the other hand, the Bulgarians used the still unclarified question of the chain of command to stave off their signature,[134] and it was only on 10 February that they sent a member of Boydeff's delegation, Colonel Popov, to Berlin to discuss the question. In Berlin Popov joined forces with Minister Draganov and together they let the cat out of the bag; afraid of English bombardment, Bulgaria wanted still stronger guarantees of her security. While these could, and were, readily granted their other demand was harder to fulfil: in the hope of conciliating Turkey, they proposed to halt their mobilization until the arrival of the German troops.[135] From the German point of view this meant that the crossing would become even more risky. No wonder, therefore, that on 12 February List protested strongly against the Bulgarian plan.[136]

In the interests of an early crossing, Hitler decided to refuse the Bulgarian request. Moreover, he now hoped to speed up their mobilization and to complete it, if possible, on 24 February. On 21 February he wanted to finish the bridge construction, move the armoured divisions stationed in the Dobrudja – which were not dependent on the bridges – into Bulgaria as cover against Turkey, and simultaneously provide anti-aircraft batteries of VIIIth air corps for the defence of Sofia. The crossing proper was to take place three days later.[137] As a result of the endless delays, OKH was now giving vent to its anxiety; it was feared that preparations inside Bulgaria could not be completed in time for the attack to start on schedule, that is early in April.[138]

While these decisions were being made, things were going somewhat better at the Twelfth army. By 15 February the following forces of stage I had arrived in Rumania: XXXXth army corps with 9th armoured and 60th motorized divisions, XIVth army corps with 5th and 11th armoured divisions, XXXth army corps with 164th, 50th and 72nd infantry divisions. On 16 February stage II consisting of XVIIIth army corps with 5th and 6th mountain divisions, 2nd armoured division, 73rd infantry division and 125th infantry regiment was scheduled to start rolling east. Though its rearguard, consisting of supply trains, would not reach Rumania before the end of March the bulk of the fighting forces could be expected on the Danube late in February.[139] It seems that Berlin now considered the Russian danger less serious, for Hitler had ordered SS 'AH', originally part of stage I to stay in France to participate eventually in operation 'Attila'; its place was taken by 16th armoured division, hitherto subordinated to the German army mission in Rumania and now transferred to the Twelfth army.[140] The weather had now improved to such an extent that Benzler could report on 12 February that the Danube was free from ice and that bridge-construction could begin.[141] As a result of these factors, List and his officers now hoped that it would be possible to keep to Hitler's timetable and cross the Danube on 24 February.[142]

List, however, was heading for yet another disappointment. In the middle of the month the weather that had caused the ice to disappear from the Danube also made the snow melt; the Rumanian air fields were deep under water and it was impossible to bring up further planes to reinforce the single fighter and dive bomber groups that had already arrived. On 17 February, Halder noted that this would cause further delay.[143] On the next day the Twelfth army reported that:

'Heerestrasse' [i.e. the bridge construction] and the Danube crossing on 21 and 24 February are possible for 12th army, but not for VIIIth air corps.

On the assumption that the weather stays good, the Rumanian air fields can be ready by 25 February.

It is impossible to have supplies [for VIIIth air corps] ready in Bulgaria before 2 March ...

Bulgarian mobilization complete on 28 February at the earliest, Since prerequisites for entry not given, 12th army proposes:

a. 'Heerestrasse' not before 28 February.

b. No Danube crossing before 2 March.

OKH forwarded the report to OKW, recommending that List's request be granted; it would be possible to start 'Marita' on time in any case, while the end of the operation depended not so much on its starting date as on Turkey's attitude. If the latter were to interfere 'Barbarossa' might well have to be cancelled altogether.[144]

Quite unexpectedly, List's request to have the crossing postponed by a few days received support from another quarter. On 15 February the Bulgarians, to whom Hitler's decision had been communicated, protested that a German entry on the 24th would wreak havoc with their own still incomplete mobilization.[145] Behind this request Richthofen suspected renewed fears of foreign intervention, and on 18 February Ribbentrop accordingly assured the Bulgarians that there was not even 'the smallest ground' for anxiety.[146] Coming as it did on top of the difficulties encountered by the Luftwaffe, Hitler saw no choice but to comply; on 19 February he decided that 'Heerestrasse' was to take place on 28 February, the crossing itself on 2 March.[147] His decision formed the basis of yet another timetable, according to which the first forces of stage I were to arrive on the Greek frontier on the 8th, the deployment of stage II in Bulgaria to be completed on 29 March. Depending on the weather, which might make it expedient to advance or postpone the date by a few days, the attack could then start on 7 April.[148]

Possibly because he feared they might come up with yet more objections, Hitler did not communicate his decision to the Bulgarians. To the latter, however, knowledge of the date appeared to be of the greatest importance. Throughout February the Soviet pressure on Bulgaria had continued, culminating in an ostensibly innocent warning by Vyschinski on 20 February.[149] In order to reinsure themselves, the Bulgarians were preparing a note for the Kremlin, in which they explained that their accession to the Tripartite Pact was in no way directed against Russia. They wanted to deliver this note on the eve of 'Heerestrasse', which was also the day before the entry of the first German forces – those stationed in the Dobrudja – into Bulgaria was scheduled.[150] On 19 February Filov therefore asked no less than three times when the bridging was supposed to start, claiming that all preparations indicated that it would take place very early and requesting 'a few days advance notice'.[151] All he could get in reply, however, was the statement that the operation had not yet been cleared.[152] Sofia was left in the dark for another few days, and it was not until 26 February that Richthofen announced Hitler's decision.[153] Even then the Bulgarians did not receive complete satisfaction; in the interests of keeping Turkey out, Hitler at the last moment decided to alter his plan, refused the Bulgarian request to have the Dobrudja group march ahead of the rest of the forces, and instead ordered them to move simultaneously with the Twelfth army.

A full six weeks behind the original schedule, Twelfth army was now ready to cross the Danube. The weather, which had caused a major part of the delay, remained uncooperative; on 27 February, rain and fresh snow were again threatening the bridge-construction.[154] Though this obstacle was overcome, the operation was and remained a risky one; for it had not yet been possible to obtain full security for its flanks. True, negotiations with both Turkey and Yugoslavia were far advanced, but the reactions of both countries remained to be seen.

VICTORY AND FAILURE IN THE SOUTHEAST

We left German–Turkish and Bulgarian–Turkish negotiations at a crucial point, i.e. when the Turks had conceded to the Bulgarian demand that third parties be left out of the talks between them. This concession, made on 13 January, undoubtedly presented a major breakthrough; from now on, it could be expected that the Turks were willing to arrive at a speedy agreement.

The moves designed to secure operation 'Marita' against armed Turkish intervention have been described elsewhere,[155] so that it is enough to give a brief outline here. On 20 January the Turks handed Sofia a proposal for a joint Bulgarian–Turkish declaration, which was duly turned over to the Wilhelmstrasse for approval.[156] The most conspicuous feature of the Turkish draft was a long preamble, stating that the aim of the declaration was to maintain 'the quiet and the peace in the Balkans', and referring to the preamble of the Bulgarian–Turkish accord of 15 January 1940, which said that Turkey and Bulgaria were 'in perfect accord about the maintenance of the peace in the Balkans and of the neutrality proclaimed by the Bulgarian government'. Article 1, the only one that is relevant to our discussion, said that 'Bulgaria and Turkey regard abstinence from any attack as a cornerstone of their foreign policy'. Both Richthofen and Sofia thought the Turkish draft was acceptable.

The foreign ministry took a different view of the matter. Weizsäcker examined the draft, then pointed out that the reference to the Bulgarian–Turkish declaration could not be allowed to stand; its obvious aim was to compel Bulgaria to pursue a policy of neutrality, and thus prevent her accession to the Tripartite Pact.[157] Ribbentrop on 27 January decided to endorse his state secretary's objection, but since he suspected that the Turks would be unwilling to concede the point he had Richthofen ask the Bulgarians to make a counter proposal. Article 1 now received new formulation at the hands of the German foreign minister: 'each of the two signatories commits itself, in accordance with the previously expressed desire for neutrality, not to support an attack conducted through its territory upon that of the other'.[158] This, of course, would deny Greece precisely the sort of diplomatic protection Turkey was trying to obtain for her.

If the Germans were satisfied with their own device, the Bulgarians were not. Early in February their fears lest the entry of German troops expose them to a Turkish attack were roused again;[159] they were supported by the German military attaché in Ankara, General Rohde, who argued that Turkey's entry into the war was inevitable unless Germany offered to respect a zone of 50 km from her frontier.[160] For reasons that have already been explained, however, this idea could not be accepted, or at least not openly. As the melting of the ice on the Danube made the crossing appear imminent, Bulgarian–Turkish relations rapidly approached a crisis. On 12 February the Bulgarians purported to know 'for certain' that an invasion by the Turkish army was imminent;[161] on 13 February the rumour spread rapidly in Ankara that German troops had already crossed the Danube and were marching south and made war appear inevitable.[162] In a remarkable document, OKH on the next day laid down its plans for such an eventuality. Should the Turks enter the war, it would be possible to:

a Launch a simultaneous attack on Greece and Turkey, while restricting the objectives with regard to the former. Such an attack was to start on 7 April 'at the latest'.

b Invade Turkey after fulfilling the objectives in Greek Thrace and the subsequent regrouping. Such an attack could presumably start on 14 April.

From the point of view of coordination with 'Barbarossa', OKH calculated, both plans were equally bad: both would make a postponement of that operation inevitable. Plan (*b*), however, was considered safer and OKH recommended it to OKW.[163] The really interesting point in this document is the extremely short duration envisaged for 'Marita': a single week. Obviously, so short an operation was thought possible solely because its objectives did not include the occupation of the entire Greek peninsula, but only of a narrow strip on the Aegean Coast.

Meanwhile the diplomatic crisis was passing. In his decision of 13

February Hitler followed Rohde's advice in that he ordered his army to avoid crossing the Turnovo–Burgas line to the south 'for political reasons'.[164] It is not impossible that Papen was secretly allowed to pass this decision to the Turks, for only a day later Ankara suddenly gave its consent to alter the preamble.[165] Ribbentrop now dropped his former reservations and on 17 February the Bulgaro–Turkish declaration of non-aggression was signed amidst much publicity.

While the foreign ministry thought it had achieved its object, Papen and Sofia soon found reasons for renewed anxiety. On 24 February Saracoglu declared in a newspaper interview that Turkey 'would by no means remain indifferent if her security zone were violated'.[166] On 26 February Eden arrived in Ankara, and on the same day Sofia suggested that the danger of a Turkish invasion made it impossible for both prime minister and foreign minister to be present when the Tripartite Pact was signed in the Vienna Belvedere.[167] By this time, however, the Danube crossing was so imminent that the German foreign minister could not pay much heed to such warnings; on 27 February he told Papen to announce Bulgaria's accession to the Tripartite Pact on the next day, and, should the Turks adopt an aggressive attitude, say that 'the Führer has stated that the military security measures taken by Germany in the Balkans are not directed against Turkey but against the British gaining a foothold in Greece. These decisions are irrevocable and the Führer does not issue such statements as a joke. If, however, the Turks are looking for a reason to start a war, they should say so.' From this *démarche* Ribbentrop expected a 'cleansing' effect.[168]

Matters, however, did not get as far as that. Due to an error the telegram reached Papen only on 1 March, and when he delivered the message Saracoglu received it 'in a very friendly way'.[169] This was followed by a personal letter from Hitler to President Inönü, in which the German dictator gave assurances that the measures taken by the Wehrmacht in the Balkans were 'in no way intended to be directed against the territorial or political integrity of Turkey', and that 'immediately after the dangers mentioned [i.e. the English ones] are removed the German troops will leave Bulgaria . . . and Rumania likewise. He had ordered his forces to remain at a sufficient distance' from the Turkish frontier. The letter was conciliatory in form and contents, and Inönü was gratified. On 4 March Papen could report that it had been received with satisfaction.[170]

In the nick of time, Hitler had succeeded in securing his left flank against foreign intervention. Considerable as this success indubitably was, it was nevertheless incomplete; diplomatic failure was waiting on his right flank.

*　　*　　*

Early in December, it will be remembered, German–Yugoslav negotiations aimed at obtaining Yugoslav cooperation, or at least connivance, in the liquidation of Greece had reached deadlock.[171] The Hitler–Cincar Markovic conversation of 28 November resulted, nine days later, in a statement from Belgrade that 'Yugoslavia is willing to discuss with the Reich government and the Italian government the possibilities of signing a non-aggression pact.'[172] At that time, however, Hitler had already launched his attempt to end the Italo–Greek war, and the Yugoslav note was therefore left unanswered. It was only on 21 December – that is, on the very day when negotiations with Turkey were also resumed – that the Wilhelmstrasse shook off its two-week lethargy and renewed contact.

By then, circumstances had changed. On 28 November Hitler had pressed for a non-aggression pact; he was willing to grant Salonika to Yugoslavia, and emphasized that 'Germany did not ask for anything, not even the right of passage for troops'.[173] By the end of December, on the other hand, 'Barbarossa' was a settled matter; and further, the relationship between it and 'Marita' had been thoroughly clarified by OKH. Though 'directive No. 20' of 13 December prudently advised that the use of the Yugoslav railways was not to be reckoned with, the possibility of shortening the build-up for 'Marita' from ten (as originally planned) to six weeks was too tempting to be disregarded. On 21 December, therefore, Ribbentrop answered Cincar Markovic that:

The Führer and I . . . gave consideration to the proposal . . . that a non-aggression pact be concluded between Germany, Italy and Yugoslavia . . . the conclusion of such a pact would of course not meet the specifications for the strengthening of Yugoslavia's relations with the Axis powers that we had envisaged in the conversations with Cincar Markovic at the Berghof and Fuschl.[174]

Because of 'Barbarossa', a non-aggression pact was not simply insufficient; it was positively dangerous, as it would allow Yugoslavia to close her frontiers with impunity to the passage of German troops and war material. The Yugoslavs, on the other hand, knew nothing of 'Barbarossa' and were – or pretended to be – surprised. After all, Cincar Markovic politely reminded Ribbentrop, the proposal for a non-aggression pact had come from Hitler himself.[175]

Deadlock again followed. With most of the delays in the build-up for 'Marita' still in the future, Hitler may have hoped that the matter could be dispensed with; in any case, he did not renew the contacts. The Yugoslavs, on the other hand, could not rest content with their successful parrying of Hitler's thrust; the German troops streaming into Rumania were too dangerous for that. A diplomatic reconnaissance appeared to be in order, as long as it did not commit Yugoslavia to anything. Sometime after the middle of January, therefore, the Prime

Minister, Cvetkovic, indicated his willingness to go for talks in Germany to Gregoric, whose services had already been utilized in a similar manner by Cincar Markovic in November. Gregoric fulfilled his task in an admirable way, for he promptly incorporated the suggestion at the end of a long epistle in which he explained that the talks between Hitler and Cincar Markovic had failed because of Italy's defeats and the influence exercised by England's friends. Cincar Markovic was described as a 'civil servant' who 'did not see things clearly'. Would the Führer agree to meet Cvetkovic in person? Not so, it seemed. Several days passed and no answer came from Berlin.[176]

Hitler, however, was in no position to ignore the Yugoslavs for long. On 26 January a telegram from Rumania made it clear that in List's opinion the only way to avoid further delay to 'Marita' was to use Yugoslav railways for the transportation of anti-aircraft units.[177] OKH agreed with the fieldmarshal, and on 29 January submitted a proposal to this effect to OKW.[178] Though Hitler did not ratify the plan – he may have been afraid lest the generals' impatience spoil his chances of winning over Yugoslavia, and had Keitel issue a directive reaffirming his original instructions[179] – he now saw himself compelled to accept the offer transmitted by Gregoric.[180] After some obscure wrangling, the visit was arranged for 14 February.[181]

In preparation for the meeting, Ribbentrop's principal military adviser prepared a memorandum analysing the question of railway transport through Yugoslavia. The question, Ritter explained, should be divided into three parts: 1. During the troop-movements to Rumania. 2. After the entry into Bulgaria. 3. After the start of operations against Greece. For stage 1, he explained, it was too late. Stage 2 was still possible, and its implementation would be greatly welcomed by the *Chef de Wehrmachttransportwesen*. As to stage 3, the foreign ministry was of the opinion that once the trains were rolling to Bulgaria it would not be difficult to redirect them to Greece. To this memorandum a note, entitled 'passage through Yugoslavia' was appended, reading as follows:

No troops
No war material (weapons and ammunition)
But everything else: supplies, sanitary services, trucks, horses, etc. Trains of German Red Cross for the sick and wounded in both directions. On the way back, empty carriages.
Number: 10 trains daily.
Transports to Bulgaria only, not to Greece.[182]

Since the number of trains supposed to bring supplies into Bulgaria before the Danube crossing was one hundred and twenty-eight,[183] a quota of ten a day to pass through Yugoslavia could present a very considerable fraction of the total. The relief to the overburdened

Rumanian railways, particularly in the Dobrudja, would be tremendous and was certainly worth bargaining for.

The Yugoslavs, however, were tough bargainers. Upon inquiries being made Prince Paul had – on approximately 20 January – assured both Metaxas and the American envoy, Colonel Donovan, that Yugoslavia would fight rather than allow German troops to cross her territory.[184] On 14 February Cvetkovic and Cincar Markovic put up such a determined resistance that the question simply never rose at all. The Prime Minister started his conversation with Ribbentrop with a flat denial that he had ever charged Gregoric with any mission; on the contrary, his decision to travel to Germany was the result of a conversation between the journalist and Schmidt, during which 'the two gentlemen' had concluded that a visit might be useful. For the rest, Yugoslav policy aimed only at keeping the peace in the Balkans. Ribbentrop tried to counter this by saying – somewhat unconvincingly – that the Tripartite Pact to which the two Yugoslav gentlemen were asked to put their signature was aimed at 'preventing the extension of the war', and 'did not represent a treaty of alliance against England'. Germany, too, would have preferred not to fight in Greece, but British machinations there – remember the Salonika Front? – made a clash inevitable. If, Cvetkovic countered, throwing the British out of Greece was Germany's objective, Yugoslavia would be willing to assist; she could try to mediate in a diplomatic solution for the Italian–Greek war and then construct a neutral Balkan block, also including Turkey, with the aim of keeping the British out. The pre-requisite, of course, was that Germany should also stay out. What did the Reich foreign minister think of such a plan? Not much, answered a somewhat surprised Ribbentrop. Frankly, he doubted whether it was possible to drive the British out by peaceful means.[185]

Hitler's attempt in the afternoon of the same day to succeed where his foreign minister had failed similarly suffered defeat. The Yugoslav premier scarcely listened to the exposition of the Führer's plans; instead, he kept returning to his own scheme for a diplomatic solution and a neutral Balkan bloc. Hitler never even had the chance to raise the all important question of transit, or perhaps he sensed that raising it would contribute nothing to disarming the Yugoslavs. As to Cvetkovic's plan for a diplomatic solution, he was as sceptical about its prospects as his foreign minister; but he agreed to have the proposal transmitted to Rome which, for appearance's sake, was still presented to the world as the Axis-appointed arbitrator on all Balkan questions. Having dealt with the Führer's plans in such an exemplary fashion Cvetkovic, always aware of the menacing presence of the German divisions in Rumania and intent on gaining time, had the cheek to ask for a meeting between Hitler and Prince Paul.[186]

Hitler, of course, had no use for a plan which would oblige Germany to stay out of the Balkans.[187] Not wanting to appear as the disturber of the peace, however, he did not care to say so but left this task to Mussolini. The latter received a strongly doctored record of the conversations, bristling with professions of unbounded loyalty to the Axis partner and giving special emphasis to the Führer's opinion that 'the whole conception of Yugoslavia entering into an alliance with states like Turkey, which had a pact with England, in order to exercise pressure on England was irrealistic'.[188] The trick worked, and the Duce swiftly replied that the Yugoslav proposal smacked of an attempt to revive the Little Entente which was 'in accord with the mentality of Beneš'.[189] This served Hitler's purpose well enough. On the other hand, his pressure on Cvetkovic now began to have the effect of pushing Belgrade and Rome into each other's arms; the former hoped that by separate negotiations with Italy it would be shielded from Germany, while the latter planned to exploit Yugoslav fear of Germany and to negotiate a bilateral Italo–Yugoslav accord directed, like that of 1937, against Germany.[190] This, though ostensibly intended to link Yugoslavia more closely to the Axis, did not suit Berlin at all, and Mussolini was told to desist.[191]

The attempt to get Yugoslavia into line with the liquidation of Greece had thus failed for the second time. Needless to say, the military were unhappy with the fact; not only had the prospect of utilizing the Yugoslav railways been postponed into the indefinite future, but the right flank appeared insecure in view of the 700,000 troops Yugoslavia was reported to have concentrated on her eastern border.[192] It was with growing apprehension that List requested information about the outcome of the conversations with Yugoslavia, and particularly as to whether the 'transit of German equipment or troops was discussed'.[193]

The Serbs had put on a brave show, but could not maintain their opposition forever. The growing concentration of German troops in Rumania spoke a stronger language than moral exhortations from England's friends;[194] and on 24 February Prince Paul agreed to go to Germany.[195] The meeting between him and Hitler took place on 4 March, and we know its details from a summary Ribbentrop sent Heeren two days later. After his usual harangue about the inevitability of Germany's victory, Hitler cleverly argued that after the liquidation of the British in Greece the German troops would not stay in the Balkans indefinitely; if Yugoslavia failed to stake her claim to Salonika, the city might fall to the Bulgarians or to the Italians. 'Visibly impressed' by these remarks, Prince Paul said that, although his personal sympathies were for England, Yugoslavia had no choice but to consider the course offered by Germany. He expressed the fear that agreement on his part would lead to revolution in Yugoslavia, then took his leave.[196]

Immediately after his return from the Berghof Prince Paul summoned a crown council to discuss the German demands. A thorough examination of the courses open to Yugoslavia resulted in the conclusion that accession to the pact, however distasteful, was the least unpalatable course – provided some conditions could be fulfilled.[197] Two days later a list of these conditions was presented to Heeren. If Yugoslavia signed, would Germany and Italy guarantee in writing that:

1. The sovereignty and territorial integrity of Yugoslavia will be respected.
2. No military assistance will be requested of Yugoslavia and also no passage or transportation of troops through the country during the war.
3. Yugoslavia's interest in a free outlet to the Aegean Sea through Salonika will be taken into account in the reorganization of Europe.

An affirmative answer, Cincar Markovic claimed, would 'make it much easier for the government to agree to the desired policy'.[198] By now, the German troops had already entered Bulgaria and were rapidly marching southward. Although Twelfth army headquarters was complaining about the congestion in Bulgaria and continually pointing at the Yugoslav railways as the only possible solution,[199] Heeren, in his comment on the Yugoslav demands, expressed the opinion that they presented a *conditio sine qua non*. Unless they were granted, further talks would be necessary, and by the time these got under way the entire question of passage would be outdated. What was more, the Yugoslavs were clearly determined to resist the demand for transit; they were even reported to be mining their railways.[200] Under the circumstances, it must have seemed to Hitler that partial success securing his flank and linking Yugoslavia to the Axis was better than no success at all, and on 8 March he wrote to Mussolini that he on his part was ready to agree to the Yugoslav demands.[201] No answer has been found, but on 9 March Heeren was instructed to give a positive reply to most of the Yugoslav requests. Germany was ready to guarantee Yugoslavia's sovereignty and territorial integrity; no passage for troops would be required; no military assistance against Greece would be asked for, and Salonika was to be awarded to Yugoslavia. On the other hand, Yugoslavia could not be released from article III of the pact as regards the rendering of military support by the signatories of the treaty in such cases as it applied.[202] The Yugoslavs, however, were not satisfied; they insisted that although prepared to support the reorganization of Europe 'politically and economically', they did not want to sign an obligation that might involve them in a war with the USSR and the US. Persuasion, Heeren reported, was unavailing.[203]

The ensuing deadlock lasted for only one day. On 11 March Heeren reported that there was 'strong agitation' in the population and the army caused by rumours that Germany had presented Yugoslavia with an ultimatum.[204] Confirming Prince Paul's fears of a revolution, this report must have had its effect on Hitler, for on 12 March he conceded even this Yugoslav demand:

Taking into account the military situation, Germany and Italy assure the Yugoslav government that they will not, of their own account, make any demand for military assistance.

This represented a great victory for the Serbs; with unparalleled nerve, they proceeded to demand even more. 'For compelling domestic reasons' they wanted to have the German declaration published.[205] This went too far; Berlin had already consented to publish her submission to Yugoslavia's other demands, but to publicly confirm the fact that Yugoslavia's accession was really a lot of humbug was a request which Hitler could not grant. There were, Ribbentrop concluded, limits to everything.[206]

After months of sidestepping, the moment of truth had dawned for Yugoslavia. German troops were streaming into neighbouring Bulgaria; Hungary and Rumania were already occupied. Caught in a ring of steel the Belgrade government capitulated on 17 March.[207] The actual signative took place in Vienna on 25 March in the presence of the representatives of Germany, Italy, Japan, Hungary, Rumania, Bulgaria and Slovakia. By dragging their feet for so long, the Yugoslavs had shown quite unequalled courage in the face of a state so much stronger than themselves. They achieved all their demands, effectively undoing the act of accession before it ever became known to the world. They even obtained Hitler's consent to the publication of those concessions – all except one. In the end, this was to prove Yugoslavia's undoing.

ON THE EVE

'HEERESTRASSE' clicked the teleprinter at the headquarters of Twelfth army on the evening of 27 February; 'Heerestrasse' went the order to a score of subordinate units next morning, triggering off feverish activity everywhere. At three points along the Danube, ships were brought into position and moored to the river bed; pontoon bridges were built and secured; anti-aircraft batteries moved into position to protect them. By the evening of the same day, the bridges – from west to east, at Bechet, Turnu Magurele and Giurgiu – were ready. On 1 March the first anti-aircraft units passed over the bridges on their way to Sofia and Burgas.

List's plan foresaw the entry into Bulgaria in four columns. The extreme right wing, consisting of parts of VIIIth air corps and of XVIIIth army corps, would brush the Yugoslav frontier on its way to

Sofia and, using road No. 1, would march south to the Rupel Pass through the valley of the Struma. The bulk of XXXXth corps was to march over the bridge at Turnu Magurele, but 60th motorized division, although subordinate to that corps, was referred to the bridge at Bechet in order to avoid congestion. The XIVth army corps marched further east through Giurgiu, while 5th and 11th armoured divisions raced over the frontier between the Dobrudja and Bulgaria and deployed against Turkey, their first units reaching the frontier as early as 4 March. Generally speaking the march went according to plan; serious delays took place only on road No. 1, where the weak Bechet bridge was temporarily put out of action. The section of the road near Orjechovo – which was bad in any case – was blocked by snow, delaying the units of VIIIth air corps and XVIIIth army corps behind it. Furthermore, it was essential to throw forward a screen to cover the Greek frontier at its most vulnerable point opposite the Rupel Pass. For this purpose units of 2nd armoured division received priority on road No. 1, as did 6th mountain division which was loaded on transport units and dispatched to the border, where it took up positions on 4 March. The movements of these units resulted in the rest of XVIIIth army corps being dispersed over extraordinarily long distances.

The movement of the infantry and mountain divisions across the Balkan mountains involved unusually difficult hazards created by the weather and the terrain. Inevitably, the marching columns were dispersed and strung out, and took some time to get together again. The motorized advance guards of 50th, 72nd and 164th infantry divisions, following hard on the heels of 6th mountain division, reached the sectors allocated to them in the Nevrokop, Pasmalki and Nestali areas on 8 March.

The high command of VIIIth air corps also started to march on 2 March. Aided by the favourable weather, the transfer of the flying units of the corps was completed on the same day. The ground organization ended its deployment on 8 March. The anti-aircraft units generally marched in conjunction with the army units they were supposed to protect, the main forces being concentrated round the Danube bridges and in the passes of the Balkan mountains. The anti-aircraft units detailed for the protection of the bridges stayed in their positions until the bulk of stage I had crossed on 8 March, then departed for their scheduled positions round Karlovo, Sofia, Turnovo, Burgas and the quarters of 6th mountain division.[208]

While these movements were going on inside Bulgaria, stage II was completing its disentrainment in Rumania. Possibly as a result of the Bulgarian protests on the eve of the crossing, Hitler had once more been impressed by the need to protect his rear against the Russians. He therefore reversed his previous decision to detach 16th armoured division from the German army mission in Rumania and send it into Bulgaria, and instead had SS 'AH' division reincorporated into the transports of stage II.[209] The division was brought up from Metz, marched across the Danube and concentrated round Sofia.[210] On 13 March stage III was expected to start arriving in Rumania. Consisting of high commands XIth and Lth army corps, 46th, 56th, 76th, 183rd, 198th, 294th infantry and 4th mountain divisions, as well as corps troops and supply trains, its tail stretched to 2 April.[211] On 5 March Hitler, who the previous day had received Papen's description of the friendly reception of his letter by Inonü, considered that 'the danger from Turkey can now be disregarded'.[212] This presented OKH with an opportunity it had been hoping for for some time. The divisions of stage III were, in accordance with the deployment order of Twelfth army, earmarked to relieve 5th and 11th armoured divisions in their task of covering the Turkish frontier. After the end of 'Marita' they were to form part – still under the command of Twelfth army – of that arm of army group south which was to advance into Russia from Rumania.[213] If marched into Bulgaria, they would clearly have to be marched out again. Pointing to the positive attitude of Turkey, OKH on 7 March asked OKW whether the transfer of that stage to Bulgaria could not be dispensed with altogether. An answer was requested within 11 days.[214]

While these movements were going on in Bulgaria and Rumania, the objectives of the operation remained unclear. Moreover, it was not even certain that it was to be carried out at all. Throughout the winter, contacts between Berlin and Athens had continued.[215] Using various channels, the Greek government tried to convince Hitler that there was no intention of throwing the Italians out of Albania, that Greece 'had not wanted to fight against Italy, but was forced to by England' and that the best solution would be the occupation of the whole of Albania by German troops.[216] Simultaneously, we have indications that various German proposals were brought to the attention of the Greek government.[217]

The reason why these efforts failed is shrouded in mystery. For one thing, Hitler may have thought that the Greek offers were insincere; and with reason, for on 12 February King George told the American minister that 'should Germany before attacking propose that Greece make peace with Italy the answer will be that Greece must consult her ally; should Germany offer any other compromises the reply will be refusal since acceptance would only mean eventual enslavement as in Rumania's case'.[218] While it is easy to dismiss these words as lip service to the allied cause, Hitler probably regarded anything that reached his ears as additional proof that the Greeks were wholly in the hands of Britain and therefore unable to get out of the war. By no means could he give up the attainment of his objectives in Greece, i.e. the ejection of the British and the occupation of Salonika and the Aegean Coast as a barrier against them. On the other hand, he may have hoped that the presence of the Wehrmacht in Bulgaria would to some extent at least obtain what diplomatic means had repeatedly failed to do; in other words, that the Greeks would give up this area without war.

Understandably, the Italians were greatly disturbed by this possibility. Fear of German intentions in Greece had already led them to reject help in Albania, and they now hoped that it would still be possible to put an end to the whole affair before their allies could arrive on the scene and steal the show.[219] On 26 February, however, disturbing news arrived from Berlin; OKW was reported to be hoping that the Greeks could be induced to make peace before the Wehrmacht intervened, and 'leading German circles' were said to be in favour of an arrangement that would involve Greek concessions in return for avoiding a war with Germany.[220] To Mussolini this was shocking news, and he ordered Marras 'to make [Berlin] understand that Italy intends to defeat Greece . . . it is a question of prestige, and nobody should understand this better than the German military.'[221] Marras's remonstrations apparently failed to make much of an impression on the German senior officers, for on 3 March Lanza recorded 'a secret German communication' in his diary: 'the troops of the Reich will march very slowly toward Salonika in order to allow the Greeks plenty of time to consider the opportunities of surrendering without resistance'.[222] On the next day he noted that 'the [German] foreign ministry still hopes Greece will give in without a fight'.[223] In a remarkable entry dated 3 March, Halder noted that:

We must be clear about the following:
a. Does the political leadership attribute any value to the early arrival of the first German troops on the Greek frontier, in order to make it clear to the Greeks that our troops will arrive before those of Mr Eden, who is now in Athens? . . .
As to (a.): OKW welcomes anything that can contribute to the early appearance of German troops on the Greek frontier.[224]

Although they may not have been quite sure of the best way to intimidate the Greeks, it would therefore seem that the Germans did in fact hope to manage without war. On 7 March Marras again reported that the impression existed that 'the imposing concentration of German forces in the Balkans aims at obtaining a great political success avoiding, if possible, a new conflict', and that Twelfth army, in the hope of making the Greeks think twice, was advancing rather slowly toward the south.[225] This time Rome was furious; Anfuso let the Germans know that the attempt to make Athens give way 'did not interest us', and Guzzoni telephoned that it was 'inadmissible' that the German troops should occupy Greece peacefully while 'our [men] fight and die'. 'Seldom,' noted Lanza, 'had the atmosphere between Rome and Berlin been so cold'.[226]

If the Germans did not, after all, make peace with Greece the reason was not Mussolini's fear lest he be robbed of his laurels but the landing in Greece of relatively strong British forces. From January onward the Greek general staff had been conducting talks with the commander-in-chief of the British Empire forces in the Middle East, General Wavell, as to how to meet the growing German menace. Both sides quickly realized that British aid would perforce be of a symbolic nature, since they did not dispose of the troops and material needed to offer serious resistance. Although the British wanted to send aid anyhow the Greeks insisted that this would only provoke Germany without serving any military purpose, and it was finally agreed to defer the despatch of British reinforcements until the Germans gave final proof of their intentions by crossing the Danube. The decision was passed on to Berlin via Belgrade.[227] Hitler, however, needed a secure flank for his attack on Russia and could not stake 'the decision over the hegemony in Europe' on a Graeco–British promise. He therefore ordered his troops to enter Bulgaria on 2 March. Five days later the first units of a British force totalling some three divisions started to disembark at Piraeus. To Hitler, this looked very much like a confirmation of what he had suspected all along; nothing but German armed force would dislodge the British.

The results were twofold. On the one hand, Berlin now categorically rejected all peace feelers extended from Athens – and of these there were plenty, for various Greek circles, though refusing to renounce any part of the national territory, were desperately hunting for a diplomatic solution that would stave off the impending disaster. On 6 March Pangalos, formerly the Greek dictator, approached Erbach in the name of 'influential persons' with a plan to establish a pro-Axis government by means of a *coup d'état*, join the Tripartite Pact and terminate the war with Italy with a settlement based on the *status quo*.[228] On 11 March Mavroudis asked Erbach how a German invasion could be avoided.[229] On the next day there was an unofficial approach from the Greek army, which offered to throw the British out in return for a cease fire in Albania and the halting of the German advance in Bulgaria.[230] On 15 March the German military attaché, Clemm von Hohenberg, talked to Mavroudis who said that 'the Greek government desired nothing so much as an early peace in Albania that would preserve Greek honour and would make possible the withdrawal of the English from the continent'.[231] On 18 March Weizsäcker foiled an attempt by Riazo Rangabe to raise the subject, telling him that Greece's fatal mistake had been the acceptance of the British guarantee in 1939.[232]

On the same day Ribbentrop, obviously with an eye to putting an end to these approaches, prepared a draft telegram claiming that 'the Greek government is mistaken if it assumed that it can pass on to us the responsibility for taking the initiative in terminating the conflict. In particular, however, it seems to harbour illusions concerning the price it would have to pay for such a termination.'[233] Ribbentrop apparently reconsidered, and his draft never left the Wilhelmstrasse.

The military results of the British landing in Greece were even more important. Although 'directive No. 20' had mentioned the possibility that operation 'Marita' would be extended to include more Greek territory than just the Aegean Coast, all preparations had hitherto been made on the assumption that this would not be the case. Thus, the OKH plan of 14 February allocated only one week to the entire operation, and as late as 8 March Warlimont complained that it was not clear how far the occupation was to be extended.[234] In view of the British landings in Greece the question became even more urgent, and on 17 March it was answered in a drastic manner by Hitler; the operation, he ordered, was to be continued until the British were driven from the entire Greek mainland, including the Peloponnese.[235]

From the point of view of coordination between 'Marita' and 'Barbarossa', Hitler's decision had disastrous consequences. The numerous delays in the start of the former, as well as the continual increase in the number of troops involved, had caused OKH considerable headaches during the winter; and Hitler's decision completely upset the timetables governing the relationship between the two campaigns. For one thing, the duration of 'Marita' – that of the operation itself as well as the time required to transport the troops back northward – was extended very considerably. As a result, the chief-of-staff of Twelfth army told OKH, it was no longer possible to count on the units of the army for 'Barbarossa'. Halder himself did not go that far, and after a conference with Heusinger he expressed the hope that it would still be possible to bring up the 'fast' – i.e. armoured and motorized – divisions of Twelfth army in time to participate in the assault of army group south, for which they were earmarked.[236] On the other hand, Halder conceded that the infantry divisions, as well as AOK 12 itself, which would be required for occupation duties in the expanded area of Greece, would not be available in Rumania to take part in 'Barbarossa'.[237]

This realization led to far reaching changes in the plan for 'Barbarossa' itself. Under the original deployment order Twelfth army, after completing its tasks in Greece, was to return to Rumania and form the southern prong of army group south. Its task was to advance into Russia from Wallachia and, in conjunction with the northern prong formed by Sixth and Seventeenth armies, encircle the Russian forces in the Ukraine before they could escape across the Don. Now, however, Hitler convinced himself that the Pruth formed a formidable obstacle in front of Twelfth army, which, moreover, could count only on part of the forces earmarked for it in the original plan of deployment. He therefore decided, against strong opposition from OKH, to dispense altogether with the southern prong of army group south and to deploy *Panzergruppe* Kleist, originally supposed to supply the punch to the advance of Twelfth army, north of the Carpathians. Only comparatively weak forces, sufficient to protect the oil fields against Soviet surprises, were to remain in Rumania under Eleventh army, while Twelfth army was to stay in Greece for occupation duties. The whole change amounted to a considerable reduction of the offensive power of army group south, which would have six infantry divisions less to attack with.[238] This was ultimately to have far reaching consequences.[239]

The order to occupy the entire Greek mainland had yet another result. In spite of all alterations, Halder on 16 March still hoped it would be possible to start the Russian campaign – minus the infantry divisions of Twelfth army – on the date originally envisaged, provided Hitler complied with the OKH's request not to march stage III into Bulgaria, so that the latter could start redeploying for 'Barbarossa' on 10 April.[240] Hitler's decision, however, made it necessary to commit stronger forces than originally intended to operation 'Marita', and this sealed the fate of the timely start to 'Barbarossa'. On 12 March, a dispute had broken out between OKW and OKH as to which of the forces of stage III should, if necessary, be marched into Bulgaria; 183rd infantry division or 4th mountain division. Although Halder argued that the acceptance of OKW's proposal to select 4th mountain division would involve delay to 'Barbarossa',[241] Hitler allowed OKW to have its way and ordered 4th mountain division to enter Bulgaria on 19 March.[242] After Hitler's order to occupy the entire Greek mainland OKW seems to have realized its error, for Warlimont now suggested that only 4th mountain division was to be subordinated to Twelfth army, while the rest of stage III was to stay in Rumania.[243]

Now, however, the positions were reversed. Brauchitsch claimed that he needed additional forces in order to cope with the extended objectives of 'Marita', and on 22 March he got his way. High commands XIth and Lth army corps, together with 46th, 294th and 76th infantry divisions were ordered to cross the Danube and join 4th mountain division.[244] The rest of the forces of stage III were to stay in Rumania and were divided between the Russian front and the army mission.[245] Anticipating these orders, OKH had already given instructions that the forces of stage III now earmarked for Bulgaria should not march to the Dobrudja – from where they had originally been supposed to take up positions against Turkey – but concentrate in the Corabia–Craiova–Slatina–Bucharest–Oltenita area, from where they were to pass over the bridges at Turnu Magurele and Giurgiu and so on by roads Nos. 2 and 3 to the Greek frontier.[246] On 22 March List, who by now must have been thoroughly confused, received a list of the units at his disposal for the attack on Greece. These included high commands XXXXth, XVIIIth, XXXth and Lth army corps, 2nd and 9th armoured divisions, 46th, 50th, 73rd, 164th and 294th infantry divisions, 4th, 5th and 6th mountain divisions, and infantry regiment 125. The staff of *Panzergruppe* Kleist was assigned completely new tasks within the framework of the new deployment plan of 'Barbarossa', and was therefore ordered back to Bucharest. High command XIVth army corps, as well as 5th and 11th armoured divisions, were detailed for cover against Turkey 'for a limited period', and were to be back in Rumania between 10 and 18 April. SS 'AH', too, was to be back in Rumania by 3 May, which meant that it could participate in the early stages of 'Marita'.[247] Finally, the changes in 'Barbarossa' left 16th armoured division without an offensive task in Rumania, and OKH now hoped to extract it by 25 March.[248]

The picture painted by these directives is a clear one. Though OKH was making every effort to get its armoured divisions out, it was now known that neither Twelfth army nor its infantry divisions would arrive on whatever date had been selected for the start of 'Barbarossa'.[249] There followed, therefore, a series of desperate, eleventh hour measures designed to speed up the termination of operation 'Marita', not all of them successful. Thus, we find OKH asking Twelfth army to dispense with a number of army troops, a request which, because most of the units in question had already reached the Greek frontier and could not be marched back over the narrow Bulgarian roads without hopelessly disrupting the build-up of stage III, was fulfilled only in part.[250] More successful was the effort to advance the starting date of the operation. According to the most recent timetable the attack was to begin on A (= Danube crossing) + 36 days, i.e. 7 April.[251] As a result of the decision to occupy the entire mainland, however, OKW now considered the start of operations on 1 April 'desirable'.[252] On 22 March a directive to this effect, bristling with '*schnell*'-s and '*rasch*'-es was dispatched to Twelfth army.[253] Although his deployment was still incomplete, List gracefully complied and scheduled the beginning of the attack for 1 April.[254]

Finally, Hitler's decision led to a last ditch attempt by the senior staff to get the trains rolling through Yugoslavia at all costs. The problem was still as important as ever, only more so. Out of 128 supply trains scheduled to roll into Bulgaria before A day, only 80 had – because of the limited capacity of the Bulgarians to handle them –

arrived, creating a considerable backlog. As soon as the German troops crossed the Danube heavy congestion was formed in the Dobrudja, because the Bulgarians were hopelessly incapable of processing the 8 to 12 trains that were to supply Twelfth army each day. Inside Bulgaria, too, the railways were unable to fulfil even a small fraction of the requirements of Twelfth army and VIIIth air corps, the main bottleneck being the lack of locomotives. All this made it extraordinarily difficult to supply the army, and Greiffenberg duly suggested that the only way to ease up the situation was to get the trains rolling from Vienna through Yugoslavia directly into Sofia.[255]

The problem of supplying Twelfth army was not the only one that was well nigh insoluble without having recourse to the Yugoslav railroads. Even more important, because of the extremely tight timetable governing the withdrawal of the units of Twelfth army for 'Barbarossa', was the question of having the troops pass through Yugoslavia on their way back from Greece. Although the generals knew perfectly well that 'transports through Yugoslavia have been completely renounced in the negotiations with that country',[256] they kept returning to the idea with singular tenacity. On 13 March Warlimont asked Ritter if:

The assurance given to Yugoslavia . . . that upon its accession to the Tripartite Pact no troops will be transported through Yugoslavia is to be regarded as binding. Chief L points to the extraordinary importance of these transports in view of the rapid regrouping of the forces committed in 'Marita' for operation 'Barbarossa'.

Minister Ritter replies that to his mind there can be no doubt concerning the binding power of the assurances to abstain from troop transports through Yugoslavia . . . the stress is laid on the fact that TROOP TRANSPORTS [emphasis in the original] will not take place. This does not exclude a latter agreement concerning the transportation of supplies and materials.[257]

Warlimont thereupon undertook to inform the high command of the army of these facts, and did so in a letter two days later.[258] However, the matter was too important to end there. Despite the OKW directive on 16 March Halder kept wondering whether it would not, after all, be possible to utilize the Yugoslav railroads on the way back from Greece.[259] When Hitler had expanded the army's objectives in Greece the question became even more urgent; although the German radio promised that Germany would not demand rights of transit for either troops or war material,[260] OKW on 21 March demanded that 'the question of transport through Yugoslavia will be raised immediately after the accession to the Tripartite Pact, as there is no railway connection from Bulgaria to Greece'.[261] Despite everything, on 24 March Warlimont, still hoped that some arrangement would be made; and two days later Halder noted that without the use of Yugoslavia's railways operation 'Marita' would be 'exceedingly difficult'.[262]

OKW and OKH left no stone unturned in their efforts to convince the foreign ministry of the importance of opening a way through Yugoslavia, but on 25 March they had to admit defeat. On that day Yugoslavia signed the Tripartite Pact, receiving in return a written assurance that Germany would not demand the passage or transportation of troops through her territory during the war. In that the beginning of the attack was now imminent, it was too late to help Twelfth army anyhow. Only material could be expected – perhaps – to be allowed to pass through Yugoslavia on the way back.

By 25 March 1941 the deployment of Twelfth army and VIIIth air corps in Bulgaria was, for all practical purposes, complete. List has fixed his headquarters at Camkorja, Richthofen at Dzumaja. From west to east, the following forces were ranged on the Greek frontier: 6th mountain division at the extreme southwestern corner of Bulgaria; 5th mountain division with infantry regiment 125th in the Menlik area; 72nd infantry division near the point where the river Mesta (Nestos) enters Greece. All these forces were under the command of XVIIIth mountain corps. Further to the east, 164th and 50th infantry divisions were standing on the frontier under the command of XXXth corps with its headquarters at Chaskovo. The 4th mountain division was on its way on road No. 1 to join 5th mountain division. The 2nd armoured and SS 'AH' divisions were standing on the Yugoslav frontier, the one in the Kustendil area and the other further north in the Sofia–Dimotrovgrad area. The 73rd infantry and 60th motorized divisions were concentrated round Plovdiv under the command of XXXXth corps serving as strategic reserve. The 9th armoured division was stationed further to the east round Stara Zagora under the command of XIVth corps. Even farther to the east stood the two divisions which were to cover 'Marita' against Turkish intervention: 11th armoured in the Sliven–Jambol area, 5th armoured round Burgas. From the north, 294th, 46th and 76th infantry divisions, all belonging to stage III, were still on their way. Everything was getting into position when a dramatic event turned the tables: in the night of 26–27 March, a *coup d'état* overthrew the government in Belgrade.

27 MARCH AND AFTER

'I fear', Prince Paul told Hitler on 4 March, 'that if I follow your advice and sign the Tripartite Pact I shall no longer be here in six months.' Opposition to the pact was, indeed, strong in Yugoslavia. During the entire winter, when it seemed that Yugoslavia was slowly but inexorably being drawn into the orbit of the Axis, Prince Paul and the members of his cabinet were constantly pestered with warnings by the opponents of the Pact.

The most important of these were not Yugoslavs at all, but outsiders. Roosevelt, Churchill and Stalin understood Yugoslavia's importance just as well as did Hitler; because of her strategical position at the rear of the Italian forces in Albania and on the flank of the German army in Bulgaria, Yugoslavia's neutrality was not desired by any of the great powers. President Roosevelt in particular was persistent in his attempts to convince the Yugoslavs that it was in their own interest to resist Hitler; on 23 January a special emissary of his, Colonel William Donovan, arrived in Belgrade with some high sounding phrases about the preservation of national honour and a not so veiled ultimatum to the effect that if Yugoslavia allowed the passage of German troops the United States would not interfere on her behalf at the peace table.[1]

The recipient of this warning, the Prince Regent, was by this time a broken man. Even his enemies have scarcely questioned the sincerity of his sympathies for England; he had been educated at Oxford, felt like an Englishman and was married to a Greek princess. Yet his regency was to come to an end in a few months, and he did not want to hand over a country devastated by war to his nephew, King Peter II. On 18 and again on 23 February he explained Yugoslavia's position to Arthur Lane, the United States Minister; Yugoslavia would not take military action if the Germans entered Bulgaria, for to do so would clearly put her in the wrong and the need for such action would not be understood by the Croat and Slovene sections of the population. The Yugoslav army was not ready for war; even if it were, it would be impossible to do the strategically correct thing and concentrate the troops in the southern part of the country, for political considerations made it imperative that Croatia and Slovenia should not be abandoned.

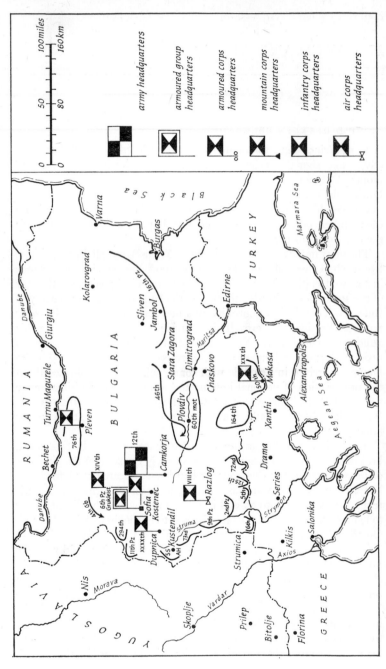

Map 1 German dispositions in the Balkans 27 March 1941

Operating from both Temesvar – where the frontier was unfortified – and Sofia, the Germans could easily cut the country in half and crush her within two weeks.[2] Roosevelt's assurance that the United States were looking 'not merely to the present but to the future'[3] was of little value to the Prince Regent; Hitler's armoured divisions were so very much nearer than any aid the American president, or for that matter the British prime minister, could promise. Yugoslavia, Prince Paul and Cvetkovic assured the United States minister, would resist attack and not allow the transportation of German troops across her territory; but that was as far as she would go. She would sign the Tripartite Pact – although not the article providing for military assistance – and would certainly not fight, even if the Germans occupied Salonika.[4]

Like their American friends, the British exercised strong pressure on Yugoslavia to resist the Nazis; unlike them, they were not prepared to take 'no' for an answer. While Lane admitted failure by pointing out to Prince Paul that the United States had never asked Yugoslavia to attack Germany or the Axis,[5] Churchill, convinced that it was the right and even the duty of great powers to sacrifice small neutrals for the sake of victory over Nazism,[6] wanted them to do just that. In his view a magnificent opportunity presented itself to the Serbs in the form of an attack on the Italian rear and flank in Albania. Such an operation, he argued, would not only crush the Italians and thus liberate Greek troops for use against the Germans but also supply the Yugoslavs with the arms and equipment they were so desperately demanding.[7] The British were as well aware of Yugoslavia's difficulties as the Americans,[8] but were apparently determined to get her into the war at all costs. When hints about possible revision – after the war, of course – of the Italo–Yugoslav frontier proved unavailing,[9] they decided to resort to underhand means. For this purpose they had even founded the so-called 'ministry of ungentlemanly warfare'.

It is very hard to say how far the Belgrade coup of 27 March was the result of the machinations of foreign agents. The first foreigners to receive notice of the possibility were, apparently, the Germans, whom Prince Paul warned against such an eventuality on 4 March and who received reports of the unrest the expected Yugoslav accession to the Tripartite Pact was causing in the population and the army one week later. The British, if their official history is to be believed, were unaware of such a possibility until 21 March, when the resignation of three Yugoslav ministers in protest against the Pact made it clear that official opinion was not at all unanimous in favouring it.[10] On 24 March the foreign minister, Eden, authorized Campbell 'to proceed at [his] discretion by any means at [his] disposal to move leaders and public opinion . . . to action to meet the situation'; two days later Churchill sent his famous telegram to his representative in Belgrade to 'pester, nag and bite . . . do not neglect any alternative to which we may have to resort if we find present government have gone beyond recall'.[11] Yet the man who was to be the brain behind the coup, General Bora Mirkovic of the Yugoslav air force, seems to have started contemplating a revolt as early as 1937, when Stoyadinovic was apparently out to turn the country into an Italian satellite.[12] Though it may be true, as some allege, that the conspirators received British aid and were promised in advance that their government would be recognized, there can be little doubt but that the origins of the *coup* were essentially Yugoslav – or rather, Serb – and not foreign.

The details of the *coup* have been described elsewhere and need not be repeated here.[13] The brain behind it was, as I have already said, General Mirkovic who was motivated by a peculiar mixture of Serb nationalism and a romantic conception of the traditional role of the Serb army in setting right erring politicians in the national interest. Its figurehead – or was he more than a figurehead? – was General Dusan Simovic, commander of the Yugoslav air force, a man who had been demoted several times for his political activities and always managed to reach the top again. On 23 March he is said to have warned Prince Paul that he would 'have trouble restraining his fliers' if Yugoslavia signed the Pact.[14] The other conspirators were air force officers, members of the Belgrade Reserve Office Club and civilians from the Serb Cultural Club. This central group formed personal contacts among Serb officers – all of junior rank – dispersed in garrisons all over the country. It seems that only a very small number of people knew the details or had been assigned specific tasks in advance. The *coup* was directed by Mirkovic from Simovic's office while the commander of the air force – either because he was a mere figurehead or because he knew he was being followed and wanted to cover up the activities of his fellow conspirators – spent the night of the *coup* at home.

Cvetkovic and Cincar Markovic returned to Belgrade from Vienna early on 26 March. A few hours later Mirkovic and Simovic decided to act that very night. That evening the commander of the air force was placed on the retired list, but this belated counter-measure no longer disturbed Mirkovic. One after the other, he summoned the officers of the air force headquarters to Simovic's office, placed them in command of the troops protecting the base and dispatched them to occupy the Belgrade police headquarters, the main post offices and telephone exchanges, the broadcasting station, the ministry of war. Special detachments were sent to arrest Cvetkovic, Cincar Markovic and other ministers. By the morning the royal palace outside Belgrade had been surrounded and young Peter's voice was imitated on the radio in a call to the Yugoslav peoples to rally behind the King.[15] By eleven o'clock the resistance of the royal guard had been broken – without, however, a shot being fired – and Peter was brought to the war ministry. By this time, the *coup* was an accomplished fact. Prince Paul, who was on his way to his estate in the north of the country, was intercepted near Zagreb, and after conferring with Macek and rejecting the latter's suggestion to call upon the troops in Croatia to suppress the *coup* returned to Belgrade. Received by Simovic, he was driven through the streets of the capital – which by now were bedecked with French, English and Yugoslav flags and were swarming with a wildly enthusiastic population – to the war ministry, where he signed his resignation as regent. Later that evening he and his family left for Athens.

A new government had now to be established. Sometime on 27 March King Peter was made to sign the proclamation which Simovic had already had read on the radio, thus restropectively legitimizing the *coup*. The next day he was crowned by Patriarch Gavrilo. Simovic became prime minister, General Illic – a friend of Mirkovic's – minister for war. The rest of the government consisted of prominent Serbs representing all legal political parties. The Slovene and Croat ministers remained at their posts, although Macek himself took several days to make up his mind to remain as vice premier. After some argument between Simovic and Groll of the Serb democratic party the ancient Nincic was hauled from his house and assigned the portfolio of foreign affairs. This was a highly significant appointment, for Nincic was chairman of the Italo–Yugoslav and German–Yugoslav societies and his tenure of the same office in 1927 was marked by friendly relations with both countries.

Nincic's appointment was the first, but not the last, indication of the course the new government was going to follow in foreign policy. On 28 March Simovic told Lane that he wanted to avoid any discussion of the Tripartite Pact; it had not been negotiated by his government and had not yet been ratified. Not wishing to provoke Germany, however, he would neither denounce nor ratify the pact, but he would resist a German move on Salonika.[16] Next day Nincic pointed out that the Pact could not be repudiated because it became effective upon signature.[17] Thus, Yugoslavia's new rulers in effect adopted the very policy against which they had risen; they realized the vital importance of Salonika, refused a British request that Eden might visit Belgrade, and carefully tried to avoid provoking Germany. True, they did agree to a secret visit by General John Dill the chief of the Imperial Staff. The latter, after conferring with Simovic, reported that he had found only confusion and paralysis in Yugoslavia. They seemed to believe that they had months in which to make decisions and more months to put them into effect.[18]

Somebody else, however, did not require months to make decisions, nor to put them into practice. To Hitler the Yugoslav *coup* came as a painful surprise. The flank which he believed had been made secure by Yugoslavia's accession to the Tripartite Pact was now threatened by the million-strong army of a government that had established itself in protest against that Pact. Drastic action seemed to be called for.

THE NEW DEPLOYMENT

'The population of the capital,' Heeren wired on 26 March, 'is universally most deeply impressed' by the signature of the Tripartite Pact. The government, he added, had to disperse a few minor demonstrations, but was 'completely master of the situation'.[19] Driving through the beflagged streets of Belgrade next morning, he must have wanted to eat his words. Heeren made his first attempt to get in touch with the new government as soon as he heard about the *coup*; arriving at the war ministry on the morning of 27 March, however, he was told that Simovic was too busy to receive him and had to content himself with a conversation with Nincic, who assured him that his own selection as foreign minister 'guaranteed the continuity of the cooperation with the Axis powers, particularly with Germany'. He personally would see to it that 'those obligations which had been assumed would also be observed'.[20] Received by Simovic on the same evening, the new prime minister tried to convince the German minister that he had always been Germany's friend.[21] On 30 March Nincic summoned Heeren to submit the statement that 'the present Royal Yugoslav government remains true to the principle of respect for international treaties which have been signed, among which the protocol signed on the 25th of this month at Vienna belongs'.[22] On the same day Heeren reported that he had learnt that the majority of the new cabinet were in favour of unconditional recognition of Yugoslavia's accession to the Tripartite Pact.[23] This was the last report Heeren was to send because, having already been instructed to exercise the greatest reserve, he was called home on the same day 'for the purpose of reporting'.[24]

To Hitler the Yugoslav attempts to save what could be saved were so much drivel. He must have received news of the *coup* as early as 1000 or 1100 hours in the morning, for Ribbentrop informed his Japanese colleague of the *Putsch* during a conversation between them. 'At this moment', the verbal report ends, 'the Reich foreign minister was summoned to the Reich Chancellery. Contrary to his original assumption that this would mean only a short absence, the discussion there lasted quite a while, so that the conversation with Matsuoka could not be continued before lunch. Thereupon the lunch which was on the programme was held in a very intimate circle [i.e. in the company of totally insignificant clerks], at first without the Reich foreign minister, who did not appear until later.'[25] It is very hard to trace the exact sequence of the events that followed. At 1155 hours Heeren's first telegram, announcing large demonstrations 'in favour of the King and the army ... and explicitly directed against accession to the Tripartite Pact' arrived in Berlin.[26] Five minutes later Halder received a telephone call ordering him to the *Reichskanzlei*. The chief of the general staff must have heard about the *coup* from another source, for he did not find it too hard to guess what the discussion with Hitler would be about.[27]

After the war much has been made of the fact that the need to prepare a campaign against Yugoslavia took the German army by surprise. The very speed with which Halder could, during his journey by car from Zossen to Berlin, prepare a plan for the invasion of Yugoslavia from no less than four directions belies this 'fact'. Indeed, he and Heusinger had always thought such an operation possible, and had studied it in October. According to their plan, it was to be carried out by XXXXth army corps, then stationed in Vienna and forming part of Twelfth army.[28] Moreover, there are indications that Halder did not limit himself to military planning, but went on to prepare the diplomatic background for the operation. In Nüremberg evidence was produced by the Soviet prosecution that he and Keitel had, in November and December 1940, got in touch with the Hungarian chief of the general staff and war minister by means of the German military attaché in Budapest. OKH, Halder explained to his Hungarian opposite number, wanted to make plans for future preventive war against Yugoslavia, to be launched in the spring. The operation aimed at excluding the menace 'at a later date' of a Soviet attack 'from the rear'. For this purpose, Germany would supply Hungary with 10 cm cannon and modern tanks to equip a mobile brigade.[29] Thus it is clear that Hitler's decision to smash Yugoslavia did not catch the army unawares. In Halder's own words later (quite different of course from his Nüremberg account) the theoretical (*gedanklichen*) preparations had been made many months earlier, and it was necessary only to complete the material preparations.[30] Even here OKH did not have to start from scratch, because the establishment of a large supply depot near Vienna in the summer of 1940 made it unnecessary to bring up supplies from the interior of the Reich and greatly facilitated the operation.[31]

On his arrival in Berlin at 1300 hours[32] the chief-of-staff found that a conference attended by Hitler, Keitel, Jodl, Göring and the Führer's four adjutants was already under way. Soon Brauchitsch, Heusinger, Rintelen and Ribbentrop were also called in. Hitler spoke in curt, tough sentences. Yugoslavia had always been an uncertain factor, especially in view of the future operation 'Barbarossa'. Serbs and Slovenes were traditionally anti-German. No document signed by a Yugoslav government could be trusted, because the danger of a *coup* was always there. As it was, the situation was not too bad, for the *coup* would have been far more dangerous if it had taken place after the start of the Russian campaign. Hitler professed himself determined to smash Yugoslavia as a political entity without waiting for the diplomatic explanations and declarations of loyalty which would surely arrive in a few days. Hungarian and Bulgarian cooperation could be depended on. The Führer then laid down the outlines of a concentric attack to be launched against Yugoslavia from Bulgaria (Sofia – Kustendil) and Austria (Graz) with strong Hungarian forces invading the country from the north and Italian troops operating from the Julian Alps. The operation was to open with a bombardment of Belgrade.

None of those present tried to dispute Hitler's decision. The need for it was only too obvious. Brauchitsch pointed out that the Führer's plans largely coincided with those prepared by the army, Göring that his air force could immediately start action against Yugoslavia from Bulgarian air fields but would require two or three days to bring up reinforcements. Hitler then instructed Jodl to outline the results of the discussion in a directive which he would sign. With that the conference adjourned.[33]

The same evening 'directive No. 25' was issued. It read:

The military revolt in Yugoslavia has changed the political position in the Balkans. Yugoslavia . . . must be regarded as an enemy and beaten down as quickly as possible.

It is my intention to break into Yugoslavia in the general direction of Belgrade and to the south by a concentric operation from the Fiume-Graz area on one side, and the Sofia area on the other, and to deal an annihilating blow to the Yugoslav forces. Further, the extreme southern region of the country will be occupied as a base from which the German–Italian offensive against Greece can be continued.

I issue the following detailed orders:

a. As soon as sufficient forces are available and the weather allows, the ground installations of the Yugoslav air force and the city of Belgrade will be destroyed from the air . . .

b. If possible simultaneously – but in no event earlier – undertaking 'Marita' will begin with the temporarily limited objective of occupying the Salonika Basin and gaining a foothold on the heights of Edessa. For this purpose XVIIIth army corps can advance through Yugoslav territory . . .

c. All forces still available in Bulgaria and Rumania will be committed to the attacks which will be carried out from the Sofia area to the northwest and from the Kustendil–Gorna–Dzumaya area to the west, with the exception that a force of about one division, with air support, must remain to protect the Rumanian oil fields. The protection of the Turkish frontier will, for the time being, be left to the Bulgarians. A German formation consisting if possible of an armoured division will stand by in the rear in support.

d. The thrust from the general direction of Graz towards the southeast

will be made as soon as the necessary forces have been assembled. The army
is free to decide whether Hungarian territory should be crossed in breaching
the frontier . . .

e. The air force will support with two groups the operations of 12th army
and of the assault group now being formed in the Graz area . . . the possibility
of bringing up Xth air corps into action from Italian bases will be considered.[34]

The Führer, Halder told Paulus when placing him in command of the
operation on the same day, had decided to invade Yugoslavia for the
following reasons: 1. To protect the flank of the offensive to be launched
from Bulgaria against Greece. 2. To gain possession of the railway line
from Belgrade via Nisch to the south. 3. To make sure of his right
flank before starting 'Barbarossa'.[35] From the point of view of Germany's overall strategy operation '25' was therefore similar to 'Marita'
in the sense that both aimed to secure the right flank of the future
Russian campaign. Moreover, Hitler's decision to invade Yugoslavia
was not without advantages from the purely operational point of view;
the army's long-standing demand to open up the Yugoslav railways
for use during 'Marita' and the redeployment for 'Barbarossa' could
now be realized, and at the same time the opportunity of circumventing
the Metaxas line presented itself. But we had better postpone discussion of these aspects of the operation for a little while.

After the conference at the *Reichskanzlei* Hitler dictated a letter to
his main ally. Yugoslavia, he explained, had been an uncertain factor
right from the beginning. At long last her attitude was now clear.
The situation was serious but not disastrous. Mussolini was asked not
to start anything in Albania during the next few days and to make
sure his left flank was adequately guarded.[36] In accordance with
Hitler's explicit instructions, Mackensen delivered the letter that very
night, dragging the Duce out of bed and causing him to complain that
the Germans had less consideration for him than he had for his
servant.[37] The following day Rintelen arrived with more detailed
military instructions, drafted by Hitler during the night; the Italians
were to redeploy their forces in Albania, stage an offensive from across
the Julian Alps and take care of the Yugoslav naval forces.[38] It seems
that Mussolini, who was none too happy about the Führer's decision
to finally settle the question of the sphere of influence to which Yugoslavia belonged, made some attempt to mediate. On 30 March Ribbentrop therefore told Ciano that the assurances Italy received from
Belgrade[39] were worthless and that the attack would go ahead.[40]

On 27 March Hitler also contacted the Hungarian and Bulgarian
representatives. The Yugoslavs, he raged, had gone stark mad. Him
whom the gods would destroy they first struck blind. Budapest and
Sofia were asked to cooperate in the liquidation of Yugoslavia and

would receive slices of her territory for their pains. Here, however, Hitler faced a disappointment; King Boris politely refused to help, while the Hungarians limited their participation to some ten infantry and armoured brigades which were to attack on 14 April. Hitler, who had originally hoped for much greater Hungarian participation and had asked General Antonescu of Rumania to evacuate Temesvar so that Hungarian troops could operate from that area now changed his plans and had General Reinhardt's XXXXIst corps march on Temesvar instead.[41]

On 28 March the forces earmarked to carry out operation '25' began to deploy. Basically, the movements that took place in the next few days can be divided into two parts: those carried out by Twelfth army, which had to redeploy its forces in Bulgaria in order to comply with the new orders, and those of Second army, newly assembled in the Graz area in preparation for an advance into the northern part of Yugoslavia. The crucial difference between the two armies was that, while Twelfth army disposed of units that were about to start their attack on Greece and required only to be wheeled round in order to face Yugoslavia, the divisions of Second army had to be hurriedly collected from all over Europe. For this reason the concentration of the forces for operation '25' is best studied in two parts.

Twelfth army started its deployment on 28 March; the order to do so arrived just in time, because List had already – in accordance with the instructions received from OKH on 22 March[42] – released the staff of *Panzergruppe* Kleist, which was just setting out on its way to Bucharest, and was about to dispatch 5th and 11th armoured, as well as SS 'AH' divisions in the same direction. This would leave Twelfth army with only three corps to carry out the attack on Greece. The XVIIIth corps was to attack in the west; XXXth corps in the east; and XXXXth corps, stationed in the rear near Plovdiv, was to serve as a strategic reserve.

'Directive No. 25', however, changed the situation completely. For one thing, it was now possible to utilize southern Yugoslavia in order to stage the attack on Greece; and this was a move which List, who was not at all eager to launch a frontal attack against the naturally strong Metaxas and Kaimaktsalan–Vermion–Olympus lines, was only too willing to carry out. He therefore moved XXXXth corps west from Plovdiv to Dupnica together with 9th armoured and 73rd infantry divisions subordinated to it. Instead of returning to Rumania, SS 'AH' moved south and joined the corps.

'Directive No. 25' had also ordered Twelfth army to stage an attack from Sofia via Nisch against Belgrade. For this purpose Kleist and his staff were called back and set up their headquarters at Kustendil. The *Panzergruppe* was assigned 294th infantry and 4th mountain divisions, as well as 5th and 11th armoured divisions. The latter two units were marched from east to west right across Bulgaria, their task of protecting the Turkish frontier being taken over by 16th armoured division which had come down from Rumania and deployed on an extremely long front from Kolarvograd through Sliven to Stara Zagora. Kleist naturally regarded his own attack as Twelfth army's most important task and therefore demanded 60th motorized division as reinforcement. List would have preferred to use the division in support of XXXXth corps, but Halder, who together with Hitler overestimated Yugoslavia's fighting power, supported Kleist and the commander of Twelfth army had to give way.[43]

While very considerable changes took place in the deployment on the eastern and western frontiers of Bulgaria, the situation on her southern border remained basically unchanged. The 2nd armoured division was transferred south and placed under the command of XVIIIth corps for the purpose of outflanking the Metaxas line by a lunge over Yugoslav territory, while 4th mountain division, as already mentioned, was taken back northward and placed under Kleist. The only force that remained virtually unaffected by the changes was XXXth corps deployed in western Thrace opposite Xanthi. All in all, Twelfth army thus shifted the bulk of its forces to the west in a series of complicated and very difficult – because of the quality of the Bulgarian roads and the weather – movements; on the other hand, it had been necessary to bring up only two divisions (16th armoured and 198th infantry) not originally earmarked for 'Marita', none of which was to see action.

If the movements of Twelfth army were greatly hampered by the state of the Bulgarian road network, it did at least have its units within a reasonable distance of their new deployment areas. No so Colonel General von Weich's Second army, which was detailed to carry out the attack on Yugoslavia from the north. When first allocating forces for operation 'Marita' the Wehrmacht had had at its disposal a large number of divisions unengaged on any operation, among which OKH was free to choose. In March 1941, however, such divisions as were not used as garrisons in the occupied territories or engaged in reorganization within the plan for the enlargement of the army were for the most part incorporated in a series of vast movements from west to east and from east to west; there was no 'free' reservoir of forces OKH could send to Yugoslavia, and the divisions of Second army had therefore to be taken from those earmarked for 'Barbarossa'. In order to understand the problems connected with the concentration of Second army, as well as the all-important question of the effect of this concentration on the build-up for 'Barbarossa', it is necessary to delve a little into the history of the latter.

The plans laying down the details of the army build-up for 'Barbarossa' were prepared by Heusinger's operations department and submitted to Halder on 29 January,[44] together with the deployment order to which they were appended. Four days later Halder explained them to Hitler. The principle governing the proposed timetables was that of delaying the introduction of the maximum capacity railway schedule for as long as possible, partly in order to avoid giving up the camouflage and partly for economic reasons.[45] The need to preserve the camouflage for as long as possible also dictated that the majority of the forces, including practically all the 'fast' (i.e. armoured and motorized) units, were to be brought up at the last possible moment. The build-up was divided into four stages, the first of which was already in progress at the time of Halder's report.[46] The second, comprising 17 divisions, was scheduled to start rolling east at a rather leisurely pace in mid-March and to last until mid-April.[47] The third and fourth stages, scheduled to start moving on 12 and 25 April respectively, included between them the majority of the units involved in the build-up and, unlike their predecessors, were to employ the maximum capacity railroad schedule. The 'fast' forces were concentrated in stage IV, while the tail of the transports was formed by the armoured and motorized divisions coming up from the Balkans. The strategic reserves for the Russian campaign were not included in this build-up; they were to start rolling only after the beginning of hostilities in a fifth stage.[48]

Although OKH had warned OKW on 31 January that after 10 March it would no longer be possible to introduce major changes in the build-up,[49] on 17 March Hitler abolished the entire right wing of army group south and thereby forced OKH to revise its plans. On 21 February Halder sent an officer to explain the army build-up to OKW, which consequently ordered the other two branches of the Wehrmacht to prepare their own schedules for incorporation into that of the army.[50] The overall OKW timetable was not to be ready before mid-March.[51] Until that time only 2500 out of the 17,000 trains comprising the build-up had run to the east, mainly carrying infantry divisions;[52] the beginning of the concentration of the 'fast' divisions was still five weeks away, while that of the various army troops did not start until 19 March.[53]

This, then, was the situation of the 'Barbarossa' build-up at the time of the Yugoslav *coup*: its timetable had only just been laid down, its transports were proceeding at a rather leisurely pace on a peace-time railway schedule, and the majority of the forces had not yet moved from the bases where they were engaged in regrouping and training. At the same time as these west–east movements, 21 divisions – mostly of second class quality – were engaged on a series of movements from east to west. The purpose of this manoeuvre was to deceive foreign agents – as well as the troops themselves – into thinking that Germany was preparing for an invasion of England in the spring.[54]

It is extremely hard to say when all these preparations were supposed to end and the invasion of Russia to start. Historical opinion has mostly named 15 May as the day, but 'directive No. 21', on which this opinion is usually based, merely says that those preparations requiring more than eight weeks were to be completed by that date. During the important conference of 5 December 'end May' was specified.[55] In fact, since the starting date would take the weather into account, it is doubtful whether the beginning of the attack could have been determined at so early a date; late in March it was still open, with 15 May as the *terminus post quam*.[56] On 24 February Halder raised the idea of securing the equipment of the reserves before that of the divisions to be supplied with French material, which according to this suggestion were to be ready only on 1 June.[57] Since five crucially important armoured divisions were involved, the very fact that such a suggestion could be raised shows that no date earlier than June was envisaged. This, even before the extension of the objectives of 'Marita' on 17 March made it impossible for the infantry divisions of Twelfth army to arrive on time. All in all, it is unsafe to place the date for the projected invasion of Russia than the first week of June.

What was the effect of Hitler's decision to invade Yugoslavia on the build-up for 'Barbarossa'? Having analysed the latter in some detail, we are now in a position to supply an answer that is more than a mere guess. To begin with, it is perfectly clear that the redeployment of Twelfth army with more than half of all the forces allocated to both 'Marita' and '25' could not have any effect on 'Barbarossa' because this army had practically all its units in Bulgaria. As to Second army and the OKH reserves for '25', it would seem that the detachment of twelve divisions from the gigantic build up for 'Barbarossa' and their diversion to the south could hardly have disrupted the latter to a very large extent, particularly as it had scarcely even got under way. A comparison of the time-tables of stages II and III of 'Barbarossa' with a list of those forces committed in the Balkans[58] shows that, when the Belgrade *coup* took place, OKH was forced to detach a grand total of 4 divisions – 1st mountain, 79th, 125th and 132nd infantry – from the transports of stage II and send them southward. As none of these forces had yet started on their way to the Russian border,[59] it was not even necessary to 'divert' them; rather, a gap was opened in the last phases of stage II, a gap which could be, and was, filled up from the OKH reserves.[60] Since the timetable of stage III does not include any of the forces listed as forming part of Twelfth and Second armies,[61] the rest of the units which transferred to the Balkans because of the *coup*

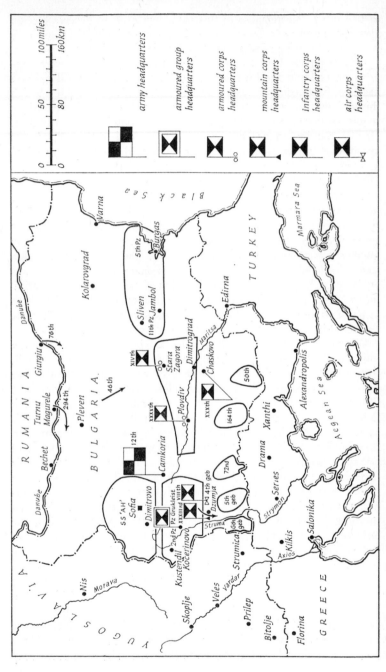

Map 2 German dispositions in the Balkans 6 April 1941

came from either stage IV or from the OKH reserves for 'Barbarossa' (the starting date for the transportation of these latter was still a very long way off). These forces were: 14th, 8th and 19th armoured divisions, 100th, 101st ('light') motorized divisions, SS 'das Reich' and 16th motorized divisions, and SS infantry regiment 'Grossdeutschland'.[62] When the *coup* took place these forces had to be hastily scraped together from France,[63] the Reich and Czechoslovakia.[64] Out of the 29 divisions that were in one way or another involved in the Balkan campaign only one – 14th armoured – had already been transported to the east.[65] Since the forces taken out of stage II could be, and were, replaced by units from the OKH reserves for 'Barbarossa', while the transportation of those included in stages IV and V was still some time away, the delay caused by the outbreak of the Yugoslav campaign to the build-up for 'Barbarossa' was limited to the time needed to prepare the OKH reserves for transportation. Even this delay, however, could be made up later on because of the very leisurely timetable governing stage III.[66]

For the purpose of concentration Second army was divided into two parts. The infantry divisions under high commands XXXXIXth, LIInd and LIst army corps were deployed in the Graz–western Styria area, which could be reached by three railway lines with a combined capacity of 78 trains per day; this meant that the combat elements of two infantry divisions could be brought up each day, while the rear services had to be disentrained in the Vienna–Salzburg area (with a total capacity of 192 trains a day) from where they were to march by road. The 'fast' units of Second army comprising 8th and 14th armoured and 16th motorized divisions, were concentrated under XXXXVIth corps in the Nagykanisza (western Hungary) area, which could be reached by only one railway line with a capacity of 12 trains daily and two roads. Here the tracked vehicles were brought up by rail, while the motorized columns and services marched by road.[67] The XXXXIst corps with SS 'das Reich' and some army troops was concentrated in the Banat, and once there, subordinated to Twelfth and not to Second army.[68] As to the OKH reserves, consisting of 12th and 19th armoured as well as 100th and 101st ('light') motorized divisions, they never got the chance to deploy at all before the campaign was as good as over.

The air force, too, redeployed in preparation for operation '25'. During the night of 27 March Göring ordered eleven groups of fighters and bombers to be concentrated round Vienna in three days. These forces were then subordinated to General Lohr of the Luftwaffe, who now united VIIIth and XIth air corps under his 4th air fleet. On 31 March, the forces of XIth air corps moved up to the Yugoslav frontier. Here they were further reinforced by units of Xth air corps coming from Sicily. In addition, General Lohr now disposed of 7th airborne division, earmarked for the occupation of Lemnos and other islands, which was now moved to Plovdiv for the purpose.[69]

How much delay to the beginning of 'Marita' was caused by operation '25'? Since 'Marita' was originally supposed to start around 1 April and in fact started on the 6th, the difference can hardly have been of the greatest significance. In its original version, the plan for operation '25' called for an intensive air bombardment of Belgrade and the ground installations of the Yugoslav air force to be carried out by Richthofen's VIIIth air corps on 1 April; the invasion of Greece was to start on 2 or 3 April; the attack on Yugoslavia on 12 April. This, then, was a staggered attack, each force going into action as soon as it was ready.[70] On the afternoon of 29 March, however, Paulus presided over a conference in which List, Weichs and Kleist took part as well as their respective chiefs-of-staff. It was agreed that operation 'Marita' would succeed more quickly if brought into closer relationship with '25', that is if XXXth corps delayed its attack on the Metaxas line until 2nd armoured division and XXXXth army corps redeployed in order to circumvent it.[71] Consequently OKH issued a new timetable according to which the bombardment by the Luftwaffe and the beginning of 'Marita' were postponed to 5 April, so as to make it possible for 2nd armoured division to complete its deployment and circumvent the Metaxas line by a lunge over Yugoslav territory on the same day. The attack from the Sofia–Kustendil area was to start on 8 April, while Second army was to attack on 12 April 'with the forces then available to it'.[72] On 2 April this timetable was still being adhered to,[73] but one day later Hitler overrode OKH and endorsed List's request to postpone the bombardment of Belgrade and the opening of 'Marita' by another 24 hours.[74] These dates were adhered to, except for the starting date for Second army; breaking into Yugoslavia from the east, *Panzergruppe* Kleist made such rapid progress that it was decided not to wait for the arrival of all Weich's forces but make a 'flying start' on 10 April. Thus, it is clear that such delay as 'operation 25' caused to 'Marita' was largely due, not to any difficulty in bringing up additional forces, but to the desire to start operations against Greece and Yugoslavia simultaneously; in the eyes of OKH and OKW the advantages of outflanking the Metaxas line clearly outweighed those of an early start of 'Marita'. The course of the campaign was to prove them right.

THE DUAL CAMPAIGN

We have seen that Yugoslavia's refusal to allow German troops to operate from her territory faced the Wehrmacht with such difficulties that, after the *coup*, it was considered worthwhile to postpone 'Marita' by a few days in order to make this possible; under the same token, Belgrade's uncertain attitude had 'bedevilled'[75] Anglo–Greek planning for months. As a result, the *coup* caught the allied forces in Greece in a singularly difficult position.

The Greek general staff started to consider the possibility of German intervention as early as December 1940. It was clear from the outset that if it did materialize the bulk of the army would have to remain in Albania, since to redeploy part of the forces in Thrace would mean that the Greeks would find themselves inferior in numbers and equipment on both fronts. The decision to leave the bulk of the army in Albania meant, of course, that the units in Macedonia and Thrace would be very much inferior to the German forces opposing them, an inferiority which could be remedied by British help, or by Turkish or Yugoslav intervention, or both.[76]

During a series of conferences in mid-January, the Greeks presented their strategical problem to the British. Both Yugoslavia and Turkey, Metaxas thought, were likely to stay neutral in face of the German–Bulgarian threat to Greece. Since the Greek army had 14 of its divisions in Albania only 4 incomplete divisions could be spared to reinforce the frontier guards in Thrace. As the German force being concentrated in Rumania was at that time estimated at 12 divisions Papagos thought that 9 British divisions would be needed to reinforce the Greek army in Thrace. Assuming Yugoslavia stayed neutral, the combined Anglo–Greek forces could then be deployed opposite the Bulgarian border from the Vardar (Axios) in the west to the Maritsa (Evros) in the east, thus covering Salonika but not eastern Thrace. If carried out in time the deployment of such strong forces might influence Yugoslavia and Turkey in Greece's favour.

General Wavell, however, replied that he did not have sufficient forces available. All he could spare from North Africa were two or three divisions and a few dozen tanks. This, Metaxas countered, was insufficient; it would contribute but little to Greek strength while giving Germany an excuse to attack. He therefore rejected the immediate dispatch of these forces.

This left Papagos with no choice but to try and deploy the five or six divisions he now thought he could spare from Albania into the best possible positions. With his weak forces, the Greek chief-of-staff reasoned, it was hopeless to try and hold eastern Macedonia and western Thrace, particularly as the Metaxas line was at its weakest in the west near Mount Belles and could be outflanked by the Germans who thus cut off the north-eastern part of Greece. From the military point of view it was therefore better to abandon eastern Macedonia and western Thrace altogether and deploy on the much shorter and more easily defensible Kaimaktsalan–Vermion–Olympus (Aliakhmon line, in

British terminology) line stretching from the Aegean to the Yugoslav frontier.

Here, however, the question of Yugoslavia's attitude came in. Politically the abandoning of Salonika involved in Papagos's plan would mean the forfeiture of such chance as there was that Yugoslavia could intervene on Greece's side, since she would then be cut off from British help. If Yugoslavia was to be brought in, therefore, Salonika had to be held. What was more, the plan assumed that Yugoslavia would stay neutral and not allow the passage of German troops; otherwise, the latter could outflank the proposed line via the Monastir Gap. If this assumption were not correct, it would be better to withdraw still further and deploy on the Olympus–Aliakhmon–Venetikos–Mount Vasilitsa–Merjani–Graeco–Albanian frontier.

On 22 February Papagos explained his conclusions to the British. Assuming Yugoslavia stayed neutral and did not allow German troops to enter, he said, the Greek army and such British forces as could be brought up should deploy on the Kaimaktsalan–Vermion–Olympus line. This, Papagos explained, meant abandoning the whole of Thrace and Greece's second city; before such an important decision could be made he thought it necessary to try once more to ascertain Belgrade's attitude. A coded message was sent to the British minister in Belgrade.[77]

The British seem to have taken a different view of the results of the conference. On 2 March strong formations of Twelfth army moved into Bulgaria; on the same day Sir John Dill, returning from Ankara where he had unsuccessfully been trying to bring in the Turks, asked Papagos why he had not pulled his troops back to the Kaimaktsalan–Vermion–Olympus line. Taken by surprise, Papagos answered that he had not yet had any reply from Belgrade. It is not clear whether the Greek or the British account of these events is correct; there may have been a misunderstanding, caused by the fact that Papagos was considerably more optimistic than either the British or his own government concerning Yugoslavia's attitude. It is quite clear, however, that both the Greeks and the British grossly overestimated the speed of the German advance across Bulgaria. Papagos and Dill thought the attack might start within 15–20 days of the Danube crossing, whereas the Germans at this time were thinking more in terms of 36 days.[78] Thus, Papagos still had twenty days in which he could have withdrawn his troops, but he did not know this, and perhaps did not want to know. This error, whether deliberate or not, made him on 2 March refuse the British request to withdraw his forces from Thrace, because he feared that in the process they might be caught by the advancing columns of the Wehrmacht. Instead, he decided on a new plan; he would leave such forces as were already manning the Metaxas line in position, while deploying the rest of his divisions and such British forces as would arrive on the Kaimaktsalan–Vermion–Olympus line. By thus splitting up his forces Papagos hoped to be able to move them forward or backward at short notice according to Yugoslavia's attitude.[79]

The difficulties did not end here. On 8 to 9 March the Greeks and the British conferred in Athens with Colonel Peresitch of the Yugoslav general staff. No definite conclusions were reached, but the very fact that the talks could take place demonstrated the supreme folly of abandoning Salonika prematurely. While Papagos was thus encouraged to hold on in Macedonia, Churchill took a different view of the matter; he evidently did not believe that Yugoslavia could be brought in, and therefore demanded why on earth the Greeks were holding so many forces in Albania, where he could see no hope of victory without such intervention.[80] Caught in this cross fire Papagos stuck to his dispositions until, on 25 March, the signing of the Tripartite Pact by Yugoslavia seemed to justify the British view. The latter accordingly offered Papagos transport to move his forces back from Thrace to the Kaimaktsalan–Vermion–Olympus line.[81]

'Just as this decision was being taken' the Belgrade *coup* again turned the tables. Unlike Hitler, who immediately made up his mind to disregard any possible diplomatic assurances and took the military measures necessary to smash Yugoslavia, the Greeks and the British were not at all clear about the significance of the *coup*. On the one hand, the nagging fear lest the Yugoslavs should allow German troops to operate from their territory could now be finally discarded. On the other the new Belgrade government quickly came to realize the dangerous situation into which it had thrust itself and exercised great reserve in its dealings with the allies.[82]

There followed a few days of uncertainty. On 28 March the British considered that Simovic 'could maintain the unity of the country, in any case in the south'. It was hoped that the Yugoslav army, whose morale was supposed to be high, would stage an offensive against the Italian rear and liquidate them 'in two or three weeks'. The Germans, in the meantime, were supposed to be held up by the 'difficulty of the ground and communications on the Balkan frontier'.[83] Papagos regarded the *coup* as a vindication of his demand to hold on to Salonika, and was eager to push forward the Greek and British forces that had in the meantime occupied the Kaimaktsalan–Vermion–Olympus line.[84] This, however, was not done, possibly because the Greek government under Alexander Koryzis – Metaxas having died on 19 January – feared lest the presence of British troops in Salonika would present Germany with a *casus belli*, or because the Simovic government continued to vacillate.[85] Thus the allied forces remained split, with Greek divisions occupying the Metaxas line and also joining British forces on the Kaimaktsalan–Vermion–Olympus line. Meanwhile, the Yugoslavs

also disappointed Papagos. Not only did a conference between him and
the deputy chief of the Yugoslav general staff on 3–4 April result in
Belgrade rejecting out of hand the proposal to attack in Albania,[86] but
the Yugoslavs refused to adhere to Papagos's strategic plan and to
concentrate the bulk of their army in southern Serbia in order to prevent the outflanking of the Metaxas line and prevent a link between the
Germans and the Italians from being formed (a link which would cut
them off from Greece). The adoption of this strategically correct plan
meant the abandoning of more than 50 per cent of Yugoslavia's
national territory, and this was a decision which Simovic and Co. could
not bring themselves to make. All they did was to allocate one army – or
rather, one corps – of four divisions for the protection of South Serbia.
The rest of the Yugoslav army with its million men and eight armies
remained where it was, that is strung out all along the very long
frontiers of the Kingdom.[87]

The resulting dispositions were suicidal. In Greece Papagos kept the
bulk of his forces – some 14 divisions – on the Albanian frontier.
Whatever was left over was spread over two different lines of defence.
Three and a half divisions held the Metaxas line. Three others, joined
by approximately three British divisions with some artillery and
armour, held the Kaimaktsalan–Vermion–Olympus line. All three
forces depended for the protection of their flank and rear on a single
Yugoslav corps. Should the Germans succeed in breaking through this
corps rapid and total disaster was inevitable. Yugoslavia and Greece
would be cut off from each other, the Metaxas and the Aliakhmon lines
outflanked, and the Greek army in Albania threatened at the rear.
After that, it would be a small matter to mop up the rest of the allied
and Yugoslav forces separately.

With General Paulus coordinating overall strategy, the Germans
were quick to exploit the situation.[88] The early morning of 6 April
witnessed a spectacular bombardment of Belgrade. Besides the losses it
caused among the civilian population of the capital it destroyed the
central organization of the Yugoslav army and thus rendered communications between the widely dispersed armies even more difficult.
At the same time XVIIIth and XXXth army corps began to prod the
Metaxas line opposite Serres and Xanthi. However, the line was very
well constructed and the fortifications made the best possible use of the
exceedingly difficult terrain, so that even heavy artillery failed to make
much of an impression. The Greek forces fought with the utmost
tenactity and won the admiration of their opponents. Although local
advances were made everywhere, in general the line held. At noon on
7 April Twelfth army had to reckon with the possibility that its forces
operating against the line would not be able to overcome the unexpectedly tough Greek resistance.

While the Greeks were holding out in the north the campaign was being decided elsewhere. Advancing westward into Yugoslavia, 9th armoured and 73rd infantry divisions under high command XXXXth army corps initially made good progress in the direction of Skoplje, but the third division subordinated to the corps, SS 'AH', ran into such stiff resistance on the part of the Yugoslav third army during the night of 6–7 April that it was doubtful whether the corps would be able to carry out all its tasks, i.e. reach the Albanian frontier, break through Monastir and Florina to the south, and secure its own northern flank against counter attacks. The smaller hook by 2nd armoured division across Yugoslav territory likewise enjoyed a good start, and the division reached Strumica in the morning of 6 April after fighting its way through the Yugoslav frontier guards. At this point, however, the division found itself unable to disengage and create sufficient room for manoeuvre to enable it to turn south. Throughout the day and most of the following night it was thus prevented from carrying out its tasks.

The morning of 7 April was the critical moment of the campaign, and the only one during which Twelfth army headquarters had to give serious consideration to possible important changes in the overall plans.[89] Confronted with the failure of both his 'right hooks' to disengage and turn south, List toyed with the idea of dispensing with the smaller of the two, subordinating 2nd armoured to XXXXth corps, bringing up 60th motorized division,[90] and dispatching the lot to Florina. While maintaining the threat to the Greek army in Albania and to the flank of the Kaimaktsalan–Vermion–Olympus line, this move would mean the abolition of an essential part of the original plans, i.e. cutting western Thrace off from the rest of Greece and capturing Salonika.

List's anxiety turned out to be unnecessary. On the morning of 7 April XXXXth corps finally broke through the third Yugoslav army and resumed its advance to Skoplje, with units of SS 'AH' proceeding rapidly through Veles and Stip to reach Monastir two days later, thus threatening the flank of the main Anglo–Greek position on the Aliakhmon. Farther east 2nd armoured division repulsed a counter attack on its flank, then wheeled south and started to descend the Vardar valley. A regular race now developed between the tanks of 2nd armoured and 5th mountain division, which had broken through the defences of the Struma Valley. It was won by a Captain Kapherer of 2nd armoured, whose advance unit was approaching the city on the night of 8–9 April. Cut off from the rest of the army, 60,000 of the best Greek troops still resisting in the Metaxas line now laid down their arms. Next morning the Germans entered Salonika.

In only three days the forces of Twelfth army had thus succeeded in breaking through the first Greek line of defence and occupying their second largest city. Its units were now facing the second and most important line of defence, while the occupation of Monastir by SS 'AH' severed the most important road from Greece to Yugoslavia and made it possible to mop them up separately. In Yugoslavia, three different forces were engaged on this task. From the area west of Sofia, *Panzergruppe* Kleist with 5th and 11th armoured, 60th motorized, 4th mountain and 294th infantry divisions started its advance into Serbia on 8 April, encountering stiff resistance. In a great many cases, roads had been destroyed. Fighting their way through the Yugoslav Fifth army Kleist's divisions occupied Nisch on 9 April, thus opening the way to Belgrade from the south. It was only after the fall of Nisch that Halder changed his orders, for he now realized that he and Kleist had overestimated the strength of the Yugoslav resistance in this area and therefore allowed List to detach 5th armoured division from the *Panzergruppe* and send it back south to reinforce the three divisions of XXXXth corps.[91]

Meanwhile other forces were also advancing on Belgrade. From Temesvar General Reinhardt's XXXXIst corps with SS 'das Reich' and SS infantry regiment 'Grossdeutschland' was descending on the city. Originally this corps had been supposed to attack only on 12 April, but Halder overruled Reinhardt's objections and made him start two days earlier.[92] The rapid advance of *Panzergruppe* Kleist convinced OKH that it was also possible to bring forward the starting date of Second army's attack from the north and northwest and on 10–11 April such divisions as had arrived got off to a 'flying start' without waiting for the concentration to be completed. The 14th armoured division advanced almost without encountering opposition through Croatia, where the enemy troops, in so far as they were not engaged in active fighting between Serbs and Croats, threw their weapons away and deserted *en masse*. The Germans reached Zagreb two days ahead of schedule on the evening of 10 April, while on 11 April the division linked up with the Italian Second army advancing from Fiume. The 8th armoured and 16th motorized divisions started to descend the Drava and the Danube in the direction of Belgrade on 11 April, reaching Novi Sad on the same day. Thus, the Yugoslav capital was threatened from no less than three directions: from the south by Kleist, from the north by Reinhardt, and from the northwest by Weichs. After 11th armoured had occupied the Avalla heights dominating the city on the evening of 12 April the honour of being first to enter it fell to an enterprising Captain Klingenberg from SS 'das Reich' who, 'with a few men', crossed the Danube during the night and hoisted the swastika on the German legation on the morning of 13 April.

So rapid was the advance on Belgrade that neither Second nor Twelfth army ever got the chance to concentrate all their forces.[93]

On 13 April Halder discussed the halting of six divisions with Brauchitsch,[94] and definite orders went out the following day.[95] Some of the divisions earmarked for Second army never even got the opportunity to come anywhere near Yugoslavia; this refers to 100th ('light') motorized and 1st mountain division, both of which were transported directly from Germany to their scheduled deployment areas on the eastern frontier,[96] and especially to 19th armoured division, whose men never even got the faintest inkling that they had been earmarked for Yugoslavia.[97]

After the fall of Belgrade Second army continued operations with only three of the divisions originally allocated to it. The 16th motorized and 8th armoured marched south along the Drina, while 14th armoured was sent to occupy Sarajevo. In addition Kleist's *Panzergruppe* was transferred from List to Weichs, who ordered it to turn to the southwest along the Morava valley. On 14 April its tanks occupied Krusevac. By that time the Yugoslavs had decided to give up, and sent over officers to negotiate a surrender. Though the actual treaty of capitulation was signed only three days later – the main delaying factor being that, after the flight of King Peter and his government, there was nobody left in Yugoslavia with authority to sign – the campaign was as good as over.[98]

After the occupation of Thrace and Macedonia, List too was left with only a fraction of his forces to continue operations against Greece. In the east XVIIIth corps with 2nd armoured, 5th and 6th mountain divisions was advancing along the coast from Salonika and preparing an assault against the right flank of the Kaimaktsalan–Vermion–Olympus line. Further to the west XXXXth corps, its three divisions now reinforced by 5th armoured, was menacing the same line on its left flank. List believed that, as a result of the extraordinary natural strength of the Anglo–Greek positions and particularly as the retreating allies had blown up all the bridges over the Vardar, a frontal attack on the line would be very difficult. He therefore decided to exploit the successes gained in southern Serbia. While 9th armoured advanced to the west and linked up with the Italian army in Albania north of the Ochrida Lake on 10 April,[99] the rest of the corps, headed by SS 'AH', started moving south in the direction of Florina, threatening to outflank the entire Kaimaktsalan–Vermion–Olympus position and to cut off the Greek army in western Macedonia and Epirus. This move had been foreseen by Papagos and the British commander, Wilson, on 8 April and the latter decided to abandon Edessa and to move what British forces he could muster to the Veue Pass in order to protect the exposed left flank. Papagos should for his part have taken his own right flank back from western Macedonia to a line running from the west coast near Santa Quaranta across the Pindus to the Aliakhmon, but he was reluctant to take this decision because he feared – with justice, as it turned out – that to retreat before the Italians would lead to the disintegration of Greek morale. On 12 April he did in fact issue these orders, but by then it was too late. Arriving before the Veue Pass on 11 April, SS 'AH' and 9th armoured found the going unexpectedly tough. It was only late on the 12th that, after hard fighting, they succeeded in breaking through 19th Australian infantry brigade and 1st armoured brigade group. By then, however, both German divisions had run out of petrol and ammunition and were unable to follow up their success.

Meanwhile XVIIIth corps – now consisting of only two divisions[100] – was advancing against the right flank of the Kaimaktsalan–Vermion–Olympus position, 9th armoured operating along the coast and 6th mountain further inland. The two divisions crossed the Vardar on the 11th and reached the mouth of the Aliakhmon the following day. After forming a bridgehead across the river on 13 April the German forces collided with the New Zealand troops forming the right wing of the British positions. Falling back on the Olympus Pass the New Zealanders resisted with considerable success, and were still holding out and blocking the way southward on 15 April. Their courage, like that of the defenders of the Metaxas line, was to no avail; as so often happens to troops occupying a static position in mobile warfare, the battle was being decided elsewhere. Having been supplied during the night, the columns of XXXXth corps resumed their advance southward on 13 April, threatening to cut the British off from the now disintegrating Greek army in Albania. To protect his right flank against a counterattack which he still thought might be launched by that army,[101] a cautious List now detached SS 'AH' from the main axis of advance of XXXXth corps and sent it westward in the direction of Koritsa. Far from counter-attacking, however, the demoralized Greeks gave way and thus allowed the Italians to occupy the town without resistance on 15 April. With 9th armoured division crossing the upper Aliakhmon and reaching Servia on the next day, the British forces on the Olympus found themselves surrounded on both flanks. Following a decision made by Wilson three days earlier they now started falling back across Thessaly to Thermopylae, leaving in their wake 20,000 Greek troops who, being less well endowed with motor vehicles, failed to escape in time and were captured by the Germans.

While this move was being carried out Wilson met Papagos for the penultimate time. Although he recognized the need for the British withdrawal from the Olympus Papagos felt understandably bitter towards this ally who had not succeeded in giving any real help and who was now leaving his armies in Albania in the lurch. Despairing of further resistance he asked Wilson to consider the complete evacuation of the British forces in order to avoid Greece further devastation. Wilson referred the request back to Cairo and London and on 17 April received the reply that, if the Greek government agreed, the evacuation could go ahead.

The Greek government, however, was in no position to agree to anything. On 18 April the Prime Minister, Koryzis, committed suicide; the following day the British commander met what was left of the Greek government, but they were unable to reach a decision. While Papagos and Wilson were debating whether it was possible and worthwhile to make a prolonged stand at Thermopylae, the initiative was taken from their hands by General Tsolakoglu commander of the Greek army in Epirus. The latter now saw his forces threatened in the rear by SS 'AH', which had advanced south from Koritsa through the Metsovo Pass and occupied Gianina. Determined to avoid a humiliating surrender to the Italians he asked Papagos for authority to negotiate a surrender to the Germans. Should this consent not be forthcoming, he added, the army would take matters into its own hands. Papagos reacted to this *pronunciamento* by censuring and then dismissing the rebellious general, but this did not disturb Tsolakoglu.

There followed one of the strangest episodes of the entire war. On 20 April, in his eagerness to escape the Italians, Tsolakoglu approached the Germans and sent an officer to their commander on the spot, SS General Sepp Dietrich. After some talks the latter gave the Greeks very generous terms providing for the cessation of hostilities between Germany and Greece at 1800 hours the same day. A few hours later List arrived at Dietrich's headquarters and, insisting that Tsolakoglu did not have the authority to surrender anything but his own troops, compelled the unfortunate Greek general to sign a second and much less generous accord on the next day.[102] Despite this humiliation Tsolakoglu had achieved his main objective, i.e. avoiding surrender to the Italians. List next asked Cavallero to stop his advance into Greece so as not to obstruct the armistice, and Cavallero referred the matter to the Duce. Mussolini was beside himself with rage and insisted that the Greeks should surrender to him, too. His demand was referred to Hitler via Guzzoni and Marras. According to Halder, Hitler had originally given his tacit consent to List's move in the hope of presenting his ally with a *fait accompli*, but the trick failed and he could not stake German–Italian friendship on a question of preserving Greek honour. He therefore disowned the agreement signed by the commander of Twelfth army and dispatched General Jodl to Salonika to sign yet another armistice, the third, to which the Italians, too, would be a party.[103] Tsolakoglu protested at this indignity but he had no choice. Early on the 23rd the third agreement was signed, to come into force at 2300 hours of the same day.

While the Greeks surrendered the British did not fare much better. They had started their withdrawal from the Olympus across the plain of Thessaly on 16 April, but were caught on the way by a sudden improvement in the weather which brought in its wake inevitable attacks by the Luftwaffe. The retreating British forces were hotly pursued by the Germans, who were now divided into three groups. In the east, XVIIIth corps was preparing for a frontal attack on Thermopylae, with 2nd armoured operating along the coast and 6th mountain more inland. The 5th armoured passed through the gap opened by 9th armoured and SS 'AH' at Veue, and racing down the centre of Greece, followed hard on the heels of the retreating Australians and reached Lamia in front of the Thermopylae on 21 April. In the east, 'AH' was advancing almost unopposed to Arta and beyond.

The battle of the Thermopylae was fought by 2nd armoured and 6th mountain divisions. While the former attacked frontally along the coast, a regiment of the latter under Colonel Jassi tried to repeat the classical manoeuvre of outflanking the pass. However, Jassi's mountaineers were forestalled by the tanks of 2nd armoured division, supported by the Luftwaffe, which succeeded in breaking through the British positions and occupying Volos on 22 April – just in time to open the way to 5th armoured. This relatively fresh division – it had followed on the heels of XXXXth corps without quite succeeding in overtaking it, and had seen but little action for several days – was the only one, besides SS 'AH', which continued the advance southward. Its tanks reached Thebes on the 25th and hoisted the swastika over the Acropolis on the 27th. By now the British were retreating across the Isthmus of Corinth into the Peloponnese, where they embarked in whatever ships Admiral Cunningham could muster. An attempt to cut them off by landing paratroopers on the Canal of Corinth on 26 April failed; although the paratroopers encountered no great difficulty in occupying the city they came too late to halt the British, and also failed to prevent the demolition of the railway bridge across the Canal.[104] This failure, however, was of little consequence; 5th armoured did not find it hard to construct an emergency bridge over the flat western end of the Canal, while SS 'AH' crossed the Gulf of Corinth by boat near Naupaktos and landed in the Peloponnese on 27 April. The last engagement with the British took place on 28 April at Nauplion and Kalamat, where 5th armoured and SS 'AH' encountered a total of 9000 British soldiers who had failed to get away on time and were taken prisoner. With the arrival of a small German unit at the southern end of the Peloponnese on 29 April the dual campaign was over.

Before turning his attention to Russia again it remained for Hitler to exult in his victory and divide the booty. On 4 May a big victory parade was held in Athens, including among others an Italian unit which List, after much bickering, had been forced by Hitler to accept.[105] The booty taken west of the Pindus was allocated to the Italians, the Bulgarians took the booty found in Thrace, while the Germans, after taking their pick of the rest, left everything else to the Italians.[106] In accordance with an order signed by Hitler on 12 April,[107] the Balkan cake was cut up and divided. For himself the Führer took the territory which used to belong to Austrian Styria, enlarged by a strip some 60 miles wide and 6 to 10 miles deep. Hungary got back her territory in the north of Yugoslavia up to the historical frontier. The Banat, delimited in such a way so as to exclude the Bor copper mines (which Hitler wanted for himself, though they had been thoroughly destroyed by the retreating Serbs) was also to return to Hungary, but the Führer decided to postpone this step until he could 'compensate' Rumania with Bessarabia.[108] South Serbia went to Bulgaria as far as the ethnical frontier, while Germany took over the military administration of Old Serbia. After an acrimonious debate with Italy, who advanced enormous demands including the whole of Croatia, it was decided to recognize the independent Croat republic proclaimed by Ante Pavelic, and Mussolini had to limit himself to Bosnia, Dalmatia and Montenegro, as well as an enlarged Albania. Greece lost Thrace, which went to Bulgaria in fulfilment of Hitler's promise to grant her an outlet to the Aegean, while the rest of the unhappy country was entrusted to a Quisling-style government constructed by General Tsolakoglu. Because of his eastern plans, Hitler did his best to denude the newly conquered territories of German troops; although List was given the impressive title 'commander-in-chief of the German troops in the Balkans', Greece was largely garrisoned by Italian troops, with only three German divisions – 5th and 6th mountain, and 164th infantry – remaining behind.[109] As to Serbia, she was at first garrisoned by those forces of Second and Twelfth armies that were earmarked for the OKH reserves for 'Barbarossa', i.e. 4th mountain, 60th motorized, 132nd, 183rd and 294th infantry divisions – and then turned over to four specially-formed security divisions.[110] All these arrangements, of course, were made with the specific intention of sparing Germany the burden of garrisoning yet more countries so as not to diminish the number of divisions that would be free for the east. However, the hurried character of the entire German–Balkan campaign made it impossible for all the occupied territories to be thoroughly policed, a fact which was one of the main causes for the success of the subsequent guerrilla movement.

From the strategic point of view, the most remarkable aspect of the German campaign in both Yugoslavia and Greece was its gross overestimation of the enemy. To operate against the six weak divisions which Papagos could, with the greatest difficulty, spare from Albania the Germans had brought no less than 18 first class divisions to Rumania and Bulgaria, with the result that many of them (46th, 76th, 198th, 294th infantry, 16th armoured) never saw action at all even when the campaign had been extended to include Yugoslavia, too. As to the latter country, only four divisions and one regiment (8th and 14th armoured, 16th motorized, and SS 'das Reich' and SS infantry regiment 'Grossdeutschland') out of the twelve divisions brought up for it saw action, and they alone were able to bring the whole operation to an end in less than half the time allocated to it. Out of the 29 divisions involved in the Balkans in one way or another, only 10 – or scarcely more than half those originally assigned to Twelfth army – saw action for more than six days. Because of the bad transport situation in southeastern Europe, and particularly because of the need to start 'Barbarossa' at an early date, this gross overestimate of the enemy's forces and fighting abilities was a serious blunder.

There was, however, one more operation which Hitler wanted to carry out before turning his undivided attention to the east. Crete, potentially the most valuable part of Greece, had not been included in the essentially defensive plan for 'Marita'. Throughout the winter the island was scarcely mentioned in the German documents. Sometime about the middle of April, however, Hitler allowed himself to be persuaded that the occupation of the island was, after all, worth his while.

'SPRUNG NACH KRETA'

Perhaps the most interesting question about the German *Sprung nach Kreta* is not how it was carried out, but why. In September and October 1940, it will be remembered, the Germany navy had pointed to Crete as the most valuable target to be captured in an eventual operation against Greece; it was to Greece what Trondheim and Narvik were to Norway, i.e. the most important naval and aerial base. The island was the ideal starting point from which to dominate the eastern Mediterranean from the air; also, situated as it was on the flank of the Italian advance and subsequent retreat in North Africa, it could play an important role in support of the offence or defence there. Crete, in short, was an important base within the framework of the war against the British in the eastern Mediterranean and its capture, as Hitler did not fail to grasp, within such a framework made perfect strategic sense.

In the winter and spring of 1941, however, most of these advantages disappeared. For one thing, nothing was now further removed from Hitler's intentions than a large-scale offensive in the eastern Mediterranean. The war in North Africa had largely lost such strategic objective as it had had previously; late in February the British advance was halted, April saw a stormlike advance across Cyrenaica by Rommel, and May stalemate before Tobruk. OKH was none too happy about Rommel's advance – in their eyes, it was but a diversion from their much more dangerous trap in Greece – but in any case the danger of the whole of North Africa being lost to the Axis had been removed, and if any new steps were still needed to consolidate the situation there it would be considerably more reasonable to attack Malta as a base. At present the latter was causing large chunks of Rommel's supplies to be sabotaged. The trouble with Crete, then, was not that it had lost its strategic value for warfare in the eastern Mediterranean; rather, that Hitler had lost interest in the Mediterranean.

Why, then, did he decide on the capture of the island? There are two possible explanations.[111] One is that Crete would serve as a natural barrier between Alexandria and the Aegean, preventing the British from entering the latter and thus securing the important maritime oil route from Constanta via the Dardanelles to Italy. This was the reason Hitler himself gave in his speech to the Reichstag on 4 May.[112] The other explanation lies in the ambitions of the Luftwaffe, or rather in those of its commander-in-chief, Reichsmarschal Göring, and those of the commander of its only parachutist division, General Kurt Student. The latter was anxious that his élite force should be involved in more important missions than hitherto, and during March he prepared a plan for an airborne attack on Crete. Though favourably impressed by the economy of the scheme, Keitel and Jodl thought that the paratroopers would do better to expend their energies in occupying Malta and on 15 April they summoned Student in an attempt to make him modify his views. Student, however, replied that Crete with its sausage-like form and single main road was a suitable target for his men, whereas the better communications inside Malta would make it possible for the enemy to confront them rapidly with overwhelming forces. In order to justify his plan for an attack against Crete rather than Malta he proposed that the capture of the former should be only the first stage in a series of 'leap frog' attacks in the eastern Mediterranean. At this stage Göring seized upon the plan; he saw it as an opportunity to avenge his humiliation in the battle of Britain and to substantiate his claim that 'his' air force could win campaigns all by itself without help from the army. It was Göring who presented the plan to the Führer on 21 April without, however, being very enthusiastically received, for Hitler had no use for leap-frogging from Crete to Cyprus and beyond.[113] Göring nevertheless persisted and his persistence finally bore fruit, for on 25 April Hitler issued his 'directive No. 28' for the operation which, appropriately, was named 'Merkur':

As a base for air warfare against Great Britain in the eastern Mediterranean we must prepare to occupy the island of Crete. . . For the purpose of planning, it will be assumed that the whole Greek mainland including the Peloponnese is in the hands of the Axis powers.

Lack of a strategic objective is shown clearly by the fact that, while this directive endows the operation with an offensive purpose (and one which, not surprisingly, was never acted upon) Hitler himself, in his speech to the Reichstag, said it was defensive. Far from being part of any coherent strategy, therefore, 'Merkur' was little more than a sop to Göring, whose air force was destined to play a subordinate role in the coming Russian campaign. Hitler evidently feared that the ambitions of his air force commander might run away with him, for he took care to order that the 'transport movements [for "Merkur"] must not lead to any delay in the mounting of undertaking "Barbarossa"', and that 'after the occupation of the island all or part of the forces must be ready for new tasks'.[114] To make doubly sure, he instructed the army to keep in Greece only such forces as were indispensable for supplying 'Merkur'.[115] This operation was hamstrung before it began.

Under the energetic leadership of General Student planning nevertheless went ahead. In addition to his own 7th parachute division he got 5th mountain division, which was one of the units earmarked to stay in Greece for occupation duties, and also managed to lay his hands on a regiment of 5th armoured division, a unit OKH was in no particular hurry to withdraw because it was not scheduled to take part in the initial phases of 'Barbarossa'. These forces were to be transferred to Crete by the transport planes of XIth air corps and by a fleet of barges escorted by some Italian torpedo boats, while the fighters and dive bombers of VIIIth air corps, now flying from advanced bases in Scarpanto, Phaleron and Eleusis, were to act in close support. The operation as a whole was put under the command of General Lohr of 4th air fleet, a fact which gave lead to jealousy in the army.[116] The actual descent was to be made at three places: in the west near Maleme, in the centre near Retimo, and in the east near Heraklion. In each of these areas there was an air strip which had first to be captured and which could then be used to land reinforcements and heavy equipment. Since Lohr was convinced that Maleme was the most important objective, he entrusted its capture to the 1st assault regiment, an élite unit within the élite unit that was 7th paratrooper division.

On 20 May after a delay of three days caused by the necessity of bringing up the necessary fuel,[117] the operation started. For our purposes the actual operations are of importance only in so far as they were relevant to Hitler's overall strategy (in fact they contributed very little). The paratroopers encountered unexpectedly stiff resistance to their attack, because the defenders – a motley array totalling some 40,000 men, half of whom had been evacuated from Greece and retained neither their equipment nor their organization – had been forewarned about every detail of the German plan. A copy of the paratroopers tactical manual had even fallen into their hands and was put to good use.[118] Under the indifferent command of General Freyberg, the Australians, New Zealanders and Greeks fought tenaciously, assisted by *unmensliche Freisschärler* from the population.[119] As soon as the landings started the entire Alexandria squadron of the British navy left port and began cruising round the island, foiling with some loss of life, German attempts to get through by sea during the night of 20 to 21 May.

The crisis of the battle came at noon on 21 May. Until that time none of the three air strips had been captured, and the paratroopers, greatly outnumbered and with their supplies running out, were in a desperate position. An attempt to land reinforcements on the beach near Retimo failed because the New Zealander's machine guns riddled the planes with bullets before anybody could get out. The paratroopers landed near Retimo and Heraklion in particular were almost annihilated. During the afternoon of the same day, however, the men of 1st assault regiment finally succeeded in occupying the air strip at Maleme, at least to the extent of driving the British artillery away into the surrounding hills. Despite the intensive fire it was now possible to land a regiment of 5th mountain division, complete with some light artillery, on the air strip. Although 1st assault regiment was by now too exhausted to take a further part in the battle and the transport planes were prevented from departing and destroyed by artillery fire, the crisis of the battle was over.

22 May was the great day of the Luftwaffe. Pitting itself against the British fleet, it proved that, granted favourable weather, ships were no match for planes. Six cruisers and four destroyers were sunk, many other ships damaged. The entire fleet fled back to Alexandria, its tail between its legs. Meanwhile 5th mountain division started its counterattack, working its way from Maleme to the east; though the Australians, New Zealanders and Greeks had up to this point proved more than a match for the German paratroopers who were handicapped by the loss of part of their equipment, dispersion and unfamiliarity with the terrain, they could not successfully resist General Ringel's well organized mountaineers whose chain of command was intact. Although hard fighting occurred in many places the German drive to the east was irresistible. Chania, the main town on the island, fell on 27 May and with it Suda Bay, the main harbour. On 29 May Ringel's forces, advancing against opposition that was rapidly disintegrating, linked up with the surviving paratroopers at Retimo and Heraklion. The latter group, having been reinforced from the air, had already succeeded in taking the air strip. By that time the British evacuation was well under

way. It was completed on 1 June when a German unit caught up with a British rearguard which was trying to board ship near Sfakia and, after a tough fight, took the rest prisoner.

With the occupation of Crete Hitler had shot his last bullet in the eastern Mediterranean; from now on, all his attention would be focussed on the Russian front. Although early in June the naval high command made desperate attempts to persuade Hitler to use Crete as a base for 'the opening of intensive operations against the English bases and fleet in the eastern Mediterranean',[120] the Führer did not regard the island as a highway to the Middle East but as a *cul de sac* whose only function, if any, was to form an obstacle between Alexandria and the Axis maritime traffic in the Aegean. It was, moreover, a *cul de sac* which was increasingly costly to hold, because a British-instigated guerrilla movement was soon under way and Hitler's fear of a possible attempt at invasion made him invest considerable resources in its fortification during the years 1942–3.

Finally, the Cretan episode had yet another important result. German losses in Crete were extremely heavy – a study made immediately after the event admits 1032 dead and 2097 missing, which meant more fatal casualties than the Wehrmacht had suffered during the entire Balkan campaign – and the losses in material, particularly aircraft, were also considerable. Most important, however, was the fact that the back of the only German paratrooper division was broken for good. 'The day of parachute troops', Hitler told Student shortly after the end of the campaign, 'is over.'[121]

ON THE EVE OF 'BARBAROSSA'

We now come to the last part of this study, to an analysis of the troop movements back from the Balkans to the Russian front and the relationship between the German campaigns in the Balkans and operation 'Barbarossa'. In the whole history of World War II it is hard to find another question which has aroused so much discussion and which has received so many superficial answers.[122]

Long before the Balkan campaign was over, indeed before it even started, OKH had a cool look at this problem. It was a difficult one, to be sure, but its size was nowhere near what is usually believed. While a grand total of 152 divisions had been assigned to the Russian campaign,[123] only 29 – or less than one-fifth of the total – had in one way or another been involved in the Balkans, and this number includes not only the numerous units that had never seen action but even those which, like 19th armoured, never even knew they had been designated for the Balkans.[124]

A second look at the problem reduces its size still further. Out of the above mentioned 29 divisions, three – 5th and 6th mountain, as well as 164th infantry – were to stay in Greece on occupation duties. Out of the remaining 26 large units, 11 – including 2 armoured, 1 motorized, 1 mountain and 7 infantry divisions – were earmarked for the OKH reserves for 'Barbarossa', whose transportation to the east was not supposed to start until after the beginning of the campaign.[125] Thus, OKH was left with only 15 divisions – or some 10% of the total – plus, of course, VIIIth air corps to deal with before the beginning of 'Barbarossa'.

On 4 April 1941, two days before the start of 'Marita' and '25', Heusinger submitted to Halder the timetables prepared by his operations department for the transportation of the forces. Like everyone else Heusinger overestimated the Yugoslavs and based his calculations on the assumption that operation '25' would not be over until 30 April.[126] Since the journey back from Greece and Yugoslavia would, on average, require ten days, while another three weeks were needed for the physical and technical refreshment of the troops, it was hoped that it would be possible to complete it by the first days of June.[127] In accordance with this calculation new timetables for 'Barbarossa' were drawn up. Stage III, far from being delayed, was actually shifted forward by one week and planned to start moving on 8 April. This was probably designed to prevent any loss of time that might have resulted from not exploiting the railroads. On the other hand, this stage was 'stretched out' from 25 April to 20 May, the maximum capacity plan under which it had originally been supposed to move being replaced by a – very relaxed – peace-time schedule averaging 300 trains a day.[128] This, then, meant that the movements of the 17 divisions forming that stage – none of which had anything to do with the Balkans – were slowed down and stretched out over a much longer period than had originally been intended. Furthermore, Heusinger's new draft divided the former stage IV into two parts, IVa and IVb. The former was to consist of 9 infantry divisions supposed to run between 23 May and 2 June, the latter of 12 armoured and 12 motorized divisions (including some coming from the southeast) and was to run from 3 to 23 June. Both stages were to employ a maximum capacity railway schedule.[129]

By the middle of April, however, it was obvious that the assumption on which these timetables were based was hopelessly unrealistic; the war against Yugoslavia would be over long before the end of the month, while operations against Greece were at this time being continued with only 7 out of the 18 divisions originally allocated to List.[130] On 12 April the OKH reserves for Yugoslavia were halted; on 13 April, those of 2nd and 12th armies; and on the day after, a further three divisions.[131] According to the schedule (ten days transportation + three weeks refreshment = one month) that was required before they could be ready for the east, all these forces – a total of eleven divisions, or almost exactly the number that had been diverted to Yugoslavia – could have been shifted into the extremely leisurely timetable of stage III. So, for that matter, could those forces from stage IVa which had not been involved in the Balkans and which, assuming that the Russian campaign was in fact supposed to start on 16 May, should have been ready by 5 May at the very latest. This change would in turn have made it possible to exploit the fact that those forces which continued operations against Yugoslavia after the fall of Belgrade also started their withdrawal about 23 April – in accordance with Heusinger's schedule, it should therefore have been possible for them to be incorporated in the last transports of stage IVa. In short, the unexpectedly rapid termination of operation '25' ought to have made it possible to move the whole transportation schedule forward. Such changes were not only possible; they had been explicitly provided for by Brauchitsch, who was only too aware of the impossibility of estimating exactly the duration of operations in Greece and Yugoslavia.[132]

Another factor was also operating in OKH's favour. Because of the rapid occupation of Yugoslavia many of the divisions earmarked for 'Barbarossa' could be marched back over those very Yugoslav roads and railways which OKH had fought, tenaciously but unsuccessfully, to open up before the Belgrade *coup* took place. This applies in particular to 46th and 73rd infantry, 5th and 9th armoured and SS 'AH' divisions, all of which had originally formed part of Twelfth army and would have had to march back from Greece in any case.[133] Also, Hitler's 17 March decision to dispense with the right wing of army group south meant that Eleventh army in Rumania would not participate in the initial assault and that the four divisions of Twelfth army which were allocated to it had all the time in the world to march back through Bulgaria without reference to Heusinger's grand timetable.[134] Thus the number of divisions which had to be extricated and refreshed before the start of the Russian campaign went down to eleven.

The question, then, is why the timetables for the 'Barbarossa' build-up were not revised when it became clear that operations in Yugoslavia and Greece were easier and less prolonged than had been expected. The answer is that, to some extent, this was done. Thus, a revised timetable for stage IVb drawn up on 22 April transferred 52nd and 26oth infantry divisions from stage IVa to V, that is the OKH reserves, while their place was taken by 1st mountain and 101st 'light' motorized divisions, both units that had been brought up for operation '25' and were released on 13 April.[135] Also, 4th mountain division was incorporated by Heusinger in stage IVb, but was taken out again when it became clear that the Hungarians, from whose territory it was supposed to advance, would not join in the initial assault.[136]

An examination of the evidence, however, suggests that much more could have been done. Thus, 14th armoured division, arriving at its refreshment area near Berlin on 3 May, must have been ready for the east on the 24th of the same month but was in fact dispatched there only on 6 June.[137] The 19th armoured, instead of being shifted into stage III, calmly continued its training at Augustdorf and was sent to the east only on 12 June.[138] SS 'das Reich', released by Second army on the day after the fall of Belgrade, was kept waiting until the same day,[139] while SS infantry regiment 'Grossdeutschland' had to wait four more days.[140] Finally the examples of 8th and 16th armoured divisions prove convincingly that the Yugoslav operation should never have caused 'Barbarossa' to be postponed by five weeks. It had originally been planned that 8th armoured should travel to the Russian border on 13 May; taken out of stage IV for operation '25', it was released by Second army on 23 April and must therefore have completed its refreshment round 24 May, i.e. scarcely two weeks behind schedule. Yet it was another three weeks (19 June) before it was sent to the east.[141] Still more interesting is the example of 16th armoured, a unit which, it will be remembered, had not seen action in the Balkans because its task consisted of guarding the Bulgaro–Turkish frontier. Released by Twelfth army on 21 April, this division was back in Bucharest for refreshment on 25 April,[142] and must therefore have been ready to move east on 15 May, that is only three days later than the date originally planned for it within the framework of the original stage IV build-up; however it was not sent there until sometime between 6 and 10 June.[143] These two examples make it abundantly clear that the refreshment of numerous forces from the Balkans, and particularly from Yugoslavia, was complete ten to twenty days before they were actually sent to the eastern front and only a short time behind the original schedule. Without doubt, there must have been compelling reasons which prevented the full exploitation of the unexpectedly quick termination of the Yugoslav campaign.

These reasons are not difficult to establish. Halder's diary bristles with references to various units, none of which had anything to do with the Balkans, and whose equipment and training were not yet complete as late as the end of May 1941. Long before the Yugoslav campaign was in sight an entry reads: 'the conversion of tanks into underwater tanks will require 12 weeks'.[144] Allow another few days for transportation and 'Barbarossa', for which these machines were vital,[145] could not start before the first days of June. As early as 3 April Halder was aware that the last infantry division would not be ready before 20 May, and even this could be achieved only by equipping a number of armoured and motorized divisions with captured French material.[146] Throughout May Halder was recording the difficulties encountered in supplying such diverse units as 100th armoured brigade, 13th, 17th and 18th armoured divisions and 14th and 18th motorized divisions, units which may have had nothing in common except for the fact that they had not been connected in any way with the Balkan campaign.[147] Indeed, it is hardly possible to open a history of any 'fast' unit that took part in the war against Russia without being struck by the belatedness with which it was supplied with its full motor vehicle park. Thus, the so-called *Panzerzüge*; before the Yugoslav *coup* it had been decided five of these should be constructed but they were not ready for transportation to the east until mid-June, after finally receiving French supplies.[148] The 10th motorized division did not receive its equipment until after marching east on 10 June, and even then the vehicles had to be collected piecemeal from ... Germany, Belgium, Holland and France![149] The 20th armoured, 14th, 18th, 25th and 36th motorized divisions were all supplied with French vehicles, but even so the postponement of their movement to the east was again being considered on 20 May. Indeed, the problems created by the general shortage of equipment, particularly motor vehicles, were not limited to only the 'fast' units. At the time of the German offensive against Russia, no less than 92 – or 40% – of the army divisions had to be supplied, wholly or in part, with French material.[151] Since the losses in material resulting from the Balkan campaign were extremely limited,[152] it is quite clear that lack of equipment of all kinds would have prevented 'Barbarossa' from starting before the end of June even if neither 'Marita' nor '25' had come into the world.[153]

To some extent, this hypothesis is borne out by the 'Barbarossa' timetables themselves. Thus, we have already noted the remarkable fact that 52nd and 260th infantry divisions, neither of which had anything at all to do with the Balkans, were for some unexplained reason taken out of stage III build-up to which they had originally belonged[154] and transferred first to stage IVb and then to V.[155] On 25 May, moreover, the timetable of stage IVb underwent thorough revision. On the one hand, 4th mountain division was referred to the OKH reserves; on the other, seven new divisions were now added to that stage, raising its total number of units to $24 - 1 + 7 = 30$ divisions. The forces added to stage IVb were: 3rd, 9th, 12th and 13th armoured, 8th infantry, 3rd and 20th motorized divisions.[156] Of these, the belated appearance of 9th armoured alone in the timetable may be ascribed to the Balkan campaign: this had been released by Twelfth army after helping to break through the Veue Pass. For the others, we possess some remarkable information. An entry in Halder's diary, reading 'the last infantry division will be ready on 20 May'[157] may very well explain the otherwise incomprehensible inclusion of an infantry division in a stage of the operation which, for reasons of camouflage, had been intended to include only 'fast' units. We know that 13th armoured division was ready for the east only 'at the last moment' – in this case 28 May.[158] As for 3rd motorized division, its belated incorporation in the time-table is explained by the fact that it received its motor vehicles only at the very last moment before travelling to the east on 6 June.[159] Thus, it is possible to explain the late appearance of three out of the six divisions in question by their imperfect material preparation. We have no infor-mation about the other three; but it is interesting that on 29 May a further delay in transporting another six fast units to the east (20th armoured, 3rd, 10th, 14th, 18th and 25th motorized) was being con-sidered,[160] and that the date of the arrival of the last 'Barbarossa' division, SS 'AH', and its deployment area was dictated not by any transportation difficulties but by the fact that the general shortage of vehicles prevented its timely refreshment.[161] These details make it quite clear that, irrespective of the Balkan campaign, the offensive against Russia could not have started much earlier than it did.

A word should be said here about the effect of 'Merkur' on the start-ing date of 'Barbarossa'. It is obvious that the land and airborne troops participating in this operation bore no relation to the Russian campaign since none of them was supposed to take part in it.[162] On the other hand, the fact that Hitler made his decision to occupy the island about a fortnight after Heusinger had compiled his revised timetable for 'Barbarossa' meant that OKH now saw difficulties in transporting VIIIth air corps to the east on time.[163] In addition, the Cretan business forced the army to leave in Greece two mixed and four light anti-aircraft battalions which had originally been earmarked for Russia.[164]

At a conference held in Salzburg on 12 May with Jodl as president, these problems were thrashed out. As for the anti-aircraft battalions, the army finally conceded that it would be possible to delay their with-drawal from Greece until 25 May without thereby endangering the timely start of 'Barbarossa'. A more difficult problem was the transpor-tation of VIIIth air corps; after some discussion, the army agreed to provide for the transfer of most of the corps from Craiova to Oderberg between 28 May and 9 June.[165] Within two weeks, however, the air force upset this arrangement and demanded that the corps should be transported to East Prussia instead.[166] Acceptance of this demand would involve a delay of no less than ten days in the start of 'Barba-rossa'; since the deployment could not be camouflaged after the start of stage IVa, that is after 23 May, the Russians would thus have some six weeks advance warning, during which they would be able to 'thoroughly change their dispositions'. For this reason OKH insisted that *B* day should remain 22 June, and after OKW had compelled the air force to accept Suwalki instead of East Prussia it had its way.[167] Thus it is clear that, although 'Merkur' caused Halder more than one anxious and angry moment, there can be no question of it delaying 'Barbarossa'.

IN PERSPECTIVE

With the withdrawal of the last divisions from Greece and Yugoslavia, the German campaign in the Balkans came to an end. It remains to (*a*) say something about the fate of the two countries during the next four years, and (*b*) consider the place of the Balkan campaign in the history of World War II.

Although often very dramatic, marked as it is by heroic resistance and the most brutal repression, the fate of Greece and Yugoslavia is not of the greatest importance in the history of World War II. In June 1941 Hitler had no intention of pursuing the war in the Mediterranean further; consequently, the two countries became a backyard instead of the forward base they could have been and which, for a brief period, had been intended to become. Moreover, it was a backyard which was both indispensable and expensive to hold. Indispensable because of the raw materials it contained; expensive because of the guerrilla movements which were soon in full swing – aided as they were by the character of the terrain, and by the fact that the Wehrmacht did not have time to thoroughly police the newly conquered areas – and because of Hitler's anxiety, which was not without reason, lest the allies might attempt a landing in Crete and Greece from their bases in North Africa. Such an invasion would have created just the situation Hitler had tried to prevent when undertaking operation 'Marita' in December 1940: it would have threatened the rear of his armies in Russia. In 1943, therefore, he went to great trouble and expense to strengthen and fortify the long and exposed coasts of the region – in itself, an impossible task. Thanks to Roosevelt's opposition to Churchill's plans, his fortifications were never put to the test; however, this did not save Hitler from the need to maintain many more troops in the area than he would have liked – by 1944, there were 125,000 German soldiers fighting the partisans in Yugoslavia alone.

Ferocious and widespread as it was, it was not the guerrilla movement which finally turned the Germans out of Greece and Yugoslavia. Nor was it any military operation conducted on their soil. The two countries were considered as being of so little strategic importance that they were by-passed by all the great military movements of the war. It was only in 1944, under the threat of being cut off from their home-country by the Soviet advance in Rumania and Hungary, that the German armies, still unbeaten, started to retreat. In the process, they handed Greece over to the British in return for a safe conduct from the islands. In Yugoslavia, on the other hand, Tito's partisans were strong enough to take over the country without foreign intervention.

As part of World War II, the German campaign in the Balkans has many aspects. Thus, among other things, it was the last of Hitler's 'pragmatic' or 'tactical' conquests. Whatever our view of Hitler's subsequent invasion of the Soviet Union, there can be no doubt but that here we are dealing with something qualitatively different from everything that went before. For, although it was perfectly possible to define that invasion in purely rational, politico-military terms, these do not completely explain why it took place. 'Ideological', 'historical' and 'biological' factors also played a part in Hitler's decision: it resulted more than any other except perhaps for his determination to exterminate the Jews, from his programme, which has been standing there, quite regardless of the circumstances of the moment, for about twenty years.[168]

Conversely, there is nothing programmatic in the origins, development or execution of the Balkan campaign. In this sense, the latter stands on a par with Hitler's violation of the Versailles Treaty, the rearmament of Germany, the remilitarization of the Rhineland, the annexation of Austria, Czechoslovakia, the wars against Poland, France, England. However desirable and important, whether planned in advance or the result of external circumstances, none of these presented the great 'goal' which alone could justify and fulfil the National Socialist 'revolution'.[169] Rather, they were a – more or less essential – prelude to that goal.

'If someone had said two years ago', Hitler told a visitor early in 1941, 'that one day I would be standing with my armies from Norway to Spain, I would have had him declared insane.' Whatever the truth of these words when applied to other countries, there is no indication that the Führer had ever included the occupation of Greece and Yugoslavia in any of the manifold versions of his 'programme'. Here is a war which Hitler neither planned nor, except for a short period in October and November 1940, wanted. A war which, perhaps more than any other, was dictated by purely political and strategic considerations, a means toward a very definite end. As such, it proved to be the last of its kind. In Hitler's crusade against Russia means and ends were inextricably connected; here was another kind of war. Later still, with the initiative snatched from his hands, the distinction loses any meaning, since there was no longer a programme to be realized.

Thus, Hitler's war in Greece and Yugoslavia was a pragmatic one *par excellence*, one which, perhaps more than any other, was the result of circumstances and not of advance planning. It was also the last of the successful German *Blitzfeldzüge*.[170] A mountain of military literature notwithstanding, the secret of the lightning war remains, to me at least, something of a mystery. I have not yet been able to discover a factor which, by its presence or absence, will make it possible to explain the success of certain campaigns of this kind and the failure of others. However, it would hopefully not be too rash to say that there is a limit to what even the best conceived, best led, best executed and most spirited of *Blitzfeldzüge* can achieve. These limits are presumably set by the odds which the particular campaign faces. That is, past a certain point, the best imaginable plan executed in the best possible way cannot overcome disparity in forces and resources. German successes in the early years of the war pushed this frontier steadily backward. But, however elastic the frontier – and the Balkan campaign did not require any very great elasticity on its part, since the German forces were so clearly superior – it, too, has a breaking point. In Russia, the breaking point was reached and passed. Thus, although Hitler was still destined to win many a battle and gain many a tactical victory, the Balkan campaign was the last one that brought strategic success in the classical, Clauzewitzan sense; i.e. the last one in which 'a series of battles' compelled the enemy 'to bend to our will'. The very facility with which this aim was achieved may have encouraged – although it certainly did not create – Hitler's determination to try his luck against even the greatest odds; for, to him, the Balkan campaign had proved that 'the German soldier can do anything'.[171]

Finally, the Balkan campaign marks the apogee of Hitler's meteoric career. Never again after 31 May was he to confront the world with such unlimited – and, to all appearances, justified – confidence. After six years of diplomacy and two of war Hitler had reduced France to impotence, thrown the British out of their last continental foothold, and either conquered or reduced to satellite status most of the other states of non-Soviet Europe. True, there were still a few sore thumbs – Spain being a prominent one – but these could easily be dealt with after the destruction of the Soviet Union, but although on the verge of success, Hitler ultimately failed to achieve this aim.

CONCLUSIONS

Perhaps the most striking aspect of Hitler's Greek and Yugoslav policy in the years 1940-1 is the difference in his attitude towards the two countries. On the face of it the existence of such a difference seems rather surprising, for the two countries have much in common geographically, historically, politically and economically. Both Greece and Yugoslavia belong to southeastern Europe. Both had benefited from the peace treaties of 1919 and their general orientation in foreign policy was therefore pro-western. While Germany did not really have territorial claims against either, both regarded Italy as their most dangerous enemy.[1] Their economies being based on the export of surplus agricultural products and raw materials, their relations with the highly industrialized Germany economy could not but be basically similar.

Despite these factors, German policy towards the two countries developed along entirely different lines. That this was so was not merely a matter of expediency – or rather, as so often happens, expediency was dressed up in high sounding principles. To Germany Greece was very much more remote and less important politically, economically and strategically than Yugoslavia. While the latter was watched with interest and often courted, the former was looked upon with some indifference. In order to consolidate his alliance with Italy Hitler did not hesitate to renounce any active interest in Greece; on the other hand, he behaved in an entirely different way over Yugoslavia, causing one crisis after the other within the Axis and deliberately leaving the question of whose sphere of influence she belonged to unanswered until the occupation of the country in 1941.[2] These differing attitudes were then formally laid down in a geo-political system assigning Greece to the 'Mediterranean', and thus to Italy, while Yugoslavia was assigned to the ill-defined and controversial area of the 'Balkans'.[3]

This division of southeastern Europe into a 'Mediterranean' and a 'Balkan' region explains why Hitler, who so consistently and categorically opposed his colleague's designs on Yugoslavia, regarded his Greek plans with an indifference bordering on encouragement. Indifference even turned into encouragement when he decided after the plans for a landing in the United Kingdom had been abandoned to transfer the war to the 'periphery'. Viewed in this context the possession of the Greek mainland, most particularly as a bastion of Axis warfare in the eastern Mediterranean seemed worth while. At the Brenner, on 4 October 1940, Hitler apparently gave his ally the green light.

Hitler's subsequent decision to invade Greece was caused neither by his fear that the Balkans might explode nor by an anxiety lest the British should bomb the oil fields. It was the result of offensive, not defensive, considerations. It was the Italian failure to occupy Greece and the fact that nothing could be expected from Graziani's army in Egypt that determined his action. Compared with North Africa Greece, of course, was only 'a second rate substitute'; a substitute, moreover, which had the advantage that it could be reached without being dependent on Italian consent and cooperation.

Thus, the first German plan for an attack on Greece was born. Its character was offensive, its purpose to widen the basis for Axis warfare in the eastern Mediterranean. Like Hitler's authorization of Mussolini's plans in October, like the German offer of help in Egypt and like the plan to capture Gibraltar and cross to North West Africa, the *raison d'être* for this decision was the war against England.

Though the way to Greece did not pass through the Italian sphere of influence, it did pass through a region which the Russians insisted on regarding as within their own security zone. Partly because of this but also for much more important reasons, Hitler tried to bring about a *rapprochement* with the USSR. However, Molotov's visit to Berlin on 12 to 13 November made it clear to Hitler that the Soviets would resist his penetration of the Balkans; also, that they would stand in his way wherever they could. Since he felt himself too weak militarily and economically to carry out the war against England *a l'outrance* with such an untrustworthy neighbour at his rear, he decided to smash Russia as soon as possible. It would be a mistake to try and pinpoint the date of this decision with too much accuracy. Hitler was known for his prolonged vacillations, and it is possible, indeed probable, that he took some time to make up his mind. Thus, the period from approximately 13 November to 1 December is characterized by conflicting declarations and contradictory actions. Hitler declared his determination to smash Russia on one hand, and issued 'directive No. 18' for the conduct of the war against England in the Mediterranean on the other; ordered *Gefechtstände* to be constructed on the eastern front, yet tried to win Yugoslavia over to cooperate in the extension of the war to the eastern Mediterranean.

Early in December these vacillations came to an abrupt end. The 'peripheral' strategy in the western Mediterranean was reduced, then abolished altogether. Hitler would probably have liked to do the same in the eastern Mediterranean, but here things were less simple. He saw himself compelled to support the defeated Italians in Libya, and tried to find a diplomatic solution for the Italo–Greek war. Although the details of this attempt are singularly obscure, it would seem that its failure must be laid squarely at the door of the Greeks, and perhaps the British.

Because of his scheduled Russian campaign, and the danger caused to its flank by the presence of the British in Greece, Hitler could not allow the war in Albania to go on indefinitely. This led to the second German plan for an invasion of Greece, the so-called operation 'Marita'. This plan had but very little in common with its predecessor. Its character, aims and objectives were entirely different. Above all, it was part of another whole framework. Hitherto Hitler had, at any rate *pro forma*, assigned Greece to the 'Mediterranean', an Italian sphere of influence which he entered only reluctantly and for an ostensibly limited period of time. Now, however, Greece and the Greek operation were lifted out of their 'Mediterranean' context and reincorporated into the 'Balkans', all of which had by one means or another to be secured as a basis for the attack on the Soviet Union.

Hitler, then, did not have one but two plans for an invasion of Greece, separated from each other by approximately two and a half weeks. During this period the Führer must have hoped to dispense with the Greek operation. He therefore suspended negotiations with the three countries whose cooperation or neutrality were needed for the purpose and made approaches to Athens. Only after failing to find a political solution for the Greek affair did he resume on 21 December diplomatic preparations for 'Marita'.

The plan for attacking Greece now fell entirely under the gigantic shadow cast by the scheduled war against Russia – to which it was an essential preliminary. The relationship between the two campaigns was more complicated than is usually realized. The latter could not start before the former, securing its flank and tying down some of its divisions, was over. These facts were realized from the very beginning and, as the requirements of the Greek campaign skyrocketed because of the danger of Soviet, Turkish and possibly Yugoslav intervention they caused OKH considerable concern. Because of what was planned for the east it was essential to bring matters in Greece to a conclusion as soon as possible, but the start of the operation suffered successive delays because of the weather, Bulgarian obstinacy, Yugoslav reluctance and Soviet threats. Efforts to speed up the end of the affair by sending German forces to Albania similarly met with failure.

Hitler's preparations for the invasion of Greece put Yugoslavia in a position that was both weak and strong. It was weak in that Yugoslavia saw herself surrounded on all sides by the military force of the Axis; it was strong in that her attitude would in the last resort determine whether Hitler's design for a short and 'small' war in southeastern

Europe was, after all, practicable. In addition, there was the problem of the Yugoslav roads and railways, the importance of which has been grossly underestimated by historical scholarship. Hitler did not treat Yugoslavia 'like a prima donna'[4] just for the sake of having her sign a – worthless – Tripartite Pact. It was the railways which he – and even more than him, his generals – were after, and it was only because Cvetkovic had been too clever for him that he had to content himself with the empty gesture that was Yugoslavia's signature of the Tripartite Pact. To him 25 March 1941 was the confirmation of failure, not the beginning of success.

The question of the relationship between the German campaigns in the Balkans and their offensive against Russia is an extremely complicated one and should be approached with the greatest caution. Here we must recall the 'traditional view' – in so far as there is one – of this question. It is generally assumed that, while 'Marita' was, though with some difficulty, coordinated with 'Barbarossa' it was the unexpected decision to smash Yugoslavia that made it necessary to delay the start of the Russian campaign.

This view seems to need modification on several important points. Although it is true that 'Marita' and 'Barbarossa' were coordinated, this coordination became very strained long before the Yugoslav *coup* because of the long delays imposed on the former. When the British landed in Greece on 7 March Hitler decided to extend the objectives of 'Marita' and occupy the entire Greek mainland, thereby straining the coordination between the two campaigns to breaking point and making the arrival on time of part of the forces for 'Barbarossa' impossible. Thus, the famous question whether the British landing in Greece did or did not contribute to the delay in operation 'Barbarossa' must be answered with a yes and a no; yes in that, by triggering off countermeasures, it threw the coordination between 'Marita' and 'Barbarossa' out of gear and made the timely start of the latter doubtful; no in that it contributed practically nothing to prolonging military operations in Greece.

As for the Yugoslav campaign, it was far less 'unexpected' in a military sense than is usually believed. Although it drew forces from 'Barbarossa', it cannot really be said to have delayed, much less disrupted, its build-up. It should not have caused any delay at all to 'Marita', and such postponement as did occur was not strictly necessary. In more than one sense the Belgrade *coup* can be said to have come at exactly the right moment from the German point of view. Its overall effect on the Balkan campaign was to speed up considerably the military operations and particularly the transport of troops from 'Marita' back northward.

The factor which really determined the starting date of 'Barbarossa' was, it seems, the general shortage of equipment in the German army. However this may be, it is clear that many units from both 'Marita' and '25' could have been brought up considerably earlier than they were, a fact which proves that whatever delay was caused to 'Barbarossa' did not primarily result from the Balkan campaigns.

From Greece and Yugoslavia Hitler went on to occupy Crete. Although this island was potentially the most valuable prize to be won in the Balkan campaign, it must remain doubtful whether its capture served any strategical aim at all. Rather, it was the result of the personal ambitions of two generals, who for a short time succeeded in capturing Hitler's imagination.

This study should not be allowed to end without saying a word about the kind of consideration that guided Hitler in his attitude towards Greece and Yugoslavia. Hitler's strategy was not always dictated by reason, or in any case not by reason alone. 'Ideological' and 'spiritual' factors, not to mention 'biological' ones, often played a very important part in his reasoning, strengthening or weakening his determination to fight this or that particular opponent, leading him to under- or over-estimate this or that factor. To a quite remarkable degree, this kind of consideration is absent from Hitler's policy towards Greece and Yugoslavia. With the possible exception of Crete, where the Fuhrer's admiration for 'hard' men jumping out of the sky is sometimes supposed to have played a part, it seems perfectly possible to explain his thoughts about, his appreciation of and attitude to these countries on rational grounds. In discussing the subject there is no need to refer to any unusual aspects of his mentality, which would certainly be necessary when exposing his ambivalent attitude to England or his gross under-estimation of Russia. To a large extent, this rational attitude derives from the fact that Greece and Yugoslavia were, after all, only a small item in Hitler's strategy. Perhaps the number of problems encountered in this small item should teach us that no study of history can be detailed enough.

NOTE ON SOURCES

Nowadays the superabundance of source material on World War II has become something of a *cliché* to be mentioned in prefaces. Although this superabundance is as real in our subject as in any other, large tracts of the theme of this book have nevertheless not been adequately covered so far. Thirty years after, there still exists no single study of Hitler's Yugoslav policy.[1] Greece is in a somewhat better position, though among the numerous accounts of the antecedents of the Italian attack on her there is none that is really satisfactory in the sense of utilizing both Italian and German sources. No single work covers the entire Balkan campaign in anything like a comprehensive manner, and the conquest of Yugoslavia in particular has been neglected.[2] The crucial question of the relationship between the German campaign in the Balkans and the one they later waged in Russia has received lots of superficial answers but no serious consideration.

Thus, the subject at hand presents a number of large gaps on which no adequate work has been done so far. In order to at least partly fill these gaps all the usual printed sources, both diplomatic and military, have been used. Most of them, and certainly the more important ones, are too familiar to be mentioned here.

Unprinted, but scarcely less well known, are two large and important sources of evidence, the one diplomatic, the other military. In this book much use has been made of the records of the German foreign ministry, particularly the files of the Büro Reichsaussenminister, the Staatssekretär and the Unterstaatssekretär, as well as a number of less important files. The diary of the German Naval High command – a microfilmed copy of which can be found at the Admiralty, London – has also been quoted frequently. Both sources have already been used by hundreds of scholars, parts of them have been published in various contexts and in editions, so that they scarcely need any further introduction.

Far less well known is a large mass of unpublished military material, both Italian and German. The Italian military sources utilized consist of two files, entitled '*Esigenza "E"*' and '*Esigenza "G"*', both of which are available on microfilm. These contain orders, letters, directives and circulars originating in the Italian armed forces high command and the army high command, pertaining to the Italian plans for attacks on Yugoslavia and Greece respectively. This material is absolutely indispensable in any attempt to unravel the complex of German–Italian, German–Yugoslav–Greek and Italian–Yugoslav–Greek relations culminating in the Italian attack on Greece on 28 October 1940. In addition to these two, a number of smaller unnamed files containing material on the development of the Italo–Greek war and German–Italian relations while it was going on have been used.

Even more important than the Italian military material is a large number of German military files of various origins centring around the German campaigns in Greece and Yugoslavia. To the best of my knowledge, no attempt has so far been made to systematically use this first class, direct and reliable, though extremely dry and technical, material in an attempt to reconstruct the preparations, execution and results of the Balkan campaign. The evidence in question consists mainly (but not only) of various forms of *Balkan Akten* of the command posts involved down to the level of armies; that is, records of the armed forces high command, the army high command, Twelfth and Second army high commands and records of *Panzergruppe* Kleist, the most important (in size as well as in quality) unit subordinated to these, which occupies a place between that of a corps and an army. Practically all the material used, consisting of *geheime Kommando* – and *Chefsachen*, stems from Ia (operations) department of the command posts involved. This material, too, is available on microfilm. In terms of availability alone it would even be possible to get right down to the *Akten* and *Kriegstagebücher* of the individual corps and divisions involved, except that this would be a Herculean and, in the present context, to some extent a useless task, because most of the more important details can be found in the records of the higher commands.

Finally, special mention should be made of a number of studies by German officers or ex-officers, which are often highly interesting and which, unfortunately, have not been published. Under German military practice many of the senior command posts had their own officer responsible for putting the operations carried out by those posts into something very much resembling a historical treatise or article. This resulted in such specialized studies as 'Der Balkanfeldzug der 12. Armee – Generalfeldmarschal List', by Captain E. Wisshaupt, written shortly after the campaign by a person who had personally taken part in it. Studies not unlike these were also written by some German officers after the war, mostly in reply to specific questions posed by allied interrogators. This is a kind of material to which historical scholarship would do well to devote more attention.

NOTES

CHAPTER I

1 Mario Roatta, acting chief-of-staff to the Italian army high command.
2 *Documents on German Foreign Policy* (London, H.M. Stationery Office, 1956–, cit: *DGFP*), series D, volume x, doc. No. 343.
3 Enno von Rintelen, German military attaché in Rome.
4 German support in food, supplies, hospitals etc. was indispensable to the operation; Roatta memo No. 143, 9.7.1940, 'Italian Military Records' (IMR)/126/000590–602. The most important question was that of vehicles; after all possible sources had been enumerated Marshal Pietro Badoglio, chief of the Italian Stato Maggiore Generale (cit: Stamage, SMG) still saw no way of filling up his car park without German help. V. Roatta to Stamage, No. 12581 di Prot., 6.8.1940, *ibid.*/000763–67; Badoglio memo No. SMG Sez. Op./1, *ibid.*/000759–60; and Badoglio to the army high command (Superesercito), No. 1772 Op., 8.8.1940, *ibid.*/000617.
5 Hitler to Mussolini, 16.2.1943, printed in *Hitler e Mussolini, Lettere e Documenti* (Milan, Rizzoli, 1946) p. 153.
6 Cf. Ph.W. Fabry, *Balkan-Wirren, 1940–1941* (Darmstadt, Wehr und Wissen Verlagsgesellschaft, 1966, cit: Fabry, *Balkan*) pp. 10–12.
7 Hitler's speech to the Reichstag, 4 May 1941, printed in E. Domarus, *Hitler, Reden und Proklamationen, 1932–1945* (Munich, Süddeutscher Verlag, 1962) IV, 1698.
8 *DGFP*, D, VI, No. 229. The text of the pact is somewhat ambiguous, as it does not make it clear whether Germany's political disinterest extends to the whole of southeastern Europe or to Bessarabia only. This ambiguity was deliberately introduced by Ribbentrop, who thereby fell short of fulfilling Hitler's instructions to declare, if necessary, the Reich's political disinterest 'even as far as the Dardanelles'. Ribbentrop memo for Hitler, 24.6.1940, *ibid*. x, No. 10.
9 In 1939 German production of oil ran at 3.5 million tons annually; operational reserves stood at 2.5 million tons; and wartime requirements were estimated at 10 to 12 million tons. For what Rumania could do, and did, to alleviate this situation, v. the appendices to A. Hillgruber, *Hitler Köning Carol und Marschal Antonescu* (Wiesbaden, Steiner, 1953).
10 In 1939, Germany's deficit (consumption minus production) in copper amounted to 336,000 tons, of which Yugoslavia could supply 35,000; in lead, to 186,000 tons, of which she could supply 74,000; in aluminium, to 1,167,000 tons of which she could supply 371,000; in tin, to 38,000 tons of which she could supply 34,000. V. F. Friedensburg, *Die Rohstoffe und Energiequellen im neuen Europa* (Berlin, Gerhard Stalling, 1943).

11 M. Toscano, *Le origini diplomatiche del Patto d'Acciaio* (Florence, Sansoni, 1956), p. 221.

12 Attolico–Weizsäcker (German secretary of state) conversation, 31.3.1939, *DGFP*, D, VI, No. 140.

13 Unlike Italy (whose own industrialization was only one step ahead of that of the Balkan states) and France (hit by the economic depression) Germany in the thirties was able to absorb an almost unlimited quantity of raw materials, and supply machinery and equipment in return. This she started doing on a grand scale in 1936, under the direction of Dr Shacht. Purchasing raw materials offered by the Balkan countries at prices well above those of the world market, Germany quickly became their dominant trading partner. V. A. and V. Toynbee, *Survey of International Affairs, the World in March 1939* (London, Oxford University Press, 1952) pp. 259ff; also O. F. Marzari, 'The Balkans, the Great Powers and the European War, 1939–1940' (unpublished University of London Ph.D. thesis, 1966) pp. 13–17.

14 G. Ciano, *Diary, 1939–1945* (New York, Doubleday, 1946, cit: Ciano, *Diary*) entries for 15, 16.3.1939. Like England and France, Italy on this occasion withdrew its ambassador from Berlin under a pretext.

15 Speech on the 20th anniversary of the establishment of the first *fasci italiani di combattimento*, printed in B. Mussolini, *Scritti e Discorsi*, Edizione Definitiva (Milan, 1939) XII, 154–60.

16 During the talks between the German chief of OKW and the Italian vice-minister of defence on 6.4.1939 it was explained to the Italians that in the Führer's view Germany's basic eastern orientation should not, in view of the 'great economic importance' of the Balkan countries to the preparation for war, impede 'joint economic penetration' there 'in the first stage'; Keitel–Pariani conversation, 6.4.1939, *I Documenti Diplomatici Italiani* (Rome, Libreria dello Stato, 1952–, cit: *DDI*) series viii, vol. XIII, appendix III d. The Führer next sent Göring to Rome with the message that although Yugoslavia 'belonged one hundred percent' to Italy's sphere of influence this only meant that Germany 'did not wish to make an exclusive claim to southeastern Europe', and would not 'act unilaterally in carrying out major economic actions there'. Göring–Mussolini conversation, 15.4.1939, *DGFP*, D, VI, No. 205.

17 Ciano, *Diary*, entry for 5.7.1940. On another occasion, Mussolini told an unenthusiastic Hitler that he 'could not stand' the Yugoslavs; Mussolini to Hitler, 22.11.1940, *DGFP*, D, XI, No. 381.

18 Marzari, *The Balkans*, pp. 38–9.

19 Ciano, *Diary*, entry for 9.3.1939.

20 Marzari, *The Balkans*, pp. 41–2; J. B. Hoptner, *Yugoslavia in Crisis, 1934–1941* (New York, Columbia University Press, 1962) p. 136.

21 *Foreign Relations of the United States* (Washington, Government Printing Office, 1957–, cit: *FRUS*) 1939, I, doc. No. 82. V. also the verbal of the Mussolini/Ciano–Teleki/Czaky conversation, 20.4.1939, printed in M. Adam, *Allianz Hitler–Horthy–Mussolini* (Budapest, Akademiai Kiado, 1966) doc. No. 55.

22 Hoptner, *Yugoslavia in Crisis*, p. 120.

23 A telegram of 4 April in which the Italian foreign minister instructed his ambassadors in Paris and London to spread discreetly rumours that the Albanian expedition was designed to contain Germany is printed in Toscano, *Patto d'Acciaio*, p. 223; and there is reason to believe that it is correct in substance. Marzari, *The Balkans*, pp. 52–3.

24 Keitel–Pariani conversation, 6.4.1939, *DDI*, viii, xiii, appendix iii d.

25 Göring–Mussolini conversation, 15.4.1939, *DGFP*, D, vi, No. 205. The talks ended in an uneasy compromise: 'Yugoslavia. Friendly attitude while waiting for further developments in the internal policy of the country and the prerequisite of Yugoslavia's adopting a clear pro-Axis line. Germany to recognize Croatia as being purely in the Italian sphere of influence'. *Ibid.* No. 211.

26 Ciano, *Diary*, entry for 26.5.1939.

27 *DGFP*, D, vi, No. 271.

28 V. Macek, *In the Struggle for Freedom* (New York, Speller & Sons, 1957) pp. 189–90. The person with whom Mussolini was treating finally turned out to be a Belgrade spy; Hoptner, *Yugoslavia in Crisis*, pp. 138–9, 141.

29 Hitler–Ciano conversation, 12.8.1939, *DGFP*, D, vii, No. 43.

30 'Handelpolitische Verträge, Jugoslawien', Bd. iii, German Foreign Ministry Records (GFM)/8498/E597109–18. The treaty granted all Yugoslavia's copper production to Germany (incidentally forcing the Yugoslavs to seize the mines from their French owners) and also provided for the shipment of large quantities of lead, tin and zinc. In return, Yugoslavia was to have aircraft and guns. The agreement was confirmed and extended on 12 May 1940; v. the embassy in Belgrade to the foreign ministry, 12.5.1940, *DGFP*, D, ix, No. 237.

31 Ciano to Indelli, 4.10.1939, *DDI*, ix, i, No. 600.

32 R. Brugere, *Veni, Vidi, Vichy* (Varves, Calmann-Levy, 1944) pp. 165–6.

33 For details about the allied plans for a landing in Salonika v. *Die Geheimakten des französichen Generalstab*, ed. Auswärtiges Amt (Deutsches Weissbuch Nr. 6, Berlin, 1941).

34 For reports about Yugoslav fears, v. Mamelli (Italian minister in Belgrade) to Ciano, 16, 17.4.1940, *DDI*, ix, iv, Nos. 96, 97, 103; Fornari (councillor in Athens) to Ciano, 18.4.1940, *ibid.* No. 126; Butti (director of the European and Mediterranean affairs department at the Italian foreign ministry) to Ciano, 18.4.1940, *ibid.* No. 131.

35 For what it is worth, this account of Soviet–Yugoslav relations – about which very little is known – has been taken from Hoptner, *Yugoslavia in Crisis*, pp. 173–8.

36 Cf. F. Siebert, *Italiens Weg in den Zweiten Weltkrieg* (Frankfurt am Main, Athenäum, 1962) pp. 416ff.

37 In summer 1940 Italy had 73 divisions under arms, of which 24 were stationed overseas. Only 19 of the 49 divisions at home had reached their full establishment in men, animals and vehicles. The artillery was hopelessly outdated. Three more or less complete armoured divisions were equipped with tanks so light as to be useless. In Libya 4 motorized divisions were unable to move off the roads and were far below nominal strength. All infantry and mountain divisions disposed of 2 regiments only.

With some 1400 aircraft the quality of the air force was unknown. The navy was the best of the three services, but like the air force it suffered from lack of fuel. F. Rossi, *Mussolini e lo Stato Maggiore* (Rome, 1951) ch. 1.

38 For a good assessment of Mussolini's war aims and strategy during the spring of 1940, v. E. Faldella, *L'Italia e la Seconda Guerra Mondiale* (Rome, Cappelli, 1959) pp. 65–9, 128–62.

39 Stato Maggiore Esercito/Ufficio Storico: *L'Avanzata fino ad Sidi el Barrani* (Rome, Libreria dello Stato, n.d.) p. 185.

40 Printed in Faldella, *L'Italia* . . ., p. 145. An offensive was also planned in Italian East Africa; elsewhere Italy was to limit herself to '*chiudere le porte della casa*', in Badoglio's words.

41 Ciano, *Diary*, entry for 9.4.1940.

42 R. Graziani, *Ho difeso la Patria* (Rome, Garzanti, 1948, cit: Graziani, *Patria*) p. 189; G. Santoro, *L'Aeronautica italian nella Seconda Guerra Mondiale* (Rome, Esse, 2. edizione, 1957) pp. 77–8. Graziani was not happy about the plan; according to him the Yugoslavs were strong enough to tie his troops down indefinitely.

43 Anfuso (Ciano's *chef de cabinet*) memo, 23.1.1940, *DDI*, ix, III, No. 194; Ciano, *Diary*, entry for 10.5.1940.

44 *DDI*, ix, IV, No. 642.

45 F. Halder, *Kriegstagebuch* (Stuttgart, Kohlhammer, 1962–1963, cit: *KTB*/Halder) I, 255, entry for 11.4.1940; Spakter memo, 23.4.1940, 'Deutsche Botschaft Rom. Geheimakten 1940', GFM/2281/480553–57. The latter source quotes the Italian secretary of state.

46 *KTB*/Halder, I, 277, 283, entries for 4, 9.5.1940.

47 *Ibid.*, 309, entry for 21.5.1940.

48 This is a recurring theme in Hitler's speeches in the last years before the war. From the time OKH allocated for the Yugoslav campaign of 1941 (24 days instead of the actual 11) it is clear that his respect was genuine.

49 But not Greece; asked by the Yugoslav minister about her attitude, the Greek minister president on 14 May answered that 'Greece would in such a case stay neutral in spite of the Balkan pact, and only shoot at anybody who attacks Greece.' Erbach (German minister in Athens) to foreign ministry, Nr. 210 v. 15.5.1940, 'Staatssekretär, Akten btr. Griechenland', Bd. i, GFM/449/222710.

50 Hoptner, *Yugoslavia in Crisis*, p. 177; A. and V. Toynbee, *Survey of International Affairs, the Initial Triumph of the Axis* (London, Oxford University Press, 1958) p. 242.

51 *DGFP*, D, ix, No. 138.

52 Thomas–Keitel conversation, 26.4.1940, *ibid.*, ed.'s note, p. 240.

53 On 17 May Roatta had asked for deliveries of German war material to Italy on the grounds that, as the latter had planned to enter the war in 1945, she was unprepared to enter now; Rintelen to OKH/Genst. d.H/ Att. Abt., Nr. 55/40 g.Kdos v. 17.5.1940; OKW/Ausland to OKH/Genst. d.H/Att. Abt., Nr. 63/40 g.Kdos v. 23.5; and Rintelen to OKH/Genst.d. H/Att. Abt., Nr. 60/40 g.Kdos v. 28.5.1940. Rintelen to OKH/Genst.d. H/Att. Abt. file, item No. AL/1007 at the Imperial War Museum.

54 *KTB*/Halder, I, 316, entry for 23.5.1940.
55 Von Etzdorf (liaison man of the foreign ministry at OKH) memo for Weizsäcker, 27.5.1940, *DGFP*, D, IX, No. 328.
56 *DDI*, ix, IV, No. 646.
57 *Ibid.* No. 680. V. also L. Simoni, *Berlino, Ambasciata d'Italia, 1939–1945* (Rome, Migliaresi, n.d.) p. 122.
58 Mussolini to Hitler, 2.6.1940, *DDI*, ix, IV, No. 706.
59 Foreign ministry to Mackensen (German ambassador in Italy), 2.6.1940, 'Akten Büro Reichsaussenminister', GFM/F9/000365.
60 Heeren (German minister in Belgrade) to foreign ministry, Nr. 455 v. 2.6.1940. 'St.S. Jugoslawien', i, GFM/230/152237.
61 Graziani to Stamage, No. 460 di Prot., 3.6.1940, IMR/000161–62; Armellini promemoria, 2.6.1940, *ibid.*/000613; and Graziani telegram No. 337, 3.6.1940, *ibid.*/000158.
62 Heeren to foreign ministry, Nr. 377 v. 15.5, 'St.S. Jugoslawien', I, GFM/230/152207–8. That this was official policy is confirmed by the military attaché in Belgrade being requested by OKH to 'cooperate in an effort to soothe [Yugoslavia's] fears'; Heeren to OKH/Genst. d.H/Att. Abt., Nr. 400 v. 20.5.1940, 'St.S. Jugoslawien', I, GFM/230/152218. In Rome Mackensen was working in the same direction: Mackensen to foreign ministry, Nr. 785 v. 30.4, *ibid.* GFM/230/152188–89.
63 Woermann memo, 14.6.1940, 'St.S. Jugoslawien', I, GFM/230/152246; Heeren to foreign ministry, Nr. 473 v. 12.6, *ibid.* GFM/230/152243.
64 *DDI*, ix, v, No. 161. The German record of the same conversation (*DGFP*, D, x, No. 73) makes Hitler's language more restrained.
65 Badoglio directive No. 1089/Op., 4.7.1940, IMR/127/000751; Q .Armellini, *Diario di Guerra; Nove Mese al Commando Supremo* (Rome, Garzanti, 1946) p. 49.
66 Ciano, *Diary*, entry for 5.7.1940.
67 *DGFP*, D, x, No. 73.
68 *DDI*, ix, v, No. 200.
69 Unsigned SMG memo, 12.7.1940, IMR/126/000586–88.
70 Unsigned SMG memo, 12.7.1940, *ibid.*/000610–12.
71 Unsigned SMG memo, 8.8.1940, *ibid.*/000777–80.
72 Rintelen to OKH/Genst.d.H/Att. Abt., 22.7.1940, item No. 1007 at the Imperial War Museum; *KTB*/Halder, II, 35, entry for 25.7.1940.
73 Badoglio MSS note, 11.8.1940, IMR/126/000626.
74 *KTB*/Halder, II, 63, entry for 14.8.1940.
75 *Kriegstagebuch des OKW* (Frankfurt am Main, Bernard & Graefe, 1965, cit: *KTB/OKW*), I, 33, entry for 14.8.1940. Walter Warlimont was chief of 'L' (Landesverteitigung) department at OKW and its 3rd highest ranking officer.
76 *Ibid.* I, 36, entry for 15.8.1940.
77 *DGFP*, D, XI, p. 483, ed.'s note.
78 *Ibid.* No. 353, enclosure No. 2.
79 Woermann memo, 10.7.1940, 'St.S. Bulgarien', i, GFM/585/242618–19.
80 V. Ph. W. Fabry, *Der Hitler–Stalin Pakt* (Darmstadt, Fundus, 1962, cit: Fabry, *Hitler–Stalin*) pp. 257ff.

81 A creature of Ciano's, Alfieri was vain, stupid, irresponsible and so talkative that his master used him as a sure means to convey false information. V. *The Initial Triumph of the Axis*, p. 243; also Siebert, *Italiens Weg* . . ., p. 431. Funny stories about him dot the pages of the diary of his main collaborator at the Italian embassy in Berlin, Michele Lanza; Simoni, *Berlino* . . . pp. 187–8, 216, 219.

82 The only Greek export of any relevance to the Axis war industry was 180,000 tons of aluminium, equal to about 15% of German demand.

83 Grazzi to Ciano, 22.12.1939, *DDI*, ix, II, No. 688.

84 Halifax to Waterlow (British minister in Athens), 9.4.1939, *British Documents on Foreign Policy* (London, HM Stationery Office, 1952, cit: *DBFP*), series iii, vol. v. No. 112; Knatchbull-Hugessen (British minister in Ankara) to foreign office, 10.4.1939, *ibid.* No. 119.

85 Perth (British ambassador in Rome) to foreign office, 12.4.1939, *ibid.* No. 141.

86 Ciano to Grazzi, 26.5.1939, *DDI*, viii, XII, No. 35.

87 Grazzi to Ciano, 16.6.1939, *ibid.* No. 246; same to same, 8.7.1939, *ibid.* No. 512.

88 Thus, Ciano complained that the Greek press was too much in favour of the negotiations towards the signature of an Anglo–Franco–Turkish mutual assistance pact; that the chief of the Greek general staff was planning a visit to London; that Greece had called up reservists; and so on. Ciano to Grazzi, 17.6.1939, *ibid.* No. 262; same to same, 1.7.1939, *ibid.* No. 422. Grazzi to Ciano, 25.8.1939, *ibid.* viii, XIII, Nos. 240, 247, 275.

89 Weizsäcker to Mackensen, 15.4.1939, *DGFP*, D, VI, No. 203; Weizsäcker memo, 14.4.1939, *ibid.* No. 197; Marzari, *The Balkans* . . ., pp. 124ff.

90 Raeder–Cavagnari conversation, 18.5.1939, *DDI*, viii, XIII, appendix IV b.

91 Ciano–Ribbentrop conversation, 18.5.1939, *DGFP*, D, VI, No. 341.

92 *DGFP*, D, VIII, Nos. 210, 319.

93 Weizsäcker memo, 21.10.1939, *DGFP*, D, VIII, No. 287; Attolico to Ciano, 23.10.1939, *DDI*, ix, I, No. 684; Ciano to Attolico, 25.10.1939, *ibid.* ix, II, No. 7. The Italian refusal may have resulted from their appreciation of the anti-Soviet edge of the pact (e.g. De Peppo to Ciano, 6.9.1939, *ibid.* I, No. 55); however, it is just as likely that they appreciated the fact that the pact would not affect their Yugoslav plans. (Same to same, 21.9.1939, *ibid.* No. 359.)

94 Grazzi to Ciano, 6.9.1939, *ibid.* ix, I, No. 64; Ciano to Grazzi, 8.9.1939, *ibid.* No. 96; Mussolini to Grazzi, 12.9.1939, *ibid.* No. 166; and E. Grazzi, *Il Principio del Fine* (Rome, Faro, 1945) pp. 79–80.

95 *DDI*, ix, I, Nos. 543, 544.

96 Grazzi, *loc. cit.*

97 Grazzi to Ciano, 27.9, 30.9, 10, 11, 12.10.1939, *DDI*, ix, I, Nos. 457, 543, 678, 710, 729.

98 Same to same, 30.10.1939, *ibid.* II, No. 53.

99 Same to same, 27.11.1939, *ibid.* No. 349; Ciano to Grazzi, 29.11.1939, *ibid.* No. 379.

100 Attolico to Ciano, 30.10.1939, *DDI*, ix, i, No. 545.
101 Grazzi, *Il Principio* . . ., p. 98.
102 Geloso to Stamage, No. 10RP, 25.5.1940, IMR/127/000171–72.
103 The Duce, however, had 'not thrown in the sponge' over the Corfu incident; Ciano, *Diary*, entry for 10.8.1940.
104 In August 1940 Jacomini regulated many an operational detail not with the general staff but with Ciano directly, or through Benini the under secretary of state for Albanian affairs (*DDI*, ix, v, Nos. 442, 469, 508) who even communicated directly with the commander of the air force (e.g. Benini to Pricolo, No. 19520/2784, 6.9.1940, IMR/127/0000335), a remarkable procedure illustrating the extent to which the foreign ministry had a say even in minor operational detail. Visconti Prasca, too, considered himself responsible to the foreign minister when organizing the Ciano-inspired frontier incident that was supposed to open the attack on Greece (Visconti Prasca to Superesercito, No. 04420, 16.8.1940, *ibid.*/000381), so that the general staff, expressly fearing an unauthorized Ciano-adventure, took care to remind him to proceed on its own orders only before approving his request for various kinds of equipment. V. Badoglio to Superesercito, No. 1944 Op., 17.8.1940, *ibid.*/000370; and handwritten note on Sorice to Direzione Generale di Artiglieria, No. 137518/41/2, 17.8.1940, *ibid.*/000142.
105 Erbach to foreign ministry, Nr. 155 v. 12.4, 'St.S. Griechenland', i, GFM/449/222701; same to same, Nr. 210 v. 15.5, *ibid.* GFM/449/222712; *KTB*/Halder, I, 277, 305, entries for 4, 19.5.1940.
106 Cf. G. Gigli, *La Seconda Guerra Mondiale* (Bari, Laterza, 1951) p. 156.
107 Mackensen to foreign ministry, 25.4.1940, *DGFP*, D, IX, No. 165.
108 Attolico to Ciano, 22.4.1940, *DDI*, ix, IV, No. 163. The assumption that the Germans did in fact have their plans for Greece also explains the otherwise absolutely incomprehensible hints concerning a German demand for passage (in an unspecified direction) through Yugoslavia; 'St.S. Jugoslawien', I, Pol iv g. v. 29.5, GFM/230/152227, and *ibid.* Nr. 396 v. 19.5, GFM/230/152116. It also explains an interesting entry in Halder's diary, according to which Hitler hoped to interest the Italians in Crete and Cyprus, while the Bulgarian demand for an 'outlet to the Mediterranean' at the expense of Greece would 'present no difficulties'. *KTB*/Halder, II, 21, entry for 13.7.1940.
109 Seekriegsleitung memo, April 1940, 'Wünsche an Italien für dem Fall dass Italien auf eine gemeinsame Operation auf dem deutschen Kriegsschauplatz eingeht', GFM/8230/E85473–74.
110 The idea of asking Germany for a guarantee against Italy seems to have originated with the Greek minister in Berlin, Alexander Rizo Rangabe. (Woermann to embassy in Greece, 25.5, *DGFP*, D, IX, No. 318.) On 4 June a Greek request for insurance against an Italian attack, based on assumption that Germany did not want a conflagration in southeastern Europe, arrived in Berlin. (Woermann memo, 4.6.1940, *DGFP*, D, IX, No. 384.) Though we do not possess the German answer, it is quite clear that nothing came of the proposal; *ibid.* Nos. 395, 403.

111 Wiehl to the legation in Athens, 14.6.1940, *ibid.* No. 435.

112 Ciano, *Diary*, entry for 3.7.1940.

113 *DGFP*, D, ix, No. 73. The last sentence certainly presented a strange view of Metaxas, who only eight months previously was being accused of being pro-Axis and against whose regime the allies were reported to be plotting.

114 On 6 March 1941 Rintelen sent Mackensen the following telegram: 'the foreign minister requests you to delicately ask . . . whether the Italian government has in its possession any original material from which the help extended by Greece . . . to Britain before the start of the Italo-Greek war can be proved. Should this be so, we would be grateful if the material were handed over to us, since it would be well employed in diplomatic discussions here, in which this question raises time and again.' 'St.S. Griechenland', i, No. 148 v. 6.3, GFM/449/223073. The Italian reply is even more interesting: Anfuso asserted that although he had for long been working on the collection of such material, it consisted mainly of 'memoranda concerning conversations between count Ciano and the Greek minister, as well as conversations between minister Grazzi and the Greek government', so that it would be 'of but little use to us'. Mackensen to foreign ministry, Nr. 525 v. 8.3.1941, 'Unst.S. Griechenland', xii, GFM/675/258371.

115 *DDI*, ix, v, No. 200.

116 This interpretation is put forward by G. Warner, 'Italian Policy towards Yugoslavia and Greece, 1938–1940' (unpublished article at the University of Reading) pp. 6–7.

117 When, it will be remembered, he was struggling 'with all possible means' to keep 'the Balkans' quiet while at the same time authorizing the Duce to improve his strategic situation 'very much as the Führer had done in the case of Denmark and Norway'. The examination of the evidence seems to bear out the thesis that, under the Axis geopolitical system, Greece was not included in the 'Balkans'; in no case was she thus listed in any German–Italian discussion, e.g. *DGFP*, D, vii, Nos. 266, 354, 362, 591, and especially in Mackensen to foreign ministry, No. 847 v. 9.5.1940, 'St.S. Deutsch–italienische Beziehungen', ii, GFM/1571/380312, where under the heading 'Balkanstaaten–Italien', all possible states (Rumania, Hungary, Yugoslavia, Bulgaria and even Slovakia) except Greece are mentioned. The practice was also consistently followed in the diary of the German navy high command, which omits Greece from the 'Balkans' while including Hungary, Yugoslavia, Rumania and Bulgaria; e.g. 'Kriegstagebuch der Seekriegsleitung' (cit: KTB/SKL), Teil A, Heft xii, entry for 1.8.1940, GNR/3/000004.

118 'Settore danubiano-balcanico'; Ciano to Mussolini, 20.7.1940, *DDI*, ix, vi, No. 274. Though no German record of this conversation has been found it should be noted that the translation of this expression as 'the Balkans and the Danube' by the *DGFP* (e.g. D, x, No. 484) is misleading, as it creates the impression that the 'Danube' was distinct from 'the Balkans'. In this connection it is significant that the German original of the last named record retains the Italian expression.

119 E. Schramm von Thadden, *Griechenland und die Grossmächte im Zweiten Weltkrieg* (Wiesbaden, Steiner, 1955) p. 74.

120 *DDI*, ix, v, No. 386. For the Greek version of the affair, v. the official *communique* of the Agence d'Athens, 12.8.1940, 'St.S. Italien', ii, GFM/B14/002166. According to this version Daut Hoxha, a murderer with a prize of twenty years standing on his head, had been killed by Albanians, not Greeks. Somewhat naively, Rizo Rangabe hoped to have this account published in Germany, but Weizsäcker told him to forget about it. (Weizsäcker memo, 13.8.1940, *DGFP*, D, x, No. 343.) The Germans nevertheless knew perfectly well that the charges were fabricated; Panwitz (German consul in Tirana) to foreign ministry, 17.8.1940, 'St.S. Italien', iii, GFM/B14/002172.

121 Ciano, *Diary*, entries for 10 and 11.8.1940.

122 S. Visconti Prasca, *Io ho agreddito la Grecia* (Milan, Rizzoli, 1946) pp. 31–4. The proposed operation aimed at the occupation of Ciamuria only, i.e. was limited in scope. If it were to succeed, such a 'colpo di mano' could not but lead to a British landing in what was left of Greece; so much was clear even to the Italian general staff. Unsigned SMG memo, 16.8.1940, IMR/127/000382.

123 Ciano, *Diary*, entry for 12.8.1940. Ciano himself agreed with Visconti Prasca about the timing, and in defiance of Mussolini ordered him to attack in 15 days; Visconti Prasca to Stamage, No. 04220, 16.8.1940, IMR/127/000381.

124 Erbach to foreign ministry, 13.8.1940, *DGFP*, D, x, No. 333.

125 Alfieri to Ciano, 14.8.1940, *DDI*, ix, v, No. 413.

126 Ciano to Alfieri, 15.8.1940, *ibid.* No. 420. The Palazzo Chigi was apparently out to create the impression that, while the Daut Hoxha affair was to be exploited politically, any military action that might be taken would be directed against the British; Mackensen to foreign ministry, Nr. 1515 v. 14.8, 'St.S. Italien', iii, GFM/B14/0002170–71.

127 This is quite clear from the wording of the note, which mentions Greece only as a possible complication resulting from an Italian attack on Yugoslavia; it was not intended to veto an attack on Greece.

128 Alfieri to Ciano, 16.8.1940, *DDI*, ix, v, No. 429.

129 Same to same, *ibid.* No. 431.

130 Ciano, *Diary*, entry for 17.8.1940. The wording of this entry seems to show that the Italian foreign minister was under the impression that Alfieri had carried out his original instructions; otherwise, his reference to an 'eventual' attack on Greece – which he himself had just ordered to start in 15 days – is incomprehensible.

131 Armellini, *Diario di Guerra*, p. 59; Roatta to Stamage, No. 307 di Prot., Nov. 1940, IMR/126/000683–85.

132 Roatta letter No. 15801 di Prot., 19.8.1940, IMR/126/000646–47, and unsigned SMG Ufficio Op. Sez. 1. memo, 24.8.1940, *ibid.*/000631.

133 Note on unsigned SMG Ufficio Op. Sez. 1. memo, 11.9.1940, *ibid.*/000585.

134 Typewritten comment on Badoglio directive No. ES/Op./4, 11.9.1940, *ibid.*/000369. Roatta's statement that in the second half of September

everything was ready for the attack on Yugoslavia to start 'within 24 hours' (M. Roatta, *Otto Millioni di Bayonette*, Verona, Mondadori, 1946, pp. 117–18) should be taken with a pinch of salt.

135 'On 10 September general Soddu communicated that Mussolini was furious against Yugoslavia and that consequently it was necessary to hold in readiness *'Esigenza "E"* against Yugoslavia.'/ Rossi, *Mussolini*, p. 74.

136 Armellini, *Diario di Guerra*, p. 79; Badoglio directive No. 2485 Op., 12.9.1940, IMR/126/000643–45.

137 Rossi, *Mussolini*, pp. 74–5. For the significance of this order in Mussolini's overall strategy, see A. Hillgruber's interesting evaluation in *Hitlers Strategie* (Frankfurt am Main, Bernard & Graefe, 1965, cit: Hillgruber, *Strategie*) pp. 283–5.

138 Graziani circular No. 234, 4.10.1940, IMR/126/000660–61. It is probably no accident that the order dates from the day of Mussolini's meeting with Hitler, during which his ideas on Greece were also radically modified; v. below, p. 35.

139 Mackensen to foreign ministry, 17.8.1940, *DGFP*, D, x, No. 357.

140 Ciano to Alfieri, 17.8.1940, *DGFP*, D, x, No. 353, enclosure No. 1.

141 *DDI*, ix, v, No. 467.

142 Ciano, *Diary*, entry for 22.8.1940.

143 Mussolini to Hitler, 24.8.1940, *DDI*, ix, v, No. 484.

144 Schramm von Thadden, *Griechenland*, p. 74.

145 Badoglio to Roatta, No. 2016 Op., 20.8.1940, IMR/127/000373.

146 Ciano to Jacomini, 22.8.1940, *DDI*, ix, v, No. 469; Roatta to Visconti Prasca, No. 1650 di Prot., 23.8.1940, IMR/127/000361.

147 Roatta to Badoglio and Soddu, No. 1800 di Prot., 26.8.1940, IMR/127/000353–54.

148 Roatta to Ufficio di SM della R[eale] Marina, No. 3675 di Prot., 29.8.1940, *ibid.*/000349; Somigli to Superesercito, No. 35227, 26.8.1940, *ibid.*/000365–66; Armellini, *Diario di Guerra*, pp. 66, 70.

149 Badoglio to Superesercito and Supermarina, 31.8.1940, IMR/127/000345.

150 It is significant that the Italians never seem to have regarded the German 'veto' as the reason for the postponement of the operation. Mussolini himself had always wanted to wait until the end of September (Ciano, *Diary*, entry for 12.8.1940); both before and after the outbreak of war: Ciano, Jacomini, Visconti Prasca and Farrinaci agreed that Badoglio was responsible for the delay. V. Armellini, *Diario de Guerra*, p. 159; Mackensen to foreign ministry, Nr. 473/40 g. v. 18.10.1940, 'Deutsche Botschaft Rom, Geheimakten 1940', GFM/2281/481684–87. Ciano even repeated this version to the Germans (same to same, *ibid.* Nr. 500/40 v. 1.11, GFM/2281/481735–37) who, after all, ought to have known.

151 Ciano, *Diary*, entry for 17.8.1940.

152 *DDI*, ix, v, No. 484.

153 On 19 September; *DGFP*, D, xi, No. 73, and *DDI*, ix, v, No. 617. The question of what exactly was said on the occasion is controversial and will be discussed below. It should be noted, however, that both records

stress the anti-British character of the attack on Greece as described by Mussolini.

154 *DGFP*, D, XI, No. 135; 'St.S. Italien', iii, GFM/B14/002306; *ibid*. Nr. 1884 v. 19.10.1940, GFM/B14/002292; KTB/SKL, A 14, entry for 27.10.1940, GNR/3/000576. The conversations are dated 30.9, 14,19 and 25.10 respectively.

155 Ciano, *Diary*, entry for 11.8.1940; *DGFP*, D, x, p. 509, ed.'s footnotes Nos. 1, 4.

156 Rintelen memo, 28.10.1940, 'Unst.S. Griechenland', xii, GFM/675/258392–93.

157 Armellini, *Diario di Guerra*, p. 50; F. Jacomini, *La Politica dell'Italia in Albania* (Rome, Cappelli, 1965) pp. 223–4). According to the latter authority Rome 'could not make up its mind whether to opt for the small solution (annexation of Ciamuria and a new Italo-Greek accord) or a radical one (total military occupation of the country). As late as the end of August they tended to the political solution.' Ciano seems to have said something to Mackensen about 'diplomatic pressure' (*DDI*, ix, v, No. 439) while the fact that the Daut Hoxha affair was raised only two months after the actual murder may also show that Rome had decided to plunge for the 'small' solution.

158 Erbach to foreign ministry, 13.8.1940, *DGFP*, D, x, No. 333.

159 Printed in Jacomini, *La Politica . . .*, pp. 234/6. The document bears no date, but the reference to the Second Vienna Award as a solution 'being adopted' makes the days 25–7 August likely.

160 *KTB*/Halder, I, 308, entry for 21.5.1940.

161 Weizsäcker memo, *DGFP*, D, x, No. 334.

162 Woermann to the embassy in Greece, 22.8.1940, *ibid*. No. 377.

163 Woermann memo, 20.8.1940, 'St.S. Griechenland', i, GFM/449/222777.

164 Ribbentrop to the legation in Greece, 24.8.1940, *DGFP*, D, x, No. 386, where the legation is ordered not to make any positive statements. Clodius from the foreign ministry economic department also told two Greek representatives that 'Greece was risking more by her rigid attitude than by conforming to our wishes', adding that he 'did not think it was in Greece's interest to maintain her attitude until the English domination of the Mediterranean was broken'. 'Handakte Clodius', GFM/9924/E694694. Clearly, this campaign of intimidation was directed from above.

165 Erbach to foreign ministry, *DGFP*, D, x, No. 333.

166 *KTB/OKW*, I, 42, entry for 9.8.1940. How ridiculous the whole Italian hoax was is shown by the fact that while Mussolini referred to the Vitry la Charité documents Hitler had sent him, to justify his invasion of Greece, Ribbentrop himself was begging Rome for original material to prove Greece's guilt. (Cf. footnote 114 above.)

167 *DGFP*, D, x, No. 394. This threat must have been tailored especially for Rizo Rangabe's use, as Berlin knew he had opposed mobilization; *ibid*. No. 386, and *DDI*, ix, v, No. 478.

168 *DDI*, ix, v, No. 439; *DGFP*, D, x, No. 363; 'St.S. Italien', iii, GFM/B14/002193–94.

169 On 23 September; Schramm von Thadden, *Griechenland*, p. 91.

170 Jacomini, *La Politica*, p. 245, quoting Grazzi.
171 *DDI*, ix, v, Nos. 478, 490; *DGFP*, D, x, No. 387; Ciano, *Diary*, entry for 26.8.1940.
172 Simoni, *Berlino* . . ., p. 164, entry for 24.8.1940. Ciano himself wrote that Ribbentrop had referred Rizo Rangabe to Rome, because 'Germany is in perfect accord with us about everything.'
173 The Royal Greek Ministry for Foreign Affairs, *The Greek White Book* (London, Hutchinson, 1942), doc. No. 127, pp. 85–6
174 The campaign was suspended on 24 August; Panwitz to foreign ministry, Nr. 34 v. 21.8.1940, 'St.S. Griechenland', i, GFM/449/222775; Grazzi, *Il Principio*, p. 224.
175 Rossi, *Mussolini*, pp. 80–1.
176 Schramm von Thadden, *Griechenland*, p. 63.
177 Visconti Prasca, *Io ho agreddito*, p. 23.
178 Faldella, *L'Italia* . . ., p. 262; Roatta, *Otto Millioni* . . ., p. 120; Rossi, *Mussolini*, p. 82. After the occupation of Ciamuria 'a new Italo–Greek accord' would be reached; Jacomini, *La Politica* . . ., p. 224.
179 Roatta to Badoglio and Soddu, No. 1800 di Prot., 26.8.1940, IMR/127/ 000353/54; SMG Ufficio Op. Sez. 1. memo, 10.9.1940, *ibid.*/365–66.
180 *DDI*, ix, v, No. 439.
181 Armellini, *Diario di Guerra*, p. 65, entry for 28.8.1940: 'Ciano wants his war and, recent directives notwithstanding, he will probably get it.'
182 H. Greiner, *Die Oberste Wehrmachtführung* (Wiesbaden, Limes, 1951) p. 174; Rintelen to OKW, Nr. 140/40 g.Kdos v. 21.8.1940, 'Verbindungstab beim Admiralstab der königliche italienische Marine', Teil 7c, GNR/580(F)/000373.
183 *DGFP*, D, x, No. 377.

CHAPTER 2

1 Ermannsdorf (German minister in Budapest) to foreign ministry, 5.7.1940, *DGFP*, D, x, No. 119; Schulenburgh (ambassador in Moscow) to foreign ministry, *ibid*. No. 406; Talamo (Italian minister in Budapest) to Ciano, *DDI*, ix, iv, No. 379.
2 The first Vienna Award had given parts of Ruthenia to Hungary in October 1938.
3 By 19 July at the latest. V. Hillgruber, *Strategie*, pp. 144–65.
4 For details v. K. Klee, *Das Unternehmen 'Seelöwe'* (Göttingen, Musterschmidt, 1958).
5 'Directive No. 16', printed in H. R. Trevor-Roper, *Hitler's War Directives* (London, Sidgwick & Jackson, 1964) pp. 34–6. A second order, 'directive No. 17', was issued on 1 August; *ibid*. p. 37.
6 KTB/SKL, A 12, entry for 14.8.1940, GNR/3/000086.
7 Hillgruber, *Strategie*, p. 171.
8 Klee, *Seelöwe*, pp. 198–204.
9 'Führer Conferences on Naval Affairs' (printed in *Brassey's Naval Manual*, 1948, cit: FCNA) 1940, ii, 101. As early as 13 September Hitler 'did not dream' of taking the risk connected with the operation,

and after considering its abolition decided to pursue preparations further so as not to drop the 'moral pressure' on England. *KTB/OKW*, I, 76, 78.

10 *DGFP*, D, VIII, No. 514, and ed.'s note.

11 I. SKL, Teil 6 a, unsigned SKL memo, 'Frage der Besetzung der Azoren', GNR/55/001125–30. The occupation of these islands, like the 'peripheral' strategy as a whole, was directed as much against the US as against England; Hillgruber, *Strategie*, pp. 196–206.

12 For details M. Toscano, *Una Mancata Intesa Italo-Sovietica nel 1940 e 1941* (Florence, 1951).

13 OKW/WFSt/Abt.L. Nr. 33 120/40 g.Kdos Chefsache v. 28.6.1940, 'Kriegführung gegen England', 'Oberkommando des Kriegsmarine/ Weisungen OKW', vol. I, I April 1939–1 April 1941, GFM/8589/ E602749–50. This plan 'inspired by Germany' was a brainchild of OKW. An offensive from 'Transcaucasia' into Iraq with the aim of cutting British communications between east and west was being considered. OKW/WFA/Abt.L. Nr. 494/40 g.Kdos v. 21.3.1940, 'Die militärpolitische Lage im Nahen Orient', signed by Keitel.

14 *Trials of Major War Ciminals* (International Military Tribunal, Nuremberg, 1949, cit: *TMWC*) XXVII, 301.

15 *DDI*, ix, v, No. 161.

16 *KTB*/Halder, II, 45, entry for 30.7.1940.

17 *Ibid.* II, 38, 47, 72, 82, entries for 27, 31.7. 23, 31.8.1940; v. also *KTB/ OKW*, I, 17, entry for 9.8.1940.

18 *KTB/OKW*, I, 56, 64, entries for 2, 5.9.1940.

19 'Aktennotiz über die Entwicklung der Rüstungslage im Sommer 1940', 20.8.1940, printed in *KTB/OKW*, I, 968; v. also Hillgruber, *Strategie*, pp. 355–60.

20 FCNA, 1940, II, 95–7, 104–8.

21 *KTB/OKW*, I, 72, 74, entries for 10, 11.9.1940.

22 *KTB*/Halder, II, 31, entry for 22.7.1940; v. also Raeder's record of the same conference with Hitler, printed in Klee, *Seelöwe* p. 240.

23 In June Franco offered to enter the war (*DGFP*, D, IX, No. 488); however, it was not until the adoption of the 'peripheral' strategy that Hitler showed any interest in the offer.

24 *DGFP*, D, XI, Nos. 63, 97. For the entire Spanish question, v. D. S. Detwiller, *Hitler, Franco und Gibraltar* (Wiesbaden, Steiner, 1962).

25 Rintelen to OKH/Genst.d.H/Att.Abt., Nr. 67/40 g.Kdos v. 11.9.1940.

26 Ciano, *Diary*, entry for 13.9.1940.

27 v. Hillgruber, *Strategie*, pp. 232ff.

28 Gigli, *La Seconda Guerra . . .*, p. 156.

29 I. SKL, c, xiv, 'Deutsche Kriegführung im Mittlemeer, Feb.–Dec. 1941', Schniewind memo Nr. I. Op. 692/41 g.Kdos Chefsache v. 24.5.1941, GNR/51/000077–80; I. SKL, Teil xiii, Weicholz memo v. 1.1.1941, *ibid.*/000786–810; and I. SKL, c, xiv, unsigned memo v. 1.6.1941, 'Die Strategische Lage im östlichen Mittelmeer nach Balkanfeldzug und Kretabesetzung und die weitere Kampführung', *ibid.*/000082–94. Though written somewhat later than the events discussed here and partly

meant to dissuade Hitler from his Russian campaign, the strategic ideas expressed hold good for any period.

30 J. R. M. Butler, *Grand Strategy* (London, H.M. Stationery Office, 1954–) II, 372–73.

31 V. below, pp. 36–7.

32 Armellini, *Diario de Guerra*, p. 91.

33 The Ribbentrop–Mussolini talks have been interpreted in various ways, none of them satisfactory. According to T. Higgins, *The Soft Underbelly* (New York, Macmillan 1966), p. 9, Ribbentrop gave the Duce the Green light over Greece because Hitler 'recognized the need for such a small scale compensation . . . for his frustrated . . . ally', in view of his own intention to occupy Rumania. Hillgruber, *Strategie*, p. 283, regards the talks as the end of Mussolini's Yugoslav ambitions. Schramm von Thadden, *Griechenland*, p. 91, says Ribbentrop personally overestimated the Italian military machine and 'regarded Greece through Italian eyes', a view for which there is no firm evidence. W. Langer and S. Gleason, *The Undeclared War* (Washington D.C., Dept. of State, 1953) take Ribbentrop's word for a *laissez aller* over both Greece and Yugoslavia.

34 V. Th. Sommer, *Deutschland und Japan zwischen den Machten, 1935–1941* (Tübingen, Mohr, 1962) p. 398.

35 The German record is *DGFP*, D, XI, No. 73; the Italian one, *DDI*, IX, No. 617. The latter has 'full support' and 'main forces' respectively for the words in inverted commas.

36 *DGFP*, D, IX, No. 165.

37 V. below, p. 36.

38 *DGFP*, D, XI, No. 149.

39 *KTB*/Halder, II, 150, 151, entries for 25, 26.10.1940; *KTB*/*OKW*, I, 131, entry for 28.10.1940.

40 *DGFP*, D, X, No. 313, 326; *KTB*/Halder, II, 79, entry for 27.8.1940; v. also K. Assmann, 'Die Bemühungen der Seekriegsleitung um ein deutschfranzösisches zusammengehen gegen England und die Behauptung des französischen Kolonialreichs in Afrika v. 3.7.1940–27.11.1942' (a SKL study, GNR/117(P)/000464–607). In this connection it should be added that SKL, despite its interest in the occupation of Gibraltar, was as well aware as anyone of the weakness of Spain, and more interested in North West Africa (as a submarine base) than anyone else.

41 The demands are listed in *DGFP*, D, IX, No. 488.

42 On the Canary Islands; Franco to Hitler, 27.9.1940, *DGFP*, D, XI, No. 88, and Hitler–Suner conversation, *ibid.* No. 117.

43 For Hitler's basic attitude towards France, G. Geschke, *Die deutsche Frankreichpolitik 1940* (Frankfurt am Main, Mittler, 1960) pp. 12–14, 137.

44 *KTB*/*OKW*, I, 93, entry for 26.9.1940; E. Jäckel, *Frankreich in Hitlers Europa* (Stuttgart, Deutsche Verlagsanstalt, 1966) pp. 108–9.

45 *KTB*/Halder, II, 109.

46 *KTB*/*OKW*, I, 88–9.

47 E. Raeder, *Mein Leben* (Tübingen, Schlichtenmayer, 1951) p. 246.

48 Klee, *Sealöwe*, p. 114.

49 Ciano, *Diary*, entry for 28.9.1940. This time Hitler did not delegate the

task to Ribbentrop, probably because the latter was known for his anti-French views; *KTB*/Halder, II, 117, entry for 29.9.1940.

50 *KTB*/Halder, II, 118–19, 121, entries for 30.9, 2.10.1940.

51 Geschke, *Die deutsche Frankreichpolitik 1940*, p. 42. For a series of Italian pinpricks, dating from 6 September to 24 October and obviously designed to raise German mistrust of the French, v. 'St.S. Frankreich', iii, GFM/121/119851, 119891, 120051, 120077, 120079; also Rintelen to OKH/Genst.d.H/Att. Abt., App. Nr. 7 zu Nr. 56/40 g.Kdos v. 7.8.1940, and same to same, Nr. 67/40 g.Kdos v. 11.9.1940, item No. 1007 at the Imperial War Museum. So great was the Italian fear of a *rapprochement* that they contemplated the creation of an Italo–French block designed to contain Germany (*DDI*, ix, v, No. 417).

52 KTB/SKL, A 13, entry for 1.9.1940, GNR/3/000208; *DGFP*, D, XI, No. 28.

53 The French had asked for help (*La delegation francaise aupres de la commission allemande d'armisitice*, Paris, 1946, i, pp. 384, 387, 391; *KTB*/ *OKW*, I, 95, entry for 28.9.1940) and Hitler complied by releasing French forces stationed in Africa for the purpose. He then faced the Italians with a *fait accompli* and told them, in effect, to shut up (*DGFP*, D, XI, No. 96).

54 *KTB*/*OKW*, I, 102–3, entry for 1.10.1940.

55 *Ibid.* I, 109, entry for 3.10.1940.

56 Geschke, *Die deutsche Frankreichpolitick 1940*, p. 70. At that time Ribbentrop seems to have regarded Spain's entry into the war as settled.

57 *KTB*/Halder, II, 121, entry for 2.10.1940.

58 The most recent warning dated 30 September; *DGFP*, D, XI, No. 135. V. also E. von Weizsäcker, *Memoirs* (London, Gollancz, 1951) p. 244.

59 This, at any rate, was what the Germans considered the result of the meeting; *KTB*/Halder, II, 129, entry for 8.10.1940; *KTB*/*OKW*, I, 111, entry for 5.10.1940. The German record of the conversation is *DGFP*, D, XI, No. 159; the Italian one, *DDI*, ix, v, No. 677.

60 Ciano, *Diary*, entry for 4.10.1940; *DDI*, ix, v, No. 617; Armellini, *Diario di Guerra*, pp. 119–20. Schmidt, the German interpreter, noted Mussolini's interest in the announcement that the centre of war should be transferred to the eastern Mediterranean; P. Schmidt, *Statist auf diplomatischer Bühne* (Bonn, Athenäum, 1953) p. 499.

61 Simoni, *Berlino*, p. 172. Von Etzdorf also had very little information about the talks when first reporting about them to OKH on 8 October; *KTB*/Halder, II, 129.

62 *KTB*/Halder, II, 186, entry for 18.11.1940.

63 *DGFP*, D, XI, No. 191. This, exactly a fortnight after the meeting.

64 *KTB*/*OKW*, I, 124, entry for 23.10.1940.

65 KTB/SKL, A 14, entry for 25.10.1940, GNR/3/000562.

66. 'St.S. Italien', iii, Nr. 1884 v. 19.10, GFM/B14/02292, and *DGFP*, D, XI, No. 302. This question is discussed in detail below.

67 As is proved by the appearance of the word 'Autowagen' (in inverted commas) in the German original record. This is simply a too literal translation of the Italian *autocarro*, lorry.

68 V. above, p. 21, note 138.

69 Armellini, *Diario di Guerra*, pp. 97, 105–6. The text of the note is printed in Stato Maggiore Esercito, Ufficio Storico, *La prima offensive britannica in africa settentrionale* (Rome, Libreria dello Stato, n.d.), 1, 30–1. The note for Graziani ordered him to resume his attack in Egypt by 15 October at the latest; this is clearly an attempt by Mussolini's side to keep the promise he gave to Hitler during the conference. R. Graziani, *In Africa Settentrionale, 1940–1941* (Rome, Danesi, 1948, cit: Graziani, *Africa*) p. 103.

70 It will be remembered that up to this time the Italian operational plan aimed to seize Ciamuria alone. As late as 13 October Badoglio issued a directive (No. 3084) based on the assumption that this was the case. Faldella, *L'Italia . . .*, p. 268.

71 This was intended 'to teach Hitler a lesson'; Armellini, *Diario di Guerra*, p. 99.

72 KTB/SKL, A 14, entry for 21.10.1940, GNR/3/00536.

73 E. L. Woodward, *British Foreign Policy in the Second World War* (London, H.M. Stationery Office, 1970), I, pp. 509, 510.

74 KTB/SKL, A 13, entry for 13.9.1940, GNR/3/000296; *ibid.* A 14, entry for 29.10.1940, GNR/3/000594. All this does not mean that SKL was enthusiastic about the matter, because it was feared that Mussolini was planning 'LAND ACTIONS (original emphasis) only', and that the operation was beyond Italy's operational ability. However, the basic strategic importance of the question was clearly recognized.

75 *Ibid.* A 14, entry for 25.10.1940, GNR/3/000562. In relation to our interpretation of previous events the statement that in the interest of the war against England it had **basically** been agreed with the Italians that no **military** action would take place in the **Balkans** is particularly interesting.

76 *DDI*, ix, v, No. 617.

77 *KTB*/Halder, II, 152, 153, entries for 27, 28.10.1940. The operation would aim at closing the Mediterranean and driving out the British fleet. Ultimately, an advance into Iraq would deprive England of her oil.

78 *Ibid.* 148, 151, entries for 24, 26.10.1940. The Germans might perhaps be prepared to support an operation against Crete by means of paratroopers (Simoni, *Berlino*, p. 177, entry for 24.10.1940) and such plans, considered and rejected by the Italian general staff (Rossi, *Mussolini*, p. 80), seem to have been mentioned in some German–Italian staff talks, as can be inferred from a memo prepared by Rintelen for *OKW* on 23.10.1940; GNR/50/000769–70.

79 *KTB/OKW*, I, 125, entry for 24.10.1940.

80 *Ibid.* I, 132, entry for 28.10.1940.

81 *Ibid.* I, 131–2, entry for 28.10.1940.

82 Not all the German staffs agreed with this order of operations. SKL, in a memo dated 1 September, had claimed that the conquest of Crete was an 'indispensable preliminary' (in view of the transport situation) to a successful attack on Egypt. Anlage zu KTB/SKL, c, xiv, 'Lagebetrachtung des Chefs des Verbindungstabes beim königlichen italienischen Kriegsmarine' (Weicholz), pp. 10–13, GNR/112/0000920–3.

83 Hitler to Mussolini, 20.11.1940, *DGFP*, D, XI, No. 369.
84 Armellini, *Diario di Guerra*, pp. 106, 110–11, 124–5.
85 *Ibid.* pp. 111, 120.
86 Roatta, *Otto Millioni* . . . , pp. 120–2; Armellini, *Diario de Guerra*, p. 113.
   The claim frequently heard that Mussolini was pushed into his war
   against Greece by the German occupation of Rumania (v. Ciano, *Diary*,
   entry for 12.10.1940) can, I think, be safely disregarded. The Italians
   knew everything about that action before it took place (*DDI*, ix, v, Nos.
   590, 596, 615, 618) and Ciano himself mentioned it in his diary before it
   took place. (Ciano, *Diary*, entry for 8.10.1940.) Even without all these,
   it is rather unlikely that Mussolini's first reaction to the news was to
   contemplate a postponement by three months of his invasion of Greece.
   Rather – this conclusion seems inevitable – his aim was to bring it into
   the context discussed between him and Hitler at the Brenner.
87 Unsigned SMG memo, '*appunto per il Duce*', 18.9.1940, IMR/127/000315.
88 *Hitler e Mussolini, Lettere e Documenti*, pp. 61–7.
89 Rintelen to OKW/WFSt/Ausland, 23.10.1940, I. SKL, c, xiii, 'Italienische Kriegführung', GNR/50/000769–70.
90 *KTB/OKW*, I, 120, entry for 11.10.1940. The enquiry may have resulted
   from fresh rumours concerning the attack; KTB/SKL, A 14, entry for
   10.10.1940, GNR/3/000469.
91 *KTB/OKW*, I, 123, entry for 18.10.1940: 'Italian attack on Greece with
   10 divisions at the end of October (26.10?)'. V. also Rossi, *Mussolini*,
   p. 85, and E. von Rintelen, *Mussolini als Bundgenosse* (Tübingen, Wunderlich, 1951) p. 108.
92 Ciano, *Diary*, entry for 18.10.1940; Armellini, *Diario di Guerra*,
   p. 119
93 Heeren to foreign ministry, Nr. 766 v. 21.10, 'St.S. Jugoslawien', i,
   GFM/230/15235; Papen to foreign ministry, Nr. 883 v. 18.10, 'St.S.
   Griechenland', i, GFM/449/22803; *KTB/OKW*, I, 123, entry for 22.10.
   1940; Greiner, *Wehrmachtführung*, p. 182.
94 'Deutsche Botschaft Rom, Geheimakten 1940', GFM/2281/481684–87.
95 'St.S. Italien', iii, GFM/B14/002291. The date given by this telegram
   makes it quite impossible that Hitler thought he still had time.
96 *Ibid.* GFM/B14/002292.
97 *DGFP*, D, XI, No. 302. In this document, dated 7.11.1940, Ritter sums
   up the proceedings prior to the Italian attack. It appears that even though
   the warnings were raining down on Berlin during the last hours before
   Hitler's departure for France the Führer did not even authorize 'a
   friendly inquiry', not to mention a veto. It seems that a second attempt
   to stop the Italians was made by Kordt and Weizsäcker; in this case
   Hitler rejected a draft that had already been approved by Ribbentrop.
   E. Kordt, *Nicht aus den Akten* (Stuttgart, Deutsche Verlagsgesellschaft,
   1950) p. 408.
98 *DGFP*, D, XI, No. 209. In this cable Weizsäcker also told Mackensen
   that his anxiety that 'the other end of the Axis' should be treated carefully
   (in view of the Rumanian business) was shared 'in the highest places'.
99 *KTB*/Halder, II, 132, 139, entries for 10, 15.10.1940.

100 Der Sekretär des Führers: *Führers Tagebuch*, 1934–1943 (photostat), p. 66.
101 *KTB*/Halder, II, 124, entry for 3.10.1940.
102 For the technical details v. Jäckel, *Frankreich* . . ., pp. 110–15.
103 Handwritten note by Kordt, GFM/F12/000079.
104 *DGFP*, D, XI, No. 207, 208.
105 Geschke, *Die deutsche Frankreichpolitik 1940*, p. 97; Jäckel, *Frankreich* . . ., p. 114.
106 *DGFP*, D, XI, No. 212.
107 *Ibid.* No. 220.
108 Schmidt, *Statist*, p. 504.
109 The record of the conversation is *DGFP*, D, XI, No. 227 Even though Pétain himself was fairly reserved he did not stop Laval from interrupting and raising proposals that went far beyond his own; instead, he burst into an eulogy of Hitler. Jäckel's interpretation of this episode as a deliberate attempt on Pétain's side to shift the subject sounds hollow.
110 Geschke, *Die deutsche Frankreichpolitik 1940*, p. 111.
111 *KTB*/Halder, II, 152, 158, entries for 27.10, 1.11.1940; Lagebesprechung OKW/WFSt/Abt.L, 29.10.1940, printed in Klee, *Dokumenten*, p. 122. Hitler later described Petain as 'Hindenburg personified'.
112 *KTB/OKW*, 127, 129, 130–1, 135, 145, entries for 25, 27, 28, 29.10, 1.11.1940; KTB/SKL, A 14, entry for 26.10.1940, GNR/3/000577; Geschke, *Die deutsche Frankreichpolitik 1940*, pp. 81, 95–6. On 25 October the foreign ministry was 'radiant'. They 'believed they had succeeded in . . . reaching an accord with France'. (Simoni, *Berlino*, p. 178.) On 26 and 27 October Abetz reported that Laval had already taken steps to implement the agreement and that the approval of the French cabinet had been obtained. (*DGFP*, D, XI, Nos. 234, 241.)
113 Perhaps even by an immediate Ribbentrop–Laval meeting as indicated by O. Abetz, *Das offene Problem* (Cologne, Greven, 1951) p. 158.
114 *DDI*, ix, v, No. 719.
115 Woermann memo, 23.10, 'St.S. Italien', iii, GFM/B14/002301.
116 Armellini, *Diario di Guerra*, pp. 125–6.
117 *DGFP*, D, XI, No. 205.
118 KTB/SKL, A 14, entry for 23.10.1940, GNR/3/000548.
119 *DDI*, ix, v, No. 793. The demands included a rectification of the Franco–Italian border, as well as the cession of Nice, Corsica, Tunis, Somali, etc.
120 Ciano, *Diary*, entry for 24.10.1940.
121 'Akten Büro RAM', GFM/F1/000516–18. The meeting was supposed to take place on 5 November; Rintelen, *Mussolini* . . ., p. 109.
122 'Akten Büro RAM', GFM/F1/00050–51.
123 Ribbentrop to Mackensen, Nr. 6 v. 25.10, 'St.S. Frankreich', iii, GFM/121/120084–85. It is this version that is printed in *DGFP*, D, xi, No. 199.
124 Mackensen to foreign ministry, Nr. 1914 v. 25.10.1940, 'St.S. Italien', iii, GFM/B14/002309.
125 Ciano, *Diary*, entry for 25.10.1940.

126 Ribbentrop to foreign ministry, Nr. 7 v. 25.10, 'St.S. Italien', iii, GFM/B14/002308.
127 Nr. 1511 v. 26.10, 'St.S. Italien', iii, GFM/B14/002312. At 1900 hours on the 25th, the German chief of protocol, who was in Paris, had also been informed; Ribbentrop to Doerenberg, 25.10, *ibid.* GFM/B14/002311.
128 Keitel affidavit, *TMWC*, x, 523; Schmidt, *Statist auf diplomatischer Bühne*, p. 505; Weizsäcker, *Memoirs*, p. 244. Schmidt and Weizsäcker contradict each other in giving different dates for the decision and about the identity of the message that caused it. Keitel did not mention the Greek affair when informing OKW: *KTB/OKW*, 1, 128, entry for 26.10.1940.
129 KTB/SKL, A 14, entry for 29.10.1940, GNR/3/000589.
130 Greiner, *Wehrmachtführung*, p. 182; Rintelen, *Mussolini*, p. 108; *KTB/OKW*, 1, 123, 125, entries for 22, 24.10.1940; *DGFP*, D, XI, No. 225.
131 Heeren to foreign ministry, Nr. 766 v.21.10, 'St. S. Jugoslawien', i, GFM/230/015235.
132 'St.S. Italien', GFM/B14/002306; Rintelen to OKW, 23.10.1940, KTB/SKL, C xiii, GNR/3/000769–70; same to same, 25.10.1940, *ibid.* GNR/3/000782–84. Rintelen in particular seems to have regarded the attack as a settled matter and was keeping up a lively speculation as to the motives behind it.
133 *KTB/OKW*, 1, 124, entry for 23.10.1940. The claim (Schramm von Thadden, *Griechenland*, p. 93) that Jodl could not possibly have been right because otherwise Ciano would have used Hitler's *laissez aller* when scolded by the latter does not carry conviction for the following reasons: 1. Ciano did in fact raise precisely this claim. 2. As an argument it was useless, because Hitler later blamed Italy for botching up the Greek affair, not for starting it.
134 The copy sent from Rome to Berlin is Nr. 1913 v. 25.10, 'Deutsche Botschaft Rom, Geheimakten 1940', GFM/2281/481693; the one sent from Berlin to 'Heinrich' is 'St.S. Griechenland', i, GFM/449/222811.
135 Historical opinion notwithstanding, it is a fact that Hitler's journey to Italy was not characterized by any great haste. Instead of redirecting his train to Florence in the afternoon of the 25th, he spent the night of 25/26 October at Yvoir, then travelled on to Munich on 26th. From there he departed for Florence at 1800 hours on the 27th. (*Führers Tagebuch*, pp. 66–7.) Even if a direct journey is ruled out on security grounds, there was no reason why a day should be wasted in Munich.
136 Ciano, *Diary*, 22.10.1940.
137 Simoni, *Berlino*, p. 177; also Faldella, *L'Italia . . .*, p. 287.
138 While the letter itself is stamped 'forwarded by OKW teleprinter', Zamboni, an official at the Italian embassy in Berlin, at 2300 hours cabled to Rome that the German foreign ministry had received the letter and that Weizsäcker had assured him it would be transmitted to Hitler by special envoy next morning. V. M. Cervi, *Storia della Guerra di Grecia* (Milano, Sugar, 1965) p. 120.

139 This question has been examined in greater detail than is possible here in M. van Creveld, '25 October 1940; a Historical Puzzle', *Journal of Contemporary History*, June 1971, pp. 87–96.

140 *DGFP*, D, xi, No. 191.

141 According to the Italians, OKW and SMG had agreed – presumably as a result of the Brenner meeting – 'about the need to drive the English out of ALL [emphasis supplied] their positions in the Mediterranean, and if possible in the Near East, during the winter'. KTB/SKL, A 15, entry for 2.11.1940, GNR/3/000627.

142 Weizsäcker, *Memoirs*, p. 244.

143 Rintelen, *Mussolini*, p. 109. From this source it is clear that Keitel's statement to Badoglio – assuming the latter did not invent it – to the effect that he would have flown to Rome to stop the attack had he but known of it (P. Badoglio, *L'Italia nella Seconda Guerra Mondiale, Memorie e Documenti*, Milan, Mondadori, 1946, p. 51) is nonsensical.

144 *KTB*/Halder, ii, 154, entry for 29.10.1940.

145 *Ibid*, ii, 158, entry for 1.11.1940.

146 FCNA, 1940, ii, 149.

147 Etzdorf note, 28.10.1940, 'Aufzeichnungen des Vertreters des Aus- wärtiges Amt von Etzdorf', GFM/1247/337515.

148 *KTB/OKW*, i, 124, entry for 23.10.1940.

149 *Ibid.* 129, entry for 27.10.1940.

150 Ritter to 'Heinrich', 27.10.1940, 'St.S. Italien', iii, GFM/B14/002317.

151 *KTB/OKW*, i, 129, entry for 28.10.1940; also Schmidt, *Statist*, p. 506.

152 Printed in Hillgruber, *Strategie*, p. 286. Hitler also addressed some derogatory remarks to the Italians, whom he accused of being 'spies'.

153 *KTB*/Halder, ii, 29.10.1940; *KTB/OKW*, i, 147, entry for 3.11.1940.

154 *DGFP*, D, xi, No. 302; *KTB*/Halder, ii, 181, entry for 15.11.1940. There is no indication that a culprit was ever found.

155 This telegram reached Ribbentrop at 2320 hours. Together with a second despatch, in which Mackensen transmitted the text of the ulti- matum, it was *zerreis*-ed on 29 October. As Hewel signed this operation, the order is likely to have come from Hitler. V. Nr. 1945, 1946 v. 27.10, 'Deutsche Botschaft Rom, Geheimakten 1940', GFM/2281/481694, 481695–702.

156 Schmidt, *Statist*, p. 506.

157 Ciano, *Diary*, entries for 24, 25.10.1940; Armellini, *Diario di Guerra*, p. 125.

158 The German record is *DGFP*, D, xi, No. 246; the Italian one *DDI*, ix, v, No. 807.

159 *Führers Tagebuch*, p. 67.

160 Ciano, *Diary*, entry for 28.10.1940.

161 *KTB*/Halder, ii, 157, 158, entries for 31.10, 1.11.1940.

162 V. above, p. 43, footnotes Nos. 130 and 132.

163 The Italian operational plans were based on the assumption that no major complications would arise, and this assumption proved to be correct. During the conference of 15 October Ciano had said Greece

would not fight because her leaders had been bribed, and he repeated this claim to Badoglio ten days later. (Badoglio, *L'Italia* . . ., p. 48.) The Italian ultimatum to Greece carefully avoided the word 'war', and Rome regarded the fact that Metaxas did not speak of 'war at any price' as an encouraging sign. (Mackensen to foreign ministry, Nr. 523 v. 28.10, 'St.S. Griechenland', i, GFM/449/222825.) At 1445 hours they had not yet given up hope (same to same, Nr. 1950 v. 28.10, 'St.S. Italien', iii, GFM/B14/002318) while on the 29th it was the Greeks, not the Italians, who broke off diplomatic relations.

164 Weizsäcker memo, 28.10, 'St.S. Griechenland', i, GFM/449/222830; Kramarz memo, 28.10, 'Unst.S. Griechenland', xii, GFM/675/258397. The last mentioned document sums up what was known of the Greek army with the words 'the Greek army is incapable of independent military action or even of defending its country without foreign aid'.

165 Heeren to foreign ministry, 26.9.1940, *DGFP*, D, XI, No. 110; same to same, 25.10.1940, *ibid.* No. 229; KTB/SKL, A 14, entry for 30.10.1940, GNR/3/000595.

166 Mussolini's messenger boy on this occasion, Anfuso, has described them in some colourful detail in his *Da Palazzo Venezia al Lago di Garda* (Bologna, Cappelli, 1957) pp. 139–42; v. also Badoglio, *L'Italia*, p. 54.

167 Richthofen (German minister in Sofia) to foreign ministry, Nr. 498 v. 24.10, 'St.S. Bulgarien', ii, GFM/585/242744.

168 KTB/SKL, A 14, entry for 29.10.1940, GNR/3/000590; Woermann memo, 31.10, 'St.S. Bulgarien', ii, GFM/585/242753, and same to same, Nr. 518 v. 31.10, *ibid.* GFM/585/242751. The Greeks themselves counted on Bulgarian neutrality since September; A Papagos, *The Battle of Greece* (Athens, Hellenic Publishing Press, 1949) p. 252.

169 Papen (German ambassador in Ankara) to foreign ministry, Nr. 883 v. 18.10, 'St.S. Griechenland', i, GFM/449/222803.

170 Papen to OKH, 29.10, 'St.S. Turkei', ii, GFM/265/172442; Weizsäcker memo, Nr. 789 v. 29.10, *ibid.* GFM/265/172445; Fabricius to foreign ministry, Nr. 1918 v. 29.10, *ibid.* GFM/265/172443.

CHAPTER 3

1 KTB/SKL, Handakten 'Felix' 'Niederschrift über Besprechung Chefs I. SKL bei Chefs WFSt/OKW', 4.11.1940, p. 7. GNR/3/000501.

2 *KTB*/Halder, II, 164, entry for 4.11.1940.

3 *Ibid.* 154, entry for 29.10.1940.

4 Cf. Fabry, *Hitler–Stalin*, pp. 321, 346. More than anywhere else, this method is evident in 'directive No. 18' itself, where instructions are given for military measures to be taken against no less than three countries in advance of the respective political decisions and regardless of their results.

5 *KTB*/Halder, II, 102, 110, 113, 138, 144, 144–5, 147, entries for 16, 23, 26.9, 15, 20, 21, 23.10.1940.

6 The best short discussion is C. Barnett, *The Desert Generals* (London, Kimbler, 1960), chs. I, II.

7 *KTB/OKW*, I, 64, entry for 5.9.1940. Even earlier attempts were made

in July (*DDI*, ix, v, No. 161) and August (*KTB/OKW*, I, 17, entry for 9.8.1940) but had remained unanswered.

8 *KTB/OKW*, I, 73, entry for 11.9.1940.

9 *Ibid.* I, 78, entry for 14.9.1940.

10 *Ibid.* 81, 83, entries for 18, 20.9.1940.

11 'The employment of such units ... is certainly useful. But it can take place only if adequate logistic organisation is provided for, which does not seem possible given the means at our disposal.' Graziani, *Africa*, p. 112, and E. Cavenari, *La Guerra Italiana* (Rome, Tossi, 1949) II, 185.

12 Printed in Faldella, *L'Italia . . .*, p. 233. Basically, the problem was that the Germans offered integral units, while the Italians wanted to have material only; Rintelen to OKH/Genst.d.H/Att.Abt., Nr. 67/40 g.Kdos v. 11.9.1940; OKH/Genst.d.H/Att.Abt. to Rintelen, Nr. 34/40 g.Kdos v. 3.9.1940, both in bundle No. 1007 at the Imperial War Museum.

13 *DDI*, ix, v, No. 677.

14 *DGFP*, D, XI, No. 149.

15 Rintelen, *Mussolini*, p. 101; Armellini, *Diario di Guerra*, p. 105. Mussolini informed Graziani of this decision (Graziani, *Africa*, p. 103) while OKW concluded that 'discussions with the Duce very harmonic. The Italian offensive in Egypt is to be resumed between 12 and 15 October. He wants armoured fighting vehicles, particularly for the continuation of the offensive after the fall of Mersa Matruh. Führer has promised 100 ...' (*KTB/OKW*, I, 111, entry for 5.10.1940).

16 Armellini, *Diario di Guerra*, pp. 114–16.

17 Printed in Faldella, *L'Italia . . .*, p. 249.

18 *KTB/OKW*, I, 118–19, entry for 10.10.1940.

19 *Ibid.* 120, entry for 14.10.1940.

20 Graziani, *Africa*, pp. 103–6; Faldella, *L'Italia . . .*, p. 248.

21 Armellini, *Diario di Guerra*, p. 129. Mussolini was reluctant to accept German forces even after Graziani's defeat by the British on 9 December; *ibid.* p. 220.

22 *KTB/OKW*, I, 124, entry for 23.10.1940.

23 *KTB*/Halder, II, 149–50, entry for 24.10.1940.

24 *Ibid.* 150, 152, entries for 25, 26.10.1940.

25 *Führers Tagebuch*, p. 67.

26 *KTB*/Halder, II, 156, entry for 31.10.1940.

27 This clearly was the main reason; Hillgruber, *Strategie*, pp. 181, 346.

28 For details v. KTB/SKL, A 15, entry for 30.10.1940, GNR/3/000601. However, these difficulties did not prevent the despatch of German forces to Libya in January, even though shipping losses in the Mediterranean had by then grown considerably.

29 B. H. Liddell-Hart, *The Other Side of the Hill* (London, Cassell, 1948) p. 234, where Thoma himself is quoted; *KTB/OKW*, I, 150–1, entry for 4.11.1940.

30 At the same time, the conquest of Greece would secure the Italian Dodecanese Islands which, though sufficiently close to Alexandria to be of use as air bases against her, could not be utilized because it was impossible to supply them with fuel.

31 *KTB/OKW*, I, 141, entry for 31.10.1940.

32 KTB/SKL, A 15, entry for 8.11.1940, GNR/3/000650.

33 *KTB/OKW*, I, 143, entry for 1.11.1940. Halder's reaction to this shows the Germans were not taken in; 'Badoglio suggests we reinforce our mission in Rumania. (Nonsense! Wants to hold us in readiness for "Bulgaria").' *KTB*/Halder, II, 150, entry for 31.10.1940.

34 *KTB/OKW*, I, 143, entry for 1.11.1940; KTB/SKL, A 14, entry for 29.10.1940, GNR/3/000594. If the attack on Greece was comparable to the German capture of Norway, then the failure to seize Crete was comparable to a German failure to go for Trondheim or Narvik. It was this *LIMITED* [double emphasis in the original] character of the operation that surprised and embarrassed the Germans; KTB/SKL, A 14, entry for 28.10.1940, GNR/3/000582–83.

35 Schmidt, *Statist*, p. 507, whose account is usually quoted in this connection, says that it was in the 'long . . . nights of the NEXT YEAR' [emphasis supplied] that Hitler lamented the Italian action. This is an interesting statement to which I shall return.

36 *KTB/OKW*, I, 144, entry for 1.11.1940; *KTB*/Halder, II, 158, entry for 1.11.1940.

37 *KTB/OKW*, I, 144, entry for 1.11.1940.

38 G. Ciano, *L'Europa verso la Catastrofe* (Milan, Mondadori, 1946, cit: Ciano, *L'Europa*) p. 615. The British Imperial Staff would have agreed.

39 *KTB*/Halder, II, 160, entry for 2.11.1940.

40 The following account blends two different entries in Halder's diary; one recording the chief of the army general staff's notes for his report to Hitler (*ibid.* II, 159–62) and the other a transcription of the Führer's decisions at the conference itself. (*Ibid.* 163–5, entry for 4.11.1940).

41 V. above, p. 37, footnote 77. Two corps and three (or six) months were required for the operation.

42 *KTB*/Halder, II, 191, entry for 24.11.1940: 'during the last conference the Fuhrer told me: "we can go to the Straits only after Russia is beaten"'.

43 *Ibid.* II, 166, entry for 4.11.1940.

44 *KTB/OKW*, I, 150, entry for 4.11.1940.

45 KTB/SKL, Handakten 'Felix', 'Niederschrift über Besprechung I. SKL bei Chefs WFSt/OKW General Jodl am 4.11.1940', p. 2, GNR/115/000469–503.

46 Thus, the SKL diary, says that the menace to the Rumanian oil fields was to be dealt with by the 'immediate' dispatch of air force units (not mentioned anywhere else), while the German invasion of Greece, directed against Larissa and not against Lemnos, was supposed to be 'in support of the Italian offensive'. This statement is in turn contradicted by Hitler telling Halder that he wanted the Italians 'to go it alone'. (*KTB*/Halder, II, 159, entry for 1.11.1940.) A further sign of confusion is the note by the SKL diarist saying that 'two divisions of two corps' were being considered. It seems hopeless to try and unravel this tangle of conflicting, incomplete and partially nonsensical statements.

47 B. Mueller-Hillebrand, 'Der Zusammenhang zwischen den deutschen Balkanfeldzug und der Invasion in Russland' (Koenigstein/TS, 1951,

MS No. AL 1454 at the Imperial War Museum, Cit: Mueller-Hillebrand, *Zusammenhang*) pp. 4–5.

48 In this context it is interesting that, according to the Greek military attaché in Berlin, OKH was planning 'to attack the British fleet and bases in the eastern Mediterranean and for this purpose intended to establish air bases in eastern Thrace . . . in connection with advance bases in the Dodocanese. . . This German plan has nothing to do with giving assistance to Italy in Albania.' British Foreign Office Documents (unprinted, cit: BFOD), Sargent memo, 30.10.1940, C. 13139/764/19.

49 *KTB/OKW*, I, 150/51, entry for 4.11.1940.

50 *Ibid.* I, 152.

51 *Ibid.* I, 157.

52 Printed in Trevor Roper, *Hitler's War Directives*, pp. 39–43.

53 KTB/SKL, A 14, entry for 30.10.1940, GNR/3/000596.

54 For a detailed discussion v. Jäckel, *Frankreich . . .*, p. 126.

55 *KTB*/Halder, II, 155, 156, entries for 31.10.1940; *KTB/OKW*, I, 148–9, 158, 160, entries for 1, 4, 7, 8.11.1940; also *ibid.* p. 979, appendix C, No. 37.

56 *KTB/OKW*, I, 182, entry for 19.11.1940; OKW/WFSt/Abt.L Nr. –/40 g.Kdos v. 22.11.1940, and OKW/WFSt/Abt.L Nr. 79/40 g.Kdos Chefsache v. 26.11, both in Sammelmape 'Akten btr. Weisung Nr. 18', item No. M.I 4/14/620 at the Imperial War Museum. Also *KTB*/Halder, II, 179, entry for 14.11.1940. On 13 November Greiner noted that it was again intended to offer Badoglio German air force units for the second stage of the Italian offensive; *KTB/OKW*, I, 171, and *KTB*/Halder, II, 185, entry for 18.11.1940.

57 *KTB/OKW*, I, 191, entry for 27.11.1940.

58 KTB/SKL, A 15, entry for 8.11.1940, GNR/3/000666. The demand was repeated by SKL on 14 November; FCNA, 1940, ii, 154.

59 'Besprechung Innsbruck . . . Ägypten-Angriff kommt zunnächts überhaupt nich mehr in Frage.' *KTB*/Halder, II, 185, entry for 18.11.1940.

60 KTB/SKL, A 15, entry for 26.11.1940, GNR/3/000782. The lack of any reference to the threat to the Rumanian oil fields in this context is of course illuminating.

61 H. Greiner, 'Das Eingreifen auf dem Balkan 1940–1941' (MS No. AL 1039/1 at the Imperial War Museum, cit: Greiner, *Balkan*) pp. 1–2. V. also *KTB/OKW*, I, 180, entry for 19.11.1940.

62 *KTB*/Halder, II, 191, 194, entries for 24, 25.11.1940.

63 Under the programme for the enlargement of the army from 120 to 180 divisions, all divisions were required to cede some of their men and staffs for the establishment of new units; in November 1940, no less than 70 divisions had thus been made incomplete.

64 *KTB/OKW*, I, 69, entry for 29.8.1940.

65 The purpose for which the army group was moved to Poland has been the subject of some discussion. Here the views expressed by Hillgruber, *Strategie*, p. 234, are accepted.

66 *KTB*/Halder, II, 165, entry for 4.11.1940.

67 'Panzergruppe Kleist auf dem Balkan' folder, quoted by Fabry, *Balkan* p. 73.

68 *Ibid.*
69 *KTB*/Halder, II, 167, entry for 6.11.1940. Of 5th mountain division only 100th regiment was ready; the rest of the division would be ready only by end December.
70 Hitler–Teleki conversation, 20.11.1940, *DGFP*, D, XI, No. 365; Ribbentrop memo, 21.11.1940, 'Akten Büro RAM', GFM/F16/000024.
71 Fabry, *Balkan*, p. 82.
72 *DGFP*, D, VIII, Nos. 102, 237.
73 According to Warlimont: Fabry, *Hitler–Stalin*, p. 281.
74 *KTB*/Halder, II, 168, entry for 6.11.1940.
75 *Ibid.* 170, entry for 7.11.1940.
76 *Ibid.* 172, entry for 8.11.1940.
77 *Ibid.* 175, entry for 9.11.1940.
78 *Ibid.* 175, entry for 11.11.1940. Kinzel was regarded as especially suitable for the job because he had done similar work in the Balkans during World War I.
79 Perhaps because the Yugoslavs mobilized their army when it was reported, in mid-November, that the Italians would demand rights of transit to Albania; Heeren to foreign ministry, Nr. 828 v. 12.11.1940, 'St.S. Jugoslawien', i, GFM/230/152355. At the end of the month, OKW received a report from Athens to the effect that 'a German attempt to march through Yugoslavia will be resisted by force of arms'; Kramarz memo, Nr. 1401 g.Rs. v. 26.11.1940, *ibid.* GFM/230/152392.
80 In all geographic descriptions, here and henceforward, the original German map (OKH/Abt. für Kriegskarten und Vermessungswessen, Karte d. Mittelbalkan, 1941, at the map room of the British Museum) has been used. The advantage of this particular map is that it shows frontiers, roads and railways as they were at the time.

CHAPTER 4

1 *The Ribbentrop Memoirs* (London, Weidenfeld & Nicolson, 1954) pp. 148–50.
2 V. above, p. 29.
3 *KTB*/Halder, II, 32–4, 48–50, entries for 22, 31.7.1940. The most detailed description of these preparations is contained in E. Paulus, *Die Entwicklung der Planung des Russlandfeldzuges* 1940–1941 (University of Bonn Diss. Phil., MS., 1956).
4 V. Fabry, *Hitler–Stalin*, p. 321, esp. footnote No. 466.
5 For a much more detailed discussion, v. Hillgruber, *Strategie*, pp. 207–41, 351–75.
6 Rather optimistically, he hoped that suitable diplomatic action would prevent a consequent deterioration in German–Soviet relations; *KTB/OKW*, I, 115, entry for 8.10.1940.
7 KTB/SKL, A 14, entry for 30.10.1940, GNR/3/000595.
8 Sommer, *Deutschland und Japan*, pp. 461–2; also Fabry, *Hitler–Stalin*, 328–9.
9 *DGFP*, D, XI, No. 118.

10 *KTB*/Halder, II, 118, entry for 30.9.1940.
11 Fabry, *Hitler–Stalin*, pp. 324–5.
12 *DGFP*, D, XI, No. 176; *KTB*/Halder, II, 148, entry for 15.10.1940; for a detailed analysis, Fabry, *Hitler–Stalin*, pp. 343–5.
13 'Russia: Molotov 10.11. Berlin. Stalin's answer to the Führer's letter. He agrees to the explanations of the Führer. Molotov will come to Berlin. The adherence of Russia to the Tripartite Pact is then expected.' *KTB*/Halder, II, 148, entry for 24.10.1940.
14 Schulenburg to foreign ministry, 31(?).10.1940, *DGFP*, D, XI, No. 260.
15 At Florence. The Italians were surprised by the announcement of Molotov's visit.
16 Ciano, *L'Europa*, pp. 608–11. No German record of this rather informal meeting has been preserved.
17 *DGFP*, D, XI, No. 309.
18 *Ribbentrop Memoirs*, p. 151.
18a The records of Molotov's conversations with Hitler and Ribbentrop are in *DGFP*, D, XI, Nos. 326, 328, 329, 348.
19 For an analysis of the talks, v. Fabry, *Hitler–Stalin*, pp. 349–57.
20 Boris to Hitler, 22.10.1940, *DGFP*, D, XI, No. 217.
21 Richthofen (German minister in Sofia) to foreign ministry, Nr. 475 v. 15.10.1940, 'St.S. Bulgarien', i, GFM/585/242737.
22 Same to same, Nr. 518 v. 31.10, *ibid*. GFM/585/242751.
23 Where they were reported to have 34 divisions; Schramm von Thadden, *Griechenland*, p. 127.
24 Ritter to Richthofen, 6.11.1940, *DGFP*, D, XI, No. 295.
25 Richthofen to foreign ministry, Nr. 540 v. 7.11.1940, quoted in *DGFP*, D, XI, No. 345.
26 Ritter to Richthofen, 16.11.1940, *DGFP*, D, XI, No. 345.
27 *Ibid*. ed.'s Note No. 5.
28 No record of the conversation has been found in the archives of the foreign ministry; but cf. *KTB*/*OKW*, I, 179, entry for 19.11.1940.
29 Papen to foreign ministry, 22.11.1940, *DGFP*, D, XI, No. 378.
30 Richthofen to foreign ministry, 21.11.1940, *ibid*. No. 373.
31 Hitler–Draganov conversation, 23.11.1940, *ibid*. No. 384.
32 Richthofen to foreign ministry, 26.11.1940, *ibid*. No. 403.
33 Same to same, 29.11.1940, *ibid*. No. 430.
34 Draganov–Hitler conversation, 3.12.1940, *ibid*. No. 438.
35 The news of the signature of the Ribbentrop–Molotov pact sent the Turks into a 'stupor' and caused Saracoglu to request that the duration of Turkey's mutual assistance pact with England and France be extended from 5 to 15 years. V. R. Massigli, *La Turquie devant la Guerre, Mission à Ankara, 1939–1940* (Paris, Plon, 1964) pp. 247–9.
36 L. Krecker, *Deutschland und die Türkei im Zweiten Weltkrieg* (Frankfurt am Main, Klostermann, 1964) pp. 81–7. According to Massigli Ankara first heard of the project from Moscow and not from Paris; and Turkish consent was never asked because it was clear that it would not be forthcoming. Massigli, *La Turquie*, pp. 381ff., 398ff. Late in 1940 German–Turkish relations also suffered from rumours about the establishment of

British bases in Asia Minor; Woermann memo, 10.10, 'St.S. Türkei', ii,
GFM/265/172421; Fabricius (German minister in Bucharest) to foreign
ministry, Nr. 1782 v. 15.10, *ibid.* GFM/255/172424.

37 For a more detailed account v. Krecker, *Deutschland und die Turkei*,
pp. 101–3.

38 Unsigned memo, 21.9.1940, 'St.S. Türkei', ii, GFM/265/172416.

39 Papen to foreign ministry, Nr. 795 v. 20.9, *ibid.* GFM/265/172415.

40 According to Saracoglu the Turkish foreign minister 'Turkish–Soviet
relations were improving and would soon become very intimate.' Fabricius to foreign ministry, Nr. 1766 v. 12.10, *ibid.* GFM/265/172423.

41 'The [German] foreign minister called the breaking of the alliance with
England by Turkey a very desirable goal and stated . . . that in case of an
agreement between the Axis powers and Russia Turkey would probably
be very much more accessible.' Hitler–Mussolini conversation, 28.10.
1940, *DGFP*, D, xi, No. 246.

42 On 11 November he asked Papen how far he could go without destroying
Turkey; F. von Papen, *Memoirs* (London, Deutsch, 1952) pp. 465ff.

43 Schmidt, to Papen, Nr. 20 v. 28.10, 'St.S. Türkei', ii, GFM/265/172436;
Kroll (counsellor in Ankara) to foreign ministry, Nr. 898 v. 6.11, *ibid.*
GFM/265/172477; Richthofen to foreign ministry, Nr. 547 v. 10.11.1940,
ibid. GFM/265/172484.

44 Kramarz memo, Pol. I M 14669g., 'St.S. Griechenland', i, GFM/449/
222898.

45 Papen, *Memoirs*, p. 464.

46 Hillgruber, *Strategie*, p. 359, footnote No. 37.

47 No record of the conversation between Hitler and Papen has been found.
In April 1941, however, Papen recalled the Führer's instructions, 'which
aimed at bringing about a closer and more confidential relationship with
Turkey'. Papen to Weizsäcker, 8.4.1941, *DGFP*, D, xii, No. 295.

48 Papen to foreign ministry, 23.11.1940, *ibid.* No. 386.

49 Same to same, 29.11.1940, *ibid.* No. 422.

50 *Ibid.*

51 Papen to foreign ministry, 2.12.1940, *DGFP*, D, xi, No. 436. The points
were: 1. Turkish connivance with the new order in Europe. 2. A Turkish
undertaking to keep out of the war against the Axis. 3. Turkish obligations
to England, in so far as they refer to the defence of Turkish interests,
are not affected thereby. 4. The Axis undertakes not to attack Turkey. 5.
The Axis will include Turkey in the discussions on the new order in
Europe.

52 Richthofen to foreign ministry, 26.11.1940, *ibid.* No. 403.

53 Ribbentrop to Richthofen, 28.11.1940, *ibid.* No. 413.

54 Richthofen to Ribbentrop, Nr. 584 v. 28.11.1940, 'St.S. Bulgarien', i,
GFM/585/242788–89.

55 Ribbentrop to Papen, 5.12.1940, *DGFP*, D, xi, No. 454.

56 By 26 August the traditionally pro-western Prince Paul was already declaring his allegiance to Germany, which to him was 'the incarnation of
order'; Richthofen to foreign ministry, Nr. 628 v. 26.8.1940, 'St.S. Jugoslawien', i, GFM/230/152301–3.

57 *KTB*/Halder, II, 148, entry for 24.10.1940.
58 Erbach to foreign ministry, Nr. 13 v. 30.11.1940, 'St.S. Türkei', ii, GFM/265/172522.
59 Hitler–Ciano conversation, 18.11.1940, *DGFP*, D, XI, No. 353.
60 R. L. Knezevic, 'Hitler, Prince Paul and Salonika', *International Affairs*, XXVII (1951), pp. 39–44; also D. N. Ristic, *Yugoslavia's Revolution of 1941* (Hoover Institution Publications, 1966) pp. 43ff.
61 *DGFP*, D, XI, No. 320.
62 Heeren to foreign ministry, 3.11.1940, 'St.S. Jugoslawien', i, GFM/230/152333; same to same, *ibid*. Nr. 18 v. 14.11, GFM/230/152356; Ritter memo, Nr. 1940, *ibid*. GFM/230/153351; Crassel (Yugoslav senator of the German minority) memo, 16.11.1940, *ibid*. GFM/230/152378.
63 Heeren to foreign ministry, Nr. 795 v. 3.11. 'St.S. Jugoslawien', i, GFM/230/152332.
64 *DGFP*, D, XI, No. 324, and ed.'s note.
65 D. Gregoric, *So endete Jugoslawien* (Leipzig, Goldmann, 1943) pp. 113–14.
66 *DGFP*, D, XI, No. 392.
67 Ciano–Hitler conversation, 18.11.1940, *ibid*., No. 353.
68 Ciano, *Diary*, entry for 11.11.1940. Cf. also Hoptner, *Yugoslavia in Crisis*, pp. 187–8.
69 Mussolini to Hitler, 22.11.1940, *DGFP*, D, XI, No. 383. Originally the Duce had made his consent dependent on a 'demilitarization of the Adriatic', but when the Germans asked him what this meant he dropped his demand. Ribbentrop to Mackensen, Nr. 1758 v. 28.11, 'St.S. Italien', iii, GFM/B14/002395; Mackensen to foreign minstry, Nr. 2179 v. 29.11, *ibid*. GFM/B14/002396.
70 Hitler–Cincar Markovic conversation, 28.11.1940, *DGFP*, D, XI, No. 417.
71 'Conversations with the Soviet foreign minister ... satisfactory in every respect. For the time being, no agreement, which was not originally expected. The Russians apparently prepared to join the Tripartite Pact in the foreseeable future, but want to clear up a few questions first.' (*KTB/SKL*, A 15, entry for 16.11.1940, GNR/3/000713.) 'Molotov: no binding agreements. Führer not ungratified.' (*KTB*/Halder, II, 180, entry for 14.11.1940.)
72 *Tagebuch Engel*, entry for 15.11.1940, printed in Hillgruber, *Strategie*, p. 358.
73 *Soviet Documents on Foreign Policy* (ed. J. Degras, London, Oxford University Press, 1953) III, pp. 476ff.
74 *DGFP*, D, XI, Nos. 353, 369. In spite of this, the highly astute Ciano detected the change that had come over German–Soviet relations: 'I will immediately state that after Molotov's visit we speak very little of Russia, and in a somewhat different tone than that used by Ribbentrop during my recent visit... Russia is once again a country not to be trusted, of whom it is best in view of the present circumstances to seek for ourselves her friendship rather than her hostility, but whose neutrality must be constantly and attentively watched.' Ciano, *L'Europa*, p. 616.
75 Hitler–Teleki conversation, 26.11.1940, *DGFP*, D, XI, No. 365.
76 *KTB/OKW*, I, 179, entry for 19.11.1940. Jodl also told the air force to

discontinue its study concerning dispositions in case of a two-front war; *ibid* 188, entry for 25.11.1940.

77 Schulenburg to foreign ministry, 26.11.1940, enclosure, *DGFP*, D, XI, No. 404.

78 *KTB/OKW*, I, 190, entry for 26.11.1940.

79 In February 1945 Hitler told Bormann: 'my decision was made immediately after the departure of Molotov ... I decided ... to settle the account with the Russians in the first fine days.' *Le Testament Politique de Hitler, Notes Recueilles part Martin Bormann* (Paris, Hachette, 1959) pp. 95–6.

80 Hitler estimated them at 80 divisions.

81 *KTB/*Halder, II, 198, entry for 27.11.1940; Mueller-Hillebrand, *Zusammenhang*, pp. 5–7.

82 FCNA, 1940, ii, 149–56.

83 There is a very lucid exposition in Schramm von Thadden, *Griechenland*, pp. 143–4; also Hillgruber, *Strategie*, pp. 345–6.

84 Ribbentrop to Mackensen, 'Akten Büro RAM', GFM/F1/000504–9.

85 The record is *DGFP*, D, XI, No. 312.

86 *Ibid*. No. 352.

87 OKM/SKL/I.Op. Nr. 2510 g.Kdos Chefsache v. 22.11.1940, GNR/96(P)/000993.

88 'Unst.S. Frankreich', i, Nr. 1157 v. 11.11, GFM/587/243349–52; 'St.S. Frankreich, iii, Nr. 23 v. 16.11 and 1533 v. 23.11, GFM/121/12079.

89 *KTB/*Halder, II, 180, entry for 18.11.1940.

90 *KTB/OKW*, I, 184, entry for 21.11.1940; *DGFP*, D, XI, No. 354. Cf. also Jäckel, *Frankreich*, pp. 132–4.

91 Detwiller, *Hitler, Franco und Gibraltar*, p. 70.

92 *KTB/*Halder, II, 211, entry for 5.12.1940; *KTB/OKW*, I, 204, entry for 5.12.1940. The Italian defeats in Egypt, commencing on 9 December, forced Hitler to change his mind, but this time the object was no longer to attack Great Britain strategically or to reach the Suez, but simply to save the Italians from complete collapse.

93 P. Bor, *Gespräche mit Halder* (Wiesbaden, Limes, 1950) p. 180.

94 Particularly at the Ribbentrop–Ciano meeting of 4 November.

95 *DGFP*, D, XI, No. 383. It is impossible to prove that Mussolini had deliberately timed his letter announcing the attack to miss Hitler; E. Wiskemann, *The Rome–Berlin Axis* (London, Collins, 1967) p. 276.

96 Armellini, *Diario di Guerra*, p. 157.

97 Ciano, *Diary*, entry for 4.12.1940.

98 Armellini, *Diario di Guerra*, p. 162.

99 No verbal record of this conversation has been found in the archives of the German foreign ministry. Cf. Simoni, *Berlino*, pp. 187–8, and D. Alfieri, *Dictators Face to Face* (N.Y. University Press, 1955) p. 107.

100 Hitler–Alfieri conversation, 7.12.1940, *DGFP*, D, XI, No. 477.

101 Fifty German transport planes had already been offered and accepted with thanks. However, Xth air corps which was at the same time transferred to southern Italy to help against the British was 'strictly forbidden any participation ... in the Italo–Greek conflict, and Greek territory

was to be respected. This order apparently applies also to the naval base at Suda Bay, which has been constructed by the British. No political repercussions on Greece should occur in these circumstances.' Mackensen to foreign ministry, 11.12.1940, *DGFP*, D, xi, No. 494.

102 Schramm von Thadden, *Griechenland*, p. 138.

103 *KTB*/Halder, ii, 212, entry for 5.12.1940.

104 *KTB*/*OKW*, i, 219, entry for 8.12.1940.

105 *Ibid.* 222, entry for 10.12.1940.

106 *DGFP*, D, xi, No. 488.

107 Printed in Trevor Roper, *Hitler's War Directives*, pp. 44–6.

108 According to Argyropoulos's post-war account, printed in Schramm von Thadden, *Griechenland*, pp. 217–18.

109 According to Maniadakis's post-war account; *ibid.* p. 151.

110 Knatchbull-Hugessen to foreign office, 16.12.1940, BFOD, c 13593/764/19.

111 It is remarkable that in none of the great British sources about World War II (Butler, Woodward, Buckley, Churchill, Eden) is there the slightest hint of the existence of German peace feelers in December 1940.

112 Nichols memo, 15.10.1940, BFOD, R7789/764/19. It is curious that the possibility of bombing the oil fields is not mentioned in this memorandum.

113 Foreign office to Palairet (minister in Athens), *ibid.* R7648/764/19; Nichols memo, 28.10.1940, *ibid.* R8079/764/19.

114 Campbell to foreign office, 5.12.1940, *ibid.* R8788/764/19.

115 Foreign office to Campbell, 11.12.1940, *ibid.*

116 Hoare to foreign office, 5.12.1940, *ibid.* R8824/764/19.

117 Palairet to foreign office, *ibid.* R8788/744/19. Metaxas's statement was later confirmed by the head of the economic department of the Greek foreign ministry who explained why Greece had rejected the German overture for the resumption of economic relations; same to same, 17.12.1940, *ibid.* R8940/764/19.

118 Foreign office to Knatchbull-Hugessen, December 1940, *ibid.* R8824/764/19; same to same, 16.12.1940, *ibid.*

119 Palairet to foreign office, 24.12.1940, *ibid.* R8940/764/19.

120 Quoted in Schramm von Thadden, *Griechenland*, p. 150. This explanation, however, fails to account for the fact that in the years before the war Metaxas, who had received military training at a German staff college, was considered a Germanophil.

121 King George to King George, 17.11.1940, BFOD, R8933/764/19.

122 C. Buckley, *Greece and Crete* (London, H.M. Stationery Office, 1952) p. 17.

123 Knatchbull-Hugessen to foreign office, 16.12.1940, BFOD, c 13593/764/19.

124 Erbach to foreign ministry, Nr. 59 v. 11.12.1940, 'St.S. Griechenland', i, GFM/449/222978.

125 Same to same, 20.12.1940, *DGFP*, D, xi, No. 540. This declaration may have had something to do with the desire allegedly expressed by the German government for the Greek government to proclaim that the war

'was not directed against Germany and that Greece would not be inclined to allow British forces to land on Greek mainland thus opening front against Germany'. Headquarters RAF Middle East to Air Ministry, No. 483, 16.12.1940, BFOD, R8940/764/19.

126 Erbach to foreign ministry, Nr. 68 v. 16.12.1940, 'St.S. Griechenland', i, GFM/449/222979–80.

127 Palairet to foreign office, 24.12.1940, BFOD, R8940/764/19.

CHAPTER 5

1 KTB/SKL, A 15, entry for 16.1.1941, GNR/3/000646; Kramarz memo, 5.12.1940, 'Unst.S. Griechenland', xii, GFM/675/258384. The latter source quotes a report dated 21 November and said to be confirmed by others.

2 Buckley, *Greece and Crete*, pp. 14–16. Winter made the construction of the airfields slow work, and they were ready just in time for the Germans to use.

3 *KTB/OKW*, I, 204, entry for 5.12.1940.

4 KTB/SKL, A 14, entry for 13.12.1940, GNR/4/000082.

5 *KTB*/Halder, II, 214, entry for 5.12.1940.

6 Mueller–Hillebrand, *Zusammenhang*, p. 10.

7 This measure, too, shows that the attack on Greece was now coordinated with the one on Russia; the occupation of the entire Greek mainland would obviously prolong operation 'Marita' and endanger the timely completion of preparations for the Russian campaign. V. Greiner, *Wehrmachtführung*, p. 243.

8 Printed in Trevor Roper, *Hitler's War Directives*, pp. 46–8.

9 For the games, v. F. von Paulus, *Ich stehe hier auf Befehl!* (Frankfurt am Main, Bernard & Graefe, 1963) pp. 109ff.

10 Printed in Trevor Roper, *Hitler's War Directives*, pp. 49–52.

11 For a much better description of the plans than can be given here, v. A. Philippi – F. Heim, *Der Feldzug gegen Sowjetrussland, 1941 bis 1945, ein operativer Uberblick* (Stuttgart, Kohlhammer, 1962) ch. 1.

12 *KTB/OKW*, I, 204, entry for 5.12.1940. Only the four months from June to September were considered suitable for operations in Russia; in May the ground was still likely to be soft with the melting snow, while the Russian winter could be expected to arrive in October.

13 *KTB/OKW*, I, 204, entry for 5.12.1940; *KTB*/Halder, II, 270, entry for 3.2.1941.

14 *KTB*/Halder, II, 176, entry for 12.11.1940.

15 *Ibid.* 188, entry for 18.11.1940; *KTB/OKW*, I, 179, entry for 19.11.1940.

16 *KTB*/Halder, II, 188, entry for 19.11.1940; 'directive No. 20', printed in Trevor Roper, *Hitler's War Directives*, pp. 46–8.

17 The Greeks did in fact have such plans; Papagos, *The Battle of Greece*, pp. 182–93.

18 *KTB*/Halder, II, 193, entry for 25.11.1940.

19 The roads were, from west to east: 1. The Sofia–Dupnica–Seres road following the Struma Valley. This two-laned and comparatively good road led directly to the narrow Rupel pass with its great defensive possi-

bilities, and had therefore been avoided by the Bulgarians in 1913.
2. The Sofia–Nevrokop–Drama road, a second class road even by Bulgarian standards. 3. The Plovdiv–Smolian–Xanthi road, for the most part as good as No. 1 but leading over several passes up to a height of 4000 feet and therefore impassable in bad weather. 4. The Haskovo–Nastanli–Komotoni road, of the same category as No. 2, but with passes 5000 and 6000 feet high. 5. The Adrianopol–Alexandroupolus road running through the Turdza Valley, marked on the OKH map as being of the same quality as No. 1, but reported to be in such condition that certain sections were passable for light vehicles only. Moreover, it was too close to the Turkish border to be serviceable. The description is based on OKH/Abt. für Kriegskarten und Vermesungswesen, *Militärgeographische Beschreibung von Nordost Griechenland*, pp. 16–19.

20 *KTB*/Halder, II, 195, entry for 26.11.1940.
21 For the Zeitzler mission, cf. Fabry, *Balkan*, p. 76.
22 Papagos, *The Battle of Greece*, pp. 318–20.
23 *KTB*/Halder, II, 198, entry for 27.11.1940.
24 *KTB/OKW*, I, 207–8, entry for 5.12.1940; Greiner, *Wehrmachtführung*, p. 243. In the latter case, the forces engaged would not be available 'for other use' before mid May.
25 Greiner, *Wehrmachtführung*, pp. 242–3.
26 *KTB*/Halder, II, 211–13, entry for 5.12.1940.
27 Greiner, *Balkan*, pp. 6, 7.
28 OKH/Genst.d.H/Op.Abt.(IM) Nr. 31098/40 g.Kdos v. 14.12.1940, GMR/427/8005357–59.
29 Printed in Fabry, *Balkan*, p. 78.
30 *KTB/OKW*, I, 224, entry for 11.12.1940.
31 *Ibid.* On 20 December the following changes were introduced: high command XXXth army corps was included in stage I build-up, high command XVIIIth army corps in stage II, high command XIth army corps in stage III. *Ibid.* I, 240, entry for 20.12.1940.
32 *KTB*/Halder, II, 220, entry for 10.12.1940.
33 G. Blau, *The German Campaign in the Balkans (Spring 1941)*, Washington D.C., Dept. of the army, 1953, p. 11.
34 *KTB*/Halder, II, 238, entry for 20.12.1940.
35 Fabricius to foreign ministry, 21.12.1940, *DGFP*, D, XI, No. 544; Jodl directive, 21.12.1940, *ibid.* No. 556.
36 *KTB*/Halder, II, 242–3, entry for 24.12.1940.
37 *Ibid.*
38 OKL/Obdl/Gen.Qu./Genst.4.Abt.(I) Nr. 76/40 g.Kdos v. 28.12.1940, 'Zeittafel "Marita"', signed by Jodl, item No. MI/14/655 at the Imperial War Museum.
39 *KTB/OKW*, I, 247, entry for 6.1.1941.
40 OKW/WFSt/Abt.L Nr. 33 460/41 g.Kdos Chefsache v. 6.1.1941, 'Unternehmen "Marita"', signed by Jodl, item No. MI/14/655 at the Imperial War Museum.
41 Oberkommando der Truppen des deutsches Heeres in Rumänien/Ia to OKH, Nr. 08/41 g.Kdos v. 7.1.1941, GMR/426/8004601–3.

42 Anlage zu Ob.Kdo.d.Tr.d.deu.H. in Rum./Ia Nr. 03/41 g.Kdos Chef-sache v. 8.1.1941, 'Eintreffübersicht der unterstellten Verbände', GMR/426/8004629–30.

43 Ob.Kdo.d.Tr.d.deu.H. in Rum./Ia to the German army mission in Rumania, Nr. 59/41, g.Kdos, 13.1.1941, GMR/426/8004486.

44 Greiner, *Wehrmachtführung*, p. 249; *KTB/OKW*, I, 259–60, entry for 25.1.1941.

45 Cf. Fabry, *Balkan*, pp. 136–7.

46 Greiner, *Wehrmachtführung*, p. 249; *KTB/OKW*, 259–60, entry for 10.1.1941.

47 Greiner, *Wehrmachtführung*, p. 249.

48 OKW/WFSt/Abt.L Nr. 44 410/41 g.Kdos Chefsache v. 10.1.1941, signed by Warlimont, item No. MI/14/655 at the Imperial War Museum. V. also Bürckner (chief OKW/Ausland) to Ritter, 11.1.1941, *DGFP*, D, XI, No. 644.

49 A memorandum of 12th army to this effect, dated 17.1.1941, is printed in L. Hepp, 'Die 12. Armee im Balkanfeldzug 1941', *Wehrwissenschaftliche Rundschau*, v (1955) pp. 213–14.

50 E. Wisshaupt, 'Der Balkanfeldzug der 12. armee – Generalfeldmarschal List' (MS No. AL 679/1–2 at the Imperial War Museum) pp. 4–5.

51 *Ibid.*

52 *KTB*/Halder, II, 244, entry for 16.1.1941.

53 Anlage zu OKW/WFSt/Abt.L Nr. 33 460/41 g.Kdos Chefsache v. 6.1.1941, 'Beabsichter Ablauf von Donnau-Ubergang (=D Tag) bis zum Angriff gegen Griechenland', item No. MI/14/655 at the Imperial War Museum. According to this draft, motorized units of stage I were to reach the Greek frontier on D+5; the infantry units of the same stage on D+19; the motorized units of stage II on D+29; and the infantry on D+39.

54 *KTB/OKW*, I, 255, entry for 9.1.1941.

55 Alfieri, *Dictators Face to Face*, p. 106.

56 Ciano, *Diary*, entry for 10.12.1940.

57 *KTB/OKW*, I, 241, entry for 20.12.1940.

58 Ciano, *Diary*, entry for 21.12.1940.

59 *KTB/OKW*, I, 243–4, entry for 30.12.1940.

60 *Ibid.* 245–6, entry for 4.1.1941.

61 For Xth air corps, v. Hitler to Mussolini, 5.12.1940, *DGFP*, D, XI, No. 452; Mackensen to foreign ministry, 6.12.1940, *ibid.* No. 460; and Führer directive, 10.12.1940, *ibid.* No. 487.

62 *KTB*/Halder, II, 252, entry for 24.1.1941.

63 *KTB/OKW*, I, 253–5, entry for 9.1.1941.

64 Printed in Trevor-Roper, *Hitler's War Directives*, pp. 53–5.

65 As if to emphasize this, Hitler had just scrapped what was left of operation 'Felix'; *KTB/OKW*, I, 255, entry for 9.1.1941.

66 Marras to the ministry of war, Nr. 2648/A., 4.1.1941, IMR/129/000067–71.

67 Mussolini to Cavallero, undated, IMR/129/000065.

68 Cavallero to Mussolini, '*appunto per il Duce*', undated, IMR/129/000050–52.

69 Guzzoni to Cavallero, No. 5383/Op., 11.1.1940, IMR/129/000080.

70 Cavallero to Stamage, No. 18/65951, 17.1.1941, IMR/129/000053–54. For the Italian chief-of-staff's view of the whole question of German aid in Albania cf. also U. Cavallero, *Commando Supremo* (Bologna, Capelli, 1948) pp. 44–6, 49–50, 63, 66, 71, 75–6.

71 Roatta memo, 18.1.1941, 'Logistica ed Operazione in Albania', IMR/129/000041–44.

72 Rintelen, *Mussolini*, pp. 121ff.

73 *KTB*/Halder, II, 246, entry for 17.1.1941.

74 *KTB/OKW*, I, 268, entry for 8.1.1941.

75 *KTB*/Halder, II, 244, 246, entry for 16.1.1941.

76 *KTB/OKW*, I, 273, entry for 22.1.1941.

77 Gandin memo for Guzzoni, 1.2.1941, IMR/129/000032.

78 *KTB*/Halder, II, 249, entry for 21.1.1941.

79 For the attempts to win over Bulgaria cf. above, pp. 72–5.

80 V. above, p. 85.

81 Richthofen to foreign ministry, Nr. 633 v. 23.12.1940, 'St.S. Bulgarien', i, GFM/585/242829; Ribbentrop to Richthofen, 27.12.1940, *DGFP*, D, XI, No. 570.

82 Weizsäcker memo for Ribbentrop, 2.1.1941, *DGFP*, D, XI, No. 594.

83 Ritter memo for Ribbentrop, *ibid*. No. 593.

84 Hitler–Filov conversation, 7.1.1941, *ibid*. No. 606.

85 Ribbentrop–Filov conversation, 7.1.1941, 'Geheimakten Schmidt', GFM/67/47550–81.

86 OKW/Ausland to foreign ministry, 10.1.1941, *DGFP*, D, XI, No. 644.

87 *KTB*/Halder, II, 252, entry for 24.1.1941.

88 Ribbentrop to Schulenburg, Papen, Heeren and Erbach, 7.1.1941, *DGFP*, D, XI, No. 615.

89 Schulenburg to foreign ministry, 8.1.1941, *ibid*. No. 624; Papen to foreign ministry, *ibid*. No. 634.

90 *SDFP*, iii, No. 482.

91 Weizsäcker memo, 17.1.1941, *DGFP*, D, XI, No. 668. In Moscow, an identical note was handed to Schulenburg by Molotov. However, the Soviet foreign minister tried to sugar the pill by asking the ambassador why the USSR had never received a reply to her proposal to join the Tripartite Pact. Schulenburg to foreign ministry, 17.1.1941, *ibid*. No. 669.

92 Weizsäcker memo, 20.1.1941, *ibid*. No. 678.

93 *KTB*/Halder, II, 249, entry for 20.1.1941; Hitler–Mussolini conversation, 20.1.1941, *DGFP*, D, XI, No. 679. In the Wehrmachtführungstab Warlimont anxiously asked Jodl whether the *démarche* meant that 'Marita' would lead to a conflict with Russia; but the Chef WFSt did not think so. *KTB/OKW*, I, 268, entry for 18.1.1941.

94 On 6 December Papen bitterly complained to Ribbentrop that he and Hitler had themselves instructed him to give the Turks assurances against a German attack, and suggested that unless the talks were resumed the Turks would be driven irrevocably into the arms of England. (Papen to foreign ministry, 6.12.1940, *DGFP*, D, XI, No. 459). On 14 December he reported that his fears had apparently been justified, for Saracoglu

resented German reluctance and warned that there could be 'no question' of Turko–Bulgarian negotiations. Same to same, 14.12.1940, *ibid*. No. 515.

95 Ribbentrop to Papen, 21.12.1940, *ibid*. No. 548.

96 On 24 December Saracoglu told Papen 'he was glad that it was still Germany's intention to find a new basis for a relationship of greater trust'. Papen to foreign ministry, 24.12.1940, *ibid*. No. 559.

97 Same to same, 10.1.1941, *ibid*. No. 624.

98 Richthofen to foreign ministry, Nr. 41 v. 17.1.1941, 'St.S. Bulgarien', i, GFM/585/242888o.

99 It has been argued that the Turkish agreement was the result of British pressure. The assumption is that London wanted to protect the Straits against the Bulgarians and possibly the Germans. Since the Turkish army was believed to be inferior to the German-supplied Bulgarian one London is supposed to have given Ankara the go ahead. Cf. H. Batovski, 'Pour une alliance balkanique en 1941' (*Revue d'Histoire de la Deuxieme Guerre Mondiale*, vol. 19, 1967, No. 74, pp. 11–12); also D. Kitsikis, 'La Grece en face à l'invasion allemande dans les Balkans' (unpublished article, 1968) pp. 7–8, who credits Churchill with the belief that, as late as January 1941, it was still possible to bring Bulgaria into an anti-German Balkan block. The evidence brought forward to support this view is, in the present writer's opinion, rather slight. In the case of both Bulgaria and Turkey, the available sources have not so far made it possible to say with any certainty whether they were Hitler's cynical jackals or his innocent victims.

100 Richthofen to foreign ministry, 13.1.1941, *DGFP*, D, xi, No. 648.

101 Weizsäcker–Draganov conversation, 13.1.1941, *ibid*. No. 649.

102 V. Weizsäcker memorandum for Ribbentrop, 14.1.1941, 'St.S. Bulgarien', i, GFM/585/242862, in which the state secretary explained that Bulgarian demands were unacceptable. Ribbentrop finally agreed to promise Bulgaria 'access to the Aegean Sea approximately in the size of the area of the Maritsa and the Struma estuaries', but instructed Weizsäcker to formulate the promise in such a way as to make it possible for Germany 'in certain circumstances' to 'dispose of the glacis on Greek soil extending from Edirne to the southeast'. *DGFP*, D, xi, No. 656.

103 Weizsäcker memo, 15.1.1941, *ibid*. No. 658.

104 Richthofen to foreign ministry, 23.1.1941, *ibid*. No. 693.

105 Anlage zu Ob.Kdo d.Tr.d.deu.H. in Rum./Ia Nr. 03/41 g.Kdos Chefsache v. 8.1.1941, 'Eintreffübersicht der unterstellten Verbände', GMR/426/8004629–30.

106 Ritter to Richthofen, 15.1.1941, *DGFP*, D, xi, No. 660.

107 OKW/WFSt/Abt.L Nr. 44 030/41 g.Kdos Chefsache v. 21.1.1941, signed by Warlimont, item No. MI/14/655 at the Imperial War Museum.

108 Hitler–Mussolini conversation, 20.1.1941, *DGFP*, D, xi, No. 679.

109 Ritter memo, 15.1.1941, *ibid*. No. 662. Benzler was 'responsible to the foreign minister for seeing that all matters of foreign policy in connection with operation "Marita" remain firmly in the hands of the foreign ministry'.

110 The German summary of the negotiations is in Benzler-Killinger to Ritter, Nr. 143 v. 26.1.1941, 'St.S. Bulgarien', i, GFM/585/242930–31.

111 Weizsäcker memo, 24.1.1941, *DGFP*, D, xi, No. 704.

112 Richthofen to foreign ministry, Nr. 69 v. 23.1.1941, 'St.S. Bulgarien', i, GFM/585/242909; *KTB/OKW*, 1, 279–80, entry for 25.1.1941.

113 Ritter memo, 23.11.1940, *ibid.* GFM/585/242910.

114 The equipment in question included pontoon bridges, aircraft, anti-aircraft batteries and cannon. For the whole question v. Fabry, *Balkan*, pp. 84–7.

115 Between 25 and 28 January.

116 *KTB/OKW*, 1, 283, entry for 28.1.1941.

117 *KTB*/Halder, ii, 252, entry for 24.1.1941.

118 *KTB/OKW*, 1, 279–80, entry for 25.1.1941; Greiner, *Wehrmachtführung*, p. 254.

119 *KTB*/Halder, ii, 255, entry for 27.1.1941.

120 Ritter memo, 27.1.1941, *DGFP*, D, xi, No. 719.

121 *KTB/OKW*, 1, 279–80, entry for 28.1.1941.

122 Benzler-Killinger to Ritter, Nr. 143 v. 26.1.1941, 'St.S. Bulgarien', i, GFM/585/242930–31.

123 *KTB/OKW*, 1, 285, entry for 29.1.1941; *KTB*/Halder, ii, 261, entry for 28.1.1941.

124 For the political situation versus Yugoslavia, v. above, pp. 78–80, and below, pp. 124–9.

125 Due to congestion on the Rumanian railways stage III buildup could not start rolling before the first crossed the Danube. OKW/WFSt/Abt.L Nr. 33 460/41 g.Kdos Chefsache v. 6.1.1941, 'Unternehmen "Marita"', item No. MI/14/655 at the Imperial War Museum.

126 *KTB/OKW*, 1, 284, entry for 28.1.1941; also Jodl to Ritter, 28.1.1941, *DGFP*, D, xi, No. 724.

127 OKW directive, 31.1.1941, *DGFP*, D, xi, No. 738.

128 ObKdos d.Tr.d.deu.H. in Rum./Ia Nr. 241/41 g.Kdos v. 4.2.1941, 'Feststellungen und Bemerkungen anläslich der Reise des Herrn Oberbefehlhabers nach Giurgiu am 3.2.1941.' GMR/426/8005061; Wisshaupt, 'Der Balkanfeldzug . . .', p. 4.

129 The text of the order (Nr. 050/41 g.Kdos Chefsache v. 31.1.1941, signed by Brauchitsch) is printed in *KTB*/Halder, ii, 463–9, app. 2.

130 This was the result of a dispute between Hitler and OKH as to the direction of the main advance. True to Clausewitzan theory, OKH had insisted that the main purpose of the attack was to destroy the enemy armed forces; for this purpose, it wanted an advance with strong forces on Moscow as the most important centre where the Russians would presumably have to stand and fight. Hitler, on the other hand, was more interested in ideological and economic goals and wanted to capture Leningrad and the Ukraine first. In 'directive No. 21' he had his way to the extent that army group centre was directed to halt at Smolensk and sent strong forces to the aid of army group north with the task of capturing Leningrad. In its deployment order OKH tried to get round

this conception by making army group north so strong that it could fulfil its task on its own; the advance on Moscow was served by the allocation of exceptionally strong forces to army group centre, while army group south was greatly weakened, especially in comparison with the Soviet forces assumed to be stationed opposite it. Cf. Philippi-Heim, *Der Feldzug* . . ., pp. 42–8.

131 14 out of 18 divisions of 'Marita' were earmarked for army group south, forming about one third of its total strength of 47 divisions.

132 *KTB*/Halder, II, 269–70, entry for 21.2.1941; *KTB/OKW*, I, 298, entry for 3.2.1941.

133 OKW/Ausland to foreign ministry, 2.2.1941, *DGFP*, D, XII, No. 39.

134 For details v. Fabry, *Balkan*, pp. 142–3.

135 Warlimont memo, 12.2.1941, 'Botschafter Ritter, Bulgarien', i, GFM/ 839/281568–69.

136 *KTB*/Halder, II, 279, entry for 12.2.1941.

137 OKW directive, 14.2.1941, *DGFP*, D. XII, No. 51.

138 Ritter memo, 3.2.1941, *ibid*. No. 7.

139 OKH/Genst.d.H/Op.Abt.(I) Nr. 704/41 g.Kdos v. 14.2.1941, 'Transportentwurf "Marita"', GMR/426/8004620–21.

140 *KTB*/Halder, II, 263, entry for 29.1.1941.

141 Benzler to foreign ministry, Nr. 22 v. 12.2.1941, 'St.S. Bulgarien', ii, GFM/274/177685.

142 V. Fabry, *Balkan*, p. 145.

143 *KTB*/Halder, II, 283, entry for 17.2.1941.

144 OKW/WFSt/Abt.LIH/Op. Nr. 44 186/41 g.Kdos Chefsache v. 18.2. 1941, GMR/782/5508532–33.

145 Richthofen to OKH/Genst.d.H/Att. Abt., Nr. 173 v. 15.2.1941, 'Botschafter Ritter, Bulgarien', i, GFM/839/281565.

146 Richthofen to foreign ministry, 18.2.1914, 'St.S. Bulgarien', ii, GFM/ 274/177711; Ribbentrop to Richthofen, Nr. 72 v. 19.2.1941, *ibid*. GFM/ 274/177713.

147 OKW/WFSt/Abt. L Nr. 44 187/41 g.Kdos Chefsache v. 19.2.1941, GMR/782/5508531.

148 Anlage zu OKW/WFSt/Abt.L Nr. 33 460/41 g.Kdos Chefsache v. 19.2.1941, 'Zeittafel "Marita"', signed by Warlimont, *ibid*./782/ 5508527–30. According to this order, IIIrd echelon was – in the interest of 'Barbarossa', of course – expected to stay in Rumania.

149 Richthofen to foreign ministry, Nr. 214 v. 22.2.1941, 'St.S. Bulgarien', ii, GFM/274/177735.

150 Same to same, Nr. 222 v. 24.2.1941, 'St.S. Bulgarien', ii, GFM/274/ 177744; same to same, Nr. 223 v. 24.2.1941, *ibid*. GFM/274/177745; (transmitting the text of the Bulgarian note) and same to same, Nr. 224 v. 25.2.1941, *ibid*. GFM/274/177748.

151 Richthofen to foreign ministry, Nr. 198 v. 19.2.1941, *ibid*. GFM/274/ 177715; same to same, Nr. 199 v. 19.2.1941, *ibid*. GFM/274/177720; same to same, Nr. 201 v. 19.2.1941, *ibid*. GFM/274/177721.

152 Killinger to Richthofen, 20.2.1941, 'Deutsche Legation Bucharest, Militärisches', GFM/3710H/E036659.

153 Ribbentrop to Richthofen, Nr. 102 v. 25.2.1941, 'St.S. Bulgarien', ii, GFM/274/177756.
154 Wisshaupt, 'Der Balkanfeldzug . . .', pp. 7–8.
155 Krecker, *Deutschland und die Turkei*, pp. 130–41; Fabry, *Balkan*, pp. 105–17.
156 Richthofen to foreign ministry, Nr. 48 v. 20.1.1941, 'St.S. Bulgarien', i, GFM/585/242887; same to same, Nr. 50 v. 20.1.1941, *ibid.* GFM/585/242889–90.
157 Weizsäcker to Ribbentrop, 21.1.1941, *ibid.* GFM/585/242901–2.
158 Ribbentrop to Richthofen, Nr. 46 v. 27.1.1941, *ibid.* GFM/585/242934.
159 Richthofen to foreign ministry, Nr. 136 v. 6.2.1941, *ibid.* ii, GFM/274/1777648–49.
160 *KTB/OKW*, I, 310, entry for 7.2.1941.
161 *Ibid.* 320, entry for 12.2.1941.
162 Richthofen to foreign minister, Nr. 171 v. 15.2.1941, 'St.S. Bulgarien', ii, GFM/274/177687–88.
163 OKH/Genst.d.H/Op.Abt. Nr. 225/41 g.Kdos Chefsache v. 14.2.1941, item No. A1 835 at the Imperial War Museum.
164 OKW directive, 14.2.1941, *DGFP*, D, XII, No. 51.
165 Richthofen to foreign ministry, Nr. 169 v. 14.2.1941, 'St.S. Bulgarien', ii, GFM/274/177762.
166 Papen to foreign ministry, 20.2.1941, *DGFP*, D, XII, No. 67.
167 Richthofen to foreign ministry, Nr. 234 v. 26.2.1941, 'St.S. Bulgarien' ii, GFM/274/177762.
168 Ribbentrop to Papen, 27.2.1941, *DGFP*, D, XII, No. 102.
169 Papen to foreign ministry, Nr. 1914 v. 1.3.1941, 'St.S. Türkei', ii, GFM/265/172649; same to same, 2.3.1941, *DGFP*, D, XII, No. 119.
170 Hitler to Inonü, 1.3.1941, *DGFP*, D, XII, No. 113; Papen to foreign ministry, 4.3.1941, *ibid.* No. 122.
171 V. above, pp. 78–80.
172 Heeren to foreign ministry, 7.12.1940, *DGFP*, D, XII, No. 467.
173 Hitler–Cincar Markovic conversation, 28.11.1940, *ibid.* No. 417.
174 Ribbentrop to Heeren, 21.12.1940, *DGFP*, D, XI, No. 549.
175 Heeren to foreign ministry, 23.12.1940, *ibid.* No. 551.
176 Gregoric to Schmidt, 20.1.1941, *ibid.* No. 708 enclosure.
177 Benzler–Killinger to Ritter, Nr. 143 v. 26.1.1941, 'St.S. Bulgarien', i, GFM/585/242930–31.
178 *KTB*/Halder, II, 261, entry for 28.1.1941; *KTB/OKW*, I, 285, entry for 29.1.1941.
179 Keitel directive, 31.1.1941, *DGFP*, D, XI, No. 738.
180 Hewel memo, 29.1.1941, *ibid.* No. 730.
181 The Yugoslavs were apparently left in the dark about Hitler's decision, for it was not until Gregoric raised the subject twice with Schmidt and Ribbentrop that an invitation for Cvetkovic and Cincar Markovic went out. V. Schmidt–Gregoric conversation, 4.2.1941, *ibid.* No. 10, and Ribbentrop to Heeren, 6.2.1941, *ibid.* No. 20.
182 Ritter to Ribbentrop, Nr. 23/41 g.Kdos Chefsache v. 5.2.1941, 'Bot-

schafter Ritter, Griechenland', iv, GFM/962/302217–18; to which there is appended an unsigned note, GFM/962/302216.

183 Anlage 1 zu OKH/Gen.Qu./QuI Nr. I/0317/40 g.Kdos Chefsache v. 21.12.1940, 'Vorläufige Ubersicht für die Zugfolge', signed by Halder, bundle No. MI/14/655 at the Imperial War Museum.

184 Hoptner, *Yugoslavia in Crisis*, pp. 204–5; Lane to Hull, 25.1.1941, *FRUS*, 1941, II, 939.

185 Ribbentrop–Cvetkovic conversation, 14.2.1941, *DGFP*, D, XII, No. 47.

186 Hitler–Cvetkovic conversation, 14.2.1941, *ibid*. No. 48.

187 'Englische Einflüstrung!' he remarked to his associates; Etzdorf memo, 17.2.1941, 'Aufzeichnungen des Vertreters des Auswärtiges Amt von Etzdorf', GFM/1274/337579.

188 Ribbentrop to Mackensen, Nr. 56 v. 14.2.1941, 'St.S. Griechenland', i, GFM/449/2230467.

189 Bismarck to foreign ministry, Nr. 326 v. 15.2.1941, 'St.S. Jugoslawien', ii, GFM/230/152501.

190 For the Italo–Yugoslav negotiations v. Hoptner, *Yugoslavia in Crisis*, pp. 208–9, 211–12.

191 Simoni, *Berlino*, p. 274; Rintelen to Weizsäcker, Nr. 108 v. 27.2.1941, 'St.S. Deutsch–Italienische Beziehungen', GFM/B13/001572.

192 Richthofen to foreign ministry, Nr. 136 v. 6.2.1941, 'St.S. Bulgarien', ii, GFM/274/177648–49.

193 Benzler memo, 18.2.1941, 'St.S. Jugoslawien', ii, GFM/230/152513.

194 Of these there were many, both in- and outsiders; v. below, p. 139.

195 Heeren to foreign ministry, 25.2.1941, *DGFP*, D, XII, No. 84.

196 Ribbentrop to Heeren, 7.3.1941, *ibid*. No. 130.

197 V. Hoptner, *Yugoslavia in Crisis*, pp. 219–21. The Yugoslavs agreed that a refusal to sign would mean war; that Yugoslavia would quickly lose such a war; and that accession to the pact was the only way, not only to keep Salonika out of much more uncongenial hands, but also to obtain some protection against Hungary and Italy.

198 Heeren to foreign ministry, 7.3.1941, *DGFP*, D, XII, No. 131.

199 Wisshaupt, 'Der Balkanfeldzug', p. 13; also below, pp. 136–7.

200 Richthofen to foreign ministry, Nr. 286 v. 8.3.1941, 'St.S. Jugoslawien', ii, GFM/230/152550.

201 Foreign ministry to Mackensen, 8.3.1941, *DGFP*, D, XII, No. 138.

202 Ribbentrop to Heeren, 9.3.1941, *ibid*. No. 144.

203 Heeren to foreign ministry, 10.3.1941, *ibid*. No. 145; same to same, 11.3.1941, *ibid*. No. 149.

204 Same to same, 11.3.1941, *ibid*. No. 151.

205 Same to same, 12.3.1941, *ibid*. No. 156.

206 Same to same, 14.3.1941, *ibid*. No. 165.

207 Same to same, 17.3.1941, *ibid*. No. 173.

208 AOK.12/Der Chef des Generalstabes/Ia Nr. 595/41 g.Kdos v. 20.3.1941, 'Bericht über Versamlung und Vormarsch der 12. Armee bis zum Erreichung der "Marita" Gliederung durch die Masse der Infanterie Divisionen', signed by Greiffenberg, pp. 4–6, GMR/427/8005343–45.

209 AOK. 12/Ia Nr. 0151/41 g.Kdos Chefsache v. 8.3.1941, GMR/426/
8004616.
210 P. Hausser, *Waffen SS im Einsatz* (Göttingen, Plesse, 1953) p. 42.
211 Anlage 60 zu OKH/Gents.d.H/Op.Abt.(I) Nr. 704/41 g.Kdos, 'Transportentwurf III. Aufmarschstaffel "Marita"', 8.3.1941, GMR/426/
8004617.
212 OKW/WFSt/Abt.L Nr. 44274/41 g.Kdos Chefsache v. 6.3.1941, item
No. MI/14/655 at the Imperial War Museum.
213 *KTB*/Halder, II, 315, entry for 17.3.1941.
214 Greiner, *Wehrmachtführung*, p. 266.
215 Schramm von Thadden, *Griechenland*, p. 173.
216 Fabricius to foreign ministry, Nr. 78 v. 16.1.1941, 'St.S. Griechenland',
i, GFM/449/223015; Papen to foreign ministry, Nr. 43 v. 16.1.1941, *ibid.*
GFM/449/223012; Erbach to OKH, Nr. 189 v. 26.1.1941, 'Unst.S.
Griechenland', xii, GFM/675/258377-78; Thomsen to foreign ministry,
Nr. 478 v. 24.2.1941, *ibid.* GFM/449/258375.
217 Steinhardt (US ambassador to Russia) to Hull, 1.3.1941, *FRUS* 1941, ii,
652; same to same, 2.3.1941, *ibid.* 653.
218 Mcveagh (US minister in Greece) to Hull, 12.2.1941, *ibid.* 644-5.
219 Guzzoni memo, 'appunto per il Duce', 24.2.1941, IMR/129/000023-6.
220 Marras to ministry of war, No. 813/A., 26.2.1941, *ibid.*/129/000022.
221 Guzzoni to Marras, No. 6814/Op., 28.2.1941, *ibid.*/129/000014. On 1
March the military attaché reported that he had carried out these instructions: Marras to SMG, No. 861/A., 1.3.1941, *ibid.*/129/000012.
222 Simoni, *Berlino*, p. 211.
223 *Ibid.*
224 *KTB*/Halder, II, 299, entry for 3.3.1941. The chief of staff did not think
that prospects for the desired peaceful settlement were very good; *ibid.*
303, entry for 5.3.1941.
225 Marras to Mussolini, No. 990/A., 7.3.1941, IMR/129/000011; same to
same, No. 991/A., 7.3.1941, *ibid.*/129/000010.
226 Simoni, *Berlino*, p. 212.
227 Papagos, *The Battle of Greece*, pp. 310-17.
228 Erbach to foreign ministry, Nr. 172 v. 6.3.1941, 'St.S. Griechenland', i,
GFM/449/223075.
229 Same to same, Nr. 274 v. 11.3.1941, *ibid.* GFM/449/223016.
230 Same to same, 12.3.1941, *DGFP*, D, xII, No. 155.
231 Clemm von Hohenberg-Erbach to foreign ministry, 16.3.1941, *ibid.*
No. 170.
232 Weizsäcker memo, 18.3.1941, *ibid.* No. 180. Though Rizo Rangabe
claimed to be acting on his own, OKW had intercepted his instructions.
233 Ribbentrop note, 18.3.1941, *ibid.* No. 179.
234 *KTB/OKW*, I, 352, entry for 8.3.1941.
235 *Ibid.* 360, entry for 18.3.1941. According to Halder's rather unlikely
account, Hitler's aim in ordering the operation extended was 'to form a
basis for the domination of the eastern Mediterranean from the air'.
KTB/Halder, II, 318-19, entry for 17.3.1941.
236 *KTB*/Halder, II, 319, 322, entries for 17, 19.3.1941.

237 *KTB/OKW*, 360–1, entry for 18.3.1941.

238 Before 17 March 12th army, forming the right wing of army group south, was supposed to attack with 46th, 56th, 76th, 183rd, 198th and 246th infantry divisions. Four of these would still be available to 11th army replacing it, but not for participation in the initial assault. Anlage Ia zu OKH/Genst.d.H/Op.Abt.(IN) Nr. 050/41 g.Kdos Chefsache v. 31.1.1941, 'Kräfteübersicht', GMR/335/6291229–34; and Anlage Ia zu OKH/Genst.d.H/Op.Abt.(IN) Nr. 050/41 v. 24.3.1941, 'Kraftgliederung, Stand v. 24.3.1941', *ibid./335/6291398–401*.

239 For a much better description of the grounds for and the consequences of Hitler's decision to alter the plan of the attack on Russia v. Philippi-Heim, *Der Feldzug . . .*, pp. 49, 60. The weakening of army group south and the alteration in its dispositions forced Rundstedt to attack frontally and made him lag behind the other two army groups. This resulted in Hitler's decision of August 1941 to detach strong forces from army group centre and send them to the Ukraine, instead of going to Moscow. In the opinion of such experts as Halder and Guderian this decision cost Hitler the Russian campaign.

240 *KTB*/Halder, II, 314, 315, entry for 16.3.1941.

241 *Ibid.*

242 AOK.12/Ia Nr. 517/41 g.Kdos v. 12.3.1941, GMR/426/8005040; AOK.12/Ia Nr. 521/41 g.Kdos v. 12.3.1941, *ibid./426/8005039*.

243 *KTB/OKW*, I, 363, entry for 18.3.1941.

244 AOK.12/Ia Nr. 0184/41 g.Kdos Chefsache v. 22.3.1941, GMR/426/8005026–27. As it turned out, none of these forces was to see action.

245 AOK.12/Ia Nr. 578/41 g.Kdos v. 18.3.1941, *ibid./426/8005034*. 56th infantry division was detailed to the Russian front, 198th infantry division to the army mission.

246 AOK.12/Ia Nr. 560/41 g.Kdos v. 16.3.1941, *ibid./426/8005036*; AOK.12/Ia Nr. 615/41 g.Kdos v. 21.3.1931, *ibid./426/8004665*.

247 Anlage zu OKH/Genst.d.H/Op.Abt.(I) Nr. 492/41 g.Kdos Chefsache v. 22.3.1941, *ibid./6285501–2*.

248 *KTB*/Halder, II, 322, entry for 19.3.1941.

249 V. below, p. 151.

250 OKH/Genst.d.H/Op.Abt.(I) Nr. 493/41 g.Kdos Chefsache v. 22.3.1941, GMR/426/8004862; AOK.12/Ia Nr. 0191/41 g.Kdos Chefsache v. 24.3.1941, *ibid./426/8004866–67*.

251 'Zeittafel "Marita"', 19.2.1941, 'Marine-Archiv, Mittelmeer', II, 8, GFM/M176/005639–44.

252 OKW directive, 22.3.1941, *DGFP*, D, XII, No. 195.

253 OKH/Genst.d.H/Op.Abt.(I) Nr. 492/41 g.Kdos Chefsache v. 22.3.1941, 'Ergänzende Weisung für 12. Armee', GMR/329/6285495–500.

254 Wisshaupt, 'Der Balkanfeldzug . . .', p. 13.

255 AOK.12/Der Chef des Generalstabes/Ia Nr. 595/41 g.Kdos v. 20.3.1941, 'Bericht über Versammlung und Vormarsch der 12. Armee bis zum Erreichung der "Marita" Gliederung durch die Masse der Infanterie Divisionen', signed by Greiffenberg, pp. 8–10, GMR/427/8005347–49.

256 *KTB/OKW*, I, 353, entry for 12.3.1941.

257 *Ibid.* 354–5, entry for 13.3.1941.
258 *Ibid.* 357, entry for 15.3.1941; OKW/WFSt/Abt.L Nr. 44 320/41 g.Kdos Chefsache v. 15.3.1941, signed by Jodl, item No. MI/14/655 at the Imperial War Museum.
259 *KTB*/Halder, II, 314, entry for 16.3.1941.
260 Ristic, *Yugoslavia's Revolution of 1941*, p. 81.
261 *KTB/OKW*, I, 365, entry for 21.3.1941.
262 *KTB*/Halder, II, 329, entry for 26.3.1941.

CHAPTER 6

1 Langer and Gleason, *The Undeclared War*, pp. 396–8.
2 Lane to Hull, 18.2.1941, *FRUS* 1941, II, 645–6.
3 Hull to Lane, 22.2.1941, *ibid.* 947.
4 Lane to Hull, 23.2.1941, *ibid.* 947–8; same to same, 15.3.1941, *ibid.* 955; same to same, 16.3.1941, *ibid.* 955–6; same to same, 16.3.1941, *ibid.* 956; same to same, 21.3.1941, *ibid.* 962–3.
5 Same to same, 22.3.1941, *ibid.* 964–5.
6 In 1939 he wrote that it was the right and the duty of Great Britain to abrogate the principles she was trying to reaffirm for some time, and that small nations should not be allowed to tie the hands of the great powers which were fighting for their freedom. W. Churchill, *The Second World War* (London, Cassell, 1949) i, 657.
7 Churchill to Roosevelt, 10.3.1941, *FRUS* 1941, II, 951–2; Churchill to Cvetkovic, Churchill, *The Second World War*, III, 141.
8 Woodward, *British Foreign Folicy*, pp. 530–1, 537–8.
9 *Ibid.* 532.
10 *Ibid.* 541–2. On the other hand Eden was 'desperately searching for ways ... to encourage the national spirit which I was sure was strong in Yugoslavia'; A. Eden, *Memoirs, the Reckoning* (London, Cassel, 1965) p. 226.
11 Eden, *Memoirs*, pp. 227–8; Churchill, *Second World War*, III, 142.
12 For Mirkovic's background v. Hoptner, *Yugoslavia in Crisis*, pp. 250–3.
13 Basically there are three distinct views of the *coup*: 1. that of its opponents, mostly ex-members of the legitimate Yugoslav government, who denounce it as a criminal or at least mistaken attempt, more or less inspired by foreign intervention, to alter the country's policy in an irresponsible way leading to national disaster. 2. That of the conspirators themselves, in whose eyes it was just retribution for a government that had abandoned Yugoslavia's traditional pro-western policy and bowed to Nazi aggression out of fear and desire. Though causing Yugoslavia to be overrun, they argue, the *coup* decisively contributed to victory over Nazi Germany by forcing Hitler to postpone his attack on Russia. 3. That of the communists, to whom it was a working-class revolt against a capitalist government which had sold out to the Nazis.
14 Ristic, *Yugoslavia's Revolution of 1941*, pp. 75–6.
15 For the text, 'St.S. Jugoslawien', ii, GFM/230/152598.
16 Lane to Hull, 27.3.1941, *FRUS*, 1941, II, 969.

17 Same to same, 29.3.1941, *ibid.* 969–72.
18 S. O. Playfair, *The Mediterranean and the Middle East* (London, H.M. Stationery Office, 1956) II, pp. 74–5.
19 Heeren to foreign ministry, 26.3.1941, *DGFP*, D, XII, No. 211.
20 Same to same, 27.3.1941, *ibid.* No. 219.
21 Same to same, 28.3.1941, *ibid.* No. 225.
22 Same to same, 30.3.1941, *ibid.* No. 235.
23 Same to same, No. 315 v. 30.3.1941, 'St.S. Jugoslawien', ii, GFM/230/ 152683.
24 Rintelen to Heeren, 28.3.1941, *DGFP*, D, XII, No. 232; Ribbentrop to Heeren, 30.3.1941, *ibid.* No. 236.
25 Ribbentrop–Matsuoka conversation, 27.3.1941, *ibid.* No. 218.
26 Heeren to foreign ministry, 27.3.1941, *ibid.* No. 214.
27 *KTB*/Halder, II, 330, entry for 27.3.1941, and ed.'s note.
28 *Ibid.* 131, 134, 140, 143, entries for 10, 12, 15, 18.10.1940.
29 *TMWC*, vii, 331–2. The Soviet prosecution here quotes the testimony of one Stephen Ujszaszyn (ND USSR–155) during the trial of Keitel.
30 Bor,*Halder*, p. 182.
31 Blau, *The German Campaigns*, p. 47.
32 It is here that the difficulty in timing lies. According to Halder the conference lasted from 1300 to 1430 hours. From the *Documents on German Foreign Policy*, however, it would appear that Hitler, together with Ribbentrop, spent the time from 1310 to 1325 hours in conversation with the Bulgarian minister (*ibid.* D, xii, No. 215) and from 1415 to 1420 with the Hungarian one (*ibid.* No. 216). The military conference which Halder attended may conceivably have been held in between, but this would leave open the question why Ribbentrop (and Hewel, who took the record of Hitler's conversations with the ministers) had to be called in later.
33 OKW/WFSt/Abt.L(IM) Nr. 44 791/41 g.Kdos Chefsache v. 27.1.1941, 'Besprechung über Lage Jugoslawien', printed in *DGFP*, D, XII, No. 271.
34 Printed in Trevor-Roper, *Hitler's War Directives*, pp. 61–2. The invasion of Yugoslavia never received a proper name and was known as 'operation 25'.
35 *TMWC*, vii, 238; also Paulus, *Ich Stehe hier . . .*, p. 125.
36 Hitler to Mussolini, 27.3.1941, *DGFP*, D, XII, No. 224.
37 Ciano, *Diary*, entry for 28.3.1941; Mackensen to foreign ministry, 28.3. 1941, *DGFP*, D, XII, No. 226.
38 Rintelen, *Mussolini*, pp. 136–7.
39 On 29 March; Guzzoni to Cavallero, No. 7674/op., 29.3.1941, IMR/129/ 000080.
40 Rintelen memo, 30.3.1941, *DGFP*, D, XII, No. 237. Cf. also G. Perich, *Mussolini nei Balcani* (Milan, Longanesi, 1966) pp. 88–9, entries for 31.3, 1, 2, 5.4.1941.
41 Greiner, *Wehrmachtführung*, 277, 278; *KTB*/Halder, II, 332, entry for 28.3.1941; also Reinhardt's own description in US Military Tribunal, *Trials of War Criminals* (cit: TWC), case 12, vol. x, p. 1047, and Hausser, *Waffen SS*, p. 42.

42 V. above, p. 136.

43 *KTB*/Halder, II, 338–9, entries for 29.3, 4.4.1941.

44 'Very good work!' commented the chief-of-staff, *ibid.* II; 262, entry for 29.1.1941.

45 The abolition of all civilian traffic under a maximum capacity railway schedule would obviously hurt industrial production, which was planned to reach its peak in the spring.

46 *KTB*/*OKW*, I, 299, entry for 3.2.1941. The timetable of stage I is Anlage 2a zu OKH/Genst.d.H/Op.Abt.(IN) Nr. 050/41 g.Kdos Chefsache, GMR/430/6401931.

47 The timetable is Anlage 2b zu OKH/Genst.d.H/Op.Abt.(IN) Nr. 050/41 g.Kdos Chefsache, GMR/430/6401932.

48 *KTB*/*OKW*, I, 300, entry for 3.2.1941; the timetable for stage III is Anlage 2c zu OKH/Genst.d.H/Op.Abt.(IM) Nr. 050/41 g.Kdos Chefsache, GMR/430/6401933; that of stage IV Anlage 2d zu OKH/Genst.d.H/Op.Abt.(IN) Nr. 050/41 g.Kdos Chefsache, *ibid.*/335/6291487.

49 OKH/Genst.d.H/Op.Abt. Nr. 050/41 g.Kdos Chefsache v. 31.1.1941, GFM/M346/015827.

50 *KTB*/*OKW*, I, 332–3, entry for 21.2.1941.

51 *Ibid.* 349, entry for 8.3.1941.

52 *KTB*/Halder, II, 311, entry for 14.3.1941.

53 OKH/Genst.d.H/Op.Abt.(III) Nr. 340/41 g.Kdos Chefsache v. 7.3.1941.

54 For operation 'Haifisch', as the mock landing was named, v. OKW/WFSt/Abt. Nr. 44 277/41 g.Kdos Chefsache v. 12.3.1941, 'Archiv der Marine, "Barbarossa", OKW Weisungen', i, GFM/M175/00511–16. According to this gigantic plan of deception the troops being deployed on the Soviet frontier were being told that their real task lay in the west, whence they would be transferred only at the last moment.

55 *KTB*/*OKW*, I, 204, entry for 5.12.1940.

56 Mueller-Hillebrand, *Zusammenhang*, pp. 14–15.

57 *KTB*/Halder, II, 292, entry for 24.2.1941. 1 June is also the date given by a memorandum on the oil situation, OKW/W.Rü/LI V/Qu/FHQu of 24 January, item No. MI/14/688 at the Imperial War Museum.

58 As printed in B. Mueller–Hillebrand, *Das Heer* (Frankfurt am/Main, Mittler, 1956) II, 155–6; also *KTB*/*OKW*, I, 1134, appendix D.

59 Footnote 47 above. The divisions in question were supposed to start rolling east between 29 March and 7 April.

60 Mueller–Hillebrand, *Zusammenhang*, pp. 15–16. In the present account the figures given by the actual timetables have been preferred to those in *KTB*/Halder, II, 347, entry for 4.4.1941, with which they partly conflict.

61 Footnote 48 above, stage III did, however, include 52nd and 260th infantry divisions, which we shall meet again.

62 The SS divisions in particular were supposed to move east only at the last moment; Hausser, *Waffen SS*, p. 43.

63 Those coming from France had been idle for months following the cancellation of operation 'Felix'. On 11 February OKW had already put these divisions at the free disposal of OKH. *KTB*/*OKW*, I, 317.

64 Bor, *Halder*, p. 182.

65 R. Grams, *14. Panzerdivision* (Pozdun, Henning, 1957) p. 16.
66 Mueller-Hillebrand, *Zusammenhang*, pp. 15–16.
67 Blau, *German Campaigns*, pp. 42–8.
68 *KTB*/Halder, II, 332, entry for 28.3.1941.
69 Greiner, *Wehrmachtführung*, p. 276.
70 OKW/WFSt/Abt.L Nr. 44 382/41 g.Kdos Chefsache v. 28.3.1941, 'Vorschlag für die Ubereinstimmung der deutschen. . . Operationen gegen Jugoslawien', item No. MI/14/626 at the Imperial War Museum.
71 Blau, *German Campaigns*, p. 30.
72 OKW/WFSt/Abt.L Nr. 44 406/41 g.Kdos Chefsache v. 31.3.1941, signed by Warlimont, item No. MI/14/655 at the Imperial War Museum; also *KTB*/Halder, II, 337, entry for 30.3.1941.
73 OKW/WFSt/Abt.L Nr. 44 433/41 g.Kdos Chefsache v. 2.4.1941, 'Zeittafel für der Freigabe des Anlaufs der Operationen "25" und "Marita",' signed by Warlimont, item No. MI/14/655 at the Imperial War Museum.
74 OKW/WFSt/Abt.L Nr. 44 450/41 g.Kdos Chefsache v. 3.4.1941, signed by Keitel, *ibid.*; also *KTB*/Halder, II, 343, entry for 3.4.1941.
75 Bulter, *Grand Strategy*, II, 458.
76 The present account has deliberately been kept as concise as possible and is based on Papagos, *The Battle of Greece*, pp. 308ff.
77 *Ibid.* p. 324; also Churchill, *Second World War*, III, pp. 87–8. According to Eden Papagos concluded the talks by saying that 'in view of this dubious attitude of the Yugoslavs . . . it was not possible to contemplate holding a line covering Salonika, and that the only sound line in view of the circumstances was the . . . Aliakhmon'. Eden, *Memoirs* , p. 202.
78 Papagos, *The Battle of Greece*, p. 325; Churchill, *Second World War*, III, p. 89; Eden, *Memoirs*, p. 201. The Anglo-Greek miscalculation was even worse than these figures suggest, because they assumed that the Germans would be able to reach not only the Bulgaro–Greek frontier but even the Kaimaktsalan–Vermion–Olympus line within 15–20 days. The originator of the error seems to have been the British military attaché in Sofia, according to whom the Germans could cross Bulgaria 'in ten days or less'. Earle (US minister in Sofia) to Hull, 7.2.1941, *FRUS* 1941, II, 643–4.
79 Eden, *Memoirs*, pp. 210–13.
80 Churchill, *Second World War*, III, 96.
81 Papagos, *The Battle of Greece*, p. 326.
82 V. above, p. 143.
83 Butler, *Grand Strategy*, II, 458–9.
84 *Ibid.* 449.
85 Eden, *Memoirs*, pp. 233–4.
86 Dill to Churchill, 4.4.1941, printed in Churchill, *Second World War*, III, 154.
87 For a concise description of the deployment of the Yugoslav army v. Greiner, *Wehrmachtführung*, pp. 278–9.
88 For the detailed German plans, v. Anlage zu OKW/WFSt/Abt.L Nr. 44 478/41 g.Kdos Chefsache v. 6.4.1941, GMR/780/5506820–21.

89 Back in Austria Göring was using the slow advance of Twelfth army in order to attack the army as a whole; *KTB*/Halder, II, 355, entry for 7.4.1941.

90 This, it will be remembered, had been List's original plan which he was prevented from carrying out because of Halder's support for Kleist. V. above, p. 149. As it turned out, both List and Halder were equally right or wrong.

91 List had wanted to do this on 8 April, but at that time Halder had refused to authorize the change. The reversal of his position on 9 April may have had something to do with a dispute he had with Brauchitsch (with Hitler supporting him) as to whether or not to send part of the forces of XXXXth corps to the Albanian frontier to link up with the Italians. Halder, who did not consider the Italian front was in any danger, resisted this move, and since he was over-ruled he may have wanted to reinforce the corps in carrying out what he regarded as its main task, i.e. the outflanking of the main Anglo-Greek positions. *KTB*/Halder, II, 356, 357–8, entries for 8, 9, 10.4.1941.

92 This was another result of the List–Kleist dispute. Following new information reaching OKH on 4 and 5 April, suggesting that the Yugoslav forces in southern Serbia were stronger than suspected, Halder began to fear lest he had erred in overruling List. Afraid that he would have to reinforce XXXXth corps with Kleist's *Panzergruppe* and thus cancel the attack on Belgrade, he made Reinhardt start earlier than the latter would have liked. *KTB*/Halder, II, 345, 349, entries for 4, 5.4.1941.

93 OKH had taken 30 April as the last day for Yugoslavia, but in fact it was as good as over by 14 April; Bor, *Halder*, p. 185. V. also Hitler–Alfieri conversation, 7.4.1941, *DGFP*, D, XII, No. 290.

94 76th, 79th, 46th, 198th and 125th infantry, 60th motorized divisions; *KTB*/Halder, II, 364, entry for 13.4.1941.

95 1st mountain, 76th, 79th, 125th and 198th infantry, 101st 'light' motorized; *ibid.* II, 365, entry for 14.4.1941. 60th motorized division was apparently not halted because it reappears in *ibid.* 368, entry for 15.4.1941, as continuing its advance together with 11th armoured.

96 OKH/Genst.d.H/Op.Abt.(III) Nr. 502/41 g.Kdos Chefsache v. 12.4.1941, signed by Paulus, GMR/430/6402039–44; *KTB*/Halder, II, 350, entry for 5.4.1941.

97 A. Krull, *Das Hannoverische Regiment 73*. (Hannover, Regimentkameradschaft 73., n.d.) pp. 90–2. 73rd regiment was part of 19th armoured division.

98 V. Hoptner, *Yugoslavia in Crisis*, pp. 290–2. Ironically, it was Cincar Markovic who had to sign the surrender.

99 This was done at the command of Brauchitsch, who must have been inspired by Hitler directly. Halder for his part saw in it the influence of political reasoning on military operations, and opposed the move on the grounds that the manoeuvre represented an unnecessary diversion from the main task of XXXXth corps. In this he was right, for the corps did in fact waste two days before Veue. *KTB*/Halder, II, 355–6, 358, 359, entries for 9, 10, 11.4.1941.

100 5th mountain division had been withdrawn to prepare to take the Aegean islands.

101 In List's opinion 27 Italian divisions did not suffiicently bind the 14 Greek ones; Wisshaupt, *Der Balkanfeldzug*, p. 34.

102 For details v. Cervi, *Storia della Guerra di Grecia*, pp. 348–51.

103 *KTB*/Halder, II, 364–5, entries for 21, 22.4.1941; also Greiner, *Wehrmachtführung*, p. 284. In private Hitler assured both Dietrich and List that in their place he would have done the same.

104 Another aim of the operation was to prevent the Canal, which was important for the shipping of oil from Rumania to Italy from being blocked; *KTB*/*OKW*, I, 385, entry for 22.4.1941.

105 Greiner, *Wehrmachtführung*, p. 284.

106 Rintelen to SMG, Nr. 190/41, IMR/129/000942; SMG to Rintelen, 26.4.1941, *ibid.*/000971.

107 OKW/WFSt/Abt.L(IV/Qu) Nr. 00630/41 g.Kdos v. 12.3.1941, signed by Keitel, GMR/780/506803–5.

108 *KTB*/Halder, II, 391, entry for 2.5.1941.

109 *KTB*/*OKW*, I, 398, entry for 30.5.1941.

110 *Ibid.*; also OKH/Genst.d.H/Op.Abt.(IS) Nr. 42241/41 g.Kdos v. 9.5.1941, GMR/427/8005186–87.

111 After the war, it was suggested by various British authors that the German capture of Crete was dictated by Hitler's desire to help the Arabs and the French against the British in Iraq and Syria. The available evidence does not support this interpretation. The entire business was rather marginal in Hitler's mind, and such limited German aid as was flown to the Middle East went through Rhodos.

112 Domarus, *Hitler Reden* . . ., IV, 1699; also Playfair, *The Mediterranean and the Middle East*, II, 128.

113 The present account is based on B. H. Liddell-Hart, *The Other Side of the Hill* (London, Cassell, 1948) pp. 238ff.

114 'Directive No. 28', printed in Trevor-Roper, *Hitler's War Directives*, pp. 68–9.

115 'Directive No. 29', *ibid.* pp. 69–71.

116 *KTB*/Halder, II, 389, entry for 1.5.1941, and ed.'s note.

117 V. Playfair, *Mediterranean and the Middle East*, II, 130; also Blau, *The German Campaigns*, pp. 127–8.

118 Liddell-Hart, *The Other Side of the Hill*, p. 240.

119 Wisshaupt, *Der Balkanfeldzug* . . ., p. 48. An investigation conducted by the Germans after the campaign revealed that the *Freischärler* had not been so *unmenschlich* after all.

120 Unsigned SKL memo, 1.6.1941, 'Die strategische Lage im östlichen Mittelmeer nach Balkanfeldzug und Kretabesetzung und die weitere Kampführung', p. 3, I. SKL, xiv, GNR/51/000082.

121 Liddell-Hart, *The Other Side of the Hill*, p. 242.

122 Lack of space prevents a fuller discussion of the problem in this context. Cf. M. van Creveld, 'The German Attack on the USSR; the Destruction of a Legend', *European Studies Review*, Jan. 1972, pp. 69–86.

123 Including 123 in the first line, 21 in strategic reserve, and 8 in Norway,

where they were to launch operation 'Silberfuchs' under the command of OKW; Mueller-Hillebrand, *Das Heer*, II, 102.

124 V. OKH/Genst.d.H/Op.Abt., Schematische Kriegsgliederung (item No. AL 755 at the Imperial War Museum) where, among those of other fronts, there is a systematic comparison of the forces in the Balkans with those in the east at various dates from May 1940 to June 1941.

125 *KTB*/Halder, II, 387, entry for 30.4.1941. By 13 July OKW considered the Russian campaign won and ordered the two armoured divisions to stay in Germany; OKW/WFSt/Abt.L(I.Op./IIOrg.) Nr. 441179/41 g.Kdos Chefsache v. 13.7.1941, signed by Halder.

126 *KTB*/Halder, II, 327, entry for 4.4.1941.

127 *Ibid.* 353, 395, entries for 7.4, 5.5.1941; Mueller-Hillebrand, *Zusammenhang*, p. 19. For detailed plans of the refreshment and the principles behind it v. OKH/Genst.d.H/Gen.Qu./Abt.I(Qu.2) Nr. I/0333/41 g.Kdos Chefsache v. 8.4.1941 signed by Halder.

128 *KTB*/Halder, II, 417, entry for 17.5.1941. The timetable for stage III echelon is Anlage 2c zu OKH/Genst.d.H/Op.Abt.(IM) Nr. 050/40 g.Kdos Chefsache, GMR/430/5401933.

129 *KTB*/Halder, II, 347, 349–50, 365, 387, entries for 4, 5, 14, 30.4.1941; Mueller-Hillebrand. *Zusammenhang*, p. 20. The timetable for stage IVa. is Anlage 2d zu OKH/Genst.d.H/Op.Abt.(IN) Nr. 050/41 g.Kdos Chefsache, GMR/430/6401934; that of stage IVb. Anlage 2e to the same, *ibid.*/6401935. Neither table bears a date, but since Heusinger reported about them to Halder on 15 April they must have been prepared between 4 and 14 April.

130 V. above, p. 161.

131 *KTB*/Halder, II, 362, 364, 365, entries for 12, 13, 14.4.1941; Mueller-Hillebrand, *Zusammenhang*, p. 17; Blau, *The German Campaigns*, pp. 150–1.

132 ObdH/Genst.d.H/Op.Abt.(IaIM) Nr. 644/41 g.Kdos Chefsache v. 7.4.1941, GMR/430/6402054–59.

133 46th infantry started its march back from the Prilep-Bitolj area after handing it over to the Bulgarians on 7 May; AOK.12/Ia Nr. 1155/41 g.Kdos v. 3.5.1941, GMR/427/8005285, and AOK.12/Ia Nr. 1153/41 g.Kdos v. 5.5.1941, *ibid.*/8005236. 73rd infantry left Greece for Belgrade on 10 May, but was then halted in the same area until the termination of 'Merkur'; AOK.12/Ia Nr. 1146/41 g.Kdos v. 4.5.1941, *ibid.*/8005203, and AOK.12/Ia Nr. 1218/41 g.Kdos II. Ang. v. 11.5.1941, *ibid.*/8005190. 5th armoured division left Salonika by rail on 31 May through Yugoslavia; AOK.12/Ia Nr. 1086/41 g.Kdos v. 1.5.1941, *ibid*/8005292. SS 'AH', the last of the 'Barbarossa' units to leave Greece, left Salonika on 27 May via Yugoslavia for refreshment near Prague; AOK.12/Ia Nr. 1123/41 g.Kdos v. 3.5.1941, *ibid.*/8005279.

134 These were 50th, 72nd, 76th and 198th infantry divisions. For their movements, v. AOK.12/Ia Nr. 1127/41 g.Kdos v. 4.5.1941, GMR/427/8005280–81; AOK.12/Ia Nr. 1166/41 g.Kdos v. 18.4.1941, *ibid.*/8005299; and AOK.12/Ia Nr. 1008/41 g.Kdos v. 20.4.1941, *ibid.*/8005297–98.

135 OKH/Genst.d.H/Op.Abt.(IM) Nr. 722/41 g.Kdos Chefsache v. 22.4. 1941, GMR/430/6402064.

136 OKH/Genst.d.H/Op.Abt.(III) Nr. 975/41 g.Kdos Chefsache v. 25.5. 1941, *ibid.*/6402127–33; also *KTB*/Halder, II, 446, entry for 7.6.1941. The division, no longer needed for the initial attack, was referred to the OKH reserves.

137 Grams, *14. Panzerdivision*, pp. 22–3.

138 Krull, *Das Hannoverische Regiment 73*, p. 92; also OKH/Genst.d.H/ Op.Abt.(III) Nr. 975/41 g.Kdos v. 25.5.1941, GMR/430/6402127–33.

139 *Ibid.*; *KTB/OKW*, I, 383, entry for 21.4.1941.

140 *Ibid.*; KTB/OKH/Genst.d.H/Op.Abt.(Ia), entry for 29.5.1941, GMR/ 306/6259708.

141 *Ibid.*; also Anlage 2d zu OKH/Genst.d.H/Op.Abt.(IN) Nr. 050/41 g.Kdos Chefsache v. 31.1.1941, GMR/335/6291487.

142 Mueller-Hillebrand, *Zusammenhang*, p. 21.

143 Anlage 2d zu OKH/Genst.d.H/Op.Abt.(IN) Nr. 050/41 g.Kdos Chefsache, GMR/335/6291487; and OKH/Genst.d.H/Op.Abt.(III) Nr. 975/41 g.Kdos v. 25.5.1941, *ibid.*/6402127–33.

144 *KTB*/Halder, II, 301, entry for 3.3.1941.

145 For details cf. P. Carrell, *Hitler's War on Russia* (London, Harrap, 1964) pp. 23–5. The tanks were to spearhead the attack by Guderian's *Panzergruppe* across the river Bug.

146 *KTB*/Halder, II, 343, entry for 3.4.1941.

147 *Ibid.* 395, 417, 421, 424, 427, entries for 5, 17, 20, 21, 22.5.1941.

148 The *Panzerzüge* were freight trains adapted to carrying and rapidly unloading armour and material for use in occupying bridges, strongholds, etc. Cf. OKH/Genst.d.H/Op.Abt.(IN) Nr. 517/41 g.Kdos Chefsache v. 26.3.1941, GMR/430/6402022; OKH/Genst.d.H/Op.Abt. (I) Nr. 1042/41 g.Kdos Chefsache v. 28.5.1941, *ibid.*/335/6291920; and OKH/Genst.d.H/Op.Abt.(III) Nr. 8225/41 g.Kdos v. 10.6.1941, *ibid.*/ 6291920.

149 A. Schmidt, *Geschichte der 10. Division* (Bad Nauheim, Pozdun, 1963) pp. 88–9.

150 *KTB*/Halder, II, 421, entry for 20.5.1941.

151 Mueller-Hillebrand, *Das Heer*, II, 105.

152 *Idem, Zusammenhang*, p. 24; *KTB*/Halder, II, 381, entry for 25.4.1941.

153 As it was, the tanks for about 1¾ armoured divisions were produced in the last six weeks preceding the start of 'Barbarossa'; Jodl memo, 'Stellungnahme zuer Rüstungfertigung', 3.12.1940, printed in G. Thomas, *Geschichte des deutschen Wehr-und Rüstungwirtschaft, 1918–1945* (Bopard am/Rhein, Haroldt Boldt, 1966) pp. 436–7; also *KTB*/ Halder, II, 292, entry for 25.2.1941. Even so the campaign was started without any reserves.

154 V. above, p. 151, footnote No. 61.

155 Cf. the timetable of stage IVb. (Anlage 2e zu OKH/Genst.d.H/Op.Abt. (IN) Nr. 050/41 g.Kdos Chefsache, GMR/430/6401935) and the revised version of 25 May as quoted in footnote No. 143 above.

156 *Ibid.*

157 *KTB*/Halder, II, 343, entry for 3.4.1941.
158 *Ibid.* 417, entry for 17.5.1941; and G. Tessin, *Verbände und Truppen der deutschen Wehrmacht und Waffen SS im Zweiten Weltkrieg, 1939–1945* (Frankfurt am Main, Mittler, n.d.) p. 266.
159 G. Dieckhoff, *3. Infanterie Division, 3. Infanterie Division (mot.), 3. Panzergrenadier Division* (Göttingen, Börries, 1960) pp. 90–1.
160 OKH/Genst.d.H/Op.Abt.(I) Nr. 947/41 g.Kdos Chefsache v. 29.5.1941, GMR/430/6402124.
161 *KTB*/Halder, II, 458, 459, entries for 20, 21.6.1941. The fact that this division – whose presence was considered crucial to the start of 'Barbarossa' – did not go into action until 27 June (Hausser, *Waffen SS*, p. 44) lends credence to the view that the campaign could have been started without waiting for the last division.
162 Mueller-Hillebrand, *Zusammenhang*, p. 23.
163 *KTB*/Halder, II, 407–8, entry for 12.5.1941. As for XIth air corps, its bombers and anti-aircraft units were released by Hitler as early as 14 April; 'directive No. 27', printed in Trevor-Roper, *Hitler's War Directives*, pp. 65–8.
164 *KTB*/Halder, II, 433, entry for 28.5.1941.
165 OKW/WFSt/Abt.L Nr. 44708/41 g.Kdos Chefsache v. 12.5.1941, 'Protokol der Besprechung am 12.5. 1800 Uhr bei OKW/WFSt/Abt.L in Salzburg', GNR/3/000706.
166 *KTB/OKW*, I, 397, entry for 26.5.1941.
167 KTB/Genst.d.H/Op.Abt.(Ia), entry for 28.5.1941, GMR/306/6257080; *KTB/OKW*, I, 397, entry for 28.5.1941.
168 For this aspect of the Russian campaign v. the excellent article by H. R. Trevor-Roper, 'Hitlers Kriegsziele', *Vierteljahrshefte für Zeitgeschichte*, VIII (1960), 121–33.
169 Assuming, of course, that such a goal existed in the first place; that is, that the justification of Nazism was not just Hitler's personal craving for power.
170 The word *Blitzfeldzug* is used here in preference to the more common *-Krieg*. From the German point of view, the early years of World War II were not a war at all but a series of campaigns; and when a war finally developed, Germany was lost. Cf. the enlightening analysis in A. Milward, *The German Economy at War* (London, 1965).
171 'Dem deutsche Soldat ist nichts unmöglich!' was the phrase he used in his speech of 31 May.

CONCLUSIONS

1 For Greece, this was true only from 1939 onward.
2 Which Mussolini resisted.
3 Or, alternatively, to the 'Adriatic' which was part of the 'Mediterranean'. This was the definition adopted when the Nazis wanted to calm their allies down.
4 Jodl's phrase at Nüremberg.

NOTE ON SOURCES

1 Consider the recent account by J. Wuechst, *Jugoslawien und das dritte Reich* (Stuttgart, Seewald, 1969) a historiographical monstrosity.

2 It is remarkable that, while there are a number of studies concerning German operations in Greece (e.g. A. Buchner, *Der deutsche Griechenland Feldzug* (Heidelberg, Vowinckel, 1957) there is none on Yugoslavia.

BIBLIOGRAPHY

I UNPRINTED SOURCES

A DIPLOMATIC

1 German
'Akten Büro Reichsaussenminister', GFM, F1, F9, F16
'Aufzeichnungen des Vertreters des Auswärtiges
    Amt von Etzdorf', GFM, 1247
'Botschafter Ritter, Bulgarien,' Bd. i, GFM, 839
'Botschafter Ritter, Griechenland', Bd. iv, GFM, 962
'Deutsche Botschaft Rom, Geheimakten 1940', GFM, 2281
'Deutsche Legation Bucharest, Militärisches', Bd. 2/8, GFM, 3710H
'Geheimakten Schmidt', GFM, 67
'Handelpolitische Verträge, Jugoslawien', Bd. ii, GFM, 8498
'Handakten Clodius', GFM, 9924
'St.S. Bulgarien', Bds. i, ii, GFM, 585, 274
'St.S. Deutsch–italienische Beziehungen', Bds. i, ii, GFM, B13, 1571
'St.S. Frankreich', Bds. ii, iii, GFM, 121
'St.S. Griechenland', Bd. i, GFM, 449
'St.S. Italien', Bds. ii, iii, GFM, B14
'St.S. Jugoslawien', Bds. i, ii, GFM, 230
'St.S., Türkei', Bd. i, GFM, 265
'Unst.S. Franreich', Bd. i, GFM, 587
'Unst.S. Griechenland', Bd. xii, GFM, 675

2 British
British Foreign Office Documents (at the Public Record Office),
    vols. FO/371/24385, 24919, 24920, 24921.

B MILITARY*

1 German
a. Army
AOK.12/Ia, 'Balkanakte', GMR, 1. frame 426 8004389
AOK/12/Ia, 'Balkanfeldzug, Sammelakte', GMR, 1. frame 426 8004706
AOK.12/Ia, 'Marschbefehle, Rückmarschbewegnungen nach d.

* Not all files mentioned under this heading have names. In case they do not,
  the title given is just a rough indication of the contents.

Balkanfeldzug', GMR, 1. frame 427 8005128
Chef d. Heeresnachtrichtenwesen, 'Aufmarschanweisung
  für 12. Armee', GMR, 1. frame 329 6285489
OKH/Genst.d.H/Op.Abt., 'Aufmarschanweisung
  Barbarossa', GMR, 1. frame 335 6291366
OKH/Genst.d.H/Op.Abt., 'Barbarossa', Bd. ii, GMR,
  1. frame 335 6291544
OKH/Genst.d.H/Op.Abt.(IS), 'Bulgarische Grenzreglung in
  Jugoslawien', GMR, 1. frame 329 6285656
OKH/Genst.d.H/Op.Abt., 'Entwurf zur Aufmarschanweisung
  Barbarossa', GMR, 1. frame 335 6291208
OKH/Genst.d.H/Op.Abt.(Ia), 'Kriegstagebuch',
  27 Mai – 4 September 1941, GMR, 1. frame 335 6291235
OKH/Genst.d.H/Op.Abt., 'Schematische Kriegsgliederung',
  IWM, item No. A1 755
OKH/Genst.d.H/Org. Abt. (unnamed), preparations for
  Barbarossa and related movements, GMR, 1. frame 430 6402091
OKH/Genst.d.H/Att. Abt. (unnamed), Rintelen
  reports to OKH, IWM, item No. AL 1007
OKH/Genst.d.H/Org. Abt. (unnamed), transportation and
  relocation of German units in the period
  January–May 1941, GMR, 1. frame 430 6401880
OKW/WFSt/Abt.L., 'Akten btr. Weisung Nr.18', IWM, item
  No. ML/14/620
OKW/141, 'Sammelmape Weisung Nr. 18',
  GMR, 1. frame 782 5509140
OKW/122 (unnamed), Chefsachen relating to the
  Balkans, GMR, 1. frame 782 5508419
OKW/118 (unnamed), Italy, GMR, 1. frame 780 5506479
OKW/WFSt/Abt.L (unnamed), Strategic planning for the
  Balkans, IWM, item No. MI/14/655
Panzer AOK.1., 'Barbarossa ii, nich benötigte
  Chefsachen', GMR, 1. frame 18 7246027

b Navy
Archiv d. Marine, 'Barbarossa', GFM, M175
Marine Archiv, 'Mittelmeer', GFM, M176
OKM/SKL, 'Deutsche Kriegführung im Mittelmeer', GNR, 51
OKM/SKL, 'Die Bemühungen d. Seekriegsleitung um ein
  deutsch-französischen zusammengehen gegen England
  und die Behauptung des Französischen Kolonialreichs in
  Africa, 3.7.1940–27.11.1942', GNR, 117P
OKM/SKL, 'Handakten Felix', GNR, 115
OKM/SKL, 'Kriegstagebuch'
  Teil A, GNR, 3, 4
  Teil C, GNR, 50, 112
OKM/SKL, 'Zusammenarbeit Deutschlands, Italien, Spanien,
  Japan, Russland, Ungaren, Rumänien', GFM, 8230

c Others
Sekretär des Führer: 'Führers Tagebuch'

2 Italian
SMG: 'Esigenza "E"', IMR, 126
SMG: 'Esigenza "G"', IMR, 127
SMG: (unnamed), directives, orders and correspondence concerning
the Italo–Greek war, IMR, 129

II PRINTED SOURCES

A. COLLECTIONS OF DOCUMENTS

Adam, M.: *Allianz Hitler–Horthy–Mussolini* (Budapest, Akademiai
Kiado, 1966).
Ciano, G.: *L'Europa verso la Catastrofe; 184 colloqui con Mussolini,
Hitler, Franco, etc.* (Milan, Mondadori, 1946).
Die Geheimakten des Französischen Generalstab, ed. Auswärtiges Amt
(Deutsches Weissbuch Nr. 6), Berlin, 1941).
Documents on British Foreign Policy (London, HM Stationery Office,
1952–) series iii, vol. v.
Documents on German Foreign Policy (London, HM Stationery Office,
1956–) series D, vols. VI, VII, VIII, IX, X, XI, XII.
Domarus, E.: *Hitler, Reden und Proklamationen, 1932–1945* (Münich,
Süddeutscher Verlag, 1962) vol. IV.
Führer Conferences on Naval Affairs, printed in *Brassey's Naval
Manual,* 1948).
Foreign Relations of the United States (Washington DC, US Government
Printing Office, 1957–) vols. 1939 I, 1941 II, III.
Hitler e Mussolini, Lettere e Documenti (Milan, Rizzoli, 1946).
Le Testament Politique de Hitler. Notes Recueilles par Martin Bormann
(Paris, Hachette, 1959).
I Documenti Diplomatici Italiani (ed. Ministero degli Affari Esteri, Rome,
Libreria dello Stato, 1952–), series viii, vols. XII, XIII; series ix, vols.
I, II, III, IV, V.
OKH/Abt. für Kriegskarten und Vermessungswesen, *Militärgeogra-
phische Beschreibung von Nordost Griechenland* (1941).
Soviet Documents on Foreign Policy (ed. J. Degras, London, Oxford
University Press, 1953) vol. III.
The Greek White Book (London, Hutchinson, 1942).
Trevor Roper, H. R.: *Hitler's War Directives* (London, Sidgwick &
Jackson, 1964).
Trial of Major War Criminals (International Military Tribunal,
Nuremberg, 1949) vols. VII, X, XXVII.
Trial of War Criminals (US Military Tribunal, Nuremberg, 1950)
case 12, vol. X.

B. DIARIES

Armellini, Q.: *Diario di Guerra, Nove Mese al Commando Supremo* (Rome, Garzanti, 1946).
Ciano, G.: *Diary, 1939–1945* (New York, Doubleday, 1946).
Halder, F.: *Kriegstagebuch* (Stuttgart, Kohlhammer, 1962) vols. I, II.
Kriegstagebuch des Oberkommando der Wehrmacht, ed. P. E. Schramm (Frankfurt am Main, Bernard & Graefe, 1965), vol. I.
Simoni, L.: *Berlino, Ambasciata d'Italia, 1939–1945* (Rome, Migliaresi, n.d.).

C. TALKS AND MEMOIRS

Abetz, O.: *Das offene Problem* (Cologne, Greven, 1951).
Alfieri, D.: *Dictators Face to Face* (N.Y. University Press, 1955).
Anfuso, F.: *Da Palazzo Venezia al Lago di Garda* (Bologna, Cappelli, 1957).
Badoglio, P.: *L'Italia nella Seconda Guerra Mondiale, Memorie e Documenti* (Milan, Mondadori, 1946).
Bor, P.: *Gespräche mit Halder* (Wiesbaden, Limes, 1950).
Brugere, R.: *Veni, Vidi, Vichy* (Varves, Calmann-Levy, 1944).
Churchill, W.: *The Second World War* (London, Cassell, 1949), vols. I, III.
Eden, A.: *Memoirs, the Reckoning* (London, Cassell, 1965).
Graziani, R.: *Ho difeso la Patria* (Rome, Garzanti, 1948).
Graziani, R.: *In Africa Settentrionale, 1940–1941* (Rome, Danesi, 1948).
Grazzi, E.: *Il Principio del Fine* (Rome, Faro, 1945).
Gregoric, D.: *So endete Jugoslawien* (Leipzig, Goldmann, 1943).
Jacomini, F.: *La Politica dell'Italia in Albania* (Rome, Cappelli, 1965).
Kordt, E.: *Nicht aus den Akten* (Stuttgart, Deutsche Verlagsgesellschaft, 1950).
Liddell Hart, B. H.: *The Other Side of the Hill* (London, Cassell, 1949).
Macek, V.: *In the Struggle for Freedom* (N.Y., Speller & Sons, 1957).
Massigli, R.: *La Turquie devant la Guerre, Mission a Ankara, 1939–1940* (Paris, Plon, 1964).
Papagos, A.: *The Battle of Greece* (Athens, Hellenic Publishing Press, 1949).
Papen, F. von: *Memoirs* (London, Deutsch, 1952).
Paulus, F. von: *Ich Stehe hier auf Befehl!* (Frankfurt am Main, Bernard & Graefe, 1963).
Raeder, E.: *Mein Leben* (Tübingen, Schlichtenmayer, 1951).
Ribbentrop, J. von: *The Ribbentrop Memoirs* (London, Weidenfeld & Nicolson, 1954).
Rintelen, E. von: *Mussolini als Bundgenosse* (Tübingen, Wunderlich, 1951).
Roatta, M.: *Otto Millioni di Bayonette* (Verona, Mondadori, 1946).
Schmidt, P.: *Statist auf diplomatischer Bühne* (Bonn, Athenäum, 1953).

Visconti Prasca, S.: *Io ho agreddito la Grecia* (Milan, Rizzoli, 1946).
Weizsäcker, E. von: *Memoirs* (London, Gollancz, 1951).

D. SECONDARY SOURCES

Barnett, C.: *The Desert Generals* (London, Kimber, 1960).
Blau, G.: *The German Campaigns in the Balkans (Spring 1941)*
  (Washington DC, Dept. of the Army, 1953).
Buckley, C.: *Greece and Crete* (London, HM Stationery Office, 1952).
Butler, J. R. M.: *Grand Strategy* (London, HM Stationery Office,
  1954–), vol. II.
Cavenari, E.: *La Guerra Italiana* (Rome, Tossi, 1949), vol. II.
Cervi, M.: *Storia della Guerra di Grecia* (Milan, Sugar, 1965).
Detwiller, D. S.: *Hitler, Franco und Gibraltar* (Wiesbaden, Steiner,
  1962).
Dieckhoff, G.: *3. Infanterie Division, 3. Infanterie Division (mot.),
  3. Panzergrenadier Division* (Göttingen, Börries, 1960).
Fabry, Ph. W.: *Balkan-Wirren, 1940–1941* (Darmstadt, Wehr und Wissen
  Verlagsgesellschaft, 1966).
Fabry, Ph. W.: *Der Hitler–Stalin Pakt* (Darmstadt, Fundus, 1966).
Faldella, E.: *L'Italia e la Seconda Guerra Mondiale* (Rome, Cappelli,
  1959).
Friedensburg, F.: *Die Rohstoffe und Energiequellen im neuen Europa*
  (Berlin, Gerhard Stalling, 1943).
Geschke, G.: *Die deutsche Frankreichpolitik 1940* (Frankfurt am Main,
  Mittler, 1960).
Gigli, G.: *La Seconda Guerra Mondiale* (Bari, Laterza, 1951).
Grams, R.: *14. Panzerdivision* (Pozdun, Henning, 1957).
Greiner, H.: 'Das Eingreifen auf dem Balkan 1941' (MS No. AL 1039/1
  at the Imperial War Museum).
Greiner, H.: *Die oberste Wehrmachtführung* (Wiesbaden, Limes, 1951).
Hausser, P.: *Waffen SS im Einsatz* (Göttingen, Plesse, 1953).
Hepp, L.: 'Die 12. Armee in Balkanfeldzug 1941', *Wehrwissenschaftliche
  Rundschau*, V (1955), pp. 201–14.
Hillgruber, A.: *Hitler, König Carol und Marschal Antonescu* (Wiesbaden,
  Steiner, 1953).
Hillgruber, A.: *Hitlers Strategie* (Frankfurt am Main, Bernard & Graefe,
  1965).
Hoptner, J. B.: *Yugoslavia in Crisis, 1934–1941* (NY, Columbia
  University Press, 1962).
Jäckel, E.: *Frankreich in Hitlers Europa* (Stuttgart, Deutsche
  Verlagsgesellschaft, 1966).
Klee, K.: *Das Unternehmen "Seelöwe"* (Göttingen, Musterschmidt, 1958).
Knezevic, R. L.: 'Hitler, Prince Paul and Salonika', *International Affairs*,
  XXVII (1951), pp. 39–52.
Krecker, L.: *Deutschland und die Türkei im Zweiten Weltkrieg*
  (Frankfurt am Main, Klostermann, 1964).

Krull, A.: *Das Hannoverische Regiment 73*. (Hanover, Regimentkamer-adschaft 73., n.d.).

Langer, W., and Gleason, S.: *The Undeclared War* (Washington DC, Dept. of State, 1953).

Marzari, O. F.: 'The Balkans, the Great Powers and the European War, 1939–1940' (unpublished University of London PhD. thesis, 1966).

Mueller Hillebrand, B.: *Das Heer* (Frankfurt am Main, Mittler, 1956) vol. II.

Mueller-Hillebrand, B.: 'Der Zusammenhang zwischen den deutschen Balkanfeldzug und der Invasion in Russland' (Koenigstein/TS, 1951, MS No. AL 1454 at the Imperial War Museum).

Philippi, A., and Heim, F.: *Der Feldzug gegen Sowjetrussland, 1941 bis 1945; ein operativer Uberblick* (Stuttgart, Kohlhammer, 1962).

Playfair, S. O.: *The Mediterranean and the Middle East* (London, HM Stationery Office, 1956), vol. II.

Ristic, D. N.: *Yugoslavia's Revolution of 1941* (Hoover Institution publication, 1966).

Rossi, F.: *Mussolini e lo Stato Maggiore* (Rome, n.ed., 1951).

Santoro, G.: *L'Aeronautica italiana nella Second Guerra Mondiale* (Rome, Esse, 2. edizione, 1957).

Schmidt, A.: *Geschichte der 10. Division* (Bad Nauheim, Pozdun, 1963).

Schramm von Thadden, E.: *Griechenland und die Grossmächte im Zweiten Weltkrieg* (Wiesbaden, Steiner, 1955).

Siebert, F.: *Italiens Weg ins Zweiten Weltkrieg* (Frankfurt am Main, Athenäum, 1962).

Sommer, Th.: *Deutschland und Japan zwischen den Mächten* (Tübingen, Mohr, 1962).

Stato Maggiore Esercito/Ufficio Storico: *L'Avanzata fino ad Sidi el Barrani* (Rome, Libreria dello Stato, n.d.).

Stato Maggiore Esercito/Ufficio Storico: *La Prima Offensiva Britannica in Africa Settentrionale* (Rome, Libreria dello Stato, n.d.).

Survey of International Affairs, The World in March 1939, ed. A. and V. Toynbee (London, Oxford University Press, 1952).

Survey of International Affairs, The Initial Triumph of the Axis, ed. A. and V. Toynbee (London, Oxford University Press, 1958).

Tessin, G.: *Verbände und Truppen der deutschen Wehrmacht und Waffen SS im zweiten Weltkrieg, 1939–1945* (Frankfurt am Main, Mittler, n.d.).

Tippelskirsch, K. von: 'Der deutsche Balkanfeldzug 1941', *Wehrwissen-schaftliche Rundschau*, v (1955), pp. 49–65.

Toscano, M.: *Le origine diplomatiche del Patto d'Acciaio* (Florence, Sansoni, 1956).

Toscano, M.: *Una Mancatao Intesa italo-sovietica nel 1940 e 1941* (Florence, n.ed., 1951).

Wisshaupt, E.: 'Der Balkanfeldzug der 12. Armee – Generalfeldmarschal List', MS No. AL 679/1–2 at the Imperial War Museum.

Wiskemann, E.: *The Rome Berlin Axis* (London, Collins, 1967).

Woodward, E. L.: *British Foreign Policy in the Second World War* (London, HM Stationery Office, 1970) vol. I.